ARAB AMERICA

Arab America

Gender, Cultural Politics, and Activism

Nadine Naber

NEW YORK UNIVERSITY PRESS
New York and London

NEW YORK UNIVERSITY PRESS
New York and London
www.nyupress.org

References to Internet Websites (URLs) were accurate at the time of writing.
Neither the author nor New York University Press is responsible for URLs that
may have expired or changed since the manuscript was prepared.

Library of Congress Cataloging-in-Publication Data
Naber, Nadine Christine.
 Arab America : gender, cultural politics, and activism / Nadine Naber.
    p. cm. — (Nation of newcomers : immigrant history as American history)
Includes bibliographical references and index.
ISBN 978-0-8147-5886-1 (cl : alk. paper)
ISBN 978-0-8147-5887-8 (pb : alk. paper)
ISBN 978-0-8147-5888-5 (ebook)
ISBN 978-0-8147-5920-2 (ebook)
1. Arab Americans—Social conditions. 2. Arab American women—Social conditions.
3. Arab Americans—Ethnic identity. 4. Arab Americans—Politics and government. 5. Sex
role—United States. 6. Feminist theory. I. Title.
E184.A65N335   2012
305.892'7073—dc23   2012009401
New York University Press books are printed on acid-free paper,
and their binding materials are chosen for strength and durability.
We strive to use environmentally responsible suppliers and materials
to the greatest extent possible in publishing our books.

Manufactured in the United States of America
c 10 9 8 7 6 5 4 3 2 1
p 10 9 8 7 6 5 4 3 2 1

CONTENTS

ACKNOWLEDGMENTS

This book was born collectively, through ongoing relations with friends, colleagues, and activists. Yet ultimately, I take full responsibility for the content and any errors on the pages that follow. First and foremost, I acknowledge with deep respect and gratitude each person who participated in my research. You shared your stories with me and trusted me to write them.

This book began at the University of California–Davis in the 1990s. I was fortunate to work with Suad Joseph. She is a model of the feminist principle "lift while you climb." She opened up many doors for me. Also at UC–Davis, I had the privilege to learn from Kent Ono, who always saw the best in me and encouraged me to publish my work. At UC–Davis I was met with colleagues, friends, and mentors with whom I developed the early foundations of an interdisciplinary, ethnic studies–based feminist ethnography: Shagufta Bidiwalla, Adrianna Clay, Rosa Linda Fregoso, Ileana Labergere, Smadar Lavie, Donald Moore, Sarah Projansky, Ella Maria Ray, and Zeina Zaatari.

Arab and Arab American scholars, friends, and activists in California provided me with a sense of collective power throughout the process of research and writing. I am grateful to these community elders who supported my research whether or not we shared the same ideas or political commitments: Darwish Addassi, Kamel Ayoub, Bishara Kubein, Jamal Dajani, Manuel Dudum, Fouad Malouf, Salem Mufarrah, Alice Nashashibi, and Abeer Rafidi. Notably, my mother's childhood classmate and long-time activist, community builder, and pathbreaker, Nabila Mango, assisted me all along the way. I am deeply indebted to the many friends living in the San Francisco Bay Area who were consistently available to discuss or assist me with research matters, answer questions, or offer their homes. Among them are Marwan Abderrazzaq, Maad Abughazalah, Dena Al-Adeeb, Janaan Attia, Hatem Bazian, Lina Baroudi, Lillian Boctor, Youmna Chlala, Eman Desouky, Ron Dudum, Sema Dudum, Manal Elkarra, Noura Erakat, Laura Farha, Nadine Ghammache, Jess Ghannam, Monadel Herzallah, Emily Katz-Kishawi, Senan Khairie, Eyad Kishawi, Huda Jadallah, Manal Jamal, Chis Lymbertos, Ghada Saliba Malouf, Heba Nimr, Mona Odeh, Osama Qasem, Fadwa Rashid, Elias Rashmawi, Michel Shehadeh, Linda Sherif, and Mona Sousou. In the 1990s, I witnessed these scholars who came before me rupture the boundaries of Middle East area studies and open up new possibilities for diasporic Middle East feminist studies: Amal Amireh, Nada Elia, Joe Kadi, Lisa Suhair Majaj, Minoo Moallem, Therese Saliba, and Ella Shohat. Their work shapes this book and helped to make it possible. As I expanded this project, these generous colleagues challenged me in the most profound ways, offered me their time and energy, and provided invaluable feedback: Evelyn Alsutany, Maylei Blackwell, Piya Chatterjee, Lara Deeb, Vince Diaz, Dena Goodman, Rebecca Hardin, Sandra Gunning, Sondra Hale, Scott Kurashige, Jayati Lal, David Lloyd, Minoo Moallem, Susan Najita, Julia Paley, Elizabeth Roberts, Sarita See, Ella Shohat, Andrea Smith, Miriam Ticktin, Valerie Traub, and Ruth Tsoffar. I am deeply grateful to these colleagues for their ongoing feedback and for reading individual book chapters: Dina Alkasim, Paul Amar, Paola Bacchetta, Marc Baer, Yvette Floretz-Ortiz, Sondra Hale, Charles Hirschkind, Amira Jarmakani, Karen Leonard, Saba Mahmood, Damani Patridge, Martina Reiker, Nayan Shah, and Kate Wahl.

I am truly fortunate to receive ongoing support, insight, and inspiration from these colleagues and friends: Rabab Abdulhadi, Kali Akuno, Deborah Alkamano, Amal Amireh, Anjali Arondeker, Kathryn Babayan, Elizabeth Betita Martinez, Alisa Bierra, Adrienne Marie Brown, Linda Burnham, Lucy Burns, Louise Cainkar, Tina Delisle, Philip Deloria, Gregory Dowd, Derethia Duval, Nada Elia, Holly Fincke, Simmi Gandhi, Reem Gibriel, Gayatri Gopinath, Elaine Hagopian, Sondra Hale, Frances Hasso, Rima Hassouneh, Ilana Invincible, Mervat Hatem, Randa Jarrar, Jodi Kim,

Larry Lafontaine Stolkes, Emily Lawsin, Jeannette Lee, Sunnina Maira, Khaled Mattawa, Tiya Miles, Huli Milanese, Joe Namy, Dahlia Petrus, Eric Quesada, Andrea Ritchie, Dylan Rodriguez, Damon Salesa, Jenny Salesa, Therese Saliba, May Seikaly, Setsu Shigematsu, Andrew Shryock, Bill Sorro, and Cindy Weisner.

My involvement in these organizations provided me with a sense of home and powerfully shaped the analyses and methods that frame this book: American Arab Anti-Discrimination Committee, San Francisco Chapter (ADC SF); Arab Movement of Women Arising for Justice (AMWAJ); Arab Resource and Organizing Center (AROC); Arab Women's Solidarity Association, San Francisco (AWSA SF); Center for Political Education (CPE); Cyber AWSA; INCITE! Women of Color against Violence; Radical Arab Women's Activist Network (RAWAN); and the Women of Color Resource Center (WCRC).

Affiliations with Arab American communities in Ann Arbor and greater Detroit and with these organizations in Michigan sustained me during the writing process: Allied Media Project; American Arab Anti-Discrimination Committee (ADC, Michigan); Arab American National Museum (AANM); Arab Community Center for Economic and Social Services (ACCESS); Detroit Summer; and Palestine Office.

More than ever, I owe deep thanks to Andrew McBride, Matthew Stiffler, and Lee Ann Wang, who extended themselves way beyond the call of duty as research assistants. I also thank Paul Abowd, Rabia Belt, Chris Finley, Angela Parker, and Kiri Sailiata. I am deeply indebted to Eman Desouky and Layla Feghali, who worked as assistants and interlocutors. Graduate student Mejdulene Shomali provided invaluable insight as I worked through the significance of queer studies to this project.

My heartfelt appreciation goes to David Lobenstein for editing my work with exceptional precision and splendor and with deep respect for the stories I wanted to tell and the integrity of my ideas. I also thank these editors: Jane Cavolina, Christopher Hebert, and Heidi Newman.

These individuals with NYU Press have made the process of publishing as efficient and enjoyable as it could ever be: Eric Zinner, editorial director; series editors Matthew Jacobson and Werner Sollers; and editor Ciara McLaughlin.

At the University of Michigan, I am grateful to the staff from the Department of Women's Studies and the Program in American Culture. Research and writing were aided by these grants: Ford Foundation Post-Doctoral Fellowship, University of Michigan Vice Provost for Research Award, University of California Humanities Research Institute Fellowship, University of Michigan Rackham Faculty Research Grant, and University of Michigan Institute for Research on Women and Gender Research Grant.

My extended family has stood by me every step of the way. My parents, brothers, and sister-in-law took on extra responsibilities so that I could write this book. I am grateful to my life partner, Atef Said, who has stayed up many nights discussing ideas with me and has provided me with unconditional love and support. My son, Kinan, who pinches me, hugs me, and massages my arms while I type filled me with the joy and happiness I needed to continue. Baby Nile, you are the light that kept me shining. Finally, I have been most inspired by the people who dedicate their lives to social justice and the unapologetic truth speakers and freedom fighters whose paths I follow.

Articulating Arabness

I was born in San Francisco, three years after my parents arrived to the United States from Jordan.[1] Over the next twenty years, my family moved several times across the Bay Area, creating for me a childhood and a sense of community that was both rigidly structured and ever changing. Through-out my childhood, "culture" felt like a tool, an abstract, ephemeral notion of what we do and what we believe, of who belongs and who does not. Culture seemed to be the way that my parents exercised their control over me and my siblings. The same fight, I knew from my aggrieved conversations with friends and relatives, was playing out in the homes of countless other Arab families. The typical generational wars—about whether we teenagers could stay out late at night, or whether we could spend the night at our friends' slumber parties—was amplified into a grand cultural struggle. The banalities of adolescent rebellion became a battle between two "cultures," between rigid versions of "Arab" and "American" values. To discipline us, our parents' gen-eration invoked the royal "we," as in, "No, you can't go to the school dance, because we don't do that." Here, "we" meant "Arabs."

I hated these words. I hated these declarations of what "we" did and didn't do. And yet they worked. Sort of. I came to understand a set of unspoken rules: that Arab girls don't wear mascara or that going to a party with a boy will offend the memory of my grandparents. Sometimes I actually upheld them. Or, more often as time went on, I simply tried to hide these parts of my life from my parents. Because even worse than disobeying my parents was the threat—always present in my house, in our extended family, and in our community centers—that I might be betraying my people, a term that signified anyone from the Naber family to everyone in Jordan to all Arab Christians to all Arabs. Transgressing these unspoken rules was understood not as mere adolescent rebellion but as a form of cultural loss, of cultural betrayal. And even worse, each moment of transgression seemed to mean the loss of Arab culture to "al Amerikan," that awesome and awful word that could encompass everything from the American people to the American government to the American way of life (at least as my parents seemed to imagine it).

Our Arab community, like so many immigrant networks, was wildly diverse, comprised of Muslim and Christian Jordanian, Lebanese, Palestinian, and Syrian families. And yet our parents' generation seemed to have a remarkably similar idea of what "American" and "Arab" meant. They seemed to share a tacit knowledge that Amerika (America) was the trash culture, degenerate, morally bankrupt, and sexually depraved. In contrast, al Arab (Arabs) were morally respectable—we valued marriage, family, and close relationships. It was not only our parents who put this pressure on us. What we learned at school and from the U.S. media reinforced this dichotomy, perhaps in different terms.

But as with all products of human belief, there were caveats, and shades of grey, and matters of proportion. Our immigrant parents' generation disproportionately pressured girls to uphold their idealized demands of Arab culture. Girls' behavior seemed to symbolize the respectability of our fathers and our families, as well as no less than the continuation of Arab culture in America. Particularly as my girlfriends, cousins, and I hit puberty, the pressure seemed to intensify. I couldn't wear my trendy jeans with the tear down the side for fear that al nas (the [Arab] people) would curse my sloppy clothes and bare skin, as if the tiniest sign of rebellion would let down the entire community. By the time my friends and I graduated from high school, young women's bodies and behaviors seemed to be the key signifiers in the stereotyped distinction between Arabs and Americans. The amorphous and seemingly arbitrary pressures and distinctions and rules felt outrageous. My friends and I would joke about what would happen when we came home after going out with our American friends. One night, a friend came home late, and her mother was, as usual, waiting for her at the front door. Before she walked in, her mother remarked, "Why didn't you stay out there with the slutty girls and the trash?"

Compounding matters, our parents raised us in predominantly white suburbs and encouraged us—in certain ways—to assimilate. They encouraged us to befriend the "American kids" and helped us dress up for colonial days at school. And many of us watched our fathers change their names from Yacoub, Mohammed, and Bishara to Jack, Mo, and Bob when they arrived to their grocery and convenience stores as the sun rose. It was only later that I came to understand that they had changed their names not only for assimilatory purposes but also after being called "dirty Arab" or "Palestinian terrorist," or after customers refused to shop at their stores.

Despite this, and despite the fact that our parents were encouraging us to adopt the values of middle-class America, the fundamental message in our family and community remained: we were Arab and they were American. It felt like we were living between two worlds, one within the confines of our modest suburban homes and our Arab community, the other at school and in the streets of San Francisco. With each passing year, it seemed more and more impossible to live in such a bifurcated way. I fought with my parents all the time, and because I started to doubt which "side" of me was really me, the demands from both sides just made me want to rebel against everything.[2]

Even as I yelled at them, I knew that my parents only wanted the best for me. Due to my adolescent myopia, I had only the faintest sense of the difficulties of their lives and the concurrent struggle of their immigrant generation to foster cultural continuity in America. Just like I was with my ripped jeans, they too were trying to articulate who they were. It would be years before I grasped how each day they confronted not only the pressures of displacement and assimilation but also the realities of an expanding U.S. imperialist war in the region of their homelands and intensifying Orientalism and anti-Arab/anti-Muslim racist discourses in their new home.

More than thirty years ago, Edward Said argued that "Orientalism" is a European fabrication of "the East," that "the Orient" is shaped by European imperialist attitudes and assumes that Eastern or Oriental people can be defined in terms of cultural or religious essences that are invulnerable to historical change. Orientalism, he explained, configures the "East" in irreducible attributes such as religiosity or femininity. This political vision, he contended, has promoted the idea of insurmountable differences between the familiar (Europe, the West, "us") and the strange (the Orient, the East, "them"). Like Said, critics of Orientalism have long argued that essentialist representations of Islam are crucial to Orientalist thought. In Orientalist thought, Muslims, Arabs, and other "Orientals" are hopelessly mired in a host of social ills, the cause of which is an unchanging tradition that exists outside of history and is incompatible with civilization (Majid 2000, 7; Moallem 2005; Shohat and Stam 1994). Feminist scholars have in turn argued that this strand of Orientalist thought has constructed visions of Arab and Muslim societies either as completely decadent, immoral, and permissive or as strict and oppressive to women (Abdulhadi 2010, 470; Moallem 2005; Shohat and Stam 1994). This new Orientalism relies on representations of culture (Arab) and religion (Islam) as a justification for post–Cold War imperial expansion in the Middle East, U.S. alliance with Israel, and the targeting of people perceived as fitting the racial profile of a potential terrorist living in the United States, that is, people perceived to be Arabs, Middle Easterners, and/or Muslims.[3] New Orientalist discourses have birthed a variety of widely accepted ideas: of Arab and Muslim queers oppressed by a homophobic culture and religion; of hyper-oppressed, shrouded Arab and Muslim women who need to be saved by American heroes; of a culture of Arab Muslim sexual savagery that needs to be disciplined—and in the process, modernized—through U.S. military violence (Puar 2007; Abu-Lughod 2002; Razack 2005).[4]

The impact of Orientalism, I began to see, was everywhere. Our Arab community had a plethora of cultural and political organizations that put on music concerts, festivals, and banquets, and a range of political organizations that focused on civil rights issues and homeland politics. And yet there were no resources for dealing with the difficult issues within our families and communities. As in many immigrant communities, ours opted to avoid bringing attention to personal matters in public space and among one another. This seemed like a product of fearing both how airing potentially "negative" ideas about us could fuel anti-Arab racism and how we might judge one another for our successes or failures when it came to making it in Amerika. Such pressures manifested in a sense of internal conflict I shared with many of my peers. Throughout high school especially, many of my Arab American peers were devastated by the conflicting feelings of love, pain, and guilt toward our parents and the conflicting ideas about Arab culture that we learned from their generation and U.S. society. We joked about fleeing our community altogether—and some of us did flee. Some of us swore to each other that we would never marry an Arab. These pressures were pushing young people in our community away from each other. In addition, on my trips to Jordan to visit relatives, I learned that many of the Arabs I knew in the Bay Area had more socially conservative understandings of Arab concepts of religion, family, gender, and sexuality than their counterparts in Jordan. I was baffled: why were the stakes of culture and family respectability so high in America?

Articulating Arabness

After I survived the dual gauntlet of high school and what I understood as my parents' expectations, and after I moved away from their home, I began listening more carefully to the stories of our immigrant parents. I began asking why they came to the United States, what they experienced when they arrived, and what they dreamed of and worked for in the United States. Not surprisingly, our parents' commitments to cultural continuity were much more complicated than I had understood them to be. As the twentieth century became the twenty-first, I spent several years investigating these cultural ideas and exploring how and why they operated as such an intense site of struggle for middle-class, second-generation Arab Americans then growing up in the San Francisco Bay Area. I worked with community-based organizations and did ethnographic research with people who were between eighteen and twenty-eight years old, whose families had immigrated to the United States, primarily from Jordan, Lebanon, Palestine, and Syria. I also worked with fifteen immigrants from their parents' generation, immigrants who came to the Bay Area between the 1950s and 1970s, an era characterized by increased Arab migration to the United States, the expansion of U.S. empire in the Arab region, and the intensification of colonization, racism, and xenophobia in California.[5] I additionally worked wtih immigrants of the same age group as the second-generation young adults who are the focus of this book. All of my interlocutors were connected, in one way or another, to what many referred to as "the Arab community," an all-encompassing word representing a wide range of people and ideas.

Despite a broad diversity in family origins and religious values, and despite access to socioeconomic class privileges, nearly all of these young adults told a similar story: the psychological pressure to maintain perceived ideals of Arab and American culture felt overwhelming and irresolvable. As Nuha, a daughter of Jordanian immigrants put it, "Sometimes it can make you crazy because you can't get out. I have so many worlds and every world is a whole other world. But in your mind they're totally separated, but then they're all there in your mind together. You get to a point that you are about to explode." Bassam, a Palestinian Arab American who served on the board of the Arab Cultural Center in San Francisco during my research, placed the feeling of Nuha and so many others within the context of America at the turn of the twenty-first century:

We have real needs as a community. We are really under attack. We are being damaged severely in, and by, the U.S. There is a great necessity for proactive behavior and community building. But it conflicts with the way our young people are brought up here. I'm so sympathetic to the need to perpetuate the community and yet, I'm horrified that the methods we think we must use to do so are going to kill us psychologically in this society.

For several years, as I worked closely with teens and twenty-somethings, we shared stories about the norms and expectations of our immigrant communities. From their stories, the themes of family, religion, gender, and sexuality continually emerged. It became clear that these themes formed the backbone of the idealized concepts of Arab culture that circulated in their families and communities, and were the battleground on which they, and their parents, and the Arab community, and the looming world of America all wrangled. This struggle, over bifurcated concepts of culture, and the ways that we understand ourselves as individuals and peoples, is the first cornerstone of this book.

And once again, Orientalism was at the heart of this struggle. The dominant middle-class Arab immigrants' articulation of Arabness through rigid, binary categories (good Arab girls versus bad American girls, for example) was based on a similar framework that guided Orientalist discourses about Arabs. My parents and their peers reversed Orientalism and used its binary categories (liberated Americans versus oppressed Arab women, bad Arabs versus good Americans) differently and for different purposes. Articulating immigrant cultural identity through rigid binaries is not an unfamiliar resolution to immigrant and people of color's struggles in a society structured by a pressure for assimilation and racism (Prashad 2000; Espiritu 2003; Cohen 1999; Gaines 1996). As Vijay Prashad argues, this dynamic, while a reaction to political and historical conditions, is an attempt to depoliticize the immigrant experience where culture is articulated not as living, changing social relations but a set of timeless traits (2000, 150). In many ways, the research for and writing of this book have been haunted by culture or, more precisely, by Orientalist definitions of culture. As we will see, the uninterrogated naturalization of a dichotomy between an idealized "Arab" and "American" culture among Arab Americans—a reversal of Orientalist discourses— has momentous effects on second-generation young adults. These effects are highly gendered and sexualized. Yet this same concept of Arab culture, usually associated as it is with essentialist understandings of religion, family, gender, and sexuality among Arab communities, allows Orientalist thought to be left intact and activated. Consigned to the cultural, aspects of dynamic, lived experience come to be seen as frozen in time—essentialist Arab traditions that exist outside of history—and this is the same conceptualization that operates as the basis for the demonization of Arab communities in the discourses and practices of U.S. empire.

Within the dominant middle-class Arab immigrant discourse that circulated in my interlocutors' homes and community networks, gender and sexuality were among the most powerful symbols consolidating an imagined difference between "Arabs" and "Americans." Consider the ways some of my interlocutors described what they learned growing up about the difference between Arab and American culture:

> Jumana: My parents thought that being American was spending the night at a friend's house, wearing shorts, the guy-girl thing, wearing makeup, reading teen magazines, having pictures of guys in my room. My parents used to tell me, "If you go to an American's house, they're smoking, drinking . . . they offer you this and that. But if you go to an Arab house, you don't see as much of that. *Bi hafzu ala al banat* [They watch over their daughters]."

> Tony: There was a pressure to marry an Arab woman because the idea was that "she will stand by her family, she will cook and clean, and have no career. She'll have kids, raise kids, and take care of her kids, night and day. She will do anything for her husband." My mom always says, "You're not going to find an American woman who stands by her family like that. . . . American women leave their families."

> Sam: "You want to screw, go out with American girls. They all screw," you know . . . that was the mentality growing up.

In the quotations above, concepts of "good Arab girls" operated as a marker of community boundaries and the notion of a morally superior "Arab culture" in comparison to concepts of "American girls" and "American culture." Idealized concepts of femininity are connected to idealized notions of family and an idealized concept of heterosexual marriage. These ideals underpinned a generalized pressure for monogamy—and more specifically, for no sex before marriage—and for compulsory heterosexuality. In the middle-class communities at the heart of my study, dominant articulations of Arabness were structured by a strict division between an inner Arab domain and an outer American domain, a division that is built upon the figure of the woman as the upholder of values, and an ideal of family and heterosexual marriage.

This jumble of ideals about Arabness and Americanness was the buoy that guided, and girded—but also threatened to drown—the middle-class Arab diasporas in the Bay Area. These ideals created a fundamental split between a gendered and sexualized notion of an inner-familial-communal (Arab) domain and an external-political-public (American) domain—a split that both provided a sense of empowerment and belonging and also constrained the lives of many of my interlocutors. This split was terribly familiar to me, and at the same time, largely undiscussed both in my own life and in the larger Arab American communities. I have spent nearly a decade trying to decipher the divide within our Arab community between the internal and the external and figuring out how we find meaning and formulate a life within this split.

As my research progressed, I began interpreting the predicament of growing up in new ways. Both my parents and the parents of my interlocutors constantly referred to Arab culture—as the thing that rooted us, and often, it seemed, ruled us. This amorphous entity shaped our calendar and our thoughts, what our goals were and who our friends were. But the more I searched, the harder it became to find this culture. The concepts of "Arab culture" my parents relentlessly invoked were indeed historically grounded in long-standing Arab histories, and yet it became increasingly clear that they were just as much shaped by the immigrant journey of displacement and diaspora and the pressures of assimilation in the United States. My parents' generation, and through them my peers' and my interlocutors', have ultimately been shaped not by a ceaseless and unchanging tradition but by an assemblage of different visions of how we are to make our way in the world. This is why I refer to my interlocutors' stories as *articulations* of Arabness.[6] Articulations of Arabness are grounded in Arab histories and sensibilities about family, selfhood, and ways of being in the world but are also hybrid, syncretic, and historically contingent. Our articulations of Arabness are shaped by long-standing traditions, by the isolation of running a mom-and-pop store, by the travel of news and stories through the internet and satellite TV, by Arab responses (past and present) to European colonialism and U.S. empire, and by the words and images of contemporary media. The result is in some ways disappointing to all sides: the stories of my interlocutors expose the absurdity of the Orientalist discourse so prevalent in America, but they also expose the historical conditions in which middle-class Arab American claims to hold onto some authentic notion of Arab culture have emerged. These articulations offer a long overdue look at the way concepts of community and belonging are made across the diaspora, and provide insight into the possibilities for decolonizing Arabness or rearticulating Arabness beyond Orientalism or reverse Orientalism.

Rearticulating Arabness

As I met more Arab Americans through the late 1990s, I found that young adults were involved in diverse social arenas. I let my research follow wherever the stories, imaginations, and visions of my interlocutors would lead me. I spent a lot of time among the Arab Cultural Center's networks, the major middle-class Arab American community networks in San Francisco, where I kept meeting people who frequented Arab community events but who found their primary sense of belonging within two interconnected anti-imperialist political movements. Amid difficulties with many of their parents and the frustrating clash between rigid notions of Arab and American culture, these young adults kept talking about their involvement in either the leftist Arab movement (LAM) or Muslim student activism. The Bay Area, long a hotbed of radical politics of all sorts, had in the preceding several decades birthed this activism.

I was struck by a consistent undercurrent among these activists. Indeed, young adults certainly engaged in typical forms of political activism. They organized demonstrations and teach-ins. They developed grassroots organizing strategies. They attempted to attract other members. They wrote letters and articles and distributed them on the street corner and on the internet. They held press conferences. Yet they also developed deep-seated alliances with each other. They formed alliances, they supported each other, and just as important, they disagreed. In the process, they came up with new concepts of Arabness that challenge the dominant middle-class Arab and U.S. discourses we have seen. From their flurry of activity, from their hopes and their frustrations, I saw how these movements were generating new articulations of Arabness. I gained unique insight into the ways in which dominant Arab and American discourses can be "unhooked, transformed, or rearticulated" (Diaz and Kauanui 2001). As these young adults were actively working toward ending injustice and oppression, they were also forming new definitions of family and kinship, new ideas of affiliation and belonging, new grounds for the fostering of community. They were remaking and transcending dominant concepts of Arabness and America and putting forth new visions of the future.

LAM and Muslim student activists had different aims and ideologies but had many things in common, and their projects and campaigns often overlapped. It was the late 1990s, and self-determination for the people of Palestine and Iraq was at the top of their agendas. Their movements shared a similar analysis that the United States was engaged in a regional project that aimed to remake the Middle East according to political, economic, and military structures most beneficial to U.S. empire. They concurred that U.S. Orientalist discourses were crucial in legitimizing U.S. empire in the Middle East region. They were committed to replacing Orientalist versions of Arabness and Islam with articulations of self that were grounded in the historical and material realities of immigration and displacement, racism, and U.S.-led militarism and war. LAM's concepts of self were wrapped up in the framework of secular, leftist national liberation struggles against colonial, imperial, and racial domination. Young adults involved in Muslim student activism worked through a framework that disaggregated the categories Arab and Muslim and articulated who they are as "Muslim First, Arab Second." They defined Islam as a politically constituted religious framework for addressing racial and imperial injustice and oppression that offered an alternative to Orientalist ideas about them imposed upon them by U.S. society. At times, the articulations of self that emerged in these movements were liberatory. At times, they reproduced constraints that resembled the dominant discourses they sought to transcend. In combination with dominant middle-class concepts of "Arab culture" that we saw among Arab immigrant families earlier, rearticulations of Arabness within the leftist Arab movement and among Muslim student activists form the second cornerstone of this book.

Muslim student activists were articulating a global Muslim consciousness among a diverse assemblage of individuals of all ages and groups of all kinds. Muslim community organizations, student organizations, and educational and religious institutions; immigrants and second-generation Americans from diverse countries of origin; African Americans and white Americans; lifelong Muslims and new converts to Islam—all collaborated in shaping this global Muslim consciousness in the Bay Area. As the name implies, this global Muslim consciousness parallels efforts of Muslims worldwide to better their world. "Global Muslim consciousness" does not refer to a formal global Muslim political movement with a unified international structure or network or formal membership; its adherents throughout the world take up different issues and strategies depending on the priorities of their surroundings (Mandaville 2007; Majid 2000). In the Bay Area, the Muslim student activists I worked with share a general understanding that fighting injustice in oneself and one's society is an act of worship. In the Bay Area in the late 1990s, people involved in articulating a global Muslim consciousness focused on a set of issues that they understood to impact Muslims around the world—issues that also impact non-Muslims. They understood that as Muslim Americans, they had a responsibility to address problems emanating from the U.S. government. They took up the U.S. government's criminalization of youth of color, specifically African Americans in general and African American Muslims in particular. They also took up the U.S. war against terrorism and its impact on civilians in places like Iraq and Palestine and on immigrants and immigrant communities living in the United States.

The leftist Arab movement (LAM) is a smaller collective of primarily middle-class college students and graduates between the ages of eighteen and thirty, who bring to their work myriad histories of displacement. Their ideas parallel those of the leftist Arab movements in the Arab world and its diasporas. Most members of LAM are not also involved in Muslim student activism. Yet their efforts emerge out of interconnected histories, and they often work on similar issues, support one another's work, and come together in joint projects or campaigns.[7] LAM activists are Iraqis, Egyptians, Palestinians, Jordanians, Lebanese; men, women, queers; Christians, Muslims, agnostics, and atheists; recent immigrants and exiles, and individuals born or raised predominantly in the United States; computer engineers, nonprofit workers, service workers, artists, and students. Although this diversity contributes to a varied and often contentious set of political visions, there are certain matters that bring these activists together. During the time of my research they were focused on two separate but unified campaigns: one to end U.S. sanctions on Iraq and the other to end the Israeli occupation of Palestine. Like Muslim student activists, LAM activists shared this tacit knowledge: Iraqis and Palestinians were dying en masse; the U.S. war on Iraq was looking more and more like genocide; U.S. tax dollars were paying for this; and the world was sitting back and watching.

I tried to move equally between both of these groups of people, interviewing LAM activists and Muslim student activists alike. Yet because I had fewer avenues into Muslim religious communities compared to LAM's political community, and because the work of Muslim student activists was more diffuse, I spent more time with LAM activists. In addition, I was an active participant in LAM's work. I was a board member of the San Francisco chapters of two community organizations that were central to LAM: the Arab Women's Solidarity Association and the American-Arab Anti-Discrimination Committee. And I was employed as a manager of the building that housed the main organization LAM worked through at the time and the offices of several leftist, antiracist organizations in the Mission District. During the period of my research, I spent a lot of my time around LAM activists.

And yet, for each struggle LAM waged, I couldn't help noticing the other struggles that it silenced. Mobilized by daily images circulating in alternative media sources of dead Palestinian and Iraqi children, LAM activists operated as a community in crisis. Operating in a crisis mode meant that certain issues were privileged over others. This was most clearly evident in moments when a few members criticized the sexism or homophobia within the movement. Such critiques were met with official movement logic: the issue of sexism is secondary to the fact that "our people are dying back home." Many members, women and men alike, seemed to have internalized this potent reasoning. In this movement, as in many racial justice and national liberation solidarity movements, the official movement logic also subordinated critiques of sexism and homophobia in reaction to racism. Not only were gender and sexuality barely discussed, but the official movement discourse insisted that discussing these internal issues in public could actually endanger the goals activists were fighting for. In fact, many LAM and Muslim student activists shared the belief that U.S. Orientalist representations of Arabs and Muslims, specifically images of hyper-oppressed Arab and Muslim women and Arab Muslim sexual savagery, were among the most common images Americans saw—especially from the news media and Hollywood. In this analysis, Orientalist representations were among the many reasons why so many Americans supported U.S. military interventions in the Middle East, and why many Americans, particularly liberals, expressed profound empathy for Arab and Muslim women—perceived to be victims of their culture and religion—but little concern over the impact of U.S.-led war on Arab and Muslim human life.

In response, many activists feared that discussing sexism and compulsory heterosexuality within Arab communities would reinforce Orientalism. Both LAM and Muslim student activists tended to relegate matters of heteropatriarchy among Arab and Muslim families, communities, and organizations to the margins. The tacit belief was that activists who publicly critiqued sexism or homophobia within Arab and Arab American communities were no better than traitors to their people. The result—of yet another binary structure—was that attempts to dismantle heteropatriarchy were often confined between two extremes: untenable silence, on the one hand, and the reification of Orientalist representations, on the other. As a result, I spent my days talking with a broad spectrum of Arab American young adults about how an unspoken code meant that some issues could not be talked about; and then I spent my nights going to meetings and events where some members internalized this potent logic, perhaps in different ways and for different purposes. Movements that were inspiring so many young adults around me, while bringing social justice–based Arab and Muslim perspectives to San Francisco's political milieu, could also replicate some of the debilitating aspects of our communities.

Today, nearly any discussion of the Arab world begins with the terrorist attacks of September 11. The complexity of the Arab world, and of Islam, have for many Americans been supplanted by these devastating acts. These emotions have narrowed and simplified understandings of the world's nearly 1.5 billion Muslims, the three hundred million Arabs living in Arab nations and the millions of Arabs living in the diaspora, as well as the overlap and variety among these groups (Moore 1999; Darity 2008). I seek to enlarge our understanding and, as a result, I insist on exploring the world that predates 9/11 while also considering the ramifications of that day. To be sure, the 1990s was a different moment, one that witnessed both the crystallization of U.S. empire in the Middle East and a restriction, in its own right, of U.S. global military supremacy and the Pentagon's post–Cold War plan (Maira 2009; Mamdani 2005; Khalidi 2004).

Through an analysis of the varied concepts of Arabness within middle-class Arab American families and within Arab and Muslim anti-imperialist social movements—the two cornerstones of this book—I will interrogate the dichotomies that ensnare Arab communities as they clamor for a sense of safety and belonging in the United States. As I acknowledge the remarkable efforts of those who came to the United States from the Arab world, and analyze the innovations of their children as they seek to create new ways of living in the United States, I also hope to unlock the rigid back and forth between Orientalism and anti-Orientalism, and in the process imagine new means of articulating Arabness in America.

In the pages to come, we will meet a wide range of people, from business professionals to artists, refugees to students, people involved in cultural festivals and political demonstrations and wedding celebrations, all of whom are trying to articulate affirmative concepts of who they are in between the interconnected forces of empire and diaspora. We will see how the themes of religion, family, gender, and sexuality permeate the effort among Arab Americans to define themselves and shape the way the wider world perceives them. We will hear the stories of immigrants who came to the Bay Area from the 1950s to the 1970s, and the stories of their children who came of age in the 1980s and 1990s. We will see how both generations—in one way or another—became invested in a middle-class politics of cultural authenticity—a narrative of Arabness that prescribes what is respectable and what is stigmatized, what is normal and what is deviant. We will see instances where both of these groups reify Orientalism or reverse Orientalism's binary terms, from "bad

Arabs" versus "good Americans" to "good Arabs" versus "bad Americans," and more specifically, to "Arab virgins" versus "American(ized) whores." We will see Muslim student activists articulate a new religiously constituted politics of racial justice, gender justice, and anti-imperialism as an alternative to Orientalism and reverse Orientalism. We will see Arab feminist activists struggling to find a "home" within a leftist Arab movement. We will see Arab and Arab American activists transforming their communities from within— bringing the internalized back into the external, the private back into the public, and the cultural back to the political.

None of these stories can be understood through standard visions of American assimilation, or through the essentialist concepts of culture or religion, Arabness or Islam. Nor can they be understood through liberal feminist or queer studies frameworks that approach either patriarchy or homophobia as self-contained issues. Analyses of the relationship between nation and diaspora that fail to account for U.S. histories and structures of settler colonialism and imperial expansion are also inadequate. Here, instead, we see how the domain of "culture," of the internal—and their manifestations in concepts and practices of religion, family, gender, and sexuality—can only be fully understood by considering the domain of history and politics, of the "external." In the pages to come, we will see the devastation caused by our insistence on separating these domains and will glimpse a messier reality, where a more complete articulation of self can be found in the entanglement of cultures, histories, and politics among Arabs in America.

A Note on Method(s)
De-Orientalizing Methodology

In the course of writing this book, my interlocutors had as many questions for me as I had for them: "How is this study going to benefit us?" "How is your research going to be different from the way academic institutions in America study us?" Much is implied in these questions, including a tacit knowledge that academia, especially in the United States, tends to see "Arabs" and "Muslims" from an Orientalist perspective and to use methodologies that reinforce histories of imperial domination and racism against us (Samman 2005). Though of Arab descent, just like them, I was tainted, at least in some of their eyes, by my place in the academy. The vestiges of Orientalism, as many of us know, are nearly impossible to shake. I have drawn upon the work of Arab, indigenous, third world, and people of color scholars whose work aims at "decolonizing methodologies."[8] I have also drawn on my own understandings of local knowledges, cultural sensibilities, and political commitments among Arab Americans. I adapted the notion of "decolonizing methodologies" into the framework of de-Orientalizing methodologies, a framework, I contend, that emerges from the specific context of Arab American life at the turn of the twenty-first century.

Many scholars have noted that a huge gap exists between the actual concerns of Arab Americans and their portrayal in current academic and popular literatures. Yet few have studied what Arabs living in the United States themselves are saying about their twenty-first-century predicament. Much of the progressive political critique related to Arabs and America focuses on centers of power and domination, such as government policies and media representations, which are by definition external to the actual individuals, and the daily lives of the communities, targeted by the war on terror. This approach unintentionally reifies the centers of power by ignoring—among other things—Arab and Arab American engagements with race and intra-communal differences among Arab and Arab American communities; when we subsume Arabs and Arab Americans into the scholarship as mere targets of the war, however good our intentions, we contribute to their disappearance as human subjects and agents. My hope is that this book not only refuses, deconstructs, and de-essentializes Orientalist forms of knowledge but also replaces Orientalism with new forms of knowledge. Foregrounding the complexity of the lived experiences of subjects within a transnational feminist ethnography engenders what I hope can be an antidote to the objectifying modes of Orientalism and imperialism that shape discourse.[9] What emerges is a dynamic picture of the plurality and relationality of Arab diasporas, a dynamism that has to do with the location of Arab diasporas in relationship to multiple Bay Area histories and communities, and with the way the locality of the Bay Area emerges in terms of global facts taking on local form (Appadurai 1996).[10]

The Research

Most of my research took place in the San Francisco Bay Area between January 1998 and August 2001. My research is based upon participant observation and intensive interviews with twenty-two immigrants and eighty-six young adults, most of whom are second-generation Arab Americans from Jordan, Syria, Lebanon, and Palestine. I interviewed forty second-generation men and forty-six second-generation women. I use the term "second-generation" to refer to people born in the United States or who came to the United States before they were five years old. Although seven interviewees self-identified as gay, lesbian, and/or queer, people conceptualized sexuality in many ways—ranging from liberal notions that mapped sexuality onto an identity category (gay, lesbian, or queer) to identifying as queer to mark one's nonconformity with dominant concepts of family, gender, and sexuality. By specifying heterosexual/straight and gay/lesbian/queer research participants, I bring to focus the distinct kinds of oppression and exclusion that people whose lives do not conform to dominant sex-gender systems are forced to engage with. Yet this distinction cannot capture the complex ways sexuality is imagined and lived or the fluid and changing meanings of sexual desire, behaviors, and sexual identities that have circulated in the Arab region and its diasporas (Massad 2007; Abdulhadi 2010).

My training in anthropology significantly shaped my interest in the institutional forms of power that are critical in producing notions of cultural identity, community, and belonging, even as I was acutely aware of the pitfalls of the field's standard definitions of culture, definitions rooted in colonialist frameworks that have "contributed directly or indirectly to maintaining the structure of power represented by colonial systems" (Asad 1973). I planned to begin my research among networks where dominant constructs of "the Arab community" circulated in the Bay Area. When I developed my research design, I came face to face with anthropology's institutional structures of grants and funding, and they were much less flexible than the critical theories I had studied in my graduate courses (Gupta and Ferguson 1997). I was trained to think beyond homogeneous notions of culture, but the institutional structures expected me to craft a research design that assumed "a permanent join between a particular culture and a stable terrain" (Lavie and Swedenburg 1996, 1). Grant applications asked me to define my "field site" and to justify how the "sample" of people I planned to interview represented an equal number of individuals from my "population group" across the categories that were the focus of my research (religion, nation of origin, and gender). In the preliminary stages of my research, I tried to fit my research into this concept of one "field site," and I worked with middle-class Arab community leaders and e-mail list-serves. At the time, I conducted interviews with sixty young adults (an equal number of persons from families with Muslim and Christian affiliations) and conducted participant observation at public events and family- and community-based social gatherings related to this network.[11] Participant observation included attending social, cultural, and political events, everything from music concerts to family gatherings, weddings, parties, and film festivals to cultural festivals, political demonstrations, and press conferences. I also joined the board of a few organizations, attended Arabic language and religious courses and religious ceremonies, led workshops and events, and frequented Arab-owned restaurants and coffee shops that attracted Arab and Arab American customers. Because I was working among people actively negotiating the meaning of Arabness, I spent my time among groupings, organizations, or locations where heated discussions over cultural politics took place—Arabic language classes at colleges and universities, Arab community-based (social, cultural, and political) organizations, student groups, online Arab community list-serves, and family- and community-based events and gatherings.

I realized within the first year that these traditional research methods were foreclosing possibilities of exploring the multiplicity and contradictions of middle-class Arab communities. I took solace in poststructuralist feminist anthropology (Moore 1999; Visweswaran 1994; Abu-Lughod 1991; Haraway 1988) and feminist women of color theories of the self (Alarcón 1991; Moraga and Anzaldúa 1981; Beal 2008). I went to the exact same events and talked to the same people but saw the events differently and asked different questions. I expanded my research into new areas—a more diverse group of places that attracted Arab American young adults. These approaches, rooted in a critique of essentialist or universalist definitions of womanhood, are committed to transcending the notion of "bounded selves" and "bounded cultures" (Visweswaran 1994). They shift the focus from our standard, liberal humanist idealization of a self-contained, authentic, singular, or independent self to an emphasis on tensions and contradictions among multiple discourses (including, but not limited to, gender, race, class, and sexuality). This conjuncturalist, anti-essentialist approach calls for "an understanding of the relationship between subjects and their histories as complex and shifting . . . and for using this concept to describe moments, social formations, subject positions and practices which arise out of an unfolding axis of colonization/decolonization, interwoven with the unfolding of other axes, in uneven, unequal relations with one another."[12] It was here that my de-Orientalizing method was born.

Essential to this method is the power of the stories we all have to tell. Rather than seeking to represent the "real" Arab Americans (as opposed to the media's fictive Arabs), I came to track the historical and political conditions that give rise to concepts of Arabness, and the specific and diverse narratives through which individuals who in one way or another affiliate with the Arab region and its diasporas make claims to, negotiate, live, reject, or transform these concepts. My focus on plural narratives about Arabness brought to my attention the range of discourses and power relations that shape these stories (Abu-Lughod 1993). Even the collectivity that many Arab Americans in the Bay Area themselves referred to as "the Arab community" cannot be explained in terms of a bounded, monolithic group tied to a single geographic place.

I also drew upon transnational ethnographic methods (Lavie and Swedenburg 1996; Gupta and Ferguson 1997; Marcus 2009), which refuse the concept of bounded field sites and the illusion of "bounded groups that are tightly territorialized, spatially bounded, or culturally homogeneous" (Appadurai 1990, 196). Some Arab Americans were less affiliated with the dominant middle-class Arab community network and negotiated the meaning of Arabness within other collectivities such as Muslim student organizations, anti-imperialist political movements, and feminist and queer collectives. I decided to design the "what" and the "where" of my research not in terms of a bounded "Arab American population" but by epitomizing George Marcus's notion of "multi-sited ethnography"—where narratives emerge ethnographically by the researcher following the people (2009, 90). I followed young adults' stories, imaginations, desires, and visions where they would lead me. For instance, at Arab Cultural Center events, I met a few young adults who frequented Arab community events but found their primary sense of belonging among other Muslims. This corresponded to the growing institutionalization of Bay Area Muslim institutions, which were in turn an outcome of the increasing migrations of Muslims from various parts of the world to the Bay Area since the late 1980s. As I talked with my interlocutors, I learned of a growing trend among Arab American young adults to claim their identity as "Muslim First, Arab Second." A narrative of belonging to a global Muslim community, among Muslims from various parts of the globe, took precedence over an Arab identification.

Thus, I committed a portion of my time to participant observation in Muslim organizations where young adults articulated Muslim identity among Muslim migrants, second-generation Muslims, and Muslims with various racial/ethnic histories. My research revealed that among these young adults, a particular group forged powerful concepts of home, belonging, loyalty, and affiliation through their involvement in a transnational social and political movement focused on ending global oppression. This led me to define Muslim student activism, which was the primary entry into their involvement with transnational Muslim politics, as my second research focus. I interviewed twenty Arab American Muslim students involved in this movement and conducted participant observation at the religious education classes and social and political events that constituted their social world. I did not take up studying distinctly Christian narratives. Indeed, there are Arab Americans who are also practicing Christians and who articulate distinct concepts of cultural identity and politics that might fit in with the focus of this book. There is also a distinctly Arab Christian faith-based activism rooted in Christian forms of liberation theology.[13] Yet owing to geopolitical conditions I cover in chapter 1, such as the peak in Arab Muslim migration patterns to the Bay Area in the 1990s and the politics of war that singles out Arab Muslims disproportionately compared to Arab Christians, there was no institutionalized transnational Christian political movement that second-generation Arab Americans were joining.

I encountered and subsequently worked with another collective of transnational Arab activists, this time young adults involved in leftist, anti-imperialist protest focused on Palestine and Iraq. These activists were connected to the dominant middle-class Arab community although a general middle-class sentiment was that they were "too liberal" or "too radical." This leftist Arab movement (LAM) in the Bay Area included primarily young adults with different histories of migration, including both second-generation young adults and immigrants and refugees of the same age group. For a short time, they worked in collaboration with the recent Iraqi refugee community. I was a board member of the main organization through which LAM worked. Here, the categories "Arab," "Arab American," or "second-generation" were less significant than the narrative of leftist diasporic anti-imperialism. At the same time, differences of gender, class, and immigration history complicated, in unexpected ways, all attempts to explain this movement in categorical terms.

I also interviewed individuals whose experiences were crucial to the stories that this book tells but do not fit neatly into the above groupings. These interviews took place with community leaders who were primarily immigrants. They assisted me in locating my interlocutors' stories within relevant historical and political circumstances. To better understand my interlocutors' references to their middle-class immigrant parents, I conducted interviews with fifteen immigrants of their parents' generation who moved from Jordan, Lebanon, Palestine, and Syria to the Bay Area between the 1950s and the 1970s. I spoke to them about Arab immigrant experiences in the Bay Area during this period, a time I knew little about beyond memories that my parents and their friends shared around the coffee table. To bolster my research among second-generation Arab American Muslim student activists, I interviewed four individuals whom these students considered key Muslim community leaders. These individuals directed or were active members of major Muslim American institutions in the Bay Area.

Following Ruth Behar, I focused my interviews on "life stories" rather than "life histories"—on what she calls "the fictions of self-representation, the ways in which life is made in the telling"—so as to "elaborate the concept of the actor as engaged in the meaningful creation of a life world."

My work with Muslim student activists and activists from the leftist Arab movement documented "activist stories," an offshoot of Behar's term. Activist stories, I contend, are those of individuals who strive to be effective not just for themselves but in order to develop a broad understanding of their group within its particularized historical and political realities. While activist stories, like all ethnographic stories, are indeed fictive, I take interest in just how historically grounded and gravely urgent these stories become to my interlocutors' lives. The conditions of living in the empire bring them to tell stories about recurring lived realities of violence and the fragility of life, even as they reside far away from many of the places they are fighting for. Throughout the book, I use pseudonyms to hide my interlocutors' identities. Unless my interlocutors agreed, I avoid writing at length on matters that would reveal their identities.

Ethnographic Accountability

My relationships with my interlocutors shaped the kinds of knowledge I produced (Narayan 2003; Abu-Lughod 1991). I have an intimate familiarity with the people with whom I worked and the way they view family, culture, and politics. I also shared many political sensibilities with my interlocutors. For decades, my family was involved in the Arab Cultural and Community Center of San Francisco, an organization I turned to during the period of my research. In the late 1990s, I was an active member of the organizations that are the focus of chapters 4 and 5, the San Francisco chapters of Arab Women's Solidarity Association and the American Arab Anti-Discrimination Committee, San Francisco Chapter. I also was involved in feminist and antiwar organizations that several of my interlocutors were affiliated with, such as the Women of Color Resource Center and INCITE! Women of Color Against Violence.

Accountability in research means developing research agendas in collaboration with the agendas of interlocutors' social justice movements and their struggles for representation and self-determination (Smith 1999, 115-20; Viswesaran 1994, 32; Speed 2008). The social movements that are the focus of chapters 3, 4, and 5 prioritize interconnected agendas, such as dismantling imperial, colonial, and racial domination in their homelands and in the United States. A primary strategy of their movements was to bring counternarratives to U.S. publics that could replace the dominant U.S. imperialist representations of the Arab and Muslim region and their diasporas, representations that they argued legitimized U.S.-led wars and anti-Arab racism. Many of my interlocutors and I were engaged in a similar project that believes in the potential of Arab and Muslim counternarratives to shift the balance of powers.

On a daily basis, I, like my interlocutors, have negotiated the discrepancy between the ways dominant U.S. discourses represent family, gender, sexuality, religion, and culture among Arab Americans and the diverse ways Arab Americans live these concepts. My interpretations of their stories were shaped as much by the analyses they shared as by my own. This reciprocity of analytical work is the reason why I refer to them as my interlocutors rather than subjects or interviewees. The mutuality of our work was especially true with the women activists who are the focus of chapters 4 and 5, as their political analyses and the political projects in which they were engaged most closely resembled my own. In light of these connections, many interlocutors seemed to perceive me as "one of us." There were many times when interlocutors lost sight of my position as researcher. Such familiarity was a great honor; they saw that I was someone interested in the textures of their lives. In turn, the intimacy they showed required careful consideration and negotiation, about what I would publish and what would remain "between us" (Simpson 2007).

The principles of reciprocity and feedback shaped my research. This entailed not only reporting back with the research findings after the research was complete but also sharing research and obtaining feedback on the findings, analyses, and theories along the way (Smith 1999, 118-22). This was important for three reasons. First, my research addresses potentially sensitive matters—people's in-depth personal stories, political events that could implicate a research participant in government harassment against them, or intra-communal tensions that could be construed by other members of the community as "airing our dirty laundry in public." Thus in places where the personal and political stakes are high, I invited interlocutors to read chapters, correct mistakes, refuse publication of sensitive matters, contribute to the analysis, and provide feedback. In some places, I incorporated their responses into the book. Second, reciprocity and feedback allowed interlocutors to collaborate with me on how I was going to represent their stories. For instance, several activists whose stories I narrate in chapters 3, 4, and 5 collaborated with me on how I would refer to their political visions and affiliations. Third, reciprocity and feedback allowed me to gauge the usefulness of my research and analyses to Arab and Arab American audiences and beyond, specifically, the people whose stories I narrate in the book. Ethnographic accountability meant relating to my interlocutors not only as research participants but as theorists, scholars, and analysts themselves. At times, this went smoothly, especially when interlocutors responded with comments such as these: "Your work is incredible, poignant, and you've named, reclaimed and worked through some incredibly difficult & spectacular moments in our collective history" (on chapters 4 and 5). At other times, I entered into elaborate discussions and negotiations over responses like this: "The class dimension is severely understated. Women who leverage years of investing in their own self-betterment by being UC or Stanford grads do not bring about the same intellectual resource in defending their rights as that of a student or waitress scrounging by."

The Limits of Accountability

Writing for multiple audiences was among the most momentous challenges. I saw myself writing both for academic audiences and for Arabs and Arab Americans and their social movements (each with their own set of complexities). Challenging U.S.-led empire and war was among the social justice agendas that mattered most to the activists with whom I worked. Yet a dominant current in U.S. academia is hostile to Arab and Arab American political narratives, often censoring those that call U.S. empire into question, especially in relation to Palestine (Samman 2005; Roy 2007). The ways in which many Arabs and Muslims view the 1990s, although shared by many (often marginalized or targeted) scholars and activists throughout the world, contest much of the standard discourse prevalent in the media and supported by the government. This contested, and in many ways delegitimized, understanding of the recent relations between the United States and the Middle East is woven through my interlocutors' narratives. Indeed, it contradicts much of what our mainstream media has been telling us for the last two decades. Consider, for example, the contested discourses on May 15, the day marking the creation of the state of Israel. Celebrated by dominant U.S. and Israeli discourses as Israeli Independence Day, this day is mourned among Palestinians, Arabs, and social justice advocates internationally as *al-Nakba* (the catastrophe) for its displacement of 750,000 Palestinian refugees and destruction of hundreds of Palestinian villages. May 15 is just one of hundreds of instances of divergent visions of the world. Yet we must acknowledge and confront the imbalances of power and the ways in which, as Edward Said has written, the power to block certain narratives "from forming and emerging is very important to culture and imperialism, and constitutes one of the main connections between them" (1993, xiii).

Balancing the demands of the academy and community accountability was a constant negotiation. Tenure procedures as well as the process of publishing generally reify positivist concepts of objectivity and call for distance between the researcher and research participants. Balancing these demands, I positioned myself as an auto-ethnographer who aims to narrate each story, place it in a theoretical, historical, cultural, and political context, and provide some sort of background, analysis, commentary, or interpretation.[14] There were indeed moments where I suppressed the urge to take stronger political stances or to advocate for one collective I worked with over another. I was also concerned that some of my interlocutors would want this to be more of an activist how-to book than I was willing or able to write. I cannot control the way this book will be read. Anytime women of color and third world women write about sexism and homophobia within their families or communities they risk having their words rerouted back through a colonialist, racist, or Orientalist mindset and misinterpreted as exemplifying their people's potential for violence and backwardness. Indeed, I also risk disappointing some of my interlocutors and people of the Arab Bay Area who may not want to see a book about intra-communal tensions and hierarchies.

Mitigating the Silences

Like all projects, this one inevitably has its own biases. In airing some voices, I have no doubt I am creating some silences. My own subject position impacted the way I related to people and the reasons why I came to narrate some stories more than others. To a certain extent, my family's history of involvement in middle-class Arab immigrant community networks gave me "insider" status as well and granted me a level of respect that impacted my research. Community leaders and interviewees generally assisted me and welcomed my project. Yet at times, my subject position was a site of difference or even distance that disrupted my "insider" status, even if temporarily. My Christian religious heritage and family name, for instance, positioned me as a guest in Muslim spaces. My active involvement in certain collectives led me to more awareness about some Arab American young adults' interests and commitments than others. For instance, I was more familiar with collectives that worked in some relationship to middle-class Arab immigrant institutions and collectives that were anti-imperialist, antiracist, antiwar, and/or feminist.

I grappled with how to write about queer Arab activism as I am not an insider to these politics, and when the research began I had developed only minimal relationships of mutual trust and respect with queer Arab activists. On the one hand, I believed that excluding queer Arab narratives would reinforce the long-standing exclusion of queer narratives from Arab American histories. I took heed from queer Arab interlocutors and activists who insisted that being spoken for and represented also contributes to exclusion, erasure, and marginality. Through conversations with queer activists, I decided not to write a separate chapter on queer Arab activism. We agreed that it made more sense to weave queer Arab narratives throughout the book and to situate them in relationship to the complex web of subject positions and concepts and practices of gender and sexuality that constitute the Arab Bay Area. This would illustrate what one interlocutor explained as "showing that sexuality is part of everyone's life experiences rather than associating sexuality only with queers." I also decided to avoid the topic of theology in my discussions of Muslim student activism and to avoid in-depth representations of the previous period of the Palestinian movement and the Palestinian women's movement in the Bay Area (1970s and '80s) that I refer to throughout the book. Such a focus, I believe, would have been beyond my area of expertise and accountability and would have diluted my ability to explain the conditions most relevant to my research.

After the attacks of September 11, 2001, one interlocutor, a human rights activist, refused to continue to be interviewed. She told me that she felt objectified as an Arab woman in the United States; after the U.S. public and media had been ignoring Arab and Arab American needs for so many years, all of a sudden, a plethora of organizations and media were asking her to speak at public events and to the media. Though she appreciated what I was trying to do, she felt unable to participate in any further efforts to represent her community. The ravages of Orientalism, as we can see, manifest in innumerable ways. My book is less compelling without her voice, but her decision contains its own power, and makes its own statement. I highlight these dilemmas to take responsibility for the fallibilities of this project. Even as I consulted with my interlocutors about my decisions, I was, ultimately, the researcher, the author, and the storyteller. I edited interview material for readability and I had the final say about how their stories would be retold and interpreted.[15]

1

From Model Minority to Problem Minority

In the 1990s, Arab immigrants who had come to the Bay Area between the '50s and the '70s spoke about their early years in America with a sense of nostalgia reminiscent of conventional immigrant stories. They dwelled on positive experiences about their homelands and idealized their first years in their new country. Yet these immigrants had a distinct story about the past and the present—one that sheds light upon changing geopolitical relations between the United States and Arab- and Muslim-majority countries throughout the Cold War era and on the way these relations crept into the daily lives of Arab Americans in profound ways. In 1999, Jamal, a Jordanian who came to the Bay Area in the 1950s, told me, "At that time [in the '50s] there was no 'the ugly Arab' or 'the bad Arab' or 'the Arab terrorist.' American society wasn't the way it is now. They [Americans] opened their homes to us. I felt it later on, after twenty years in San Francisco. It was really nice in those early days."

Scott Kurashige, analyzing the status of Japanese Americans after World War II, uses the term "model minority" to refer to a racial-ethnic status in which group members find acceptance from white America by proving that they are model American citizens, an ideal that he argues is dictated by the American state (2010, 204). Many Arab immigrants with whom I worked narrate stories in which they too were perceived as model minorities. They recall an America in which they enjoyed a general proximity to whiteness and a sense of acceptance within white middle-class America up until the late 1980s and early 1990s, the period in which the United States was consolidating its growing imperial interests in the Middle East and North Africa.[1] As the Soviet Union (soon to collapse in the summer of 1991) withdrew from the world stage, the possibility of a full-scale U.S. military intervention in the Middle East opened up. This occurred almost immediately with the Gulf War, commencing in the spring of 1991. Developments in U.S. intervention in the Middle East paralleled an intensification of U.S. imperial expansion on a global scale in the 1990s. Throughout the 1990s, U.S. policy shifted toward more openly militaristic forms of expansion and a commitment to strengthening economic neoliberalism on a global scale (Foster 2005; Duggan 2003; Ong 2006).

In the 1990s, the period framing this book, Arab immigrants of the 1950s, '60s, and '70s and their children met the expansion of U.S. empire in the Middle East through their encounters with the stories the U.S. government, the corporate news media, and Hollywood tell about the Middle East, stories that reinforce the interests of the U.S. state. U.S. imperial discourses of the 1990s can be understood in terms of the new U.S. Orientalism, a discourse that constructs an imagined "Arab-Middle Eastern-Muslim" as the enemy of the nation as a justification for imperial expansion.[2] Over the years, the ways in which Arab immigrants, followed by their children, have articulated Arabness, have been entangled in the shift in their status from model minority to problem minority. Their articulations of Arabness range from ethnic accommodation or what I term, in chapter 2, the politics of cultural authenticity to the politics of anti-imperialism, the focus of chapters 3, 4, and 5. The politics of cultural authenticity and the politics of anti-imperialism represent two poles along a spectrum of articulations. Here, I map the local and global conditions in which these two poles of Arabness in the Bay Area were produced while tracing the multiple articulations in between. Cultural authenticity, by supporting an accumulation of wealth through hard work and an avoidance of associations with the decolonizing and anti-imperialist political movements of Arab homelands in U.S. public space, provides Arab diasporas with a framework for maintaining their middle-class U.S. socioeconomic status. The politics of anti-imperialism, while still at times deploying the logics of liberal multiculturalism, prioritizes the aim of ending U.S.-led war and domination in the Arab region and elsewhere. Several interconnected factors helped birth these articulations of Arabness: ongoing diasporic relationships to the homeland(s), an expanding U.S. empire, and changing immigrant and racial politics in the Bay Area, in California, and in the United States.

Articulations of Arabness are best understood through the concept of diaspora.[3] Seen through the lens of diaspora, "cultural identity is hyphenated, wherein the hyphen does not mark a simple duality between two distinct cultural heritages." The hyphen between the categories "Arab" and "American" "emphasizes the multiple local and global conditions that shape identity" and happens when different narratives of nations, classes, genders, generations, sexualities, and so on collide with one another as "interstices" or "third-space" (Bhabha 1994, 224).[4] Yet my interlocutors' stories reflect a distinct diasporic state of consciousness, a sense of belonging to a diaspora of empire.[5] Many people with whom I worked spoke out of a tacit knowledge that Arabs or Muslims living in the United States have been forced to engage with U.S. imperial discourses in their everyday lives, discourses that associate Arabs and Muslims not with the U.S. nation but with real or fictive places outside the boundaries of the United States, and against which the United States is at war. While transnational cultural studies often invokes the way in which diasporic immigration traces a route back to the formerly imperial metropole, my theorization of the "diasporas of empire" emerges against the highly invasive and shifting relations of power central to contemporary U.S. neocolonialism and imperialism. Here, empire inscribes itself on the diasporic subject within the domestic (national) borders of empire.

Methods and Terms

Virtually no scholarly research exists about Arab immigration to the San Francisco Bay Area.[6] I gathered the accounts I narrate in this chapter by spending time among community-based networks, listening to people's stories, and scouring through community-based publications. Between January 1998 and August 2001, I conducted participant observation within community-based organizations and at community-based events and gatherings that brought together Arab immigrants from Jordan, Lebanon, Palestine, and Syria. Most early Arab immigrants who set up Arab community-based collectivities in the Bay Area were from these countries. From that time until 2008, I conducted interviews with fifteen women and men who came to the Bay Area between the 1950s and the 1970s. These individuals were either heavily involved in Arab cultural politics or community-based organizations or had engaged with them from a critical perspective. All of the men were married. Four out of seven women I worked with were unmarried; three had been divorced and one self-identified as queer. This lopsided gender structure reflects a pattern in which married immigrant women of this generation were more involved in domestic forms of labor and less involved in community-based leadership compared to their male counterparts. Community-based publications authored by organizations such as the Ramallah Club, St. Nicholas Church, and the Arab Cultural Center provided me with additional material.

There exists a major discrepancy between U.S. Census and Arab American community-based accounts of the population size of Arab Americans (El-Badry 1994; Zogby 2000). Afaf Laffrey et al. argue that the U.S. Census's underestimation of the number of Arabs in America results from the absence of a category for Arabs on the U.S. Census's short form and that many Arabs are reluctant to disclose their country of origin or ancestry even on the long form (1991). As a result, it is difficult to estimate the population size and other demographic details about Arab Americans in the San Francisco Bay Area. I use the term "immigrants" as shorthand to refer to diverse immigration experiences, ranging from forced displacement (Palestinian refugees) to migration for socioeconomic mobility.[7] I use the term "Arab American" for people who live in the United States and who trace their ancestry to one or more of the twenty-two member nations of the Arab League: Algeria, Bahrain, Comoros, Djibouti, Egypt, Iraq, Jordan, Kuwait, Lebanon, Libya, Morocco, Mauritania, Oman, Palestine, Qatar, Saudi Arabia, Somalia, Sudan, Syria, Tunisia, the United Arab Emirates, and Yemen. I often use the word "Arab" and couple it with "Arab American" (e.g., "Arab and Arab American") to acknowledge the fluid and changing ways these terms operate in people's lives and to recognize people who do not have the privilege of U.S. citizenship or who do not identify with an American national identity.

Throughout the book, the terms "Arab" or "Arab American" remain contested and take on different meanings depending on the context. At times, individuals use "Arab" as a cultural and linguistic term to refer to persons from countries where the primary language is Arabic. Another definition, influenced by the Arab nationalist movements that peaked in the 1950s and 1960s, assumes that Arab is also a national identity and that Arabs share a language and a common cultural and imagined national community. Since 1945, nations whose primary language is Arabic have combined to form the Arab League, and official international discourses consider members of the Arab League to be the Arab nations.

In response to U.S. racial discourses that construct an imagined "Arab-Middle Eastern-Muslim enemy," some critics, while recognizing its arbitrary and fictive nature, use similar designations to refer to the diverse people targeted by this racial schema (Volpp 2003a; Maira 2008; Rana 2007). My interlocutors often use the terms "Arab" and "Muslim" to refer to the people who share similar experiences with this racial schema as they recognize that these categories do not map onto each other. The six countries with the largest Muslim population are Indonesia (170.3 million), Pakistan (136 million), Bangladesh (106 million), India (103 million), Turkey (62.4 million), and Iran (60.7 million) (Central Intelligence Agency 2009). None of these countries is considered Arab. Arab countries include a diversity of linguistic, ethnic, and religious groups. Religious groups include, but are not limited to, Christians, Jews, and Druze. Non-Arab ethnic minorities include, but are not limited to, Kurds, Amazighs, and Armenians. Thus, there are many challenges that come with efforts to name Arab immigrants and Arab Americans. The religious, ethnic, and linguistic diversity of the Arab region gives at least some insight into why the federal government as well as Arab individuals and communities have found reaching a consensus over who is an Arab and what constitutes Arabness to be a particularly arduous task. Suad Joseph writes,

> There are Palestinians, Iraqis, Kuwaitis, Yemenis, Saudi Arabians, Bahreinis, Qataris, Duabis, Egyptians, Libyans, Tunisians, Moroccans, Algerians, Sudanese, Eritreans, and Mauritanians; there are Maronites, Catholics, Protestants, Greek Orthodox, Jews, Sunnis, Shia, Druze, Sufis, Alawites, Nestorians, Assyrians, Copts, Chaldeans, and Bahais; there are Berbers, Kurds, Armenians, bedu, gypsies, and many others with different languages, religions, ethnic, and national identifications and cultures who are all congealed as Arab in popular representation whether or not those people may identify as Arab. (Joseph 1999, 260)

Ever since the late 1880s, when the first significant group of Arab immigrants came to the United States, the terms of identity have been contested and shifting.[8] The first significant group of immigrants was from the Ottoman provinces of Syria, Mount Lebanon, and Palestine. The federal government classified the early immigrants along with other Ottoman subjects as originating from "Turkey in Asia" (Samhan 1999, 216). Immigration reforms that were passed in 1893 led to the classification of Arabic-speaking immigrants as "Syrians" after 1899 (216). These identity categories diverged from the familial, village, or religious modes of categorization through which early immigrants tended to identify (Majaj 2000, 321). The end of the Ottoman Empire in 1917 and the emergence of distinct Arab nations that are often referred to collectively as the "Arab world" marked another shift in the identity terms deployed by both the federal government and Arab individuals and communities. For example, Alixa Naff argues that for early immigrants from Mount Lebanon, an area formerly located within the Ottoman province of Syria, the term "Lebanese" was given political legitimacy in the 1920s as a national label or identity and was adopted by most immigrants originating from Mount Lebanon (1985, 2).

On the level of federal government racial categories, a 1978 classification scheme located Arabs within the broader rubric of "persons originating in Europe, the Middle East, and North Africa" (Samhan 1999). In 1997, the Office of Management and Budget, in collaboration with various Arab American community organizations, noted a lack of consensus about the definition of an Arab ethnic category and suggested that further research be done to improve data on this population group. Census 2000 added the classification "Arab ancestry" in a separate part of the census to obtain specific information about persons from the Middle East and North Africa who identify an Arab ancestry. The federal government and the major national Arab American community organizations have yet to reach a consensus on the appropriate term for immigrants from Arabic-speaking countries. Within the field of Arab American studies, scholars have tended to refer to immigrants from the Ottoman province of Syria before 1920 as Syrian and to post–World War II immigrants as Arabs or Arab Americans.

Some Arab and Arab American activists contest the terms "Arab" or "Arab American," arguing that these terms are nationalist, exclusionary toward non-Arab minorities in the region, and limited for purposes of coalition building beyond Arab communities. Collectives of feminist and queer activists across the United States have proposed the geography-based term "Southwest Asian and North African" (often referred to as "SWANA") to include non-Arab minorities, transcend patriarchal and homophobic nationalisms, and expand alliance building between people from Arab nations and other nations in the region, such as Iran, who share similar histories with U.S. imperialism and war. Others have privileged religious identities such as Muslim or Muslim American over the nation-based label "Arab American" on the grounds that their primary loyalty is rooted in faith and the divine.

Elders and Old-Timers: The Conditions of Early Immigration

Most Arab immigrants of the 1950s, '60s, and '70s knew someone already living in the Bay Area when they arrived through family- or village-based networks. Many of these immigrants referred to themselves and their peers as the old-timers. They initially worked in factories and did menial jobs such as painting bridges and cleaning businesses and gravitated toward one another. Although most did not intend to stay, a range of factors made it increasingly difficult for them to return to their countries of origin. The 1948 war and the creation of the state of Israel meant the displacement of approximately seven hundred thousand refugees. Some of the Palestinian old-timers were among these refugees. Since then, the Israeli state has denied Palestinian refugees the right to return to their homes or villages (Aruri 2001). For other Palestinian old-timers, the ongoing conditions of Israeli military occupation and expansion made returning to Palestine increasingly unviable. Most Lebanese old-timers considered themselves visitors until the onset in 1975 of the Lebanese civil war, which contributed to a shift in their perspective, and they began to view themselves as residents. Many found the idea of returning to Lebanon after the civil war unimaginable. Nadya, a Lebanese woman who had been actively involved in leftist Arab movements in the Bay Area, was the director of a cultural arts program at a multiracial community organization in Berkeley in 2008. She told me she migrated to the Bay Area in the 1960s on her own, planning to stay only temporarily. She returned to Lebanon in the 1980s, after the civil war began. She recalled,

> I thought that was it, I was going back home to Lebanon. I gave away all of my stuff in San Francisco, got rid of everything, packed up my suitcase, took my clarinet, and went home. I got pregnant after being married in Lebanon. And then—the war. After spending a couple of nights in a shelter while pregnant, all of a sudden came the fact that I had this baby with me—and I said, I'm not gonna risk that life.

Nadya returned to the United States to stay. Old-timers who did not come in a context of war remained in the Bay Area as a consequence of the imbalance in socioeconomic opportunities in the United States compared to their countries of origin. The old-timers came to the United States during a period when dominant U.S. discourses were emphasizing racial integration and, to a large degree, assimilation (Brodkin 2002). Most of them were not exceptionally wealthy in their homelands and came primarily from families involved in trading and agriculture. Most often, their extended family members pooled funds so one or two family members could migrate to the United States. After their arrival, relations with other Arab immigrants who had already established themselves in the Bay Area allowed them to develop the means to invest in business entrepreneurship within a few years.

One old-timer celebrated the idea that "anyone can make it in America." His perspective reflects a key pillar of dominant U.S. nationalism of this period that inspired the migration of his generation to America. Most old-timers spoke to me about Arab histories in the Bay Area from the standpoint of immigrants who were, like them, entrepreneurs or business professionals. They spoke to me in celebratory ways about their elders—the Arab immigrants who came before them and had been coming to the Bay Area since the early 1900s. Many of their elders, after working as peddlers, became store owners and manufacturers. The old-timers were particularly inspired by the few elders who went on to become producers, theater managers, doctors, lawyers, and engineers. The elders had paved the way for newcomers like my interviewees to establish small businesses. For instance, the elders advanced newcomers money for a small fee.[9] Together, the experiences of the old-timers and their elders shaped what became the dominant middle-class Arab immigrant narratives that circulated the Bay Area in the 1990s, which heralded the socioeconomic success of predominantly male Jordanian, Lebanese, Palestinian, and Syrian immigrant business entrepreneurs.[10] This coincides with a broader pattern in scholarly and community-based histories that privilege this story over others—such as the stories of poor immigrants, women, queers, or social justice activists.[11]

The old-timers inherited a great deal from the elders, who were predominantly Christians from Mount Lebanon and came from Greater Syria at the turn of the twentieth century (Naff 1985; Suleiman 1999; Shakir 1997; Aswad 1974). Paralleling patterns of migration from the Arab world to the United States in general, the elders came to the Bay Area in the early 1990s out of economic necessity and for personal advancement. The old-timers were heavily influenced by their elders' immersion within white middle-class America. Many elders had become financially successful and rarely faced obstacles in white middle-class settings. At the same time, the relationship of Arab Americans to whiteness is complex and has been changing and contradictory. Before 1940, the position of Arabs with regard to race in the United States, in terms of immigration and naturalization, was unclear and often contested. This was a period in which the U.S. government used racial schemas to allow citizenship and eligibility for naturalization. The U.S. government did not permit immigrants who were not determined to be "white" by law, and as the outcome of court decisions, to become U.S. citizens. Before the 1940s, Arabs were classified both as white and not white, depending on various court decisions, as different judges and courts came to different conclusions about the "race" of Arabs. In the 1940s, however, the United States Census Bureau determined that Arab Americans were to be treated like European immigrant communities, effectively categorizing them as "white" in the eyes of the U.S. government (Samhan 1999; Majaj 2000).

By the 1960s and '70s, ideas about race had shifted in the United States, due in large part to the civil rights movement. Race became an increasingly contested term. Yet even though the biological idea of race was generally refuted, structural racism persisted (Gaines 1996; Omi and Winant 1994). Around this time, the U.S. government increasingly began relying upon the U.S. Census and racial categories for statistical information (Lopez 1996; Samhan 1999). Within this schema, a new civil rights–based racial discourse emerged that categorized people with shared histories of racial oppression into racial categories. This discourse used the language of race not in terms of biological race but to name collective experiences of racism. After the 1960s, alongside U.S. imperial expansion in the Middle East, it became clear that the long-standing question of whether or not Arabs were "white"—whether in terms of historical concepts of biological race or post-1960s concepts of community experiences with racism—was never quite resolved. As we will see, while the U.S. Census has continued to classify Arab Americans as Caucasian, U.S. media and government policies have consistently represented Arabs as different from and inferior to whites. In addition, Arab Americans have also put forth differing ideas of race, some claiming whiteness and others refuting such categorizations.

Unlike their elders, the old-timers who came to the Bay Area after world war II found themselves interacting with more and more immigrants from every Arabic-speaking country. In particular, more Arabs immigrated from the Gulf states and North Africa. And unlike the previous generation, who migrated mostly of their own volition, a rising number of postwar immigrants came as a result of displacement caused by war. Finally, postwar Arab American communities were comprised of nearly equal numbers of Christians and Muslims (Suleiman 1999, 9). Post–World War II immigration and displacement to the United States was much more diverse and dynamic than in the previous years.[12] New transnational dynamics framed the postwar period in terms of vigorous anti-European colonial nationalisms in the Arab world. In the Bay Area, unlike their elders, who self-identified primarily by family name, village of origin, or nation of origin, most old-timers shared a generalized loyalty to Arab nationalism, even as some of them established loyalties to the United States. The Arab nationalism that predominated in their homelands during this time was primarily directed at European domination (Lockman 2010; Choueiri 2000; Barakat 1993; Khalidi et al. 1991).

Arab nationalism of the 1950s emerged out of the interrelated conditions of European colonialism in the Arab region, early Zionist settlement in Palestine, and the collapse of the Ottoman Empire in the late nineteenth and early twentieth centuries (Khalidi et al. 1991; Barakat 1993; Choueiri 2000).[13]

Anticolonial Arab nationalist ideologies, while diverse, were generally based on the precept that Arab countries form an integral and indivisible whole and on a commitment to the achievement of independence and self-determination with unity. Anticolonial Arab nationalism of this period assumed that European colonialism is incompatible with "the dignity of the Arab nation and that the Arab nation rejects it and will resist it with all the means at its disposal" (Choueiri 2000, 92). This idea culminated after 1945 when several Arab countries began to engage in projects for Arab unity.[14] This was a time when the United States had just entered the political arena of Middle East politics. Britain and France were no longer in a position to maintain control of the Arab region, and the United States deemed it necessary to step in and assume the mantle of the former colonial powers as the guarantor of stability (Lockman 2010, 117). Yet the United States was not yet a global superpower and the idea that the United States was at war with Arabs had not yet become a common sentiment among Arab Americans. In fact, when I spoke with them decades later, the old-timers often waxed nostalgic about the 1950s and '60s as a simpler time, before they faced the consequences of an expanding U.S. empire in the Arab world. Monther, a Palestinian man and the founder of the Arab Cultural Center and the first local Arab TV station in San Francisco, told me,

> We were not seen as terrorists or whatever people think about Arabs today. Most people didn't know what an Arab or Palestine was. Even though there was a lot going on in our countries—Israel was created, Nasser's revolution—the U.S. was not involved like today and the West Bank was still in Jordan.

In the 1950s, American interests in the Arab region were mostly related to investments in oil companies in Saudi Arabia known as Aramco (Arabian-American oil company) (Choueiri 2000; Khalidi 2004). Also in the middle of the twentieth century, the United States replaced Britain as the superpower responsible for working out a solution to the Palestinian problem. Historian Zachary Lockman, writing on the early development of the United States' relationship with Israel during this period, argues that the Arab-Israeli conflict contributed to growing U.S. involvement in the region and that while Arabs sought the independence of a Palestinian state, Zionists fought for the creation of a Jewish state in as much of Palestine as possible. Lockman adds that the Truman administration pressured Britain to accept Zionist demands, and when an exhausted Britain turned the Palestine issue over to the New United Nations, the US (along with the Soviet Union) endorsed the UN plan to divide Palestine into separate Arab and Jewish states. A Jewish state was established in most of Palestine in 1948, and Israel refused to allow the hundreds of thousands of Palestinian Arab refugees who had fled or been expelled from their homes during the fighting to return.

Since then, the United States has attempted to reconcile its support for Israel with its relations to Arab states, "which, while friendly to the U.S., regarded Israel as a colonial-settler enclave illegitimately established on Arab land by violent means" (Lockman 2010, 118).[15] Despite these developments, the United States did not perceive Israel as a major asset until the 1960s (Khalidi 2004). For the old-timers in the Bay Area, the 1950s was not only a period of relative calm, politically speaking, but it was also a different period in intra-communal relations. In the 1950s, several old-timers contended, intra-communal differences had not yet become politically charged. Zuheir, a business entrepreneur and former president of the Jordanian American Association, expressed this analysis as follows:

I never heard such words "Muslim" and "Christian." When I graduated from college in 1957, I didn't know which of my classmates was Muslim or who was Christian, because we never asked such questions. These things just popped up later and more and more lately. Before, we never had such words "Christian" and "Muslim." We're all one family, one people.

Zuheir's words reflect the beliefs that proliferated in the Arab Bay Area in the late 1990s, that sectarian differences were a new phenomenon. Hatem, a Palestinian and leader in Muslim American institutions who came to the Bay Area in the 1970s, shared a similar analysis about a shift towards increasing intra-communal divisions based upon religious affiliation:

More recently, some elements of Arab Christianity have become attuned to thinking of Christianity as a Western construct, not as an Eastern construct. They sometimes feel distant from Muslims because they are trying to perceive themselves as part of the West, a West in an antagonistic relationship with the Muslim East. That is a learned viewpoint and needs to be challenged. Also, in some Muslim perspectives, there is the view now, more than before, of thinking of Christians as a Western concept, and they need to de-Orientalize their view.

Zuheir's and Hatem's statements concur with a growing academic and political critique about the rise of sectarianism in the Arab world in the context of growing of U.S. imperial wars (Al-Ali and Pratt 2009; Marr 2004; D. Cole 2003).

Becoming a Problem Minority: 1960s–1980s

Melanie McAlister (2001) argues that the U.S. government's conflict with Arab nationalists first took shape after 1945, when the United States supported Israel's attempt to defeat them. Like many scholars, she explains that Cold War terms determined the strategic relationship during the really important period of the 1960s and '70s when the alliance between the United States and Israel was consolidated. The United States intended to build alliances in the Arab region (e.g., Iran and Saudi Arabia) within a post–Cold War moment, or within the twofold U.S. struggle against the Soviets and against pan-Arab nationalist regimes under leaders like Nasser, who were connected to the Soviet Union's hegemony in the region (McAlister 2001). The United States confirmed its alliance with Israel in the context of the 1967 Arab-Israeli War as a proxy against the Soviets. The 1967 war began an intensification of U.S. military, political, and economic intervention in the Arab region. McAlister writes that the end of the Vietnam War produced a crisis in masculinity for the U.S. government. When Israel won the 1967 Arab-Israeli War, the United States admired Israel and considered the country a strategic ally. Aligning with Israel helped the United States recover from what McAlister refers to as "the Vietnam syndrome" (2001).

The 1970s U.S.-Arab oil crisis brought about increased U.S. government and media representations of Arab men as potential threats to American finances and American national security. The proliferation of U.S. media images portraying Arabs as the enemy of the U.S. nation paralleled the increasing significance of oil to the global economy. As U.S. policymakers and oil companies joined forces to exert pressure on the Arab world, the imperial interests that produced "the Arab" as an enemy of the nation emerged, reinforcing long-standing U.S. concepts of the uncivilized, savage, potentially dangerous, exotic Oriental, Eastern, Arab, Muslim. The 1970s brought racial images of rich, greedy Arab oil sheiks, murderers, or slave owners threatening the U.S. economy alongside images of harems and belly dancers. Amira Jarmakani argues that in the 1970s, "oil sheik images emerged in a moment of greatly intensified political conflict between the United States and the Middle East, and they reintroduced the concept of the harem as a prisonlike space for women who were, by nature, at the mercy of brutal or greedy patriarchal figures" (2008, 166). Images of greedy patriarchal oil sheiks who hoard both their natural resources and their women reinforced the idea of Arabs as a threat to American finances and American national security (174).

The 1970s was also the period of the Iranian revolution and the Iranian hostage crisis of 1979-1980, along with a rise in racialized portrayals of Arabs as the enemy Other. The United States engaged in various covert and over-expansionist projects in the Middle East such as the intervention in the Lebanese civil war in 1982 in support of Israeli objectives, and the bombing of Libya in 1986 (Lockman 2010). U.S. media images of the 1980s increasingly portrayed Arabs in general and Palestinians in particular as terrorists (Stockton 1994, 133).[16] The idea of Arabs as a threat to America conveniently rationalized U.S.-led war. By the late 1970s and '80s, predominant U.S. media images increasingly relied on constructs of Islam as an uncivilized religion within an emerging new U.S. imperial discourse of the "Arab-Middle Eastern-Muslim" as a potential terrorist threat (Hudson 1980; Said 1981; Shaheen 1984; Terry 1985; Suleiman 1988; Jarmakani 2008). According to McAlister, "In the years after the Iranian hostage crisis, an impressive array of cultural and political texts described American bodies as vulnerable to a terrorist threat mapped as Islamic and Middle Eastern" (2001, 232). Jarmakani contends that the potential Arab Muslim male terrorist counterpart is the veiled Muslim woman who represents an oppressive, hyperpatriarchal, and irrationally violent Arab Muslim culture (2008, 174).

These factors form the bases upon which U.S. politics in the Arab region have been conceptualized as enactments of empire. U.S. empire in the Arab region has worked through a range of structures, including neoliberal economic expansion and domination (Mitchell 1991; Elyachar 2005); support for the NGO-ization or the professionalization of revolutionary social movements (Incite! Women of Color against Violence 2007; Abdo 2010); support of puppet governments through the threat of military or economic domination (e.g., Jordan and Egypt); wars on countries that do not comply with imperial interests; the economic and military backing of Israeli-settler colonialism and expansion; and the circulation of media and government discourses on terrorism and Islamic fundamentalism.[17] The development of U.S. empire in the Middle East between the 1960s and 1980s marked the beginning of a new era for Arabs in the United States. In the Bay Area, a general sentiment developed in which people began to consider whether other people were suspicious of them, perceived them as un-American, or wondered whether they were connected with people the U.S. government and media were portraying as enemies of the nation. In the dominant U.S.

national narrative, Arabs in the United States were now a potential problem minority. The consensus among my interviewees was that the post–World War II era in which Arabs enjoyed a general proximity to whiteness was disrupted.

Several old-timers traced the proliferation of anti-Arab U.S. sentiment to the aftermath of the 1967 Arab-Israeli War and especially the Iranian revolution. Karam, who immigrated to the United States from Syria in the late 1970s, told me, "The U.S. stance and the ways that Iranians were represented devastated me." She said that many people she interacted with did not know the difference between Arabs and Iranians and often bought into dominant U.S. narratives. Many Arab Americans with whom I worked also became aware of a series of U.S. government policies that drew them into the increasingly fraught relationship between the United States and the Middle East. They told me how stories about these policies circulated in the community— around the coffee table, within community organizations, and at social gatherings. Some immigrants recalled Nixon's ostensible counterterrorist measure, dubbed "Operation Boulder," in 1972, which signaled the beginning of a series of FBI policies to target students of Arab descent. Presidential directives authorized the FBI to harass Arabic-speaking individuals with phone calls and visits, without evidence of criminal activity, on the assumption that they might have a relationship with "terrorist activities" in Palestine and Israel (Akram 2002, 5). The state targeted these individuals and denied them their constitutional rights.

Several immigrants mentioned the U.S. government's surveillance of Arab Americans in the 1970s, when several government agencies, including the FBI, the Justice Department, and the Immigration Department, carried out a wide-ranging campaign of investigation and surveillance of Arab Americans, including spying and wiretapping, that was ordered from the White House under the guise of uncovering the activities of persons potentially involved in sabotage (Hussaini 1974). The collective sense of belonging to a community whose homelands are becoming increasingly important to U.S. imperial expansion after 1967 ignited what many scholars have referred to as an "Arab American awakening" (Suleiman 1999). After 1967, and particularly in the late 1970s and early 1980s, throughout the United States and in San Francisco, the first pan-Arab community-based organizations were formed. This trend drew upon the heightened pan-Arab nationalist tendencies in the Arab world of this period and a current that had shaped the politics of U.S. racial-ethnic communities in which engagements with colonial, racial, and economic domination reignited movements for self-determination in the United States. The following quotation from civil rights lawyer Abdeen

Jabara's 1977 Community Day speech in Dearborn, Michigan, captures this sentiment:

> These attitudes frequently govern how people act in employing Arab Americans, promoting Arab Americans, renting or selling homes or apartments to Arabs, or in characterizing Arabs in the local media. . . . It was the July 1967 war in the Middle East that had the effect of galvanizing what had been a dormant giant. Second- and third-generation Arab Americans were confronted with a historic challenge to their self-identification.

The ways in which Arab Americans began feeling the impact of U.S. empire in their own lives in the United States crystallized the sense that one could potentially be perceived as an "enemy within," particularly if one were politically engaged in activities that countered or critiqued U.S. government policies in the Middle East. A common knowledge developed in the Arab Bay Area that activists challenging the United States' support for Israel over Palestinians could be put under surveillance, detained, or deported at any time. The L.A. 8 case of 1987 played a crucial role in shaping this common knowledge. The Reagan administration targeted seven Palestinians and one Kenyan for deportation, a civil proceeding, on charges of being affiliated with the Popular Front for the Liberation of Palestine (PFLP), then the second-largest faction of the Palestine Liberation Organization. Peter King (2005) writes that their arrest was sparked particularly by one event, whose "purpose, organizers said, was to generate donations for 'the homeland,' in particular, to provide medical care and schooling in Palestinian refugee camps."

The U.S. government claimed that the PFLP advocated world communism, making affiliation with it a deportable offense under the McCarran-Walter Act. Although FBI director William Webster testified before Congress that none of the eight had engaged in any criminal activity, the case dragged on in federal court for twenty years as the Justice Department pressured the courts to deport them. Finally, in 2007 an immigration judge ruled that the government had violated the defendants' constitutional rights.[18] Furthermore, court proceedings revealed a Justice Department contingency plan providing a blueprint for the mass arrest of ten thousand alien terrorists and undesirable Arabs within the United States (Joseph 1999).

Internment of the Psyche

The ways in which U.S. imperial structures took on local form in U.S. government practices and media discourses contributed to what I term an "internment of the psyche," or a sense that one might be under scrutiny—by strangers, hidden cameras, wiretaps, and other surveillance mechanisms of the security state, as well as invisible arbiters of the legality and normality of behavior, rendering them vulnerable to the "truths" contrived by the state—even if they were engaging in lawful activity. Particularly for political activists, living with these specters became a normative pattern of life (Naber 2006). Nayla, a Lebanese woman who came to the Bay Area as a teenager in the 1970s, said, "The L.A. 8 case scared people out of their minds. It stopped a lot of people in their tracks." The internment of the psyche worked like Foucault's "panopticism" (1979, 209), the disciplinary mechanism of generalized surveillance that brings the effects of power to the psyche. As a form of discipline, it "induces within individuals a state of consciousness that assures the automatic functioning of power" (201). The internment of the psyche became a covert and unspoken medium that linked sociopolitical institutions and the individual psyche together, "making it possible to bring the effects of power to the most minute and distant elements" (Foucault 1979) of everyday life. Several interlocutors reflected on this sense of collective fear, a fear of being monitored by the state or simply mistrusted. Karam was living in the suburbs in the late '80s. She told me this was about the time she learned that in order to survive she would have to remain silent about her heritage.

People who had enjoyed the privileges of white middle-class acceptability, whether or not they were activists, feared criminalization or social, political, or economic marginalization. Fuad, an entrepreneur who identifies with the Republican Party, is deeply invested in the ideal of assimilation, and came to the Bay Area in the 1950s, told me, "I may have my own opinion with or against what's happening, but I'm not gonna share it with the American people." Dozens of stories circulated about fathers, uncles, and family friends who owned small business and were the targets of racial slurs or actions when their customers learned they were Arab. One old-timer told me about a customer who asked for a refund for his sandwich and soda after he realized he had just purchased his lunch from an Arab. Many grocers quickly learned that changing their name from Yacoub to Jack, Mohammed to Mo, or Bishara to Bob could help expand their clientele. These stories reflect the views that many middle-class Arab immigrant business entrepreneurs shared. They understood that making it in America would require silence about U.S. policy in public spaces or even hiding one's Arab identity altogether.

As these stories show, Arab immigrant narratives of this period do not fit neatly into a category of either assimilation and racial privilege or marginality and racial Otherness. The old-timers with whom I worked expressed desires for middle-class assimilation as well as a political understanding that the discourses of U.S. empire positioned Arab diasporas as potential enemies of the nation. As we will see, another set of factors complicated Arab American identity in the aftermath of 1967: the interconnected global processes of neoliberal economics in the Middle East, militarism and war, and increased displacement and migration had been taking on local form in the changing demographics of the Arab Bay Area.

Changing Demographics: Unimagined Arab Communities

In the aftermath of 1967, more Arabs came to the Bay Area than ever before as a result of displacement and war and the migration patterns of economic neoliberalism. Fundamental shifts in U.S. immigration policy also occurred during this period. The Immigration Act of 1965 abolished the national origin quotas that had been in place since the Immigration Act of 1924. Immigrants could now enter the United States because of their skills or professions rather than their countries of origin (Cainkar 2009; Ngai 2005). Monther referred to the 1960s and 1970s as a time "when things exploded for the Arab community in San Francisco." There were more Arabs in the Bay Area than ever before, and they were more diverse in terms of socioeconomic class, religion, political ideology, and country of origin. The middle class began to diversify along the lines of grocery store owners and professionals. Monther said,

> More Arabs from Gulf States came to the Bay Area and more and more from Palestine, Lebanon, Syria, Jordan and we also saw more and more North Africans and more Muslims. Some were already educated and economically sufficient. They became professionals who came directly into banking, real estate, and engineering. Others were not—they became farmers, taxi drivers, janitors, dish-washers.

The sudden diversification of the Arab Bay Area brought about new interactions across different Arab communities. What many called "the Arab community" in the San Francisco Bay Area could no longer be described as primarily Christian and primarily Jordanian, Lebanese, Palestinian, and Syrian. Middle-class Arab immigrants who came to the Bay Area between the 1950s and 1970s formed a range of community-based collectivities in the Bay Area in the context of a rapidly expanding U.S. empire. The collective articulations of Arabness that emerged among Arabs in the Bay Area came out of the interconnected conditions of race, class, empire, and diaspora between the 1950s and the late 1990s.

From Ethnic Accommodation to Diasporic Anti-Imperialism, 1950s–1970s

Within community-based organizations and within social and family-based networks, many old-timers institutionalized a middle-class articulation of Arabness in the Bay Area. One of the first Arab organizations in the Bay Area has represented one of the largest groups of Palestinians from the historically predominantly Christian village of Ramallah. Palestinian old-timers inherited the Ramallah Club, a local chapter of the American Federation of Ramallah, Palestine (AFRP) from the elders who came to the Bay Area in the early 1900s. AFRP has remained one of the largest Arab organizations in the Bay Area, reflecting the reality that Palestinians, due to decades of engagement with Israeli colonization, have tended to be most active in maintaining collective identity and sustaining community-based institutions. Many old-timers shared the collective sense that one day Palestine may cease to exist, inspiring a plethora of community building activities. The Palestinian old-timers I worked with were primarily from Ramallah. They spoke about Ramallah nostalgically as one big family where everyone was related to one another. One old-timer told me,

> We all came from one grandfather and his wife. We then bought the building on Ocean Street in 1961. It's a social club and has nothing to do with politics. It's for bringing the family together. To socialize. To let young people meet each other. There were no other groups at the time, other than a Lebanese club and the church.

After many of the old-timers first arrived in the Bay Area, the church was a crucial institution for community building. Jameel told me,

> The Arab churches and seeing each other—Muslims and Christians—at the church functions was one of the most important things to us. Muslim guys from Syria used to come with us. We loved eating the food together. At that time, there were about twenty to thirty Palestinian families and three Jordanian families around. We were very close and the church was our base. We tried to keep our culture alive and judged each other in terms of how good we were in keeping our culture.

These stories reflect how a politics of ethnic accommodation has shaped middle-class Arab organizations in the Bay Area such as the Ramallah Club and, later, the Arab Cultural Center. These organizations have tended to celebrate both middle-class assimilation and "ethnic difference" while ignoring material realities or structural inequalities (Lowe 1996). Lisa Lowe argues that such politics diffuses the demands of material differentiation through homogenization and the incorporation of signifiers of ethnic difference (86). Immigrants who helped found the Ramallah Club tended to frame the story of the club around memories of immigrant men gathered in grocery store stock rooms. They proceeded into celebratory accounts of middle-class entre-preneurs who pooled their resources to buy the building that has housed the organization since 1961. They herald the club as a place for preserving and promoting Palestinian cultural heritage in America—a place designed solely to promulgate friendships that have "nothing to do with politics." It is a place that "brings the family together" and "lets young people meet each other."

A posting on the Ramallah Club of San Francisco's website tells the story this way: A young Palestinian couple were planning to marry in 1955 but "were just finishing college and getting started on their lives in the commu-nity and could not afford anything like a hall for their wedding reception." A leading Palestinian entrepreneur responded to this predicament. He said, "The Ramallah Club needs a hall!" He then wrote the first check for five hun-dred dollars that began the fundraising process for the property on Ocean Avenue, which is still in use today.

The story of the Ramallah Club reflects a dominant articulation of Arab-ness among middle-class Arab diasporas in the Bay Area that took shape among the old-timers of the 1950s and was consolidated in the 1970s within the framework of ethnic accommodation and a politics of cultural authen-ticity. Here, entrepreneurs accepted and rationalized a particular narrative of American assimilation that diverged from the New Deal or working-class notions of Americanism that arose in the mid-twentieth century, when America emphasized the importance of social contracts and an interven-tionist state (Gaines 1996). The middle-class politics of cultural authenticity both asserted a distinct Arab culture and supported the ideal of American middle-class success and mobility.

Another articulation of Arabness that circulated in the Bay Area dur-ing these years privileged a commitment to self-determination and decolo-nization of the Arab world. In the 1950s, some old-timers were working in solidarity with pan-Arab anticolonial nationalist organizations of the Arab region. By the early 1970s, Arab nationalism, in its various guises and modes of application, took on a distinctly socialist dimension. Arab nationalism had developed in relationship to the rise in socialist nationalist movements globally, particularly among the nonaligned countries of the third world (Choueiri 2000). Several old-timers recalled the Arab student organization at San Francisco State as one of their first experiences in forming a collective

"Arab" identity. One old-timer told me, "It included students from Algeria, Morocco, Egypt, Palestine, Jordan, Lebanon, and Syria. We were like family." He explained, "They issued membership cards with one flag that was supposed to include all the Arabs."

In general, whether they were committed to ethnic accommodation or anticolonial nationalism (or both), old-timers' access to social and economic resources facilitated the formation of their community-based institutions and the ability to purchase property to sustain them. After most old-timers graduated from college and worked for several years, they learned from their elders that opening grocery stores was their ticket to upward mobility. They gained access to socioeconomic resources similar to those of their elders, and developed similar kinds of relationships to the U.S. market economy of the mid-twentieth century. Their increasing access over the years to human capital, such as educational status and accumulation of personal savings and, in some cases, property ownership, allowed them to accumulate further capital from economic institutions such as banks and investment firms. Collective borrowing strategies provided them with start-up capital or capital to maintain businesses, and they shared networks of low-wage workers or relied upon unpaid family members. Over several decades, many old-timers used the wealth accumulated in their small businesses to invest in real estate and eventually became wealthy, inspiring many of them to move from San Francisco to the suburbs, including the San Francisco Peninsula, East Bay, and South Bay.[19] San Francisco proper became home to younger Arabs and Arab newcomers, and less to the old-timers. Despite the dispersion of middle-class Arab immigrants throughout the Bay Area, their familial, social, and political networks remained in place. This network of middle-class Arab immigrants formed a variety of pan-Arab, nation-based, and village-based collectivities over the next few decades. They also developed diverse religious institutions. Maronite Catholic, Antiochian Orthodox, and Roman Catholic were the primary Christian groups. Each group has formed its churches and church-based communities. Most Arab Muslim immigrants were Sunni Muslims, and they developed their own religious institutions.[20]

Cultural Authenticity of the 1970s and 1980s

The formation of the Arab Grocers Association in the 1970s reflected the continued process by which a dominant trend among middle-class Arab immigrants would deploy the concept of pan-ethnicity to secure their access to middle-class resources. Fuad, a leading member of the association,

told me that the Arab Grocers Association provided grocers with a mechanism for ensuring they would "get good services, better prices, and respect"
from the large companies they dealt with for their products. It helped to
"stop companies from taking domestic advantage of us because we are foreigners and don't speak the language well." The association was one of the
largest Arab American organizations in the Bay Area of this period. One
community leader told me, "We had five hundred grocers in San Francisco
at that time. We were very big. All of San Francisco's little grocers were
Arab American." As a result, Arabs from other community-based institutions often turned to the Arab grocers for help with nongrocery issues, and
the association also provided a mechanism for engaging in the politics of
civic participation and advocacy. For example, members of an Arab American Democratic club turned to the Grocers Association for help in obtaining signatures to promote the two-state solution in Palestine at the U.S.
Democratic Convention. Monther, a long-time contributor to various Arab
community organizations and a leader in this effort, told me, "This showed
people that we can come together and make changes. It inspired people.
This was around the time that the city of San Francisco started knowing
who we are."

The possibilities the Arab Grocers Association created reflect the values
of a liberal multicultural America that requires immigrants to identify as different, as Arab, in order to gain recognition. Recognition, in turn, offers the
apparent promise of equal rights and acceptance. Zuheir told me,

> Every government official who is going to run for any position in local,
> state, or federal government used to come and beg to meet with our com-
> munity and to listen to us. And we helped those who helped us. We later
> helped Mayor Frank Jordan become a mayor. And sure enough, Frank Jor-
> dan appointed six commissioners from the Arab people.

Within the framework of liberal multiculturalism, America celebrates
racial and cultural diversity as a way to suppress the more politicized mobilizations of difference produced during the civil rights movement of the 1960s.
Elizabeth Povinelli (2002) contends that "multicultural domination works . . .
by inspiring subaltern and minority subjects to identify with the impossible
object of an authentic self-identity—a domesticated nonconflictual traditional form of sociality and intersubjectivity." The nation, she explains,

> stretches its hand to them, and they are led on to perform an authentic dif-
> ference in exchange for the good feelings of the nation and the reparative

legislation of the state. This does not simply produce good theater, it inspires impossible desires: to be this impossible object and to transport its ancient meanings and practices to the present in whatever language and moral framework prevails. (6)

The Arab Grocers Association, operating within this framework, relied on liberal multicultural categories to articulate a pan-ethnic Arab identity as a strategy for gaining racial-ethnic recognition, thus reifying the ideal of racial-ethnic recognition that obscures the realities of economic-class inequality. Indeed, this move was also informed by pan-Arab nationalist trends of the Arab world of this period. In the 1970s and '80s, people who previously identified with their nations of origin or family names came together around a pan-Arab identity more than before.

In the 1970s and 1980s, the bifurcation at the heart of liberal multicultural discourse, which assumed a separation between two domains—a cultural domain on the one hand and a political domain on the other—could be seen within most middle-class Arab organizations. Lisa Lowe argues that multiculturalism is central to the maintenance of a hegemony that relies on a "persistent distraction away from the historically established incommensurability of the economic, political, and cultural spheres." In this sense, the production of multiculturalism "at once 'forgets' history" (1996, 86). This bifurcation could be seen in the formation of strictly "cultural" organizations in the 1970s and 1980s, organizations that consolidated the hegemony of "Arab cultural authenticity" as the dominant articulation of Arabness in the Bay Area. The cultural organizations worked through a weblike structure that made room for intra-communal differences of village or nation of origin or religion while connecting people to one another through the concept of a pan-ethnic Arab cultural heritage. The Arab Cultural Center is the largest and most well established of these institutions. At the time, its constituents were primarily middle-class Arabs. Old-timers spoke about the ACC as a place that attracted community support because "it was not specialized in some political disaster area but for the Arabs here . . . for all the Arabs in the area to get in touch with their culture and maintain our roots, meet each other and bring the community together." They share a collective memory of the ACC flourishing in the 1970s and 1980s because it brought people together. Many other social and cultural institutions representing villages or nations of origin were formed that reified middle-class cultural authenticity at this time. Village-based organizations like the Ramallah Club were primarily Palestinian, reflecting the significance of village-based identities in the Levant, the large numbers of

Palestinians in the Bay Area, and the disproportionate desire for cultural continuity among Palestinians. But Jordanian, Lebanese, Syrian American, Egyptian, and Yemeni organizations, among others, were also founded.[21] This plurality of affiliations involved a critical inheritance of homeland categories for organizing social differences and accommodating them into liberal, multiculturalist categories. Yet, tensions often emerged over "homeland" (nation- and village-based) and "hostland" (pan-ethnic) frameworks that often went unresolved. One old-timer told me,

> We tried to convince the community that it's important to be Arab here more than anything else. The more you live here and see the reaction of the bigger culture to the Arabs, the more you felt like an Arab organization would be a much stronger purpose to work for. What unifies everyone is how the American culture viewed us.

Amidst these different affiliations (pan-Arab, nation-based, village-based), middle-class organizations conceptualized "culture" in a separate domain from "politics" and defined "culture" as fixed and unchanging. Here, "culture" was to be expressed through the components of music, food, art, and language or through essentialist notions of kinship, relationality, and community. One old-timer told me that "culture" is what connected him to other Arabs in the Bay Area. It is the sense that "we are all part of the same world" and share "a closeness with each other." Several old-timers recalled moments where they felt closeness with another person as soon as they learned he or she was Arab. Monther told me this was not "something you teach" but something you "have to live." Old-timers also tended to hope that their generation would transmit their culture to the new generation at social events such as dinner banquets and music and language classes, thus reifying concepts of an authentic culture frozen in time and abstracted from history.

Many political organizations assumed a similar separation of politics from culture. Old-timers helped form organizations that relied upon a concept of pan-Arab American political identity that paralleled the dominant trends among middle-class Arab activists across the United States during this time. These activists were responding to the sentiment of the late 1960s and '70s—that the U.S. state and media had waged a war against them—by establishing several Arab American organizations, many that were based upon civil rights concepts of pan-ethnicity, such as the National Association of Arab Americans (1972) and the American-Arab Anti-Discrimination Committee (1981).

Arab American political organizations of the 1970s and 1980s tended to define their work in terms of civil rights or lobbying. Civil rights organizations, such as the American Arab Anti-Discrimination Committee, San Francisco Chapter, shared a commitment to claiming political rights through the concept "We are Americans, too." Their claims focused on equality for Arab Americans in government policies and in the law. Lobbying organizations such as the National Association of Arab Americans sought to promote an evenhanded U.S. policy in the Middle East, particularly in relation to Palestine. Several factors explain the centrality of Palestine to Arab American civil rights. A large majority of Arabs in the Bay Area are Palestinian. In the 1970s and '80s, Arab Americans faced racism based on racist attitudes in the United States about Palestinians (Abraham 1994). In addition, Palestine was at the center of anticolonialist Arab nationalist ideology (Khalidi et al. 1991). By often distinguishing between domestic and global issues, Arab American civil rights frameworks favored problems such as discrimination against Arabs in the United States over U.S. foreign policy issues. Arab American civil rights frameworks aimed for the acceptance of Arabs in the United States as Americans and thus often avoided asserting a transnational critique of the interconnections between U.S. imperial formations and anti-Arab discrimination in the United States.

Diasporic Anti-Imperialism

In the 1970s, '80s, and early '90s a vibrant anti-imperialist Arab movement focused primarily on Palestine. It was based in radical-socialist national liberation theory. This movement worked through political channels rather than fixed or coherent organizations, though some of the ideologies became attached to particular organizations. The dominant middle-class Arab American narrative considered such groups as outside the boundaries of community acceptability, deeming them too radical, or as obstacles to middle-class acceptability. While most activists did not explicitly advocate for middle-class assimilation, they saw themselves as people who were forced to come to the United States and make a living. Hussein, one activist from this period, told me,

> If I'm going to be here, I'm going to take care of my family until the atmosphere of war is over. But we also brought our politics with us and maintained that political commitment. The people who started the more mainstream Arab organizations here distanced themselves from what was happening and wanted to be nonpolitical.

Activists were primarily Palestinian but were also from other Arab nations and included some non-Arabs. This movement was connected to Palestine and experienced a range of sectarian solidarities and tensions. Early on, since a majority of activists were people who came to the United States at college age with a political consciousness formed before they arrived, this movement was connected through a student organization, the Organization of Arab Students (OAS). Hussein, a Palestinian exile, told me, "I was demonstrating in my high school. So were the Iraqis, the Lebanese, and people from the Gulf. All of us found a home in the OAS." OAS had dozens of chapters throughout the United States.

The support for Palestinian national liberation worked in a broader environment of leftist Arab long-distance national liberation movements, some of which also existed in the Bay Area during this period, such as supporters of the Lebanese Communist Party, leftist progressive groups within the Lebanese civil war, the Arab Labor Socialist Party–Lebanon, the National Democratic Front in North Yemen, the Yemeni Socialist Party, and the Arab Labor Socialist Party. These movements emerged within a 1960s and '70s global context of widespread anticolonial, anticapitalist sentiment for sovereignty, national liberation, and self-determination. Arab anti-imperialism in the Bay Area was shaped by global trends of the time in which nationalist movements in China, North Vietnam, Algeria, Uruguay, the Philippines, and beyond were demanding liberation from imperialist powers (Chang and Chung 1998). They were also shaped by trends within the United States and the Bay Area specifically that drew on these global trends, as we will see. Arab anti-imperialist activism strengthened in the mid-1970s as more and more young people, particularly student immigrants, claimed a seat at the table. Palestinian and Arab national struggles peaked in the '80s. Especially after the 1982 U.S.-backed Israeli siege of Beirut, more than ever before, the Bay Area Arab movements recognized that they needed to establish themselves deeply in North America. One activist told me,

> [B]ecause Lebanon was more accepted in the U.S. and seen as more civilized compared to Palestine, this moment provided us with an opportunity to talk to mainstream Arab and American organizations. After Beirut was under siege, we had a joint struggle between Lebanese and Palestinians speaking out to a larger circle than just activists.

This period birthed a new collective, the November 29th Committee for Palestine, which later became the Palestine Solidarity Committee. The aim was to avoid sectarianism and avoid turning away Americans who might prefer affiliating with a solidarity committee rather than a political party. The Palestine Solidarity Committee was a national group with a national newsletter published in the Bay Area. Throughout the '70s and '80s, activists developed a range of community-based programs that focused on political education and grassroots political organizing. The Bay Area was indeed a major hub of activism related to Palestinian and Arab national liberation. In the 1970s, activists supporting Palestinian national liberation opened the only Arabic bookstore in the United States in San Francisco's Mission District. This store included hundreds of leftist books in Arabic. Husssein told me, "We had international novels, Tolstoy, Rosa Luxemburg, all in Arabic. People never had access to progressive books like this before. People would visit the bookstore from other states and buy books in the dozens." Not all anti-imperialist politics emerged within secular leftist formations. Some Arabs, Muslim and Christian, were developing anti-imperialist politics through religious frameworks. Muslim anti-imperialist politics peaked in the late 1990s, as we will see.

Camaraderie and Exclusion

The multiple collective articulations of Arabness in the Bay Area have coexisted and intersected with one another. An overarching sense of belonging to an imagined Arab community connected these different collectivities to one another at varying moments and to different degrees. The Arab Cultural Center is a San Francisco–based institution where multiple articulations of Arabness have interacted. A plurality of Arab community-based collectivities have held meetings at the Arab Cultural Center at one point or another— forming an interconnected web or a new, unimagined, "unanticipated community" (Ono 2000). Also, while pan-ethnic collectivities shared a critique of village- or nation-based formations, their members tended to attend the annual gatherings and conferences of village- or nation-based organizations and often turned to them to meet relatives from their home countries. Members of anti-imperialist organizations often joined village-based organizations with the aim of politicizing them. The lines between the various groups that interconnected the Arab Bay Area were not always clear. Despite the realities of sectarianism and intra-community differences (family, village, religion, or nation of origin), the immigrants with whom I worked repeatedly made statements such as, "We are all one family, one people"—even if the unity to which they referred was unstable. Monther, reflecting upon intra-communal differences, told me,

Each group still wants their pride . . . they want to be Lebanese, Jordanians, Palestinians, Yemenis, Iraqis, all that. And we wanna be Christians, Muslims. There's no cement. In the '80s, there was more cooperation between groups. The ACC was the beehive and they had their meetings there (all the different groups). Yet most were Palestinians . . . and there were views that this was a Palestinian organization because Palestinians are most active of all of them.

Many internal critiques circulated within this unimagined Arab community. One critique contended that Arab community organizations unfairly prioritized Palestinian issues over others. Another, particularly among some Jordanians, Syrians, and Lebanese, viewed Palestinians with antagonism, as the "real" Arab enemy of the U.S. nation who stood in the way of their own efforts to gain acceptance in America. Some Muslim Arab Americans argued that Christians were granted more representation and leadership privileges in Arab community organizations. There were indeed more Christians than Muslims involved in Arab community organizations. Two factors contributed to this imbalance. First, the first two generations of Arab immigrants to the Bay Area up until the late 1960s were primarily Christian. Christians were already established within the community's leadership. Second, the Arab nationalist tendency underlying pan-Arab community organizations had secular Arab undertones, inspired by mostly Christian political figures and intellectuals of the early twentieth century (Khalidi et al. 1991). In the Arab world, Arab Christians tended to be particularly attracted to the ideal of pan-Arabism. Pan-Arabism offered them a more inclusive space than religious structures for organizing society, particularly since the majority of people in the Arab world are Muslim (Majid 2000).[22] There were also differences and hierarchies that were left unspoken—especially differences of socioeconomic class, gender, and sexuality. Aliya, a Palestinian old-timer who worked with the Arab Cultural Center for decades, told me, "They [the old-timers] didn't know how to outreach to the *entire* community, to the different neighborhoods where lower-income communities live inside the city, in the inner-city, even in public housing or low-income housing." I interacted with dozens of women who worked with the middle-class Arab community organizations over the years who expressed critiques of sexism and shared experiences of marginality. Aliya told me, "I faced a lot of challenges trying to do my work to build the community center by men who felt intimidated. They don't really necessarily want women here to take initiative and to take a leading role." She also thought that patriarchy was more prominent in the United

States than in Palestine because, she explained, "people there evolved in a way where they accept women in leading roles." During this period, several women leaders, such as Aliya, left leadership positions in community organizations because of the sexism and referred to them as men's clubs.

Some interlocutors argued that idealized concepts of gender and sexuality led to the exclusion of people who transgressed those ideals. Karam, who was politicized and active in racial justice, queer, and feminist movements, told me, "People in the mainstream Arab organizations couldn't handle me. I did not look like what an Arab woman should have looked like." Karam told me that at first, she stayed away from these institutions and found a sense of home in the formation of queer Arab or Middle Eastern collectives. Writing on the history of these collectives, Bay Area–based scholar and activist Huda Jadallah affirms that "although there have always been Arab Americans who have transgressed sexual and gender boundaries, the communal identities and histories of LGBT Arab Americans were largely undocumented until the 1980s." Writing on networks similar to those to which Karam belonged, Jadallah writes, "Queer Arab Americans are active members of queer communities, Arab communities, and many other communities. . . . Formal organizational structures for Arab American lesbians and gays began to emerge as part of a larger movement of lesbian and gay people of color in the United States who organized to create visible structures of support" (2003, 76). Huda Jadallah founded the first Arab American lesbian organization, the Arab Lesbian Network in Berkeley, California, in May 1989. Queer Arab American organizations changed shape over the years. As queer activist Lana told me,

> while these collectives have tended to prioritize the goal of creating a sense of home and community and promoting visibility in our community, they have supported different political causes and have explicitly or implicitly shared an anti-Zionist, anti-occupation, anti-colonial U.S. presence in South West Asia and North Africa. It can't be just about being queer—the Palestinian issue is important to us, Iraq is important to us.

In the 1980s and early '90s, Karam said, "We were seen as freaks" in the "straight Arab sphere of things." More recently, she added, things changed for queer Arabs, who felt more and more comfortable among straight Arabs. For instance, by the turn of the twenty-first century, the leftist Arab movement became a space where this convergence could be seen, as we will seee in chapter 5.

From Dormancy to Action: The 1990s
Dormancy in the Early '90s

Elders tend to remember the early 1990s as a period of dormancy in which they did not have the tools to respond to new contradictions and tensions related to the ever-diversifying demographics of the Arab Bay Area and intensifying U.S.-led war. As we will see, the 1990s brought the failed Oslo Accords, the first Gulf War, growing numbers of political and economic crises in the Arab region, and a massive increase in the number of Arab refugees and poor immigrants to the Bay Area. Mary, a Syrian woman and former president of the Arab Cultural Center, told me that the Arab Cultural Center, which had always brought people together, faced divisions during this period, and their events and gatherings increasingly diminished. She explained that there was such a massive decrease in their resources that they had only one employee who worked a few hours a week. Aliya became a board member of the Arab Cultural Center in the early part of the decade, when the ACC was what she refers to as "yet another dormant community organization." People involved in anti-imperialist movements of this time had a similar experience. As the Oslo Peace Accords were signed in 1993, major political movements committed to Palestinian liberation globally and in the Bay Area began declining. By the mid-1990s, collectives that were based upon a leftist national liberation–based politics such as the Palestinian solidarity movement and the Arabic bookstore became dormant. Yet around the same time, momentous shifts were taking place that would bring the Arab Bay Area into a new period of revival by the late 1990s. These were related to an intensified period of anti-Arab racism and a new racial consciousness sparked by the first Gulf War; the Oslo years leading up to the second Palestinian *intifada* (uprising); generational changes in the Arab Bay Area; more diverse migration patterns; and increased sectarianism.

The Consolidation of U.S. Empire in the 1990s

The first Gulf War brought one of the most intense moments in the history of anti-Arab racism up until this period, paralleled by violence directed against symbols of U.S. empire among fringe extremist groups in the United States, such as the 1993 World Trade Center bombing, which exacerbated anti-Arab racism. The 1990s also brought mounting U.S. military interventions and economic neoliberal expansion in the Arab world. For Arab diasporas, Clinton's Omnibus counterterrorism bill of 1995 added to the growing sense of belonging to a diaspora of empire. The Omnibus counterterrorism bill called for the deportation of noncitizens based on evidence known only to the government; in some cases, defendants and their attorneys did not receive a summary of the evidence. A *New York Times* article stated that there were twenty-five immigrants facing deportation or exclusion from the United States largely on the basis of secret evidence from unidentified people. All the accused men were of Arab descent or were Muslims (Smothers 1998). Media and popular-cultural representations of Arabs and Muslims in the United States also took a turn for the worse (Sabbagh 1990; Kamalipour 1995). The Hollywood film *The Siege* (1999) represents new popular-cultural representations that brought the "enemy of the nation" home—where the Arab-Middle Eastern-Muslim terrorist lives in the United States and blows up a bus in New York City, killing elderly Americans and American children. U.S. media images of Palestine and Israel hailed Arab Americans into a racial discourse that distinguished between Palestinians and Arabs, on the one hand, and Jews and Israelis on the other. Scholarly and community-based publications documented a massive rise in hate crimes against Arabs in the United States in the first five years after the beginning of the first Gulf War (American-Arab Anti-Discrimination Committee 1991; Wingfield and Karaman 1995; Sabbagh 1990; Hatem 2001). In the following quotations, young adults who entered high school and college in the 1990s discuss encounters with anti-Arab racism of this period.

> Samia: When people hear I am Arab they associate it with war. All you hear in the media is when Arabs kill people, so they assume that I am a radical or terrorist.

> Mazen: As long as the U.S. has an interest in Israel, Arabs will never be mentioned unless they're mentioned as terrorists. The closest we will ever get to being recognized is seeing Yasser Arafat on the White House lawn.

> Raydah: I always felt that either I didn't know enough to defend myself or it didn't matter how much I knew—people already labeled me. Oh, Palestinians are terrorists, or Saddam Hussein is the worst. You feel like they see all Arabs as terrorists.

> Salem: I don't know how much it matters, but I wouldn't tell people . . . at least when I first joined the company, I wouldn't tell people I was Palestinian unless someone really asked. I only told one guy I was Palestinian.

David Theo Goldberg uses the term "racial Palestinianization" to refer to the kinds of racial ideas my interlocutors encountered: "Israel is taken as an outpost of European civilization in an altogether hostile and alien environment. . . . Israelis occupy the structural positions of whiteness in the racial hierarchy of the Middle East. Arabs, accordingly—most notably in the person of Palestinians—are the antithesis" (Goldberg 2009, 116).[23] Joseph Massad analyzes racial discourses about Palestinians, arguing that parallel U.S. and Israeli racial discourses provide the logic that blames Palestinians for violence and represents Palestinians as uncivilized barbarians: "Palestinians are asked to give up violence so that Israelis can give them peace" (Massad 2010). This racial logic shaped the dominant terms of debate about Palestine and Israel in the United States in the mid-1990s, after the Oslo Peace Accords.

Arab American feminists have analyzed racial discourses of the 1990s about Arabs, stressing that sexism permeates anti-Arab racism. One strand of this diasporic Arab feminist critique argues that two images reinforced anti-Arab racism in U.S. popular culture and academia in the 1990s: that of the victim or escapee of Arab Muslim patriarchy who needs to be rescued by an American hero (Kahf 2000; Amireh 2000) or the absent Arab woman, which juxtaposes excessively patriarchal Arab men and white women who liberate themselves from Arab patriarchy while Arab women are completely absent from the scene (Saliba 1994). According to their analyses, racist media images of Arab Muslim patriarchy and misogyny help to consolidate dominant U.S. imperial discourses about an apparently backwards, uncivilized Arab Muslim culture and superior, civilized American culture. Here, racialized distinctions between the figure of the Arab Muslim woman and the white American woman reify the imperialist hierarchies between us and them/Americans and Arab-Muslims (Kahf 2000; Jarmakani 2008; Saliba 1994; Amireh 2000). Indebted to the discourse of Orientalism, this sexist racial discourse relies on arguments that assume that an essentialist Arab Muslim culture or religion, based in violence and misogyny, is the primary difference between "Arabs" and "Americans" and the primary source of global conflict.

In the 1990s, Arab American community leaders saw the consolidation of racist U.S. discourses about Arabs and Muslims take on a local form in institutional changes on the ground. For instance, queer Arab activists distinctly name the first Gulf War as a catalyst for the consolidation of queer Arab American organizing. Huda Jadallah writes,

"The first Gulf War . . . can be seen as a particularly potent moment in the history of queer Arab Americans as they bonded together for social support as Arabs in the United States. As a community, they came together to respond politically, holding educational teach-ins and fundraisers." Through a much more widespread political consciousness than before, Aliya, reflecting on her work with the Arab Cultural Center, told me,

> People stopped saying, "We're not gonna get involved in *any* political activities and we should focus more on culture." It became for us very apparent that we can no longer differentiate between the two. We're not talking about politically being active, demonstrations—that's not our job. But we had people who started coming to the Center saying, "Look, my son went to school and he was called all kinds of names because he's an Arab! What should I do about it?"

Louai, a Palestinian man, told me that he became determined to help revive the ACC after his son experienced racism. Aliya explained, "We became reactionary because of what was going on. We could not separate the need between having culture and teaching our kids the language, and at the same time, how can we make them feel safe?" As Arabs and Arab Americans were forced to face the realities of anti-Arab racism and increased U.S. military violence in the Arab region, massive demographic changes were also underway, changes that contributed to a revival in Arab American cultural politics in the mid- to late 1990s.

Changing Demographics

In the 1990s the second generation were now adults, and many were joining the leadership of community-based organizations and movements. This shift gave rise to new tensions and contradictions within Arab collectivities in the Bay Area. Jameel, an old-timer reflecting a dominant middle-class perspective, told me, "The new generation has their own agenda. They are American-born, and they want to do things differently." Jameel's remark points to the increase of second-generation activists socialized and politicized in a different geographic location and historical moment and to the way their presence brought new logics for articulating Arabness. The presence of more second-generation young adults led to a significant shift in the Arab Cultural Center's agenda. In 1997, ACC elected a new president, Monther. He told me,

> They had just started the Arab Cultural Festival, which brought together five or six hundred people. The second year, when I worked on it with Nadya, it grew to three thousand people. Old people come and say to me,

"What's this music you're playing?" and I tell them, "The youth wanted hip-hop. You had your turn. It's the younger generation's turn now."

In addition, Arab migration patterns to the Bay Area were rapidly diversifying. The Gulf War brought thousands of Iraqi refugees to the Tenderloin, one of San Francisco's most impoverished neighborhoods. A significant number of low-income North African and Yemeni Muslim immigrants also moved to the Bay Area at this time. Many became service workers, such as dishwashers, taxi drivers, and janitors (Rafidi, Howell, and Elkarra 1999). The arrival of a disproportionate number of low-income refugees and immigrants broadened Bay Area Arab communities in terms of class and religion; there were now larger numbers of Muslims and people living in poverty. Census data from 2000, although not fully representative of migration patterns, indicates that over 50 percent of the people originally from the Arab world in the Bay Area are foreign born, reflecting this increase in migration from the Arab region to the United States that culminated in the 1990s (Ahuja, Gupta, and Petsod 2004). A massive growth in Muslim-based institutions in the Bay Area came with these shifts. This came with a growing current in which Arabs who were Muslim increasingly organized their concepts of community, affiliation, and political participation in primarily religious (Muslim) terms.

The Late 1990s Revival

An expanding U.S. empire, growing anti-Arab racism, and massive demographic shifts in the diaspora sparked new collective articulations of Arabness in the Bay Area, new forms of activism, and new languages and strategies for conceptualizing community, belonging, and nonbelonging. Business owners faced engagements with racism that impacted their businesses after the Gulf War. In the late 1990s, two community activists, a Lebanese immigrant woman and a second-generation Palestinian man, spearheaded a campaign for Arab American business owners to gain minority status in the city of San Francisco. They contended that there is a tendency to view Arab business owners as violent and that this has limited their business opportunities.[24] They argued that while Arab American business dropped in 1992 during the Gulf War, they are not recognized as a minority and therefore cannot receive the support from the city that other minorities receive. Despite the lack of statistical data available about Arab Americans, they called for Arab American inclusion in the city's minority program for business owners. In 1998, the city and county of San Francisco became the first government entity in the United States to recognize Arab Americans as a legal minority class and therefore to afford them all the rights and benefits available to other minorities under the city's contracting ordinance (Rafidi, Howell, and Elkarra 1999).

An alternative response spearheaded by the Arab Culture Center leadership focused its attention on the impact of these new transnational conditions on recent immigrants living in poverty. Responding to the growth in the number of Arabs living in poverty in San Francisco in the early to mid-1990s, the president of the ACC at the time told me she worked to change the politics of the center:

> We spent the first month logging the kinds of phone calls and requests the administrator at our center was getting. Then we brought people from different parts of the community together and told them, here are the requests: an immigrant woman asked for help with an immigration case, another called about domestic violence, one person asked for a legal referral. I then said to people, "Do we want the ACC to continue to be only a meeting place or do we want to address the needs of the community?"

Aliya and her counterparts met with the mayor of San Francisco "to lobby as a community. We agreed that everyone would leave personal or small issues aside. Leave our gas stations and stores behind and go for the major thing here—we have issues."

ACC then received a grant to conduct a community needs assessment study. As Aliya put it, "We then received funding for domestic violence, children, and youth, for educational and cultural programs, then for immigrant services and health services. Since then, the Arab Cultural Center became the Arab Cultural and Community Center." The ACC became a cultural *and* social service organization that reached out to different neighborhoods where lower-income Arab immigrants from a range of countries lived "inside the city, in the inner city, even in public housing or low-income housing." The ACC also developed a closer relationship with mosques in these neighborhoods, as well as with the many communities of the Tenderloin.

This was surely not all that happened in the late 1990s. New institutions and social movements appeared: an Arab TV station, Arab broadcasters on local public radio stations, the Arab Film Festival of San Francisco, South West Asian Bay Area Queers, the Arab Women's Solidarity Association (San Francisco Chapter), *Shilla* (an e-mail network of Bay Area Arab American professionals), *Aswat* (an Arabic music choir), and new religious institutions. As we will see in the pages to come, leftist politics was revived in new form along with a globally focused Muslim social-justice, anti-imperialist con-sciousness. The political vacuum of the early 1990s had been filled.

The revival of Arab American politics also came about in the context of the profound significance of California as a hotbed of immigrant and racial politics in the 1990s. California, the largest and most racially diverse state, had undergone a massive demographic shift between 1997 and 2000. By the 1990s, half of its population was immigrants (Gibbs and Bankhead 2001). Also in the 1990s, California became a battleground of racial politics with issues ranging from tensions over four highly racialized, politically explosive campaigns to the 1992 Los Angeles Riots.[25] These events mobilized young people, primarily young people of color, into new multiracial political alli-ances and social movements (Maira and Shihade 2006). The increased reli-ance on the internet as a method for political organizing also contributed to this revival. Queer Arab, Arab feminist, Muslim, and leftist Arab political organizing of this period relied heavily on internet lists and websites. Sev-eral founders of the local chapter of the Arab Women's Solidarity Association (AWSA SF), for instance, were actively involved in Cyber AWSA, an internet discussion group including Arab feminists living in North America. Also, Southwest Asian and North African Bay Area Queers (SWANABAQ), the support group and discussion forum for lesbian, gay, bisexual, transgender, and intersex people, was founded in 2000. By 2002, they had 183 e-mail list members. The internet has deeply enhanced their efforts to build community and organize regular gatherings and parties (Jadallah 2003).

The changes of the mid- to late 1990s and through the turn of the twenti-eth century fundamentally altered concepts of Arabness. These changes were welcomed by some, and not by others. Many old-timers were now nearing retirement and were more interested in social and cultural forms of commu-nity building than political activism. Yet they were no longer waxing nostal-gic about the 1950s. They were remembering the '70s and '80s as the golden years, before the momentous changes of the '90s. As the twentieth century became the twenty-first, the year 2000 brought the beginning of the second *intifada* and unprecedented Israeli violence against Palestinians and was fol-lowed by the horrific attacks of September 11 and their aftermath, transform-ing Arab American community politics once again.

The Arab Bay Area is in constant flux. The changes that take place are shaped by the constant interplay between U.S. empire and U.S. politics of race and culture, processes of immigration and displacement, and many local conditions specific to the San Francisco Bay Area. Many Arab immi-grants who came to the Bay Area in the 1950s, like their elders before them, imagined themselves through the lens of the American dream. Many enjoyed a general proximity to whiteness and gained access to the resources required to open their own businesses. Over the years, expanding U.S. imperial ambitions in the Middle East, coupled with changing global economics and migration patterns, radically altered their communities, the way many of them perceived themselves, and the way they imagined their future. Their daily experiences, the fears many internalized on the level of the psyche, and their hopes for their communities had a great deal to do with their increasing sense of belonging to a diaspora of empire. Black British cultural studies writers have theorized the diaspora of empire in terms of people, such as Algerians in France, who reside in countries that formerly colonized them. Kobena Mercer theorizes the diaspora of empire as a "reminder and a remainder of the nation's historical past" (1994). Yet the Arab Bay Area, as it went from model minority to problem minority in the U.S. public eye, cannot be understood as a postcolonial diaspora wherein the diaspora moves into the seat of its former empire. Rather, the stories of Arabs in the United States becoming a diaspora of empire points to a moment in which the empire and its subjects exist in a transnational frame. The subjects of the current empire "over there" also reside "over here" within the empire itself.

Yet their stories reveal much more than the changing shape of U.S. imperialism in the Middle East or the way the U.S. empire constructs and portrays Arab diasporas. Their stories reveal how the logics of U.S. empire, as they take on local form in the everyday lives of Arab diasporas in the United States, are entangled in multiple forms of power such as the structures of religion, class, gender, sexuality, and immigration, as well as the changing realities of U.S. immigrant and racial politics. The stories of Arabs in the United States becoming a diaspora of empire take place in the context of the local and global realities of imperialism, displacement, and economic neoliberalism and across a spectrum of accommodationist, civil rights, and anticolonial/anti-imperial politics.

The stories in this chapter ground the remaining chapters in the historical conditions that have shaped the Arab Bay Area between the 1950s and the turn of the twenty-first century. The remaining chapters are framed by two events that defined the decade of the 1990s for the people who are the focus of this book: the first Gulf War (1990-1991) and the attacks of September 11, 2001. Punctuating this decade were also the U.S.-led sanctions on Iraq (beginning in 1990) and the second Palestinian *intifada* (uprising). The 1990s was also a distinct moment in the San Francisco Bay Area and California. In the 1990s, California became one of a small but growing number of states with a nonwhite majority (Maharidge 1996). California also continued its legacy as a battleground for U.S. racial politics, a battleground that intensified during this decade. Those battle lines were drawn in four campaigns in the 1990s that positioned California as a "pace setter in the nation's ambivalence towards immigrants and people of color" (Gibbs and Bankhead 2001). Racial-justice and immigrant-rights movements also peaked in the 1990s in California following the 1992 L.A. riots, a "flashpoint in which struggles of blacks, Latinos, and Asian Americans converged" (Gibbs and Bankhead 2001).

Historically and politically situating an ethnography of Arab American life in the 1990s challenges what has become a disempowering habit of viewing 9/11 as an essential break or rupture, more properly understood as an unprecedented "state of crisis," instead of understanding it properly as an extension if not an intensification of a post–Cold War U.S. expansion in the Middle East. Ann Stoler, for one, has called critical attention to the persistence of this "imperial formation" that "thrive[d] on the production of exceptions [such as the idea of 9/11 as a state of crisis] and their uneven and changing proliferation" (2006). My focus on the 1990s similarly resists the entrapment of Arab American studies within the idea of an entirely new, exceptional, post–September 11 moment. This approach is grounded in the wide range of studies about the relationship between U.S. empire and Arab diasporas that Arab American studies scholars had been developing long before September 11, 2001 (Suleiman 1988; Abraham 1992; Saliba 1994; Majaj 2000).

2

The Politics of Cultural Authenticity

Arab culture is about being a certain way; knowing what is *abe* (shameful); knowing how to give *mujamalat* (flattery); knowing what you're supposed to do when someone greets you; knowing how to act at *azayim* (gatherings) and weddings; drinking *shai* (tea) or coffee; talking about politics *so* much; getting up for an older person; respecting your elders; looking after your parents and taking care of them; judging people according to what family they are from; marrying through connections; gossiping and having a good reputation; going anywhere with Arabs, with your own kind, with brothers, uncles, family, cousins, but not with Americans.

This list highlights a combination of cultural ideals taken from interviews with middle-class, second-generation young adults. Here, I interrogate what I refer to as the politics of cultural authenticity, a process by which middle-class Arab diasporas come to herald particular ideals as markers of an authentic, essential, true, or real Arab culture. I map the historical and political conditions that give rise to the concepts of Arab culture that second-generation young adults learn from their parents' generation. I provide a theoretical framework for understanding young adults' engagements with apparently "intra-communal" forms of patriarchy and the pressure for compulsory heterosexuality. I also analyze the ramifications of the politics of cultural authenticity for the lives of second-generation young adults. This chapter is based upon intensive interviews with eighty-six second-generation Arab American young adults and participant observation within a range of community-based organizations.[1] I announced my invitation to interviewees on a leaflet, on e-mail lists, and by word of mouth. My invitation was met with an overwhelming response from young adults eager to tell their stories. Rather than reflecting an authentic, pure Arab culture frozen in time, idealized concepts of Arab culture are best understood as cultural sensibilities that become entangled in transnational modalities of power—U.S. Orientalist discourses and structures of colonialism and imperialism, race, class, gender, and sexuality.[2] Dominant middle-class concepts of Arab cultural identity indeed draw upon long-standing norms about religion, family, gender, and sexuality that have circulated in the Arab region for centuries. This helps explain why idealized concepts of Arab cultural identity provide middle-class Arab diasporas with a sense of cultural and historical continuity in relation to their places of origin. Middle-class articulations of an authentic Arab culture meet desires for connection, attachment, comfort, and security that come with displacement, immigrant marginality, and the pressures of assimilation.

Yet the idea that middle-class immigrants simply transmit to their children an authentic Arab culture that they brought with them from their homelands cannot explain dominant middle-class articulations of Arabness. Even with regard to the Arab region, concepts and practices of family, marriage, gender, and sexuality are very much entangled in European and U.S. histories and are constantly changing in light of socioeconomic transformations (Abu-Lughod 1998; Hoodfar 1997; Ahmed 1992; Habib 2010). Consider, for instance, articulations of Arab culture that emerged within the context of twentieth-century anticolonial Arab nationalisms. Such articulations often reified European concepts of patriarchy and heteronormativity in the context of resisting European colonization and domination (Ahmed 1992; Abdulhadi 2010). Like European colonialist discourses, such masculinist Arab nationalisms have used patriarchal and heteronormative notions of national cultural identity, notions that mark the difference between "us" and "them" through the figure of the "woman" and European concepts of sexual respectability (Abdulhadi 2010). A logic that resembles masculinist nationalisms heavily informed the politics of cultural authenticity in the diaspora and operated to circumscribe my interlocutors' lives and behavior.

In the San Francisco Bay Area in the 1990s, middle-class articulations of Arabness provided Arab diasporas with a framework for conceptualizing themselves that, to a certain extent, challenge U.S. Orientalist and racist discourses about Arabs, Muslims, and the Middle East. Yet they also advance a binary struggle between what they conceptualize as good Arabs versus bad Americans, good Arab families versus bad American families, and good Arab girls versus bad American(ized) girls. This formulation resembles what diaspora studies scholars have theorized as the incorporation of conventional concepts of nationalism into concepts of community, affiliation, and belonging within historical contexts of displacement (Axel 2001; Gopinath 2005; Clarke 2004; Hall 1994). I refer to this formulation as the politics of Arab cultural authenticity.

Specifically, the middle-class politics of cultural authenticity articulates Arab cultural identity and community through the triangulated ideal of the good Arab family, good Arab girls, and compulsory heterosexuality, all in opposition to an imagined America and its apparent sexual promiscuity, broken families, and bad women. The politics of cultural authenticity, while drawing upon conventional masculinist nationalisms, conjoins with the liberal logic of U.S. multiculturalism, a logic for imagining and performing cultural identity that becomes available to Arab diasporas upon their arrival in the United States. Liberal multiculturalism requires immigrants, people of color, and indigenous people to craft concepts of culture that are depoliticized and ahistorical (Povinelli 2002; Moallem and Boal 1999; Lowe 1996; Prashad 2000). Vijay Prashad contends, "Whereas assimilation demands that each inhabitant of the United States be transformed into the norm, U.S. multiculturalism asks that each immigrant group preserve its own heritage. . . . The heritage, or 'culture,' is not treated as a living set of social relations but as a timeless trait" (112). Conjoining masculinist homeland nationalisms with the logics of liberal U.S. multiculturalism, the politics of cultural authenticity posits an essentialist, authentic Arab identity that exists outside of history.

Moreover, while on the one hand many of my interlocutors articulate Arabness in terms of an authentic, unified Arab culture and community, they simultaneously reference internal communal differences based on nation of origin and religion, and they represent these differences in power-laden, hierarchical terms, such as good Jordanians versus bad Palestinians or good Christians versus bad Muslims. Dominant U.S. discourses about Arabs, Muslims, and the Middle East shape my interlocutors' articulations of internal Arab differences. Entangled in these overlapping, contradictory discourses, the politics of cultural authenticity is best understood as a selective assimilation strategy. As it provides middle-class Arab diasporas with a meaning system for conceptualizing a sense of belonging, empowerment, and cultural grounding in the context of displacement and diaspora, the politics of cultural authenticity also supports desires for U.S. middle-class acceptability and belonging.

In everyday life, the politics of cultural authenticity sets up various regulations and constraints that police the lives of second-generation young adults and disproportionately impact (although in different ways and to different degrees) women and queers. The politics of cultural authenticity translates conventional nationalist hierarchies between nation and diaspora into the categories "immigrant generation" and "second-generation." Here, the immigrant generation represents the pure, authentic "Arab culture," while the second generation represents its potentially impure, inauthentic Other. In the San Francisco Bay Area, the politics of cultural authenticity positions the immigrant generation as cultural authorities setting the terms for belonging and unbelonging—terms that define cultural authenticity through the concepts of "good girls" and a patriarchal, heterosexual family. The politics of cultural authenticity positions the second generation as a potential threat to the survival of Arabness in America because of their apparent potentiality for transgressions of the racial, classed, gendered, and sexualized demands of middle-class Arabness. The stories of second-generation young adults elucidate different aspects of the politics of cultural authenticity in which both generations seemed to participate, although to different degrees. I consider the politics of cultural authenticity a baseline articulation of Arabness against which the alternatives that are the focus of the remaining chapters emerge.

Arabness as Family

In the Bay Area, I spoke with second-generation young adults about the concepts of Arabness, Arab culture, and Arab cultural identity that they learned from their parents' generation. Some spoke of cultural identity in terms of music, film, and poetry. Others referenced architecture, language, and food. Across the board, one thing remained consistent: nearly everyone referred to relational concepts of selfhood and family ties and attachments as among the most fundamental aspects of Arabness. The following quotations illustrate how people articulate Arabness through concepts of family and relationality: "Arab culture is about family and the closeness of people"; "Arab culture is family oriented"; "Arabs are supposed to have connections with cousins, brothers, sisters, aunts, uncles"; and "Arab culture is about family ties and family values—an attachment to family and the love of children."

The references above are rooted in long-standing sensibilities about relationships, loyalty, affiliation, and belonging that have organized Arab societies. For centuries, concepts of family have been at the center of social organization in the Arab region (Barakat 1985; Joseph 1993; Tucker 1993). Writing about contemporary Arab societies, Halim Barakat argues that "family is the dominant social institution through which persons and groups inherit religious, social class, and cultural identities." The most common family structure in the Arab world is extended, patrilineal, patriarchal, and heteronormative (Barakat 1985; Habib 2010; Joseph 1993). Arab societies have supported an ideal of endogamy, or "marriage within the same lineage, sect, community, group, village, and/or neighborhood," reflecting the significance of strengthening kinship solidarity and avoiding the rupturing of close relationships (Barakat 1985, 157).

Paul Amar's research reminds us of the multiple forms of social unions that existed in the medieval Middle East before the period of European colonization (Amar 2010). He argues that whereas today, the heterosexual marriage bond governs the household, heterosexual marriage is only one of many kinds of social unions that made up the concept of the household. For instance, he illustrates that there was a mosaic of identities, such as servants, extended family members (including grandparents, aunts, uncles, and cousins), and guests, and various kinds of social unions between and across these identities. Laws governing the household were not only laws that governed the lives of husbands and wives. Amar thus argues that the Middle East has retained complex norms and practices pertaining to how people relate even as the modern period introduced the simpler, more monolithic social order of the nation, in which the main unit of social organization is the family and ideals of social respectability are based upon idealized concepts of family respectability that demand patriarchy and compulsory heterosexuality. With the advent of European colonization and nationalist resistance against colonization came the privileging of concepts of the respectable modern family as a strategy to prove the worthiness of Arab people in the face of European demonization and domination, which relied upon the immorality of the Arab family and Arab men. Thus came the increased pressure to build respectable nuclear heteropatriarchal families. Amar argues that European morality campaigns destroyed the complex gender and sexual order in the Middle East and purged or undermined possibilities for a diversity of social unions and relations.

While modern ideals about kinship are based upon heterosexual marriage and familial expansion and reproduction, Arab and Islamic societies have tolerated homosexuality "as long as the prolongation of the family tree is guaranteed and no possessions are lost in the homosexual relationship" (Becker 2010). At the same time, research on contemporary Muslim-majority countries illustrates that the sanctity of heterosexual marriage and the family unit places nonnormative sexual desires and behaviors at a disadvantage, enabling various degrees of exclusion (Habib 2010; Sharma 2010). This ideal has undergone significant changes due to social, economic, and political transformations (Barakat 1985; Hoodfar 1997). For instance, extended families in the Arab region increasingly do not necessarily live together. Michael Luongo's research shows that before the U.S. invasion, Iraqi society was more accepting of homosexual men (2010). Yet, generally speaking, the normative cultural ideal has expected family members to remain closely interlocked in webs of intimate relationships, to intermarry, to uphold expectations of one another, and to hold family members responsible for each other's acts (Barakat 1985; Joseph 1993).

Second-generation young adults in the Bay Area refer to concepts of family ties, loyalty, connection, and attachment as crucial to the concepts of Arabness that they learned from their parents' generation.[3] Yet as their stories show, these concepts were significantly influenced by the conditions of diaspora. For instance, in the Bay Area, several interlocutors referred to family as a marker of an authentic Arab culture that is distinct from the way the word is used in American culture. Within their stories, while "the Arab family" supports heteronormative sexuality within the framework of marriage, a patriarchal division of labor, extended kin relations, and relational concepts of selfhood, "the American family" lacks a sense of relationality and supports sexual "deviance" (homosexuality as well as sex outside of marriage, for instance). In the following stories, young adults elaborate on this apparent tension between Arab and American notions of family. Nicole grew up in San Francisco in a tight-knit Palestinian community. Her life story defies nearly every U.S. Orientalist notion about Arabs. Her parents were atheists. They did not impose many restrictions concerning dating or staying out late at night. She tells me,

> My parents were really liberal about guys. I would tell them when I had a crush on someone. I told my mom when I lost my virginity and when I freaked out about it, she's the one who got me the pregnancy test. I used to go on vacations with my college boyfriend. My father knew we were staying in the same hotel room. I've even told them I've done drugs. When I was a junior, I went on a spring break with two of my girl friends to Mexico. I met a guy there and I dated him for a year and a half. I would talk about him to my parents. I went to visit him five or six times.

At the same time, Nicole speaks about family-based relationships as the most crucial site of support and security in her life.

> Arab culture means that my life is bound up in the lives of others. . . . [M]y family and community's love has roots and gives me stability. It is my life-blood, the social glue that keeps me tied to my roots and all the networks of social relations that are my family—the ties I have to the community that nurtured me.

Tony is Jordanian. He grew up in the Peninsula, on the outskirts of the city of San Francisco. At the time we spoke he was a graduate student in business administration at San Francisco State University. Tony often expressed to me a profound distaste for the strong emotive attachments he attributed to Arab culture. He told me that he had always felt overwhelmed by his interactions with "other Arabs"—among his mother's friends, at community-based social gatherings, and at community-based institutions to which his family belonged, such as the Arab church or the Arab cultural center. In his view, "Too many people intervene in other people's lives, gossip, and pressure me to get married. They think, you're dating someone and that's it, you're going to get married. I don't want anyone to know about my personal life because I don't want to deal with all the questions."

Tony's engagements with U.S. Orientalist and racist discourses about Arab masculinity exacerbated his desire to distance himself from "other Arabs" as well as from U.S. discourses that portray Arab masculinity as potentially violent and misogynist:

> American women have a bad view of Arab men. A lot of Arab guys I know don't even admit they're Arab because people think they're terrorists, crooks, or rich. When you say you're Arab, people assume you're rich and you treat women bad. They think Arabs have money. Or if you tell them you're Arab, they'll say, "Wow, you speak English! You don't drive a Mercedes? Does your dad wear a turban?" The Arab guys I know change their names and use an English one. I never had to worry about my name, but they do it so they're not labeled. Someone hears an Arab name and thinks you're backwards.

These sorts of experiences inspire Tony to disassociate himself from what he considered the "Arab community" and from public displays of "Arab culture." He avoids Arab community-based events, he asks his mother not to play Arabic music and to avoid speaking Arabic in public, and he swears that he will never "marry an Arab." Yet it turns out that most of his closest friends are his cousins and that forms of attachment and relationality that he attributes to "Arab culture" are crucial to his life journey and his sense of being in the world:

> We [my cousins and I] grew up with so many aunts and uncles and their closeness—they were all my mom's brothers and their kids—and we ended up wanting the same thing. It's part of our culture. We stuck together as cousins. It's family. When you're together, no time passes. There's a whole gang of us. We don't need anyone else. We don't have to worry about anyone stabbing our back. We don't have to question the trust. We know for a fact, they're always going to be there.

Like Nicole and Tony—whether or not they say they affiliate with "Arab culture" or an "Arab community"—most of my interlocutors conflate the concepts of family and Arab culture and find themselves wrapped up in familial and communal relations. In other words, the idea of "Arabness as family" is immensely important to many of my interlocutors' sense of self and to their sense of being in the world. Tony's reflections below exemplify how dominant middle-class Arab American discourses deployed concepts of family to distinguish between us and them, Arabs and Americans: "When you're younger, you don't think twice about it, it didn't seem odd, and you didn't feel different. But then when you start getting older, you start looking out there and realize not everyone has that kind of family or the real closeness we have with each other."

Adel, who grew up among a Palestinian family in the East Bay, shares with me an embellished distinction between what he perceives as connected Arabs and individuated Americans. He spent most summers visiting relatives in Palestine. He worked with his father at his grocery store while attending college:

> When it comes to Americans, everyone hates their cousins. . . . [T]here is the crazy mother-in-law and lots of divorce. People don't connect with their families or with each other in general! People can go for a year without talking to their sister or not knowing what is going on with her. People aren't close to their friends like we are.

Adel's words, like Nicole's and Tony's above, illustrate how the middle-class politics of cultural authenticity signified Arabness through a sense of connection, knowing what is going on with each other, and strong emotive ties. Suad Joseph argues that dominant concepts of selfhood in Arab countries value bonding with and commitment to family more than individuation, autonomy, separateness, and boundedness (Joseph 1994, 56). Joseph uses the concept of connectivity to refer to the "psychodynamic process in which one's sense of self is intimately linked with the self of another, such that the security, identity, integrity, dignity, and self worth of one is tied to the actions of the other" (Joseph 1993). My interlocutors mobilize concepts of connectivity within a politics of authentication that is specific to the conditions of diaspora. Here, family and relationality are markers that distinguish Arabs from Americans.

Cultural Authentication: Homelands and Diasporas

Many theorists have analyzed how European colonialist discourses rely upon racialized concepts of family, gender, and sexuality to portray the colonized as backwards, barbaric, and uncivilized (Smith and Kauanui 2008; Lazreg 1994; Ahmed 1992; Moallem 2005; Shohat and Stam 1994; Stoler 1989). While European colonialist discourses have shifted and changed at different historical moments, gender and sexuality have been central to their logics (Moallem 2005, 24). Edward Said argues that European Orientalist discourses construct the Orient through crude racial and sexual stereotypes. The Arab male is thus represented as being inherently lazy and murderously violent, while the Arab female is promiscuous, immodest, and sexually licentious (1978). Dominant European and U.S. discourses have represented Arab, Muslim, and Middle Eastern women as highly sexual, exotic victims of patriarchy and misogyny as a way of legitimizing colonial and imperial domination. These same discourses have portrayed the Arab and Muslim worlds as both exceptionally homosexual and manifestly homophobic (Puar 2007; Al-Sayyad 2010; Massad 2007; Hayes 2001). Leila Ahmed shows that in their descriptions of indigenous Egyptian concepts of gender and family, British colonial discourses relied on a combination of colonialism and the language of feminism to represent Egyptian women as the antithesis of Victorian ideals of female domesticity (1992, 151). Marnia Lazreg, writing about the French colonization of Algeria, argues that the French constructed a difference between French and Algerians through representations of Algerian women's bodies (1994).

Scholars such as Franz Fanon (1963) and Partha Chatterjee (1993) have suggested that colonialist discourse, with its explicit conceptual underpinnings of European superiority over colonized people, has created a sense of division and alienation in the self-identity of the colonized people. Franz

Fanon argues that Algerian resistance to the French colonizer's attacks on Algerian cultural identity required an affirmation of the existence of national culture. He writes, "The unconditional affirmation of national culture among the colonized succeeds the unconditional affirmation of European culture among the colonizer. . . . A national culture under colonial domination . . . . is a contested culture whose destruction is sought in systematic fashion" (1963, 35). While Arab nationalism has varied in form and vision, Arab nationalist discourses have tended to rely on essentialist concepts of Arab culture. For instance, while Algerian and Egyptian histories of engagement with Europe are indeed distinct, Egyptian and Algerian nationalist elites responded to European colonialism through essentialist logics similar to those that Europe imposed upon them (Ahmed 1992; Fanon 1963). Ahmed writes that Egyptian elites borrowed idealized notions of family, marriage, and domesticity from Victorian Europeans to naturalize concepts of national unity in the face of colonial violence and domination (1992). Among these are European nationalist constructs that privilege heterosexuality and the heterosexual family, require women to be good wives and mothers, and regulate nonreproductive sexuality so that it does not protrude into public view (Mosse 1988; Edelman 1999; Parker et al. 1992; De Lauretis 1998).[4]

More broadly, feminist research on nationalism theorizes how non-Western or anticolonial nationalisms "have to assimilate something alien into their own cultures before they can become modern nations" (Radhakrishnan 1992, 86). While diverse in their gender and sexuality structures and historically distinct, elite anticolonial nationalisms have deployed concepts of "family" to naturalize concepts of "national unity" (Collins 2000; McClintock 1993). Elite anticolonial nationalisms have drawn upon the European concept that nation and family denote eternal and sacred ties whose origins similarly disappear into mythical and distant pasts (Anderson 1983). Uma Narayan theorizes the incorporation of concepts of family (and compulsory heterosexuality) and gender into an essentialist, binary logic as a reaction to "colonial attempts to eradicate or regulate customs and practices in the colonies that Western governments found unacceptable or inexpedient" (1997, 14).

Several scholars have argued that dominant Indian nationalism selectively coped with the West by mobilizing an inner/outer distinction against the "outerness" or "otherness" of the West (Radhakrishnan 1992; Chatterjee 1993). In doing so, Indian nationalist rhetoric made "woman" the pure and ahistorical signifier of the "interiority" of the nation, the domain of home, family, spirituality, and the true Indian self. This schema assumed that women's central role is to preserve culture and tradition, while men can move between both domains, participating in modern politics with their wives and daughters by their sides. As a consequence, a patriarchal and heteronormative idea became naturalized, and the interior domain of the nation, signified by the figure of the woman (as wife or mother) became something requiring protection from Western intervention and contamination (Chatterjee 1993).

In the aftermath of the Cold War, as the United States replaced Europe as the global superpower, the United States has drawn upon the dichotomous systems of thought that had underpinned European colonialist discourses. Consider, for example, the focus on the oppression of Arab women or the "Islamic homophobia" within post–Cold War discourses that mark Arab-Muslim-Middle Eastern societies as antimodern. In such instances, the United States has manipulated feminism and queer liberation for its own purposes, even while patriarchy and compulsory heterosexuality are fundamental to the social organization of the United States.[5] In the Arab world, engagements with U.S. empire have given rise to a sensibility that perceives U.S. imperial ambitions as a continuation of a European and Western threat to indigenous identities and to the survival of local cultures and traditions (Lockman 2010; Al-Ali and Pratt 2009). This sentiment has only increased with recent U.S. military and economic interventions in the region. This perception in the Arab region is also a response to global capitalism and the resultant increase in the circulation of U.S. cultural forms in the Arab world (Said 1994; Abu-Lughod 2002). This sentiment has facilitated a concept of cultural identity, particularly among elites, that affirms masculinist nationalist distinctions between an authentic local culture or civilization and a Western, Judeo-Christian Euro-American culture. Many government and media discourses in the Arab world, for instance, have deployed distinct definitions of family and gender as markers of cultural authenticity (Hasso forthcoming; Abu-Lughod 1998; Deeb 2006, 12). Frances Hasso's research about the United Arab Emirates illustrates that a perceived invasion of foreign values produces great cultural anxiety, inspiring nationalist concepts of cultural identity. In such cases of a perceived external threat or an experience of imperial violence, domination, or erasure— whether material or ideological—concepts of cultural authenticity can provide a sense of empowerment and dignity.[6]

At the same time, my interlocutors' references to the Arab family as a marker of the difference between "Arabs" and "Americans" have their roots in conventional Arab nationalist responses to European and U.S. global power. As my interlocutors reference an idealized Arab culture, they articulate Arabs as different from and superior to "Americans." Among many of my interlocutors, the logics of conventional nationalisms persist in new form—Arab culture and American culture; the Arab family and the American family.

My interlocutors' references to an idealized "Arab family" are informed by distinct diasporic conditions. In chapter 1, I discussed how Arab immigrants of my interlocutors' parents' generation speak about the challenges facing them and their communities. Some speak about a sense of social or political marginality that has resulted from experiences with anti-Arab racism and living in a country at war with their homelands. Many mention a sense of isolation and alienation that came with immigration and displacement. Many also touch upon the pressures of assimilation, which they understood would result in cultural loss, erasure, or annihilation. These conditions of immigration and displacement to the United States contribute to the process of cultural authentication in the diaspora. They set the conditions through which people draw upon concepts of "family" as a source of comfort, security, unity, or belonging in the diaspora. Consider Adel's claim above that Arabs stick together while Americans divorce. In this quotation, Adel presents Arabness—a site of strong emotive attachments, empowerment, and self-affirmation—as morally superior to an imagined America.

The concept of Arabness as family resembles discourses that many communities have relied upon for survival in the United States. Indigenous people, people of color, and immigrants and refugees have found collective strength in concepts and practices of family (Alarcón 1999; Bhattacharjee 1992; Gutierrez 1995; Espiritu 2003; White 1990; Mahalingam and Leu 2005; Baca Zinn 2000; Zaborowska 1995). Diaspora studies scholars argue that continuities between concepts of nation and diaspora help explain the profound significance of "family" as a marker of cultural distinction in the diaspora. Anannya Bhattacharjee explains that conventional middle-class Indian immigrant ideals about family and gender support a dynamic in which nationalist logics "become available for use easily by the bourgeoisie immigrant" (1992). Gayatri Gopinath shows how conventional concepts of diaspora recruit concepts of "nation" into absolutist concepts of "culture" (2005, 4). "Fictions of purity," she argues, "lie at the heart of dominant nationalist and diasporic ideologies" (2005, 4). This, she contends, explains the rigid, heteronormative, and patriarchal structures of kinship and community that underscore conventional diasporic discourses.

In distinguishing between concepts of good Arab families and bad American families, middle-class Arab diasporas remake long-standing nationalist logics for coping with the West. Within the dominant middle-class articulation of Arabness, a patriarchal and heteronormative family is a key signifier of a pure and unchanging Arab self. Despite the distinctive shifts brought about by displacement, assimilation, and racialization, the politics of cultural authenticity arranges the domain of family as a space that this Arab diaspora can call its own.

Cultural Authentication and Parental Control

Claims to cultural authenticity reinforced parental control in my interlocutors' lives. Many young adults found a profound sense of security and comfort in the concept of Arabness as family. Yet they also said that it constrained their lives and contributed to intergenerational tensions. As parents exercise their control over young adults through claims to cultural authenticity, young adults experience normative generational wars as a conflict between Arab and American culture. Many interlocutors have faced intense emotional struggles over whether they were going to live up to the demands of what their parents' generation conceptualized as idealized "Arab culture" or as a stereotypical "American culture." They understand that this idealized Arab culture requires a strong sense of family and emotional attachments and that stereotypical American culture privileges individuality, personal desires, and independence. Many interlocutors refer to weekends as sites of tension between the Arab expectation to be with family and the American desire to be with friends. Jameel grew up among a tight-knit Palestinian extended family in San Francisco. Growing up, he spent most of his time after school and on weekends with his first cousins. When we talked, he was working as a physical therapist at a hospital. According to Jameel, "It was as if you don't need anyone else. If you have anything going on in your life, family always comes first. Anything that had to do with family you had to be there, you had no choice." Referring to his own difficulties in resisting his parents' control, he relates, "The difference between Arabs and Americans is that an American kid would tell their parents, 'I want weekends to myself.'" While Jameel desired connections beyond his extended family, he told me that his parents considered this desire irrelevant or, at best, secondary.

Young adults who desired to rebel against the normative demands of cultural authenticity explain that their parents' generation marked their rebellion as a sign of cultural loss or Americanization. Ramsy is Palestinian but was born in Saudi Arabia. He moved to the United States with his family when he was five. He told me,

> I was working since I was sixteen. I was always trying to break away from the family through work because of the fact that when I didn't work, I had to take allowance from them which meant I had to listen to them ask me

where I was going when they gave me money. Economic independence for me meant freedom. I got my first job in fast food at KFC [Kentucky Fried Chicken]. Then I went up to JC Penny and I became a major buyer when I was twenty. That was good. I went into Nordstrom next and went into my own business of consulting with appointments because of school. I would always get these great clothes and I always had a sense for fashion. Arab women are very fashionable, but Arab men can't be. That's the rule. I'd always see my sister wear all these great clothes and cool things. But for me, if I'm around the family, my mom would tell me "pants with pleats." It could never be pants without pleats. Nothing too flashy, nothing striped, nothing too . . . a white shirt, blue shirt, or whatever shirt, but it can't be an orange shirt or a yellow shirt.

At the time of our conversations, Ramsy was struggling with his family over whether he would continue living with them or move out and live on his own:

I hear it from my parents, and our relatives, and our friends all the time . . . from everyone: "How come you don't live with them? *Kif y'ani tseeb bait ahlok* [How could you leave your parents' house]. Ramsy? Your parents' house is empty." It's a lot of pressure. My mom's like, "everyone is talking about us . . . they're asking me, 'Why isn't your son living with you?' How is that possible? Do you think you're American now? Do you think we're an American family where sons move away from their parents?" People always ask me, like my aunt, in front of my mom, "Oh, how come you don't live at home?" My aunt says, "Oh, look at all my kids, they would live with me until they were thirty. Some of them got married and they still stay with me."

Nuha's family is from Jordan. We met at Arabian Nights, a weekly dance club in the Mission District where the DJ spins Arabian music. My friend Raya was a close friend of hers and introduced us to one another. A few years before we met, Raya had shared with Nuha a personal story I had written. Raya had hoped it would show Nuha that she was not alone in the conflicts she had with her family. I had titled my story, "Chronic Laryngitis?" In it I wrote about my alienation growing up in the space between what I perceived as my Arab family/community and dominant white middle-class U.S. culture. I wrote about how this seemingly contradictory space left me feeling unable to fully speak in either domain. I also wrote about my journey toward claiming my voice through Arab feminist activism and community building among Arab- and people of color–based social movements. The story provided Nuha and me with instant connection and common ground from which we developed friendship, sisterhood, and support.

During the time of my interviews with her, Nuha had been torn apart by what many of my interlocutors referred to as "the double life"—where she felt she lived one life with her parents and immediate family and the other with her friends and peers. When we first began talking, Nuha was graduating with a master's degree in nutrition. Her graduation party was at a nightclub where she used to bartend. At the party, I met Nuha's aunt. Nuha had been living with her because it was one of the only living arrangements that her parents would accept outside of living with them. Nuha considered her aunt someone who was "cool," who did not intervene in her life, and who could cover for her in relationship to her parents. Living with her aunt, Nuha maintained what she referred to as "living in two worlds . . . the 'Arab' world of my family . . . and the 'American' world outside of home." At the core of this struggle was her desire to marry a man of whom her parents did not approve. According to her,

> If I decide to follow my heart, I'll go and get all this freedom, but I'll be all alone. I'll be another lonely white CEO woman who's all alone and has no one; has no family, no brothers, no nothing—'cause that's what it's like in this [American] culture. My mom keeps saying, "You better let him know how important we are to you." And I keep saying, "Whatever my relationship is with you, my relationship is with you. And then, whatever my relationship is with him, my relationship is with him." But they can't take that kind of separation—it's too American.

Nuha interprets her reality as a choice between having family and being Arab or having independence and becoming American. She articulates her Arab world as constraining and comforting and her "American world" as free, while simultaneously lonely.

In Ramsy's and Nuha's stories, the politics of cultural authenticity regulates life decisions that significantly circumscribe their lives and their sense of future possibilities. The binary of good Arabs and bad Americans, central to the politics of cultural authenticity, underscores intergenerational tensions. Jameel captures the disciplinary effects of cultural authenticity when he says that his mother referred to his rebellion as "losing ourselves to the Amerikaan." Guided by a nationalist logic that queers the diaspora or renders it impure and inauthentic (Gopinath 2005), the politics of Arab cultural authenticity assumes that immigrant parents are the authentic representatives of Arab culture and that the second generation embodies the potential for cultural loss or annihilation. In this sense, many interlocutors' struggles with their immigrant parents were as much about their relationship with their families as they were about the Arab diaspora's relationship to an imagined America.

Arab Virgins and American(ized) Whores

In my own family, my parents' generation repeatedly articulated "American culture" through concepts of gender and sexuality. My father was a shop-keeper and went to bed early, having to wake up at 4:00 a.m. to open his store in downtown San Francisco. One December evening in 1999, while my father was asleep, I joined my mother on the couch and we searched for something interesting to watch on TV. My mother held the remote control, flipping through the stations. On station after station, a similar picture of an Anglo-American male and female holding one another in romantic or sexual ways appeared on the screen. As she flipped the channel, my mother remarked, "Sleep, slept. . . . Sleep, slept. . . . That is Amerika!" She contin-ued, "al-sex alhum, zay shurb al-mai [Sex for them is as easy as drinking water]." As I listened to my mother, I recalled several experiences growing up in which people referred to al Amerikaan in derogatory, sexualized terms. Amerika was the trash culture—degenerate, morally bankrupt, and sexually perverse. Al-Arab (Arabs) on the other hand, had good families, good girls, and good morals.

My interlocutors similarly recalled stories in which individuals of their parents' generation articulated "American culture" through the language of gender and sexuality. Indeed, many second-generation young adults, like many of their parents, were invested in this articulation. Men tended to feel less constrained by idealized concepts of gender and sexuality than women, and women tended to feel less constrained than queer-identified interlocu-tors. However, in nearly every interview, gender and sexuality were central to discussions about idealized concepts of Arabness and stereotypical notions of Americanness in the diaspora.

Susu's family is from Jordan. Her parents owned a convenience store. When we met, she had been working as a secretary in a law firm in San Fran-cisco's financial district. I interviewed her at a café near the law firm. As our first conversation began, Susu shared her excitement with me about her new relationship with a man who lived in England. She had met him through an online dating site for Muslims and was preparing to meet him in person the following month. She told me that her parents did not impose tremendously rigid rules on her growing up, yet they preferred that she socialize primarily with other Arabs: "I always wanted to be a singer or dancer. But my mom would say that is trashy because all the Americans are doing drugs and having sex and we have to stick with our culture."

Jumana's family was from a small village in Palestine. Her family expected her to socialize primarily with relatives. Her brothers, sisters, and cousins constituted her primary community growing up. We first met at Lyon's, the landmark restaurant in the West Lake district of Daly City, on the outskirts of San Francisco. She told me that during high school and college she worked for her father selling cars. There, she learned the skills of business entrepreneurship. After graduating from college, she began working in the corporate world as a business administrator. Recalling her high school days, she told me,

> My parents thought that being American was spending the night at a friend's house, wearing shorts, the guy-girl thing, wearing makeup, reading teen magazines, having pictures of guys in my room. My parents used to tell me, "If you go to an American's house, they're smoking, drinking . . . they offer you this and that. But if you go to an Arab house, you don't see as much of that. *Bihafzu 'ala al banat* [They watch over their daughters]."

Nicole's parents used a similar framework as she was growing up. She explains,

"Anytime I rebelled, it was always my friends' fault—my American friends. 'They're bad.' And I couldn't work at the store, because American men picked up on me there."

Manal's parents came to the United States from Syria. They raised her, her three sisters, and her brother in a tight-knit Arab community in the East Bay. Her father was a doctor, and they grew up in a predominantly white suburban neighborhood. She has memories similar to Nicole's: "It was as if everything we don't do is what Americans do . . . that's American . . . like boyfriends . . . makeup . . . looking at guys in an American way, reading American teen magazines, having pictures of guys in your room, American music."

My conversations with young Arab American men most explicitly reveal the significance of gender and sexuality, and women's bodies specifically, to the politics of cultural authenticity. The regulatory demands of cultural authenticity require young men to become future husbands and require that their future wives uphold distinct concepts of womanhood. Young men are thus key recipients of a heterosexual marriage ideal and an ideal femininity.

Most young men I worked with had grown up hearing that Arab girls are good girls compared to American girls. The stories they had heard illustrate that the patriarchal demands placed upon young women set the terms of marriageability. Women who fail to meet these demands are unmarriageable. In this sense, the dichotomy between Arab girls and American girls underscores a demand for heterosexuality and a dismissal of nonnormative sexualities. The relationship between patriarchy and compulsory heteronormativity has been theorized as heteropatriarchy (Smith 2006; Cohen 1999). I spoke with young men extensively about the idealized notions of Arab womanhood, marriage, and sexuality with which they had grown up.

John comes from a Catholic family from Ramallah, Palestine. He grew up in a multiracial neighborhood in San Francisco until junior high school, when his family moved to the North Bay. He worked in his father's stores while growing up. He worked hard in school because he wanted to get away from the harassment and racism he regularly experienced from his father's customers. He tells me, "Getting shit from customers because they thought we were Iranian, during the Iran/Contra affair back in the '70s, or because they just didn't want to pay you is why I don't want to have a store." He was accepted to the University of California at Davis and then became an engineer in the South Bay. I met him when he was studying Arabic at San Francisco State University. When we spoke about dating and marriage, he told me that he had been dating non-Arab women—Vietnamese, Filipinas, Mexican—for many years. "I've always identified with minorities. I never felt comfortable talking to whites. You'll never find me checking out the white women." By the time he finished college, he was interested in dating and potentially marrying an Arab woman. He said,

> Part of the reason why I didn't want to pursue these other relationships was that they were not Arab. I told myself, if I'm going to go out with anyone now, I want to marry an Arab. At some points I say, "Screw it. You're never going to meet an Arab, forget it. Just marry whoever the hell you want."

Yet he struggled in his relations with Arab women because of the ideals about Arab womanhood that he heard while growing up.

> "Arab girls don't screw around"—that is what you expect: "Arab girls are good girls." And then there's the idea that "American women are evil. Stay away from them." It was made clear. There were always discussions about how bad Americans were and how lousy American women were. Because

they would divorce their husbands, they would cheat on their husbands. They wouldn't clean the house like an Arab woman. My brother was dating a Hawaiian woman but I didn't want him to marry her. . . . I couldn't really pinpoint anything bad about her . . . but the fact that she had a boyfriend— that she messed around sexually, put her in that category—American, bad. I've never dated an Arab girl, number one. I've never dated one because I guess in the back of your mind, Arabs are for marrying, not for dating. The non-Arabs, the Americans are the ones you play around with. And then you settle down and get married to an Arab. . . . I always felt that Arab women wouldn't want to hang out with Arab men because they couldn't be themselves. 'Cause they could risk being labeled as sluts and you know . . . their reputation would be ruined and then they would have that reputation for the rest of their lives and they would never marry an Arab guy.

John's relationship with his sister contributed to his difficulty in relating to Arab women. His parents placed rigid rules upon her, and she rebelled with alcohol and drugs. He spent several years mediating between his sister and his parents, which contributed to his contradictory engagement with the ideals of Arab womanhood:

It's relevant to the Arab household that my sister grew up a certain way. An American would never understand that it's not okay for my sister, at the age of thirteen, to wear makeup and wear clothes a certain way. An American would say . . . what do you care how your sister dresses? And for me, I do care about what my sister does. And so that's where there's a cultural difference between Arabs and non-Arabs or Americans.

Other men I worked with shared a similar experience growing up:

Tony: There was this thing about marrying an Arab woman because she will stand by her family, she will cook and clean, and have no career. She'll have kids, raise kids, and take care of her kids, night and day. She will do anything for her husband. It's almost like they don't make her out to be her own person. It's nice to have someone dedicated, but that's beyond dedication. My mom always says, "You're not going to find an American woman who stands by her family like that."

My mom always said, "You can't trust American women . . . they will trap you . . . they leave their families." It's 'cause my mom's seen something on TV and makes a reference to it . . . and says, "See how the American women are! They have ulterior motives. They don't really care about you.

They know how great Arab men are and they want to trap them." And then there are the endless stories of American women who walk out on their family.

Bassam: For years, I wanted to marry an Arab woman. It started when I went to Palestine, but it also was because I grew up in a broken family and wanted a whole family. It's that illusion that Arab families are whole.

Ashraf: The ultimate American conquest is to see a woman at a club, get her number, see her later, sleep with her. . . . Americans are always talking about this girl, that girl.

These quotations reflect the significance of the binary between "good Arab girls" and "bad American girls," and between "good Arabs" and "bad Americans." Reinforced by idealized concepts of Arabness as family, the politics of cultural authenticity naturalizes the heteropatriarchal concept of "good Arab girls" and heterosexual marriage, and renders them ordinary and inconspicuous.

The concepts of gender and sexuality underpinning Arab cultural authenticity rely on a logic that many theorists of gender and nationalism have interrogated. Joseph Massad argues that a crucial project for anticolonial nationalists is "not only to define gender roles in relation to each other but also to define both in relation to the nationalist project and to dissociate national identity from any colonial contamination" (Massad 1995, 470). My interlocutors' stories illustrate that Arab cultural authenticity produces social roles by gender that correspond to a similar nationalist separation of social space into interior and exterior or inner and outer Arab or American (Chatterjee 1993; Moallem and Boal 1999). Arab cultural authenticity requires Arab women to uphold premarital chastity and expects them to be ideal wives, daughters, and mothers. To a certain extent the politics of cultural authenticity also resembles U.S. Orientalism. Whereas U.S. Orientalism represents Arab culture through images of oppressed or exotic women and repressed or erotic sexualities, cultural authenticity articulates Arab culture through images of good Arab girls and heterosexual sex within marriage. This schema thus relies on the symbolic presence of the idealized Arab woman to facilitate the belief that an essential, homogenous, true Arab culture can be protected, maintained, and preserved in America. Bhattacharjee explores a similar dynamic among bourgeois Indian immigrants. She states that the immigrant bourgeoisie uses the "figure of woman to steady itself in light of shifting grounds of immigrant community." She explains that the responsibility of preserving the intra-communal private domain, which is critical to survival in the diaspora, lies with women (Bhattacharjee 1992, 38).

"You're the Only Gay Arab in the World"

> When I went to Folsom Street Fair I took pictures and showed them to my mother. I always try not to say anything but subtly show them something—that I am involved in a circle that could be gay like this one in the pictures. My mom took one look at the pictures and said, "My God! What are we doing in this country! Oh, look what this country did to us!" They definitely see it as an American thing. They don't know that there are a lot of gay people back home, that's underground . . . . [T]here are lots of things that they don't see. They want me to hide it.

I first met Ramsy through his cousin Heba in 1998. At the time, Heba told me, "He is very gay. . . . [E]veryone [in the extended family] knows it but no one wants to admit it." Ramsy and I first met at Café Flor, a popular gay and lesbian hangout in San Francisco's Castro District. After our first meeting, we continued to run into each other at hangout spots we both frequented in San Francisco and at Arab community-based events he attended with his cousins or friends. Most people I spoke to over the years who self-identified as gay, lesbian, or queer and Arab have confronted a similar schema that defines Arabness in terms of heterosexuality and Americanness in terms of sexual transgression and promiscuity.

Consider Rabia's story. Rabia's family is originally from Lebanon. She was actively engaged in queer Arab politics during the time of my research. I first met Rabia in 1998 on the e-mail list *Shilla*, a network of Arab American professionals in the Bay Area. Immediately after I announced my research project on the list and asked for participants, she replied. She told me that she was especially eager to speak out about her experience of exclusion from her immediate family as a consequence of her coming out to them as a lesbian. We made plans to meet at a restaurant in San Francisco. When I first walked in, I recognized her by the tattoo of her girlfriend's name, Amina, in Arabic script on her arm, and by the Palestinian flag sewn onto her book bag. After we began talking, I learned that Rabia was the artist who graffitied the words "Queer Arabs Exist" that I had read in large print on the bathroom wall of Café Macondo, one of my favorite cafés in the Mission District. Rabia:

My mother keeps finding ways to say I'm too Americanized, and when I tell her, "you don't know how many queer Arabs I know," she says, "They're American, they're American born, they're not Arab." My uncles would come and take me out to lunch. They would say, "Let's talk. This doesn't happen in our culture. You've been brainwashed by Americans. You've taken too many feminist classes. You joined NOW. You hate men. You have a backlash against men . . ." It was like . . . "This is what this American society has done to our daughter." They blamed Western feminism. I was so strong in defending myself that they thought that too was very American. "You chose sexuality over us. Sex is more important than your family." Which goes back to the tight-knit Arab family thing. It's all about group dynamics. And I still get that. "We [Arabs] don't do that" or "You're the only gay Arab in the world."

Ramsy and Rabia's stories point to the normative demand for compulsory heterosexuality underlying the politics of cultural authenticity. This demand operates in connection with the concept of Arabness as family and the idealization of "good Arab girls." Here we see the consolidation of heteropatriarchy through the triangulation among idealized concepts of family, patriarchy, and heteronormativity. Put differently, the ideal of Arabness as family with "good Arab women" forecloses the possibility of homosexuality. Within this logic, the survival of an imagined Arab community depends upon a good Arab family, which requires good women within the construct of heterosexual marriage. These demands, and the articulation of homosexuality as distinctly Western, operate as markers that distinguish good Arabs from bad Americans.

To interrogate the conflation of Arab culture and heterosexuality, we can turn to scholarship on sexuality in Arab- and Muslim-majority countries. This scholarship reveals that this conflation has no basis in historical realities but emerged as a reaction to European domination and, as I will argue, as a reaction to the pressures of immigration, assimilation, and racialization in the diaspora. The scholarship also shows that we must reorient conventional Eurocentric frameworks that ask whether or not Arab culture allows for "homosexuality" to a focus on the historically and culturally specific concepts of gender and sexuality that have been circulated in the region. Indeed, in the Arab region, same-sex desire and sexual relations have existed and have taken on varying and diverse forms and cannot be explained as simple consequences of engagements with the West or colonial or imperial impositions (Babayan and Najmabadi 2008; Najmabadi 2005; Habib 2010; Rowson 2008; Amer 2008; Traub 2008). In her analysis of classical Arabic—in particular the Andaluisan and Abbasid periods—Jocelyn Sharlet reveals the existence and emergence of nonheterosexual identities and locations. These indeed existed in public spaces "without having to be disciplined or brought under the sway of the heteronormative model of marriage and reproduction" (2009). Scholars such as Kathryn Babayan and Afsaneh Najmabadi have theorized the problems in "translating" sex and relevant cultural, linguistic, and epistemological practices from Islamicate contexts into European and Anglo-American "counterparts" (2008). Rather than conceptualize same-sex desire or behavior in Arab-Muslim histories through dominant modernist Western concepts of "homosexuality" or "gay identity," many scholars have instead called for a rereading of texts mindful of the multitude of practices and attitudes around desire, and the variety of homoerotic acts that defy tidy categorization (2008).[7]

Certainly, dominant discourses in the Arab region have privileged the extended, heterosexual family as a crucial schema for organizing society. Yet the conflation between homosexuality and the West or America is also not a reference to a strictly heterosexual Arab culture. In fact, the category "homosexual" is itself a Western, European construct and does not eas-ily map onto the complex forms of sexuality that have existed through-out Arab and Islamicate histories (Foucault 1978; Rubin 1997; Najmabadi 2005; Traub 2008). For instance, Afsaneh Najmabadi shows that in histori-cal periods preceding Iranian engagements with Europe, there were many same-sex practices and forms of love and desire that were not labeled or marked in binary gendered or sexualized terms (e.g., either male-male or female-female/either homosexual or heterosexual) (2005). She explains that through engagement with Europeans and European Enlightenment thought, gender binaries became increasingly important within Iran, and homosocial male spaces that Iranian men had experienced were replaced by heterosocial encounters. She explains that before engagements with Europe, sexual acts between men were seen as "acts," not as inherent forms of "desire" or as a fixed identity, as in the Western context. This, she argues, produced "types" such as the homosexual and the nonhomosexual, which became increasingly pervasive in Iran (2005). In other words, the reference to homosexuality as not-Arab, Western, or American may reveal the limi-tations of the term "homosexual" as a framing device for defining same-sex desires, acts, or identities as much as it is a strategy for suppressing same-sex desires, acts, or identities. Thus, understanding Rabia's or Ramsy's par-ents' references that "homosexuality" or "being gay" is Western or Ameri-can requires a more complex analysis than one that defines Arab culture as simply "homophobic."

Histories of Arab engagements with European colonialisms and masculinist anticolonial Arab nationalist discourses have contributed to the conflation between "homosexuality" and "the West." Masculinist Arab nationalists, responding to negative European representations of gender and sexuality among Arabs, have conflated being gay with being Western. This conflation has served as an articulation of a unified, nationalist identity in reaction to a perceived European threat. Later, it emerged in response to a perceived U.S. political, military, and economic threat. In both instances, the conflation between "being gay" and being "Western" or "American" works as a strategy for policing non-normative sexualities.

Rabab Abdulhadi illustrates that in varying periods of Islamic history, from the Caliphates (623-656) to the Ottomans (1281-1922), there has been tremendous variation and ambiguity in sexual attitudes.[8] She documents periods in which rulers burned homosexuals to periods of highly lax sexual attitudes in which homosexual literary figures thrived and rulers favored eunuchs over women and concubines. Abdulhadi argues that the advent of European colonialism brought about European colonialist attitudes that demonized Arabs and Muslims through Orientalist representations of their sexuality. Throughout a period of over one hundred years of Arab engagements with European colonialism, Arab people internalized Orientalist representations of sexuality. Anticolonial national projects represented their ability for self-reign through the development of a rigid, conservative sexual order that privileged male dominance and hypermasculinity and rendered queers as subjects of shame and deviance (2010). In the late twentieth century, contemporary Arab states have enacted rigid new sanctions on homosexuality in the face of intensified occupation by foreign forces. This new period has introduced more rigid forms of homosociality compared to previous eras, including less hand holding in public of people of the same sex. Overall, masculinist Arab nationalisms have replaced European concepts that essentialize Arab culture through negative images of Arab sexuality, with similarly essentialist concepts that reduce culture, family, gender, and sexuality to rigid abstractions that exist outside of history. Ironically, concepts of family, gender, and sexuality become a marker of the distinction between "Arabs" and "the West" even as dominant middle-class European and U.S. discourses have upheld a similar demand for compulsory heterosexuality as a marker of respectability and acceptability.

By illustrating the varied and ambiguous attitudes about same-sex desires and relations and the emergence of rigid concepts of sexuality as a response to colonialism and imperialism, Abdulhadi's analysis complicates Rabia's and Ramsy's parents' claim that homosexuality is American. Perhaps Rabia's and

Ramsy's parents relied on claims such as "you are the only gay Arab in the world" as a mechanism to control, exclude, and constrain their lives. Yet perhaps the claim also reflects the incongruity between the category "gay" and concepts of sexuality among individuals like Rabia's mother, whose sensibilities about sexuality were partly shaped in the Arab world. Is Rabia's mother claiming that there are no same-sex desires or relations in the Arab world or that there are no "gays"? While she might perceive Rabia as the "only gay Arab in the world"—perhaps this might not mean that she denies the existence of same-sex desires, actions, relationships, and behaviors among Arabs and Arab Americans. Although I did not speak in depth to Rabia and Ramsy about their sexual desires or experiences, I wonder what the categorization of sexual desire, acts, and behaviors in terms of either "gay" or "straight" among Arab diasporas obscures and what specifically about that sexuality their parents considered to be "American."

When Ramsy shows his pictures to his mother, he says he is trying "not to say anything but subtly show them something—that I am involved in a circle that could be gay like this one in the pictures." Conventional Eurocentric logics that require same-sex sexualities to fit into a neatly packaged public identity (e.g., "gay") might interpret Ramsy as a closeted gay man who has not yet realized his full gay identity yet. Queer of color scholarship provides ways of conceptualizing Ramsy's story through a different interpretation. As we saw earlier, in his extended family he is known to be "gay." In a subtle way, his family is aware of his transgression of heternormative ideals. Consider, for instance, the way they interpret his style of dress and his circle of friends. Yet their stance against his perceived homosexuality comes up when he shows his mother his pictures with a group that could be "gay." While Ramsy's mother generally denounces Ramsy's association with a group that stands out as upholding a public "gay" identity, she, like his extended family, subtly accepts a less visible, less spoken, more fluid non-normative sexuality. Here, the ideal of the extended family within the politics of cultural authenticity opens up possibilities for sexual nonnormativity, and for resistance of heterosexual marriage, as in Ramsy's and Rabia's stories, to be reincorporated into the extended family. While Ramsy avoids the demand for heterosexual marriage, he is actively involved in extended family affairs such as weddings, family gatherings, and long visits with his extended family in Palestine. The ideal Arab family, as we have seen, is constituted by "web-like relationalities" defined within an extended kinship structure (Joseph 1993). While the concept of the ideal Arab family demands heterosexuality, it does not exclude unmarried individuals. Ramsy, who resists heterosexual marriage, found himself worked back into the extended family structure through other possibilities the extended kin structure makes available. Ramsy, for instance, stands in as a representative of his parents in the United States when he travels to Palestine. He was preparing to leave for a visit to Palestine after one of our meetings:

> My mother's giving me a list of things that I have to say and I have to do, and a list of people that I have to visit. I barely know them. But because I'm my father's only son, I'm expected to go and say hi—they take it as though I'm going there to represent my father. I have two suitcases of gifts right now and I'm only going for two weeks.

Ramsy also plans to provide for his parents when they retire. Thus, while he is criticized by the family because of his avoidance of marriage, he can also be reworked back into the family. The extended family can allow varied possibilities of gender and sexuality to remain in the circuit. Jose Muñoz uses the term "disidentification" to refer to queer subjectivities that do not easily map onto Eurocentric U.S. categories of sexual identity (1999). Through this framework, he strives "to envision and activate new social relations" among minority subjects who must work with or resist the conditions of (im)possibility that the dominant culture generates (5). Disidentification refers to the negotiation between "a fixed identity disposition and the socially encoded roles that are available for such subjects" (6). In Rabia's and Ramsy's stories, multiple power-laden, socially encoded scripts collide into each other—the binary of straight Arabs and promiscuous, sexually loose Americans, the discourse of U.S. Orientalism and its sexually savage Arabs versus sexually civilized "Americans," and the more fluid Arab concepts of sexual acts and desires compared to rigid Eurocentric categories of sexual identity. Indeed, their stories cannot be explained through liberal Eurocentric frameworks that equate visibility or "coming out" with emancipation and more subtle and fluid modes of sexuality with backwardness and victimization. Ramsy's place in his extended family parallels long-standing structures of family in the Arab world in which same-sex desire or behavior exists as long as it does not threaten the reproduction of the extended family. While he refers to his circle of friends as potentially "gay," he disidentifies with coming out. He straddles a space in between, cast out as possibly "gay" and incorporated back into the patrilineal extended family structure.

A queer Arab artist who prefers to remain anonymous articulated similar confrontations with binary middle-class Arab American discourses about "straight Arabs" and "gay Americans."

Virgin/Whore. Artist: Anonymous.

Virgin/Whore. Artist: Anonymous.

In a special issue of a cyber magazine on sexuality, the artist displays a virtual collage she created called "Virgin/Whore." In it, a collage representing her as "virgin" transforms into a second collage representing her as "whore." The "virgin" collage is a series of images associated with what she refers to as her "Arab side," including pictures of *tablas* (drums), pita bread, camels, the word "Allah" (God), a Syrian flag, and a photograph that represents her family that she altered by blindfolding their eyes. The "whore" collage includes pictures associated with what she refers to as "the flip side," the "actual stuff that is part of [her] sexuality and [her] rebellion against Arab culture." It includes images of dildos next to her girlfriend's name written in Arabic, handcuffs, a blurred image of a picture that represents her parents, and a photo of Madonna. As the artist told me,

> What I am doing with the two collages is showing how they are dichoto-mous, or at least they have felt that way, and how it has been an either/or situation. Also, I think it's how my mother would see my sexuality: dirty, sinful, dark. The reason for the rollover of images is to show that the two states can't coexist.

I read the collage not as a literal representation of two distinct "cultures"—Arab and American—but as a critique of the impossible dichotomies that the artist felt were circumscribing her life. The collage represents a disiden-tification with both dominant Arab and American discourses on sexuality as well as "the moment (of collision), of negotiation, when hybrid, racially predicated, and deviant gendered identities arrive at representation" (Muñoz 1999, 7). In the collage, the dichotomy "sexually pure Arabs" versus "sexually promiscuous Americans" is a failed interpellation through which the artist's sense of being in the world emerges. Similarly, Ramsy and Rabia's inability to identify with a singular category—whether straight or gay, American or Arab—tells us more about them than do the categories themselves.

A Selective Assimilation Strategy

While the triangulation of family, the good Arab woman, and compulsory heterosexuality draws on various, colliding Arab and European discourses, it is also informed by middle-class U.S. norms and the connected U.S. logics of liberal multiculturalism. For immigrants and people of color in the United States, middle-class acceptability requires an investment in the logic of lib-eral multiculturalism. This logic requires immigrants and people of color to disavow structural inequalities such as racism and exclusion and instead to promote and celebrate essentialist forms of cultural identity (Moallem and Boal 1999; Sleeter and McLaren 1995; Lowe 1996). Several scholars have shown that essentialist forms of cultural identity among U.S. people of color, immigrants, and indigenous people go hand in hand with assimilation (Lowe 1996; Ono 2000; Cohen 1999; White 1990).

Furthermore, a patriarchal nuclear family and compulsory heteronormativity have been fundamental to white U.S. middle-class acceptability. Cathy Cohen explains that middle-class African American discourses have articulated concepts of cultural identity through a notion of an apparently distinct "African American" respectability. At the same time, she argues, this notion is shaped by white middle-class ideals of respectability. Middle-class African American discourses have claimed notions of respectability as indigenous or authentic although such notions serve the interests of Black elites. Several scholars have analyzed how middle-class concepts of cultural identity among U.S. people of color emerge as a response to dominant U.S. discourses that demonize people of color through racist ideas about their concepts and practices of family, gender, and sexuality (Collins 2000; Cohen 1999; Alarcón 1999). Gendered racism requires people of color to prove their acceptability by articulating who they are through white middle-class ideals of respectability. In Kevin Gaines's study of Black middle-class elites, he argues that U.S. racist discourses portray acts of transgressing the authoritative moral status of the patriarchal family as a racial stigma, a lack of morality, and, thus, a badge of inferiority. In this context,

> for educated blacks, the family, and patriarchal gender relations, became crucial signifiers of respectability. . . . [Thus] claiming respectability often meant denouncing nonconformity to patriarchal gender conventions and bourgeois morality. A sense of shame might also compel silences or revisions, producing a secretive family lore on any number of sensitive matters of parentage, disease, transgressive sexuality, or other behaviors or occurrences to which a real or imagined racial stigma might be attached. (1996, 6)

Among the middle-class Arab diasporas I worked with, dominant discourses privileged certain white middle-class norms about gender, sexuality, marriage, and family, and suppressed those that may be deemed transgressive, thus providing Arab Americans with a strategy to displace racist assumptions about uncivilized and barbaric gender and sexual regimes among Arabs. In this sense, as Kevin Gaines argues, rigid structures that police gender and sexuality are, in part, an example of unconscious internalized racism. Yet the preoccupation with family, patriarchy, and heteronormativity as a strategy for acceptance has the effect of blaming individuals who do not measure up to middle-class gender and sexual norms and obscuring the actual problem of gendered and sexualized racisms. By promoting white middle-class norms and avoiding a critique of U.S. imperialism, racism, classism, sexism, and homophobia, the politics of cultural authenticity facilitates access to political, economic, and social resources (Duggan 2004; Bhattacharjee 1992, 27; Burek, cited in Bhattacharjee 1992). Cathy Cohen refers to a similar strategy deployed within African American middle-class discourses that assume that conformity to particular notions of respectability "will confer full citizenship status, bringing with it great access, opportunities, and mobility" (2004, 30). It becomes particularly urgent for immigrants and people of color who strive for acceptability in white middle-class terms to embody white middle-class concepts of family, gender, and sexuality. Rooted in European Victorian ideals that assume that unmarried women's sexuality poses a threat to middle-class identity, middle-class U.S. concepts of acceptability took on a new sense of urgency in the 1990s, during the period of my research. Republicans and Democrats alike tended to converge on similar idealizations of heterosexual marriage as emblems of an idealized American national identity (Duggan 2004; Stacey 1998). Within this logic, heterosexual marriage is an emblem of respectability. Women must marry and be controlled, or men lose power (Duggan 2004; Odem 1995, 2).

While Arab cultural authenticity serves to consolidate or solidify some sense of a distinct Arab identity, it simultaneously reifies white middle-class concepts of heteronormativity and marriage, incorporating U.S. categories of respectability into its logic. Thus, Arab cultural authenticity effectively prioritizes cultural forms that represent Arabs as similar to stereotypical white, middle-class Americans. Heterosexual marriage and the prohibition against homosexuality not only preserve an idealized concept of Arabness but also model "appropriate behavior that will lead to assimilation, acceptance, access" (Cohen 2004, 20). The dominant middle-class Arab American concepts and practices of marriage not only require heteropatriarchy but prescribe which identity categories (race, class, gender, sexuality, nationality, religion) are important and what forms of relationships, attachments, and identities deserve respect. In these very specific terms, marriage ideals facilitate white middle-class acceptability.

Although most interlocutors do not discuss socioeconomic class directly, the stories of people who felt constrained by the demands of middle-class acceptability reveal the significance of class to the politics of cultural authenticity. Ramsy and Nader relate how idealized notions of "Arab culture" pressured them to establish financial security before marriage, pointing to connections between concepts of class mobility and marriageability. Ramsy:

> My parents keep saying, "What are you waiting for? It's about time." For them, it's like, "That's it. He finished school. He has his own business. The next step would be the bride." If I didn't have my business, it could have been a good excuse to say, "I'm waiting to get a job."

Nader, a disc jockey, expresses the preference to produce music over a more "acceptable" career. He encountered a code of sociability that considered financial success inseparable from marriage. In Nader's experience, his desire to produce music contradicted familial-communal norms, particularly since he was married.

> From the Arab community, I get comments every single day because I'm a DJ. Especially from women, they'll say, "I didn't think you were married." It's not that I don't act like I'm married, it's that they assume that you can't have a family and be into the arts at the same time. Some guys look at me as the enemy. They think, "What you are doing is wrong" because my brain is not locked up in what my brother and I call the real man/real job syndrome.

While men disproportionately felt pressured to uphold an arc of education, a professional career, and marriage, women shared a sense that the ideal of education and a career could be supplanted by marriage within middle-class boundaries. For many women, marrying within class boundaries took precedence over other ideals. Rime experiences the pressure to marry within class boundaries when she meets the love of her life on a trip to Jordan:

> In Jordan, my life completely turned around. I met Omar. All my life the message was that I had to marry an Arab man. I finally met an Arab man I love, but my parents are not accepting him. They say, "The guy has no money—and you're going to go live with his family." Traditionally if an Arab man is going to get married he should furnish and open a house for the girl and then get married, not get married and then worry about that stuff. My mom and him started talking and my mom kept asking him, "How about getting her an apartment after you guys get married?" He said, "I can't. I don't have the money." He said, "If your daughter wants to bring money and get me an apartment, I'll move the next day." My mom said, "If you have no money, you shouldn't be getting married." They hung up and

he called me back in three minutes and my mom's in the background say-ing *"Batlee!* [Stop!] You're not getting married!" It all comes down to our traditions—having Arab traditions.

Rime makes repeated references to an idealized "Arab culture." Yet her story illustrates how socioeconomic class informs idealized concepts of "Arab culture." The politics of cultural authenticity protects class (through marriage) in its preservation of an idealized Arab culture. In this framework, women are not discouraged from working or pursuing higher education, but it is generally men who feel the greatest pressure for economic mobility, particularly before marriage. Men generally felt pressured either to continue their family's small business or enter a professional field such as engineering, law, or medicine.

Jokes and stereotypes that played upon notions of second-generation Arab masculinity and femininity among middle-class Arab immigrant com-munities reinforce the expected gender roles. Jokes about second-generation men often focused on the image of the "store owner" or the "engineer." Jokes about women tended to relate to themes of domesticity, such as cooking or motherhood.

One evening, at a family gathering at an interlocutor's home, I was eat-ing dinner with a group of first cousins. One cousin expressed interest in an Arab woman named Samia. Between that gathering and the second gather-ing I attended, he had met with her a few times. At the second gathering, his cousins created a teasing song about her: "She's cute and she's Samia, but can she make the *bamia* [okra]?" Implicit in the chorus was a sarcastic play upon idealized notions of the Arab woman: if she can cook Arabic food, then she is marriageable.

The articulation of cultural authenticity through marriage is as much about race as it is about class. In everyday life, marriage norms also reify U.S. racial schemas fundamental to white middle-class codes of sociability. Interlocutors and their families engage with socioeconomic class in many different ways. Some identify as people of color, some as white, and some are more open than others to marrying across racial lines. Yet most people agreed that the dominant middle-class Arab discourse promoted particular ideals about interracial dating and marriage. Before Rime went to Jordan and met Omar, she spent most of her time in high school and college socializing among Mexican and Black friends. She tells me,

One day, my dad said to me, "I had a nightmare that my daughter would marry a Black man." That was because he owns a liquor store in the

Tenderloin. All his life he's been robbed and shot at and his wife's been robbed by Blacks. He blamed poor Blacks from the Tenderloin for their situation without understanding it. He couldn't understand that I had a lot of Black friends at school and that Blacks were always the first ones out there supporting Arab student movements at school. I remember when my cousin got pregnant with a guy who is half Mexican and half Black. She lied and stayed out of the house for four years in the Mission. Her family knew, but kept it secret. My mom never knew. My uncle, who is my cousin's father, heard the news and went and told everyone about it. At that point, everyone was telling my cousin, just marry him at least. All I know is the couple got in a big fight and he kicked her out and she moved back to her parents' house. She's thirty now and she's living with her parents. She's my age. She did the most despicable thing a girl could ever do in Arab culture—and they took her back.

Rime's story points to the entanglement of Arab cultural authenticity within dominant U.S. discourses that regulate marriage in racial and class terms (and prohibit white middle-class intermarriage with people of color). Dominant U.S. anxieties about interracial marriage complicate Rime's references to "Arab tradition." Her father's position as a liquor store owner in the Tenderloin neighborhood shapes the racialized and gendered imperatives that policed Rime's sexuality. His nightmare over his daughter's potential marriage to a Black man represents a threat to the securing of white middle-class norms and the forging of a critical distance between the racial Other and whiteness. Many interlocutors articulate similar ideals. Tony tells me, "It would be bad to marry someone who was white. Asian is the worst. Black . . . they would think you were joking. It's not even an option. They would never get over it. You would be the topic of discussion for the next . . . I don't know how long."

Regulation and Exclusion

The raced and classed triangulation of Arab family, good Arab women, and heteronormativity policed my interlocutors' everyday lives in different ways. Discussions with my interlocutors about marriage most clearly elucidate the hierarchies this triangulation set into play among different Arab Americans. Men and women interlocutors, whether straight or queer, expressed particular ideals about relationships and intimacy that regulated their lives long before they were expected to marry and determined an individual's marriageability. Interlocutors did not encounter the exact same marriage demands as one another. Yet they shared similar accounts of dominant middle-class Arab American ideals that require particular marriage codes. Interlocutors who had had an oppositional relationship to this marriage ideal spoke about the inner workings of the marriage norms and the specific boundaries they police in the most explicit ways.

> Ramsy: Now the issue of marriage is starting up. They're like, "When are you going to get married? It's about time." Everybody at every gathering I go to, my aunts, their friends, everybody comes up and says . . . "It's about time you bring your parents a grandson." Now I'm going home to Palestine for a visit and my mom is saying, "Maybe I should ask around and see if there's someone you would be interested in."

> Sema: The expectation was that . . . "You're gonna grow up and get married . . . yeah, you may go to college, but you're gonna get married and have kids."

> Tony: The main thing is you're going to get married and have kids. You're going to have my grandkids. It's not a question. And, you're not going to be a homosexual. That's it. In high school, it's almost insulting if you tell them you're dating. They wouldn't understand it. They would think there's going to be a problem—like she's going to get pregnant.

Here, the politics of cultural authenticity polices the bodies of unmarried women disproportionately and reinforces the significance of female sexuality to idealized concepts of Arabness. It also positions men as actors and women as objects who are to be protected. Generally, women experience the (unspoken) ban on heterosexual dating (before marriage) more acutely than men. Women:

> Lulu: I grew up with this all the time: sex is an act of love in marriage. If you're not a virgin when you get married, you're in trouble.

> Huda: As an Arab girl, I couldn't go to school dances and I couldn't date.

> Rania: The guys can do whatever they want. They can date who they want, sleep around, and they can always come back home and marry the virgin from the village . . . and they will be welcomed in the community. If we did any of these things, we could never come back. Even if I tried, no one would want to marry me.

Rime: Arabs raise their daughters with fear of having sex. They scare them and then they either conform or rebel.

In addition to highlighting the strict regulations of female sexuality, these quotations point to the double standard women and men face when it comes to marriageability and communal belonging. Despite their privileged position, many of the men I worked with seemed well aware of the difference. Men:

Tony: Anytime you have a girlfriend, you don't talk about it. No one knows about it 'cause their view of it is that if you have a girlfriend, then you're instantly going to get married. They don't understand that this might just be temporary. You don't bring girlfriends to family functions. Dating doesn't exist.

Salem: When I was younger, they thought, "It's okay, let him play around in his own way, but when it comes to marriage, we'll pick his wife for him." Even when I was younger and had a girlfriend, they didn't like her, but they didn't mind me going out with her. If I wanted to marry her, they would say "no" for sure. They thought it was a temporary thing, but I knew that if the day came when I am going to say I'm going to marry her it would be hell.

Joe: I was in college. I had a girlfriend. She was American—blonde—and we lived together. Somehow, my dad found out. I think my sister told him. So he drove four hours away from home, down to my dorm, and knocked on the door. My girlfriend answered. He took one look at her and said, "Don't think my son is going to marry you. This is just for fun."

Ramsy: My parents always said, "You do whatever you want to do, just don't let anyone find out—when it comes to getting serious about life and getting married, we'll tell you what to do."

To a certain extent, the politics of cultural authenticity associates both homosexuality and premarital sex with deviance and the interruption of cultural norms. Yet it deems homosexuality more deviant than premarital sex.

Rabia: The bottom line is premarital sex. Lesbian sex doesn't happen because Arab girls don't have premarital sex. When I came out, it was like, "That's fine that you're gay—but don't act on it."

Laura: I don't know if you can get how it's considered *haram* [forbidden] to be queer. It's not a matter of going too far, like you're supposed to be married but you're not, or you're not going out with the right kind of guy, or you're supposed to find a man and marry him, but you're not supposed to f—— him in the meantime. . . . It's much, much worse. There's a fundamental perversion associated with us.

Sema told me, "I think for queer women, it's even worse. There are quite a few lesbian activists and the stereotypes they're faced with, if they're out as lesbian—they're seen as sexual—whereas the rest of us somehow, we're not sexual. We're virgins till the day we marry."

In the context of marriage, Arab cultural authenticity takes for granted Eurocentric concepts that reduce sexuality to explicit sexual identity categories (gay or straight, homosexual or heterosexual). Coupled with the conflation of heterosexuality with "Arab culture," Arab cultural authenticity demands that heterosexuals have the option of dating (sex) or not dating (no sex), cultural acceptability or cultural deviance. Gays, lesbians, and queers are outside this schema altogether. As Samah explained, "If I'm gay, it puts sexuality in their face. It means I'm not marriageable. Even if I change, I'm still permanently marked that I had sex."

Kalam al-nas (Words of the People)

We have seen how Arab cultural authenticity is constituted by multiple regimes of patriarchy and heteronormativity that collide, instituting a binary between "Arab culture" and "American culture." Here, I analyze a culturally specific term, "*al-nas*" (the people), that operates to consolidate the boundaries of Arabness or an imagined Arab community in America and the politics of Arab cultural authenticity. My interlocutors and their parents use this term to refer to a concept of Arab people who are deterritorialized rather than living in a bounded geographic place. The concepts of *al-nas* and family reputation go hand in hand. Most second-generation interlocutors felt expected to uphold their family's reputation before *al-nas*. Women tend to discuss reputation in terms of sexuality, whereas men do so in terms of stature. Most interlocutors agree that reputation is about how other people perceive their family.

Nuha: It all has to do with our family worrying about what other people think and how other people will perceive them, as opposed to what makes them happy. They're not just worried about family, but the entire Arab community. What I do is a reflection of them.

Muna: My parents said, always, "Someone is going to talk about you. *Al-nas* are going to find something to talk about."

Lulu: First my parents wanted to send me to a hospital to fix me, then they changed their mind. They said, "You know . . . after you change, someone might see on your hospital records that you were gay." They didn't want anyone finding out "after I change" and "once I get married" that I had this dark past.

Many interlocutors state that their parents respond to their desires to transgress the ideals of cultural authenticity with questions such as these: "Do you know what *al-nas* would say about you?" Or, "Where am I going to put my head? What are other people going to say?"

Most interlocutors told me that the demand to uphold their family's reputation was especially prevalent when they attended events with other Arabs. Weddings, funerals, holiday celebrations, and *azayem* (dinner gatherings) exemplify the social spaces of *al-nas*. Interlocutors reference *azayem* more than other social spaces since they take place more often and happen within the close confines of people's homes. *Azayim* bring together people considered "family"—people related to one another through blood ties or through friendships based on strong affective bonds. For people without extended family or with few extended family members in the Bay Area, *azayim* includes "friends" who become "family" after immigration. Consider the following:

Ferris: We were very close with our aunts, uncles, and cousins—but there was the burden to go to all the family functions and to entertain guests all the time and live your life for other people, not for yourself. Be home . . . serve guests . . . be there when guests come over.

Ramsy: One time, I had these tight-ass pants on. . . . They had a slit on the side 'cause I wear boots. . . . I had this jacket on that had all these colors, striped colors on it. . . . The family called me Versace 'cause I'm always stylish. I put on what I'm going to wear and come into the room and my mom says, "YEEH!" The clothes thing always comes up because I'm always expected to show up to family things. When I was younger, I had excuses like school. Now, people expect me to show up to weddings, *azayim*, and you're not just expected to, you have to go with your parents.

To a certain extent, interlocutors inherit the concept of *al-nas* from Arab countries. Suad Joseph writes that in Lebanon, concepts of patriarchy and the ideal of strong emotive connections work within kin structures that operated in kin and nonkin relations in public and private spheres (1993, 468). Yet the concept of *al-nas* takes on new form in the diaspora. It works as shorthand for an imagined Arab community. It enhances the possibilities for the politics of cultural authenticity to regulate behaviors by rendering transgression not only as individual rebellion but as cultural loss and Americanization. The power of *al-nas* in America is that it means that one's behaviors implicate one's entire family as well as an entire "Arab people" in the United States. The concept of *al-nas* reinforces the implication of one's family within acts of transgression, cultural loss, and Americanization and thus expands the stakes placed on young adults' desires, actions, and behaviors. Its ability to police the lives of young adults lay in its reliance on the concept of an imagined community that does not require the physical presence of "the people" to which it refers.

Nicole elucidates how this sense of "Arab community" does not require the existence of "real people" but is indeed one step removed from lived realities and operates, to a certain extent, on the level of the psyche, as an effective form of control and constraint. She tells me that "none of my relatives live in the Bay Area. Growing up, my family did not interact with other Arabs. But my mom would always tell me that *al-nas* are watching us. One day, I asked my mom, 'Where are the people?' and she couldn't reply."

For Nicole, the concept of *al-nas* reflects a sense of a people attached to one another in some kind of union of shared responsibilities, or what Benedict Anderson refers to as an "imagined community" (1983). Anderson writes, "It is imagined because the members of even the smallest nation will never know most of their fellow members, meet them, or even hear of them, yet in the minds of each lives the image of their communion. . . . In fact, all communities larger than primordial villages of face-to-face contact (and perhaps even these) are imagined" (6). Feminist scholars have added to Anderson's idea that concepts of kinship underlie this concept of an imagined communion or fraternity and that the concept of "nation as a family" is an extensive metaphor spanning most, if not all, modern nation-states (McClintock 1993, 63; Williams 1996). Anne McClintock argues that "nations are frequently figured through the iconography of familial and domestic space." She refers to nations as "domestic genealogies" (1993, 63). Rita Giaca-man and Penny Johnson, writing on the first *intifada* in Palestine, argue that "family became community" when formal networks of support were break-ing down and when conditions created new and pressing needs. They argue that "the barriers between private and public and between home and poli-tics became increasingly blurred" (1989, 157–61). In the Arab region, the idea of nation as family has been crucial to the organization of society (Joseph 2000). In the diaspora, the concept of *al-nas* was crucial to the organization of an intra-communal-cultural Arab domain that could be distinguished from an outer American domain.

Al-nas not only signifies a community that is imagined but one that is diasporic, transnational, and deterritorialized. Nuha, for example, fell in love with a Muslim man, Mohammed. Her parents are Christian and did not sup-port her marriage to Mohammed.

> Nuha: My mom called and said, "Your father is freaking out because peo-ple in the community are talking about you. Even his friends in Lebanon heard you are dating a Muslim. He's saying you've ruined his reputation." So my dad called me and said, "You have to stop dating him right now." My father's concerned about what his friends and his family are going to say, not about his own beliefs. My dad says, "This is going against your society and your family." What's really bothering them is that the whole commu-nity is talking about us and my dad needs to be able to say, "I ended that."

Gender plays a key role in Nuha's story. Her assumption that her father "needs to say" he ended her relationship points to a patriarchal kinship structure where family members' behaviors reflect on the father's family name and the father's reputation is tied up with his ability to control their behavior (Joseph 1993).

> Ferris: They acted like my grandfather would be rolling over in his grave because someone saw me kissing someone at a party. You have to be on guard. You know that your wife can't wear this or that on the beach . . . kiss you in front of others . . .

> Jimmy: The other day, my friends were saying, "Let's go to strip bars." I said, "You know, I would go . . . but we live in San Francisco . . . and what if I'm walking into the place and here comes some store owner who just closed his store . . . and turns out to be one of my dad's friends . . . or what if he knows someone in our family?" My family name impacts me hugely.

The main reason I don't do those things is because I don't want to give people the pleasure of having something against my family.

While interlocutors find the concept of *al-nas* controlling, they also express a sense of care and concern about what other people think. This cautious negotiation illustrates the complex ways the family ideal coupled with concepts of a relational self "at times empowered them and at times subordinated them" (Joseph 1993, 468–69).

As Ferris's and Jimmy's comments indicate, the interpellation of subjects through the concept of *al-nas* has disciplinary effects. Kevin, a Jordanian American, articulates this by stating, "It's like being in the eye." Others use terms such as "family gossip"; "the watchdog"; or the sense that "people are watching you." Although it is imaginative, *al-nas* produces the sense of being under the scrutiny of others, whether there are in fact others around or not. *Al-nas* links idealized familial-communal notions of "Arab culture" and the individual psyche together. In this respect, *al-nas* reinforces the significance of the discourse of family and family reputation as mechanisms of control in the consolidation of an intra-communal Arab domain in the United States. Yet the politics of cultural authenticity operates on another register of belonging and nonbelonging, attachment, community, and cultural identity—that is, the register of marriage norms related to intra-communal differences and hierarchies.

Intra-Communal Difference

A series of intra-Arab hierarchies takes on new significance in the diaspora and operates in tension with the ideal of an intra-communal Arab domain in the diaspora—particularly since the idea of *al-nas*, communal unity, or cultural homogeneity in the face of an imagined America is so crucial to the politics of cultural authenticity. Among these are differences of religion (Muslim and Christian) and nationality (Jordanian, Lebanese, Palestinian, and Syrian), although these do not exhaust the broad constellation of differences within and between Arab diasporas. These differences do not necessarily imply hierarchy, conflict, or tension in official or community-based Arab politics. Political regimes—whether internal or external to the Arab region—that privilege one group and demonize the other(s), have fueled national and religious tensions to varying degrees in different historical moments. In the United States, Arab national and religious categories take on new meanings in light of dominant U.S. imperial discourses about Arabs and Muslims; Muslims and Christians; Palestine and Israel. They also take on new meaning in a Bay Area context in which Arab migrants from diverse nations of origin interact with one another in unexpected ways and where the stakes for crafting "unimagined communities" (Ono 2000) are particularly high. Community networks in which my interlocutors and their families participate tend to include predominantly Palestinian but also Jordanian, Lebanese, and Syrian Arabs. This context produced a contradictory situation in which multiple, coexisting affiliations constituted the term "Arab community." This was most clearly reflected in concepts and practices of marriage.

Earlier I explained that the politics of cultural authenticity privileges the idea of marrying an "Arab" (as opposed to marrying an "American"). Yet when lived, the ideal of "marrying an Arab" has multiple meanings that are hierarchical and contested. In some cases, marriage norms privilege marrying an Arab from the same nation of origin and with the same religious affiliation. Both generations similarly privilege marrying within religious categories over those of nation through a critical inheritance of the ideal of kinship-based endogamy from Arab nations. Suad Joseph explains that in Lebanon, for example, the kin bond can underwrite other bonds, such as the bond over religious sect. In Lebanon patrilineal, patriarchal marriage is a crucial mechanism for reproducing religious boundaries, and this paradigm is sanctioned by the state (2000, 118). Whether and to what extent families permit marrying across these boundaries depends on their political or religious beliefs and opinions. Historical realities contribute to the ways people articulate national distinctions and the values they grant to national differences. Rabia tells me that Lebanese are the least open to marrying Palestinians because, she explains, "There's an antagonism between Lebanese and Palestinians. Lebanese, especially Lebanese Christians, consider themselves more cultured. It's also because of the role the Palestinians played in the Lebanese civil war. Palestinians, especially the Palestinian Muslims, are associated with being refugees, being radical politically, and trying to take over other Arab countries."

Rabia's observation points to a discourse particularly common among the Lebanese Maronite religious sect that disassociates Lebanese identity from Palestinians and privileges Lebanese connections to Europe. Nuha's father is Lebanese Maronite, and Nuha tells me that her parents think that Lebanese are better than Palestinians. While Lebanese religious groups have varying relationships to Palestinians, a dominant Lebanese discourse tends to support an idea of Lebanese superiority vis-à-vis other Arabs. The concept of Lebanese superiority selectively highlights Phoenician history in Lebanon; Lebanese ties to France (specifically during the French mandate on Lebanon after World War I); the geographic proximity between Lebanon and Europe; and Lebanon's disproportionately large percentage of Christians (compared to Arabs).[9] The view of Lebanese superiority contributes to norms against marrying "other Arabs."

Hashem exemplifies how long-standing conventional Jordanian nationalist stereotypes about Palestinians inform his position on marrying a Palestinian:

> I identify with being Arab and the different Arab causes . . . Palestine . . . Iraq . . . but I definitely differentiate between Palestinians and Jordanians. I'm Jordanian. Their roots aren't 100 percent like mine . . . like their women, it's like that saying, "*al Falastiniyat gawiyat*." It means they're rude and ride their husbands a little bit. I believe it. I don't think I would marry a Palestinian. Not that a wife should be submissive, but they're kinda *wighat* [rude].

Hashem's remark reflects assumptions underpinning a range of Arab discourses that conceptualize Palestinians as distinct on the basis of their distinct struggle against colonization. Tony explains differences in Jordanian and Palestinian marriage patterns through their different collective engagements with military occupation and oppression: "I know a lot of Jordanian guys who don't deal with other Arab women because they think that they won't be themselves once they know you are Arab. You don't see the same thing with Palestinians. They marry each other more than Jordanians. They stick together. That's the standard. You gotta stick together."

In Tony's quotation, women's bodies and behaviors stand in for the imagined Arab community. Underlying his remark is the idea that Palestinian histories of colonization fuel a sense of necessity for intermarriage. Histories of engagement with European and U.S. discourses also guide norms related to marriage across religious lines. Nicole explains, "All my life the message was that I had to marry an Arab Christian man." Bassam told me, "I knew I was supposed to have children with an Arab woman with the same religion as us."

Hurriya is a Palestinian American from a Muslim family. She tells me that she spent a year in conflict with her parents because she was in love with a Latino man, while they expected her to marry an Arab Muslim man. She expressed how things changed when she met an Arab Muslim whom she considered marrying: "Being with an Arab Muslim man meant all the prerequisites were gone. All we had to worry about was whether we could get along, love each other, and live together. So immediately, there was the possibility of marriage. You've jumped all the hurdles and all you have to do is fall in love."

Nuha told me,

> Both my parents are Christian, but we were raised atheist. Why this reaction to Mohammed? After college, I met the love of my life, Mohammed. He's a Palestinian Muslim, and we've been dating seriously. My mom asked me whether he was Muslim or Christian and I said it doesn't matter. Then she freaked out saying that meant he is Muslim and how dare I date a Muslim. She went on to say, "Don't you know that there are fifteen thousand cases of Christian Western American women married to Muslim men and the women are in the States and the men have taken their children from them to the Muslim world and the women are in the States trying to get their children back from those horrible men?" She learned this on 20/20. Then she asked me if I was sleeping with him. I said it was none of her business. She said, "Well you know, if you are, his family is going to kill you." These stereotypes never stop. She says that he will force me to sleep with him so I will have to marry him, or that he will make me cover my hair, or he will marry more than one wife. . . . What's crazy is my mom is Armenian and her Armenian parents let her marry my dad, an Arab! And my parents are atheists! So it's not really about religion, it's that they want me to marry someone Westernized, and Lebanese Christian falls into Western.

Nuha's parents are atheists and have a mixed marriage (Armenian-Lebanese Arab). Yet they insist that she marry a Christian. In her story, the categories Muslim and Christian extend beyond religious faith/practice and maintain European concepts of modernity in which backwards polygamous Muslim men serve as key markers of the difference between East and West. Her mother associates Lebanese Christians with the modern West and lumps Lebanese Christians who belong to Eastern sects of Christianity into the category "Western" as a strategy to distinguish (Western) Christian Arabs from their (Eastern) Muslim counterparts.

Ella Shohat and Robert Stam have argued that in Hollywood Arab men are often depicted as dark rapists, integral figures in the colonial rescue fantasy (1994). Similarly, Nuha's mother imagines Muslim men as dark rapists who justify the intervention of the Western liberator to save the Western(ized) victim from "those horrible [Muslim] men." A sexual politics of colonialist discourse in which sex between Arab men and white or Western(ized) women can only involve rape underwrites Nuha's mother's statement that

"Mohammed will force [you] to have sex with him so that you will have to marry him." This Muslim-Christian binary also emerges in references to Arab Muslim parents who oppose their children's marriage to a Christian Arab. In such cases, it takes the form of bad Christians and good Muslims, or reverse Orientalism, which reifies the idea that Muslims are more authentically "Arab." Lulu elucidates this as follows:

> I grew up with this all the time, "Sex is an act of love in marriage. If you're not a virgin when you get married, you're in trouble." I fought that all the time. I would ask my mom about Lebanon. I would say, "If good Arab women are not having sex and Arab men can have sex, then who were the Arab men having sex with?" She would answer, "The Christian women." So the Christian women were the whores. That is very prevalent in my family, the Muslim virgin and the Christian whore. The whore is either American or Christian.

Rabia's mother reconfigures the Arab virgin/American whore in terms of Muslim virgin/Christian whore. She associates the category "Lebanese Christian" with the classification "Westernized Other." She conflates "Islam" and "Arabness" through an Arab nationalist discourse about a distinct Arab-Muslim civilization that juxtaposes notions of Arab Muslimness against the notion of a Christian West.[10] In her mother's view, the Lebanese-Muslim self is to be protected from the corrupted, Westernized-Lebanese-Christian Other. Yet while distinguishing herself from the Christian West, Rabia explains, "My parents are very into the mentality of 'Arabs are white.'" Rabia's parents were open to the idea of their daughters dating before marriage, yet did not support her dating men of color. Lulu explains, "My sister was really vocal about having boyfriends and they were always Black; which was always a problem."

Her parents' openness to talking about sex is atypical among interlocutors and their families. Yet it points to a general dilemma that most interlocutors' parents face in which the possibilities of marrying "other Arabs" is more likely when living in the diaspora, among Arabs from diverse nations of origin. The conditions of this "unimagined community" (Ono 2000) render the stakes for policing intra-Arab differences particularly high. Marriage is a crucial mechanism through which Arab diasporas negotiate a range of intra-communal differences and their varied relationships to U.S. codes of whiteness, Orientalism, and modernity. Regulating demands about marriage necessitate negotiations over the categories Arab, American, Jordanian, Lebanese, Palestinian, Syrian, Muslim, or Christian that take place with and through European and U.S. discourses about Western modernity and Muslim backwardness. These negotiations emerge in a context in which the way a person is perceived in relation to any of these categories has significant implications for middle-class assimilation and acceptability.

Rabia's story elucidates that the politics of cultural authenticity works within a selective assimilation strategy. Her mother's distinction between good Muslims and bad Christians provides a sense of empowerment and cultural continuity in the diaspora. Yet her mother simultaneously reinforces codes of white middle-class acceptability in identifying as white and disapproving of her daughter's Black boyfriends. Rabia's story reflects a complex process by which both generations critically inherit categories of national and religious difference from Arab homelands, and remake them with and through engagements with U.S. categories of knowledge and the challenges of immigration, assimilation, and Americanization. To different degrees, through discourses and practices about marriage, interlocutors and their parents resist assimilation by positing particular categories of identity different from U.S. or Western modernity. They simultaneously deploy particular categories as mechanisms for maintaining middle-class status.

This chapter has interrogated the analytical and historical trajectories underpinning the politics of cultural authenticity. The chapter relies on theorizations of diaspora that go beyond conventional notions of ethnicity and nation, theorizations that assume a purity of cultures that exist in a separate domain from politics. This diaspora studies approach transcends theories of tradition versus modernity (isolation versus assimilation; traditional gender and sexual repression versus Americanization and gender and sexual liberation). While the politics of cultural authenticity invokes a seemingly essentialist Arab cultural identity, this chapter shows that the politics of cultural authenticity is motivated by economic and political conditions of cultural and geographic displacement, U.S. Orientalism and empire, and the desire for middle-class status and acceptability. This chapter also shows that normative concepts of hyphenated identity that assume a mixing of two cultures (i.e., Arab and American) cannot explain the narrative of cultural authenticity. Nor can the politics of cultural authenticity be explained by linear concepts of assimilation (Brah 1996, 241). I have explained this articulation of Arabness as a complex interaction between an imagined Arab community and an imagined America—a complex entanglement between multiple histories and discourses that are transnational in scope.

I have presented the politics of cultural authenticity as historically situated and constructed. Yet I have also shown that, for second-generation young adults for whom it is both empowering and constraining, the politics of cultural authenticity is not simply imagined or fictive. It is a grounded articulation of Arabness—embedded in historical and material realities and experiences—that has lived effects. The politics of cultural authenticity sets into play a particular approach to U.S. politics that wittingly or unwittingly ignores social inequalities of race and class or the violences of imperialism, militarism, and war. In this sense, the politics of cultural authenticity works within a conventional middle-class immigrant approach to cultural identity: it prioritizes economic mobility and establishes a sense of cultural continuity while ignoring politics (Prashad 2000).

Keeping in mind the multiple, colliding histories that shape dominant middle-class Arab American forms of patriarchy and compulsory heterosexuality, we can now understand the limitations of an essentialist, Orientalist cultural analysis. My theoretical model, a diasporic Arab feminist critique, makes central a critique of the power structures of patriarchy and homophobia that are internal to Arab families and communities, while illustrating that these power structures are shaped by a range of intersecting histories and power relations. This approach takes seriously the varying historical circumstances that are entangled in middle-class Arab American regimes of gender and sexuality, such as the challenges of displacement, reactions to U.S. Orientalism, desires for middle-class status, and engagements with U.S. liberal multiculturalism. This approach also centers an analysis of the power relations that these regimes set into play—including the kinds of subjects it produces and the internal hierarchies and exclusions they enable. I have also shown that while most interlocutors find the gendered and sexualized regimes of cultural authenticity constraining, they also find claims to cultural identity and belonging comforting and empowering. In the following chapters, I continue my analysis of Arab cultural authenticity by focusing on the possibilities through which young adults contest, negotiate, and rearticulate the concepts Arab and American.

3

Muslim First, Arab Second

Rima: One of the Arab sisters who married a Black Muslim opened the Qur'an in her father's face and said, "Look, it says here, as long as he's a good Muslim." [Her father] wasn't practicing true Islam. If he did, life would be a lot different.

Mohammed: Next week, a movie is going to come out of Hollywood . . . called *Executive Decision*. It's a blatant attempt to defame Muslim brothers in Chechnya. Do you remember the number of people who died when this country shot a civilian plane flying over the Persian Gulf?

Khaled: Any Muslim who stands against injustice is labeled a terrorist. Look at Proposition 21.[1] Since we're dressed a certain way today, I guess that means we're a gang and that gives them the right to arrest us! When you talk about Prop. 21, you have to talk about Black youth in prison—and the antiterrorism bill, where Muslims all over this country are put in jail and not told any evidence against them—in America! This struggle has to be handled on many fronts. Muslims are able to connect these things because of their belief in the oneness of Allah.

In the late 1990s, Rima and the Arab sisters of whom she spoke, Mohammed, and Khaled were actively engaged in Muslim student organizations. They prayed regularly, attended the mosque, and participated in Islamic religious and educational institutions. For them, being Muslim entailed carrying out basic religious practices such as prayer and being part of the Muslim community and U.S. civil society. In the late 1990s they were among Muslims from many countries of origin, and race and class positions, who were disaggregating religion (Islam) from culture (e.g., Arab) and articulating who they are as distinctly Muslim. Rima is a Palestinian American and was twenty-three when we met. Like Rima, many young adults I worked with articulated Muslim First, Arab Second as an alternative to ideal concepts of marriage, gender, and race that underscored Arab cultural authenticity, the dominant middle-class articulation of Arabness. Many of the young adults I worked with were political activists who were also staking a claim in global and domestic politics. Mohammed exemplifies this. He is a South Asian Muslim student activist who made the above statement at a political rally aimed at ending U.S.-led sanctions on Iraq in 2000. Khaled is an African American Muslim community leader. He made these remarks at a Muslim student organization's political rally focused on raising awareness about U.S. government policies, such as the Omnibus counterterrorism bill of 1994, that disproportionately target Muslim immigrants, as well as U.S. government policies, such as Proposition 21, that disproportionately target African Americans (Muslim and non-Muslim). Mohammed and Khaled express one of the main arguments of this chapter, that the articulation Muslim First among my interlocutors came about in continuity with the emergence of a global Muslim political consciousness in the San Francisco Bay Area in the late 1990s.

Indeed, many young people with whom I worked practice Islam because they believe, because they worry about their souls, because they want to be good people in the eyes of God. Young adults' relationships to God and to the divine are, above all, the most crucial ways that Islam matters in their lives. Yet matters of faith, religious practices, understandings of piety, the way people live their piety, their relationship to God, and their level of observance are not the focus of this chapter. This chapter focuses on the ways in which some young adults are articulating a global Muslim political consciousness. These young adults participate in Muslim spaces in the Bay Area where a discourse of global Muslim social justice circulates. I use the term "Muslim spaces" to refer to mosques, Islamic educational institutions, student groups, and political events where my interlocutors were actively involved (Metcalf 1996). These Muslim spaces, and the concepts of Islam that circulate within them, are produced out of a set of historical conditions that gave rise to a vibrant period of institution building among diverse Muslims in the Bay Area in the late 1990s. These conditions include global economic neoliberalism and related changes in Muslim immigration to the Bay Area; global Muslim responses to the crystallization of U.S. empire in Muslim-majority countries; and the related rise in Islamophobic discourses and policies in the United States in the 1980s and 1990s. Within these transnational historical contexts and relations of power, in Muslim spaces and beyond, and in relationship to Islamic sacred texts and the divine, my interlocutors developed a language for rearticulating Arab cultural authenticity as Muslim First, Arab Second.[2] Through the language of Muslim First, these young adults challenge racism, militarism, and white middle-class assimilation, as well as the limitations of middle-class Arab cultural politics and their Muslim communities. They debate matters of empire, racism, family, and gender through their discussions of sacred texts, thus crafting a "religiously constituted political consciousness" (Werbner 2002a). By contextualizing concepts and practices of Islam within varied local and global histories and power relations, this chapter disrupts Orientalist notions that Islam exists outside of history.

For my interlocutors, Islam is a framework for contending with patriarchy, capitalism, empire, racism, and war.[3] Accordingly, I have followed scholars like Lara Deeb, Minoo Moallem, and Victoria Bernal in avoiding terms such as "Islamic revival" or "Islamic resurgence," which they contend suggest a return to a fixed way of life (Deeb 2006; Moallem 2005; Bernal 1994, 3). As we will see, Islam is not an untouched, timeless tradition that these young adults have "revived," but is subject to change in the context of local and global conditions, such as young adults' engagements with U.S.-led war and its varied manifestations in Muslim-majority countries and in the United States, the gendered discourses of U.S. empire, immigration patterns of and political shifts in Muslim-majority countries, engagements with racial-justice, antiwar, and Islamic-feminist discourses and movements at the turn of the twenty-first century, and a myriad of local realities related to life as an Arab Muslim in the San Francisco Bay Area at the turn of the twenty-first century.

The Emergence of Muslim First

Amina Wadud argues that for migrants, a distinct Muslim identity becomes more and more important in the United States. When migrants come to the

United States, their relationship to Islam entails "undefined qualities resulting from cultural experiences whether or not they include aspects of volition regarding an acceptance of definitions given to methods or conclusions of historical study" (Wadud 2006, 20). She explains that, in the West, people are asked to distinguish themselves and are asked questions such as, "Are you a *practicing* Muslim?" (20). To a certain extent, Wadud's argument that new concepts of Islam among immigrants are a consequence of the migration experience helps explain my research findings. Yet my research also shows that a more specific argument is needed. Identifying as Muslim First, Arab Second is a recent current among Arab immigrants and Arab American Muslims. As I illustrate below, this identification has been shaped by migration to the United States *and* historical and cultural changes in home countries. In the Arab world in the 1950s and '60s, during the period when my interlocutors' parents were growing up, a pan-Arab cultural identity predominated. This was differentiated by religious affiliation, such as Muslim or Christian, nation of origin, and village of origin. More than intergenerational differences were at play as second-generation Arab American Muslims developed a distinctly Muslim identity more than their parents had, as we will see. I worked with college students in the Bay Area, where college campuses are exceptionally multiracial. This compounded the differences between parents' concepts of religion and identity and those held by their children. While some Arab American young adults with whom I worked attended racially or ethnically diverse mosques before college, the Muslim communities they joined after entering college tended to be much more diverse.

A series of historical and demographic shifts that took place in the 1980s and '90s globally and locally propelled the shift toward a distinctly Muslim identity among these young adults. The meanings of Islam that they encountered on their campuses, at Islamic education programs, and within Bay Area Islamic institutions, reflected a new moment in Bay Area Muslim politics that was specific to a post-1980s period of massive growth in Muslim migration to the Bay Area and in Muslim-specific community-based organizations. When my interviewees' parents came to the Bay Area and established their community-based organizations in the 1960s and '70s, there was a disproportionately larger number of Christian than Muslim Arabs in the Bay Area. Moreover, while articulations of Arabness dominant in the Arab world at that time did not foreground religiosity, they were more specifically constituted by a sense of pan-Arabism *and* subsets of that identity, including religious and other differences. It is important to note that Arab nationalism, from its inception, has drawn upon Islamic histories and ideas. Indeed, in colonial and postcolonial periods, there has been less of a focus on Islam and a development of nationalism that relies, to a certain extent, on the construct of secularism and Western modernity. Thus, community-based scholar Hatem Bazian contends that Arab nationalism, in its most heightened period of anticolonial pan-Arabism, does not represent a shift away from religiosity or Islam but a moment in which secular notions of Arab nationalism were put forward while other aspects were pushed back. Arab countries have become, overall, more religiously focused in the past thirty years, a consequence of many historical factors. They include the Iranian revolution and its reverberations, shifting U.S.-Middle East relations beginning in the 1970s, Israel-Palestine politics, revivalist movements across the Muslim and Christian worlds, and a general increasing religiosity of all sorts on a global scale. The failures of Arab regimes and Arab nationalism, the failures of leftist movements in the region, and the fall of communism in general are additional factors. Rising contradictions in the structures of Arab nation-states between state and nonstate actors contributed significantly to this rising global Muslim consciousness. For instance, the growing powers of U.S.-backed dictators who ruled Arab states to the detriment of the majority of their citizens has inspired a growing disconnection between state and nonstate actors.

These conditions developed in the context of an expanding U.S. empire in Muslim-majority countries. According to Mahmood Mamdani, the rise of Islamic movements in the late twentieth century did not emerge wholesale from within Muslim-majority nations. The United States, in its zeal to counter communism and the Soviet Union, contributed to its rise. During the Cold War, the United States funded and fought "proxy wars" in other nations in Africa, Southeast Asia, and Central America rather than a head-on war with the Soviet Union (Mamdani 2005). In the late Cold War, the focus shifted to Afghanistan, specifically when the Soviet Union invaded the Central Asian nation in 1979 (119-20). In 1979, Jimmy Carter began a program of covert operations against the Soviet forces in Afghanistan (Hirschkind and Mahmood 2002, 342). This program only intensified under Ronald Reagan. Over the course of the Afghan war, the United States poured more than three billion dollars into organizations of Afghan fighters, known as the *mujahideen* (342). In addition to the *mujahideen* from within Afghanistan, the CIA actively recruited Islamic extremists from around the world, especially Arab nations, to be trained in Pakistan and to fight in Afghanistan against the Soviet forces (Mamdani 2005, 131). The United States actively encouraged the radical nature of the groups, as it found that they could make the more radical groups of Islamic extremists and *mujahideen* into more effective vehicles for the anti-Soviet struggle (155). Overall, the major influence that the funding and training from the United States had on the rise of Islamic extremism came from the CIA's recruitment and training of such extremists from a wide array of nations. This larger context contributed to the articulation of varying ideologies that characterize Islam as an alternative to the perceived failure of Arab nationalism as a mechanism for independence from Western imperialist rule.

These events preceded the period of massive growth in Muslim migration to the United States and the Bay Area, which peaked in the late 1990s. Between 1985 and 2010, Bay Area mosques increased from three to forty-eight.[4] This growth was a consequence both of shifts in U.S. immigration policies that opened the doors to more migrants from Muslim-majority countries and of large numbers of Arabs coming to work for the IT industry in Silicon Valley. The migrants came from Egypt, Jordan, Syria, Iraq, Palestine, Morocco, Pakistan, Bangladesh, and Malaysia. Scholar and community activist Hatem explains that "90 percent of all those who came during this period came to work in Silicon Valley."[5] In addition, many recent Muslim migrants came to the Bay Area as a result of political crises in their home countries—crises in which the United States was heavily involved: the Iranian revolution; the Soviet invasion of Afghanistan; the invasion of south Lebanon; the Bosnian war; and the Iraq war. Many migrants were riled by what was happening in their countries of origin or in other Muslim-majority countries before they came to the Bay Area, particularly since many felt that a global war against Muslims was emerging and that existing nationalist movements were becoming less viable as mechanisms for resisting Western intervention.

These transnational conditions contributed to shifts in the ways people affiliated with Arabness and Islam in the Arab world and in the Bay Area at the time when my interlocutors entered college. Political debates in the Arab world were grappling with the demise of Arab nationalism and the growing possibility of Islam as an alternative to the pan-Arab identity deployed by nationalists (Majid 2000, 21). One intellectual view posed that pan-Arabism was losing its meaning, particularly in light of what many saw as the catastrophes of the Gulf War in the 1990s, the end of the first *intifada* (uprising), and the failed Middle East peace process of the mid-1990s (Cainkar 2005). Islam was filling a moral, spiritual, social, and political vacuum created by the demise of Arab nationalism (Cainkar 2005). A rampant desire for a new social agenda in the Arab world and the diaspora emerged.[6] In the Middle East, South Asia, and elsewhere, Mandaville argues, young people have been at the forefront of the new Islamic movements and ideologies of the 1980s and 1990s, which were diverse in scope and entailed a wide spectrum of positions. From pluralists to communitarians to radicals, the spectrum of political affiliations among Muslim activists is heterogeneous (Mandaville 2007, 294). As we will see, these currents have taken on local form in the Bay Area in the articulation of a global Muslim consciousness. As community activist and public scholar Hatem Bazian put it,

> Especially since the first Gulf War, people began realizing that existing political and economic structures have been used to divide us and further control us. Many of us [Muslims] do not want to fall into that dynamic. A consciousness developed that sees differences as an enhancement rather than a hindrance. Sunnis, for example, can recognize differences with Shi'i Muslims but do not have to accept their religious interpretations.

Thus, the large influx of Muslims to the Bay Area in the 1980s and '90s came with a more distinct Islamic identity than previous migrants. They also shared a belief that Muslims were under attack globally and were marginalized in the United States. Riva Kastoryano explains that "when Islam is denounced, it reinforces identification with an Islamic community for Muslim migrants" (Kastoryano 1999, 195). The socioeconomic positions of Muslim migrants of the 1980s and '90's afforded them opportunities to establish institutions with a much greater level of civic engagement and activism than the previous generation, who came during the earlier migrant period, in the 1950s and 1960s. Through their civic engagement and activism, they brought their schools of thought, ideologies, and concepts of identity into U.S. publics on a much larger scale than my interlocutors' parents' generation.

One additional difference between these generations is that Arabs of the earlier migration came to the United States without much formal education, at most bachelor's degrees; their children were going to high school and college at the same time the new IT immigrants of the '80s and '90s were actively contributing to establishing Muslim organizations. The IT migrants had graduate degrees—most had master's degrees and many had Ph.D.s. According to Hatem Bazian, "one mosque in the South Bay has 600 Ph.D.s." This newly arrived critical mass of Muslim immigrants with significant access to social and economic resources had opportunities to form large-scale institutions such as the Council of American Islamic Institutions, which was founded in the Bay Area in 1994 and is now a national organization with chapters in over thirty cities across the United States.[7] Students played an important role in this period of growth. University of California–Berkeley students, for example, formed groups that expanded into three different mosques. Student organizing at the University of San Francisco culminated in the Jones Street mosque, one of the largest in that city. Hatem refers to student groups as the nucleus of this emerging community. This trend toward a massive growth in Islamic institutions in the Bay Area after 1980, a trend of which students were at the forefront, parallels a similar trend that took place across the United States (Khan 2000). A range of positions, ideas, debates, and discussions on Islam and Muslim identity in the United States emerged, and people took different positions on political and social issues. The proliferation of a distinctly Muslim sense of identity during this post-1980s period can be understood as the formation of an imagined diasporic community in which members may identify with a territorial nation-state but simultaneously identify with a global Muslim community constituted by "a sense of extraterritorial nationalism" (Kastoryano 1999, 192).

My interlocutors, second-generation Arab American Muslims, told me that their parents' generation, predominantly immigrants and small business owners, shared the sense that Islamic education was not essential to being Muslim. This differed from the post-1980s Muslim immigrants, many of whom had advanced degrees. The differences in class and education of the newer Muslim migrants significantly impacted the profound growth in the establishment of Muslim institutions in the Bay Area. Second-generation young adults attending college in the Bay Area in the 1990s were exposed to these growing institutions, and many immersed themselves in Islamic education courses and the study of Arabic, the language of the Qur'an. This was essential to the formation of a new Muslim identity, and inspired the creation of several Islamic education programs in that decade, such as the Zaytuna Institute and the Qalam Institute of Islamic Sciences.

Although these two institutions do not share the same objectives or ideologies, they are both part of a broad intellectual trend that emerged during the Islamist current of Muslim-majority countries over the last several decades.[8] Mandaville describes this intellectual movement in Egypt, for instance, as one with a social consciousness that seeks reform and transformation, privileges the plight of the poor, and draws upon Islamic notions of social justice to achieve a social order that embraces the spirit of the *sharia*. In the Bay Area, this current can be seen in the work of the Zaytuna Institute and the Qalam Institute of Islamic Sciences. The Zaytuna Institute's primary focus is teaching traditional Islam and translating it to contemporary contexts. Al Qalam was created to fill a gap for students at universities who had no training in their Islamic tradition and lacked the tools needed to challenge dominant U.S. discourses on Islam in the classroom, as well as to provide them with Islamic literacy. Individuals affiliated with these institutions use the term "traditional Islam" to refer to normative practices that have existed in continuity and have been accepted as normative over centuries among Islamic scholars. Over time, the work of these two institutions began overlapping as many youth actively involved in Muslim spaces participated in both, to different extents, contributing to the formation of a new Muslim consciousness.

As in many Muslim-majority countries, intellectual discussions that took place within the Islamic institutions my interlocutors attended in the Bay Area focus on issues including family and marriage, religious self-discipline, community building, and prayer.[9] Some discussions, such as those within Islamic education classes and mosques, were inward-focused and took place among Muslims exclusively. Others were outward-focused and often aimed to educate non-Muslims about Islam and to correct negative stereotypes about Muslims. The Orientalist-racist representations of Muslim women throughout U.S. society—in the media, education, government, and popular culture—inspired a great deal of discussion about Islamic perspectives on family, gender relations, and women's rights and responsibilities among Muslims. In this instance, outward- and inward-focused discussions merged. Young Muslims faced with these Orientalist images in their everyday lives turned to Islamic teachings to learn Islamic perspectives, then brought these outward to challenge the criticisms. Muslim student tables on campuses had informational brochures about women in Islam; Muslim student conferences, which attracted Muslim and non-Muslim audiences, included panels about women and Islam. Young men and women took questions about Islam and gender seriously, and felt it their duty to challenge negative discourses and highlight gender-egalitarian perspectives within Islam in their public work.

Student discussions about gender and Islam drew on frameworks that Muslim women scholar-activists developed and that some scholars and activists refer to as the basis of an Islamic feminist movement.[10] This movement formed in connection with a growing Islamic feminist movement in the Middle East, South Asia, Europe, and Canada, among other places (Webb 2000; Mandaville 2007; Moallem 2005). Gisela Webb traces the history of Islamic feminism in the United States in terms of a "gradual but steady emergence of a movement among . . . a critical mass of Muslim women who insist that their religious self-identity be affirmed in the midst of their acknowledgment of and striving toward solving what they see as serious problems they have faced and continue to face as women in Muslim and non-Muslim societies" (2000, xi). Webb proposes that "intra-Islamic transformation is needed and takes place through Qu'ranic texts, which are a central means for that transformation" (ibid.). This movement, which she refers to as "scholarship-activism," is the "result of formations of networks of Muslim women involved in grassroots work on issues of jurisprudence, theology, hermeneutics, women's education, and women's rights" (2000, xii-xiii). It has favored higher religious education for women and active participation in the ongoing "reading" and interpreting of the Qur'an (Barazangi 2000); women's *ijtihad* or legal interpretation for retrieving the original flexibility and balance of *shariah* and juridical interpretation; a methodology for dealing with family and family planning issues from an Islamic perspective; and alternative interpretation of the Qur'an from a female-inclusive perspective (Hassan 2000).[11]

The materials that Muslim student activists and community organizations circulated at conferences, in their classes, and in their publications did not always parallel this movement's perspectives. Yet it was clear that the movement laid an intellectual foundation, especially for young adults grappling with questions about women and gender in their families and among their peers. At the same time, these young adults felt a responsibility to respond to Orientalist and Islamophobic perceptions about the treatment of Muslim women by Muslim men and Muslim societies that many agreed informed their encounters with racism in U.S. public spaces and institutions, as we will see.

Bringing Muslim First Home

Concepts of gender egalitarianism that circulate in Muslim spaces provided my interlocutors with a framework for contesting the narrative of Arab cultural authenticity, the narrative of identity that predominated among their parents' generation.[12] As we saw in chapter 2, the middle-class Arab immigrant politics of cultural authenticity draws upon Arabist concepts that religion is part of culture.[13] For young adults active in Muslim spaces, the intertwining of religion and culture is a concept that inspires new possibilities.

Rania is a mother of three. Her parents moved to the Bay Area from Beit Haneena, Palestine. I met with her at San Francisco City College, where she was studying nursing. She was twenty-eight years old at the time, and had been actively involved in a Muslim study group for young adults. She told me that she understands Islam differently than her parents, and focuses on what she sees as her parents' ambiguous relationship to Islam. According to Rania, "We did not study Islam, did not read the Qur'an, did not pray, and my parents did not expect me to wear *hijab*."

Nidal was a college sophomore when I interviewed him. His parents had migrated from Palestine in the 1970s. He was active in Muslim student organizations and attended classes at a Muslim school in the East Bay. He was developing a relationship with a South Asian woman he had met through an online Muslim dating site. Like Rania, Nidal tells me that, to his parents, "the religion was the culture and the culture was the religion. The only thing that made us Muslim was the fundamentals, like there is only one God, Allah, and Mohammed is his last messenger, and the whole idea of heaven and hell and the line of prophets from Adam and Eve on."

While ideals about gender and marriage are crucial to the narrative of Arab cultural authenticity, young adults who identify as Muslim First questioned these ideals. Hala grew up in San Francisco. She was socialized primarily among her extended Palestinian family. She tells me that growing up, she understood that "to marry, a woman has to come from a good background, know how to cook, seem like she can be fertile and have lots of kids, and be good to her in-laws." Abdullah, a Syrian man, tells me he learned that an Arab Muslim man would be marriageable if he "came from a good family and had a good financial background." Mona, a Palestinian woman from Jerusalem, says, "Growing up, girls could rarely go out. Girls have to stay in and guys can go out until three in the morning." According to Nidal,

> All throughout my lifetime, woman is the cook, woman is the cleaner, taking care of babies, and the guy never has to clean. And if he cleans, he's a girl. This is the mentality. This is always how it's been and my sister always throughout my life was the one cleaning and I was always the one who was enjoying myself and having a good time with the guys and the *shai* [tea].

Questioning their parents' conflation of "religion" (Islam) and "culture" (Arab) formed the basis of their critique. They ask their Arab peers and their parents, "What are the things about us that are 'Arab' and what are the things that are specifically 'Muslim'?" Their study of Islam in college, at their mosques, and at Islamic education centers informs their interest in differentiating between "culture" and "religion" and has become crucial to the narrative they've crafted for selectively critiquing the patriarchal underpinnings of Arab cultural authenticity. In their estimation, patriarchy is a product of Arab culture, more than of the religion of Islam. They reconfigure the idea of being "culturally Muslim" or "Arab Muslim" into the idea of being Muslim First, Arab Second.

Zina, who comes from Jordan, was a senior in college when we met. She was active in Muslim student organizations and attended Islamic education classes after school and on weekends. I interviewed her in the financial district of San Francisco, where she was working for a temporary employment agency. She says that Islam provided her with room to ask questions, seek explanations, and interpret the Qur'an in the context of her environment:

> The culture doesn't provide answers to questions . . . it would just be *abe* [shameful] to do this or that. My mom would say, "*Mish kwais lal banat yasawu haka*" because "*al nas biyehku alaihum*" [It is not good for a girl to do that because the people will talk about her]. I hate those words, *abe* [shameful] and *nas* [the people]. I want to remove them from the dictionary. Like those people at the Arab Cultural Center festivals. . . . If the girl's talking to a guy, it's the girl who's *ilit al adab* [without manners]. The guy, he's just charming. And when I ask, "Why shouldn't she talk to him?" they answer, "Because she's not supposed to." But then I look at Islam and it takes two. Guys and girls are responsible. The woman has to respect the man and the man has to respect the woman. Islam explains *why* it's better not to do certain things for guys and girls . . . it gives you precautions, and teaches you that some rules are there to protect and secure you. Like STDs or teen pregnancy, it helps you stay away from it.

Tala was twenty-eight years old when we met. Unlike her mother and sisters, she read the Qur'an regularly, attended Islamic education classes, and studied the Arabic language primarily because it is the language of the Qur'an. According to her, the more religious she becomes, the more leverage she has over her family. She explains that her father was strict, but that it was "more culture than religion." After becoming more religious, Tala developed a new consciousness about women and work. She explains,

> Even though the *din* [religion] doesn't say that a girl can't work, my father would still say that a woman shouldn't work. But Islamically, she has every right to do so. I think if I had been religious before I got married, I would have said no, it's not *haram* [forbidden] for a woman to work. If you want your daughter to see a doctor, wouldn't you want her to see a woman doctor over a male doctor? We need women teachers. After the women in my husband's family became much more religious, they are all studying for major degrees. They finally broke out of the [Arab] culture. I'm working on my second college degree! And when it comes to working, as a matter of fact, Islamically, what a man makes is for the family and what a woman makes is her choice, whatever she chooses to do with it.

Zina and Tala contest patriarchal authority using Islamic arguments. They share the analysis that their parents were open to this because they were quoting from the Qur'an, relying upon religious doctrine. Here Islam provides them with a mechanism for challenging their parents without destroying the stability of their relationship. In fact, they said that their parents gained a newfound respect for them because of their dedication to Islam. Here, they do not fully reject their parents' regulatory demands. Rather, they reject certain demands—such as inequality between women and men in work and education—and rework others—such as the norm of heterosexual marriage—through Islam.[14]

In perspectives such as those of Zina and Tala and of many Muslim First young adults, Islam is more open to interpretation than Arabness. In their view, religion has more possibilities for differing interpretations, whereas Arab culture is more static. Of course, there are other interpretations of Islam that support a static and patriarchal view, just as there are varying interpretations of Arab culture.

Several men articulate an affiliation with Muslim First, Arab Second on the basis of a critique similar to that of their women counterparts. Tawfiq is Palestinian and grew up in the East Bay among an extended family. He was a senior in college when we met and was hoping to attend medical school. In a discussion about the difference between his concept of gender and that of his parents, he told me,

> There is no other system that gives women as much as Islam does . . . and not just gives . . . but orders a man to do. Some people say a woman can't do this or that in Islam, that she has to stay in the house and can't work. Don't listen to this. It's Arabism. That's what destroyed my sister. I wish she understood that's what destroyed her. She thinks it's Islam. In Arab culture, girls have a hundred and one rules they have to follow, but the guy can do whatever he wants. It makes me so sad. Guys and girls have to be treated with the same rules within Islam. In Arab culture, girls get depressed because it's so hard on them and guys get spoiled and end up wasting their life. I love Islam so much. You can't give one child more than the other. They each have equal rights.

The framework Muslim First opens up possibilities for young adults such as Zina, Tala, and Tawfiq to destabilize the norms of Arab cultural authenticity, to call them into question, and to create new forms of sociability. In chapter 2, we saw how the claim to Arab cultural authenticity works as a form of self-Orientalism that fixes Arab culture into a rigid binary schema of "us" and "them," "Arabs" and "Americans." This has become the target of these young adults' critique. They point out that this rigidity is impossible to live by and provides little room for flexibility, negotiation, or interpretation. This is why, when it comes to gender, they contend that Islam provides a broader ideological framework than Arab culture. At the same time, they maintain that gender roles must be organized into a heterosexual, if not patriarchal, structure.

While opting for Islam allows women like Zina and Tala to transform kinship hierarchies while maintaining family allegiances, it exacerbates intergenerational conflict and tension for others, especially when parents do not practice Islam as consistently as their children. Iman, a Palestinian woman, was in college when we met. There, she was coming to identify as Muslim, beginning to wear *hijab*, and rigorously studying Islam. She said her father was threatened by her Muslim consciousness. He equated her participation in Muslim organizations and institutions with participation in a cult. He backed his disapproval with Orientalist arguments to the effect that places where devout Muslims congregated were for brainwashing and were socially backward. At the same time, though, he found it difficult to refuse her the rights she defined as Muslim, particularly among relatives. Here, she defined certain rights as Islamic, and her parents seemed to support her. She had authority in this negotiation with her parents. Perhaps her authority had something to do with her access to educational institutions, allowing her to see herself as someone who knows more about religion than her parents.

Muslim First young adults interpret their parents' generation as tending to articulate "Arab culture" as static and unchanging. As Tawfiq says, Arabism is backwards and patriarchal, while Islam is modern and liberatory. This formulation unsettles typical immigration studies frameworks that explain intergenerational difference in terms of a vertical progression from "tradition" to "Americanization." Young adults draw on normative U.S. concepts such as equal rights and liberty, yet they weave into it their affiliation with Islam and an association between Islam and modernity and equal rights. Dominant U.S. notions of Americanization often rely upon Eurocentric ideas that assume that religiously constituted identities—particularly identities constituted through Islam—are in opposition to Americanization, assimilation, and modernity. The idea of Islam as an alternative to the "cultural traditions" of migrant parents disrupts such binaries, even as it keeps Orientalist concepts of Arab culture and modernity versus tradition in place.

Contending with Gender

Many of my interlocutors tended to idealize concepts of gender in Islam. In practice, these concepts inspired contentious debates. Several young adults and community leaders with whom I worked were at the forefront of promoting an Islamic feminist politics. This politics challenges the discrepancy between idealized concepts of gender justice and whether and to what extent their Muslim peers realize these in everyday life. These activists who were working from an Islamic feminist perspective maintained a commitment to three main principles: (1) critiquing essentialist concepts of Muslim womanhood that circulate among Muslims and reinforce patriarchy; (2) developing alternative, egalitarian interpretations regarding the position of women in Islam; and (3) calling into question contradictions between egalitarian interpretations and everyday life practices.

Some young adults point out how essentialist concepts of Muslim womanhood create a double standard for young women and men in Muslim circles. Their critique of this double standard rests on a critique of patriarchy and a normative model of heterosexual interaction. Rana, a Jordanian woman who was active in the Muslim Student Association on her college campus, says that some of her Muslim male counterparts did not interact with her on campus in order to protect her reputation, but interacted openly with non-Muslim women. Rana says, "If women interacted with men, especially non-Muslim men in public, they would get a bad reputation." Basim, a Lebanese student activist who worked with Rana, tells me,

> The double standard is when [Muslim men] won't talk to Muslim girls, but they'll have no problem talking to American girls. Muslim girls come to Friday prayer, but they won't interact with them. Right after that, you'll see all the guys interacting in a healthy group with other girls. It happens in the back of their minds, where they'll think, "Our Muslim girls are precious and we want to protect them by not interacting with them in that way. But then it's okay to go with non-Muslim girls, because it's meaningless."

According to Rana and Basim, a dominant discourse in Muslim spaces reifies the idea of woman as the marker of community boundaries. Such discourses position Muslim women as symbols of Muslim identity who must be protected in order to protect the group as a whole. This establishes that the stakes are higher for women who transgress gender norms than for men, giving men more room for movement when it comes to normative ideals of sociability and interacting with people outside of their "community."

Several scholars write that the ways in which Muslim women in North America become representatives of Muslims in public have a polarizing influence on women's lives (Khan 2000, 20; Hoodfar 1997). Their proper behavior demarcates community from outside, and reifies community control over women (Ahmed 1992). In this sense, Islam operates in ways similar to the deployment of Arabness as a marker of community boundaries, as we saw in chapter 2.

Several community leaders who worked with Muslim student activists talked with me about idealized concepts of marriage among young adults. Asma is cofounder of an organization dedicated to educating the public about Islam and a leader in the Muslim spaces in which many young adults engaged. She tells me,

> Many youth discuss gender equality in Islam and view Aisha, the prophet's wife, who was a scholar, as their role model. Yet a lot of young Muslim women just want to get married right away, have a husband and kids. Even though they use the reasoning that marriage is to fulfill half of their *din*, they become passive and romantic about marriage. I've seen a lot of bright girls who dropped out of Ph.D. programs to stay home and have no desire to go back. It's strong, among women, to desire nothing beyond mother-hood, even though there *are* those few strong women who grew up tra-ditionally, were married at sixteen or seventeen, are mothers and house-wives, and are also activists.

Asma's observations stem from a commitment to taking the relationship between interpretation and practice seriously: Asma told me that although many young women refer to aspects of contemporary Islamic feminism, in everyday life they participate in the reduction of womanhood to wife and mother. In interviews, some Muslim men acknowledged how they often reinforce this problem. Although Tawfiq, for example, points out his par-ents' unfair treatment of his sister by stating that women have equal rights in Islam, he also tells me,

> If you're a woman, you have certain responsibilities to your family so you can fulfill your religion. That's fine, have your goals and study. If you want to work, fine, but *Insha Allah* [God willing], if we ever have a baby, I expect you to put that stuff on the side for a while. I'm going to help, too, but the mother is everything for the child. Take time for the babies and kids. That's Islamic rule number one. I don't expect her to stay at home all day and clean, wash, and cook, no! [laughs] and I hope she doesn't, either. I *do* expect the guy to be the breadwinner, the main sup-porter—to do the hard work, Islamically. I want the mother to be with the baby, 'cause the mother affects the baby more than the man, *Allah-u Aalum* [God knows].

While Abdul, a college student of Syrian ancestry, tells me that he supports women's education and career goals and wants to marry someone with whom he can have good conversation, he refers to his future wife as follows:

> When I find a wife, *Insha Allah* . . . she's going to be like a treasure box for me. . . . A priceless treasure which I cannot only make happy by myself, but will also make *Allah* happy with her. She's like an endless, priceless treasure. I get this message across to all my Muslim brothers, that a wife is the most priceless thing you're ever going to have.

Tawfiq's and Abdul's remarks and Asma's critique of young women who do not have ambition beyond motherhood reflects a problem, Muslim feminists maintain, that "women are inserted into a predetermined male discourse" (Khan 2000).

Amina Wadud provides a framework for understanding Asma's beliefs, suggesting that male-dominated interpretations of Islam put particular ideals about gender and family in place that foreclose the possibility of imagining Islam any other way (Wadud 2006, 42).[15] Wadud argues that "only in a patriarchal structure is maternity the only social power open to women" (ibid.,126). Essentialist ideals of woman as the good mother, she says, entail a moral association that allows for the conception that women's sexuality and reproductive potential are meant to serve the household or the husband. Wadud suggests that more work is needed to explore "how to achieve fulfillment of family needs without patriarchy" (ibid.). It will require rethinking the principles and the patriarchal bias in primary sources and underlying notions of family in *sharia* (152)—namely, the ideas of man above woman, of man as woman's maintainer and provider, and of these roles as taken from divine sources. She believes that other possibilities exist, and are necessary and appropriate, and that the Qur'an can be read with egalitarian social, political, economic, as well as domestic arrangements in mind (153). Wadud's statements reflect a prominent debate among Muslim feminists about the inclusion of women as equal participants in the political sphere among Muslims. She contends that calls for inclusion are conditioned by a less explicit expectation for women to accept male-defined concepts of Muslim identity or Islamic feminine virtue.

Abdul's description of his future wife as a treasure exemplifies this objectification of women. While he rearticulates Arab cultural authenticity through Islam, he positions females as a symbol that essentializes womanhood in ways similar to Orientalist discourses. His perspective resembles patriarchal discourses that respond to the negative depictions of Muslim masculinity through a "defensive anxiety about manhood among Muslim men that insists on subordinating women" (Fischer and Abedi 1990 in Moallem 2005, 24). While Orientalist essentialism devalues Muslim womanhood, Abdul's statement does the reverse—it celebrates Muslim womanhood. Asma, however, reveals alternative possibilities for conceptualizing womanhood beyond the icons of victim or good wife/mother, and beyond patriarchal, classical definitions of what women should do or be. For Asma, it is not enough to look only at what people say; when looking at what people do, she says, one sees that male authority often remains in practice. As the stories reveal, Muslim First is not always coherent or unified; Tawfiq and Abdul reify dominant male-centered concepts about womanhood, and Asma calls for imagining womanhood beyond these (Wadud 2006, 21, 37, 42). In this sense, Muslim identity emerges through utterances in progress, and in talking back to texts and to each other.[16]

Muslim First also emerges through discussions about women's engagements with sexism in U.S. public spaces and with dominant U.S. discourses on Islam. Lama, a Palestinian woman college student, tells me,

> There was a guy at work who used to go around and grab all the girls and try to touch everything. I told the store manager. The other girls, he would do the same thing to them, but they didn't care, or they didn't care to do anything about it. It was total harassment. And I was like, "This is not what I'm about. This is derogatory." I filled out a report and all the other girls didn't support me. But I'm not gonna let some guy do this to me. So that was one of the things that happened to me that made me stronger, that told me, this is your identity. This is who you are, and it all happened when I was around seventeen or eighteen, when I started finding my Muslim identity. I filled out the report and he got fired. Amazing. You can't touch me!

Wearing *hijab* provides young women with a sense of autonomy in public spaces. As Hiba puts it, "It allows you to hold yourself up as a woman with respect. I don't get cat calls." Nour tells me, "People do not judge me for my body but for my mind."

Ibtisam writes in a poem, "Muslim Women Unveiled," "My body's not for your eyes to hold, you must speak to my mind, not my feminine mold."

For these women, being Muslim provides a sense of power in relationship to sexism in public spaces. In these quotations, young adults articulate a religious identity, through the practice of wearing the *hijab*, through their experiences with sexism at work, and on the streets. Their concept of womanhood entails a relationship to the divine and an affirmation of Muslim concepts of veiling. They articulate a sense of womanhood that does not privilege normative Western feminism as the ideal mechanism of women's agency and autonomy (Deeb 2006; Mahmood 2005). Coupled with the contestations about marriage and womanhood we have seen, their statements represent a perspective on gender that conflicts with dominant concepts about women and gender in Muslim spaces, dominant U.S. Orientalist concepts about Muslim women, and dominant U.S. concepts about gender that lead to a commoditization of women's bodies. These stances intervene into multiple patriarchal discourses: they insist on egalitarianism among Muslims not only in interpretation but also in practice, and they refuse to be objects of U.S. patriarchy. Moreover, they unsettle dominant U.S. frameworks that reduce discussions about gender among Muslims to discussions about an abstract, ahistorical culture or religion. As we have seen, concepts and practices about womanhood among Muslims are, to a certain extent, issues of religion and are indeed constituted by individuals' relationships to God and the divine, but they are much more than that. They are shaped by intergenerational relations and shifting historical circumstances. They take place in relationship to dominant U.S. sentiment about gender and Muslim women, and Muslims themselves do not have one particular perspective about them. Moreover, they speak, subtly, to how sexuality is imagined within all of these debates as these debates generally focus on male-female relations, thus taking for granted that all relations function within a heterosexual family.

Contending with Racial Politics: Neoliberal
Multiculturalism and Racial Justice

Young adults also craft the concept of Muslim First, Arab Second out of discussions about race. A common perspective among the young adults with whom I worked was, "Arab culture is based on racism, while Islam is based on racial equality." As with gender, they rely on a range of societal conceptions about race that are heavily informed by their engagements with U.S. histories and are located at the nexus of ideals and practice. Nada, a Palestinian college student, tells me,

> Arabs, especially because they own stores in poor Black, Asian, or Latino neighborhoods, think that whites are so nice and then they blame certain races for social problems. But in Muslim circles, we learn about the Qur'an, and that even though Allah creates you from different tribes and clans to know each other, we're color blind. The only perfect person is Allah. We're

all human, and our skin has nothing to do with the treatment we deserve. A lot of sheiks are preaching, when a lot of the people are immigrants, that in Islam we don't see color and we shouldn't treat a Black person differently than a white person.

Khaldoun, referring to the mosques during Ramadan, says, "You have people of all origins—Indopaks and Arabs of all origins, you have Sri Lankans, Bosnians, and all these people, and they're all coming together because they're all in this local community." Hussein explains,

The mosque I attend is predominantly Arab. Last Ramadan, a Black man, so dark, *Ma Sha Allah,* was leading the prayer every night in front of five hundred people and everyone would go after the prayer and kiss him and hug him, and I just said, "Just if only those people, who talk about Islam and make it so bad, if they were here to see it, they would see, it's nothing about color." We have Chinese Muslims in our mosque and after the prayer we hug and kiss each other in a loving way, just because we say, *"La Ilahi Il Allah"* [There is no deity except God]; that bond means so much. I mean, I've hugged and kissed in a loving way, Filipinos, Blacks, Chinese, whites, you name it. They're all in the *masjid* [mosque] together and there's never anything between us.

Referring to the same verse Nada refers to, he stated,

There is no color in Islam. . . . In the mosques, they repeat it a hundred million times to get the point across: "We have created you in tribes or clans so you can get to know one another; but the better ones of you are the ones who fear Allah the most." It doesn't depend on color or anything. And the more I'm reading this *aya* [verse] the more I'm trying to get this Arab mentality away.

All three Muslim young adults point out underlying middle-class migrant assimilation politics that require distancing from U.S. racial Others to achieve assimilation and Americanization. Young adults such as Nadia, Khaldoun, and Hussein invoke instead a perspective that circulated in Muslim spaces in the Bay Area and that deployed a particular *aya* in the Qur'an that people interpret this way: "There is no color in Islam." This *aya* critiques the U.S. racial structures that immigrant parents' discourses affirm, through a logic of racial neoliberal multiculturalism that peaked in the 1990s and that "retreats from race." Neoliberal multiculturalism, which began to take shape under the first Clinton administration, "condemns racism and makes racism appear to be disappearing" (Melamed 2006). Neoliberal multiculturalism "recognizes racial inequality as a problem, and it secures a liberal symbolic framework for race reform centered in abstract equality. . . . Antiracism becomes a nationally recognized social value and, for the first time, gets absorbed into U.S. governmentality" (Melamed 2006, 20). To a certain extent the dominant Muslim institutions in which Nada and Tawfiq were involved recognize racial politics through a similar logic that identifies the structural racism in which they contend recent immigrant communities engage. Yet they idealize Muslim spaces as ones where race disappears. Not everyone, however, accepted that the ideal of colorblindness was indeed a reality in Muslim spaces. Several interlocutors refer to the racial politics within many Bay Area mosques as a "perceived colorblindness" that ignores racial hierarchies among Muslims. They took an active role in calling for a commitment to taking racial inequalities seriously. Tawfiq tells me,

> Because Arabic is the language of the Qur'an, and because the prophet was Arabic, Arabs are seen as the most excellent people. It's ingrained in their minds, in the other Muslims' minds. Whenever I'm with a Muslim group I feel like there are more eyes on me, especially if I'm the only Arab there. It's affected me. Arabs have been given a high position and it always made me feel a little higher, which I hated so much. I feel like I should be respected a little more, *Astaghfirullah al azeem* [I seek the forgiveness of God], but it's going away now. I'm humbling myself more.

Maya, a Palestinian woman who recently graduated from college and is active in Arab and Muslim social service organizations, tells me,

> It becomes better to be Arab in Muslim circles and people look up to you if you're an Arab, thinking that you must know Islam more because you speak Arabic and therefore you must be a better Muslim than I am. Arabs are very arrogant about their ethnic background, especially because of the language. They're uptight. It's really appalling. But it's the dream of every Muslim to marry an Arabic-speaking person, but Arab men in particular use that a lot in discriminating against the rest of Muslims, especially the African Americans, and if left on their own, if not checked by Pakistanis and Indians, they would completely roll over the rest of Muslims.

Tawfiq and Maya's quotes reflect a tension between two differing politics of race among Muslims—or between neoliberal multiculturalism and antiracism/racial justice. Hatem, an antiracist/racial-justice activist, summarizes this distinction:

> I still feel like race is one of those areas that is taboo in the Muslim community. People mention the *aya* [there is no color in Islam]. They may have the theology but not know what it really means to articulate being antiracist. Even though they have a good analysis that does not mean they have been able to overcome race. People are still socializing away from African Americans in particular and there is value for white converts over African American converts and there are structural differences in resource distribution. For example, the resources mobilized for an African American mosque are limited compared to the immigrant or even to white converts—even though 20 percent of Muslims in the U.S. are African Americans in terms of numbers. You don't see them represented in imagery or leadership. Some students have been able to overcome or at least to work through this because they have been placed in a diverse campus environment where their consciousness is being tested through the fire in organizing situations.

Several interlocutors bring similar concepts that fuse religion with U.S. racial discourses as a strategy to open up possibilities of gaining leverage over their parents, particularly in matters concerning interracial marriage. Since migrant parents tend to place more pressure on their daughters to marry someone who is Arab, struggles over interracial marriage were more common among women. Basem refers to himself as "Muslim first, but Arabic speaking." Like most Muslim First youth, he believes a woman's religion is more important than what he referred to as her race or ethnicity. He tells me, "I want to love her for her Islam. Marrying a Syrian, or Iraqi, is not important to me." Asma, who works closely with young adults, explains that young Muslim women upheld an idealized notion of marrying a devout Muslim that took precedence over other aspects of who they were (race, ethnicity, etc.):

> Youth want to marry practicing Muslims like themselves. A lot of the girls want to marry scholars, Muslim scholars, and the guys want to marry a *mujahidah* [freedom fighter]—it's amazing. They don't want to marry an ordinary Muslim. Once, a young woman had a list of all the qualifications she was looking for and it was like the ideal Muslim male, who doesn't watch TV, doesn't listen to music, like someone she's cloned! It's totally unrealistic, but a lot of these girls want to marry these types of individuals.

Women disproportionately told me stories about relying on the Qur'an to convince parents to support marriage across racial lines. Rima told me a story:

> These sisters married the Black Muslims . . . one of them opened the Qur'an in her father's face and was like, "Look, it says here, as long as he's a good Muslim." She put her father on the spot. "If you're a Muslim, you have to deal with this." But after they married, the parents sent the younger daughter back home because they were afraid she was going to marry a Black Muslim.

Rania, of Jordanian descent, was engaged to an Indonesian Muslim. She says, "My parents were silent because of their guilty consciences. They must have thought, 'Allah is going to come one day. This guy is a good man, how could you say no? It's in one of the *hadiths* [the words and the deeds of the Prophet Mohammed].'" According to Jamila, a community leader,

> This generation is really not racist, but they're being made racist by their parents who are trying to get them to marry within their own. Race gets played out within marriage, and race issues are debated through Qur'an, between parents and youth. Kids are really smart, they know Islam. Parents can't say "no" to interracial marriage. Parents can't get away with it. It's when parents know that the kids don't know Islam, that's when they make up things to sell their point of view. Like, they'll say, "Islam says so and so." Or "No, it doesn't say so." But usually kids are smart enough to be able to challenge their parents. All they have to do is go to any scholar and ask his point of view.

From their position as predominantly middle-class college students who have access to college education in the United States and to Islamic education classes, these young people mobilize particular *aya* from the Qur'an to defend a politics of race and gender. Women in particular gain power from neoliberal multiculturalist concepts of race in Islam to unseat the racial constructs against what many of their immigrant parents refer to as "the Blacks and the Chinese."

Islamophobia as a Discourse of Empire

Earlier, we saw how local and global events—Muslim migration patterns in light of a booming IT industry in the Bay Area, alongside a range of U.S.

imperial interventions in Muslim countries—contributed to the emergence of a distinctly Muslim identity in the Bay Area in the 1980s and 1990s. Here, I take up second-generation Arab American young adults' engagements with Islamophobic discourses about Muslims that were prevalent in the 1980s and 1990s in the context of U.S. expansion in Muslim-majority countries. Taken together, my interlocutors' stories can be read as an archive of how Islamophobia works and of the significance of Islamophobia to the articulation of Muslim First, Arab Second. As my interlocutors' stories show, Islamophobia works as a form of imperial racism and as a mechanism that fuels many young adults' commitment to a distinctly Muslim identity and, for some, a commitment to become social justice activists. Hatem Bazian, who worked as a mentor to Muslim students at the University of California at Berkeley, told me that students' daily confrontations with views that associate Muslims with terrorism catalyzed their involvement in social justice activism. In Hatem's words,

> In the classroom, the Muslim student is transformed into a terrorist. There is a political strategy of creating political support for U.S. foreign policy. It comes straight from teachers. Every day, students ask me, "What should I tell my teachers?" Teachers say racist things in class like, "Muslims are more inclined to engage in terrorism, because when they die they go to paradise and terrorism doesn't have pain for Muslims as it does in other cultures." Or "Muslim men aren't afraid to die because when they die they believe they will be given seventy-five virgins in heaven." That's in a classroom discussion!

Nearly all the students with whom I worked recalled an incident that they or one of their friends or family members encountered in which signifiers such as their names, physical features, or mode of dress led others to perceive them as "Muslim" and therefore as foreigners and potential threats to "America." Nuha, a college student active in a Muslim student organization, explained, "We get everything from a spit in the face at the Emeryville Shopping Center . . . to the statement . . . 'Go back home'. . . which was made to someone in the City Hall of Berkeley. 'Go back home' is standard operating procedure."

Maysoun, a Palestinian woman, recalled an incident that took place when she was in high school during the first Gulf War: "I was at a private school and my teacher was from Texas and I had my hand up and he was like, 'Put your other hand up.' And he was like, 'That's how all of you need to come, with your hands up.'" Mazen, a college student, remembered an encounter he had in high school with a student in the cafeteria: "It was after the Oklahoma bombing. Even though the individuals criminally charged for the Oklahoma bombing were neither Arab nor Muslim, the junior class president came up to me and said, 'Women and children, too?'"

In the incidents above, Islamophobia operates as a form of imperial racism. My interlocutors are implicated in the long-standing European and U.S. discourse that conflates Islam with violence and terrorism as a justification for war (Alsultany 2012; Ono 2005, xxxii; Moallem 2005; Rana 2007; Volpp 2003a; Naber 2006). Here, imperial racism works through the framework of two interconnected logics: cultural racism and nation-based racism. "Cultural racism," like Orientalism, "is a process of 'othering' that constructs perceived cultural (e.g., Arab), religious (e.g., Muslim), or civilizational (e.g., Arab and/or Muslim) differences as natural and insurmountable (Balibar 1991, 17-28; Goldberg 1993; Moallem 2005). I build upon Minoo Moallem's analysis of contexts in which religion may be considered "as a key determinant in the discourse of racial inferiority" (Moallem 2005, 10) and Balibar's argument that "race," when coded as culture, can be constituted by a process that makes no reference to claims of biological superiority but instead associates difference and inferiority with spiritual inheritance (Balibar 1991, 25). In such instances, "culture can also function like a nature, and it can in particular function as a way of locking individuals and groups a priori into a genealogy, into a determination that is immutable and intangible in origin" (22). As in European histories of antisemitism, histories of Islamophobia have deployed biological features in the racialization process, but "within the framework of cultural racism" (ibid.).[17] In other words, bodily stigmata become signifiers of a spiritual inheritance as opposed to a biological heredity (ibid.). I use the term "cultural racism" in cases where violence or harassment was justified on the basis that persons perceived to be Muslim were seen as inherently connected to a backward, inferior, and potentially threatening Islamic culture or civilization. I use the term "nation-based racism" in ways that draw upon Kent Ono's theory of the racialization of the category "potential terrorists" and David Theo Goldberg's argument (1993) that Western discourses racialize to refer to the construction of particular immigrants as different from and inferior to whites, based on the concept that "they" are foreign and therefore embody a potential for criminality and/or immorality and must be "evicted, eliminated, or controlled" (Ono 2005).

The interplay between culture-based racism and nation-based racism explains the process by which my interlocutors in the stories above are perceived not only as a moral, cultural, and civilizational threat to the United States but also as a security threat. The mapping of cultural racism onto

136 << MUSLIM FIRST, ARAB SECOND

nation-based racism has been critical in generating support for the idea that going to war "over there" and enacting racism and immigrant exclusion "over here" are essential to the project of protecting national security. Throughout histories of U.S. imperialist actions in Muslim-majority nations, cultural and nation-based racism have operated transnationally to justify U.S. imperial ambitions and the simultaneous targeting of persons perceived in the diaspora to be Arab, Middle Eastern, or Muslim (Moallem 2005, 8; Young 2001, 25-44).

Gender permeates interlocutors' confrontations with Islamophobia. Women disproportionately share stories in which others perceive them as foreign or as victims of misogynistic Muslim men because they wear the *hijab*. My interlocutors' confrontations with dominant U.S. discourses on the *hijab* are rooted in long-standing European and U.S. Islamophobic and Orientalist discourses. European Orientalist discourses have long portrayed the practice of veiling, which itself can vary from the loose draping of a scarf around one's head to the covering of one's whole self with the exception of hands, feet, and a small opening for the eyes, as a sign of Muslim backwardness. Whether depicting veiling as a marker of Muslim misogyny or as a sign of exotic, mysterious sexuality, European discourses have scripted Islam as a premodern, unchanging, and unsophisticated mode of being in the world, thereby scripting Muslims as savage, barbaric, and uncivilized peoples. European discourses on the veil have been charged with the significance of colonialism and war throughout different periods of European colonialism in Muslim-majority countries. During the period of British colonialism in Egypt, for instance, British government officials used arguments about the veil—as a symbol of Egyptian backwardness—to justify colonization (Ahmed 1992). Here, the Western association of veiling with repressed sexuality and backwards religion was written onto the practice of veiling, and those colonial arguments were marshaled against colonized nations and, at later times, internalized by colonized peoples. Leila Ahmed reveals how support for veiling in Egypt came to be interpreted as resistance to colonialism and opposition to veiling seemed to represent support for Western modernity. We have seen the persistence of European discourses on the veil in which the veil becomes entrapped within totalizing discourses of tradition versus modernity or oppression versus liberation in the French ban on the *hijab* in public establishments in 1994. Banu Gökariksel and Katharyne Mitchell have argued that in France, veiling became an indication of a person's ability to "advance" culturally as a citizen who chooses not only her own liberation from tyranny but also her participation in the modern, civilized nation (2005). The attempt to force women to unveil, they argue, forces conformity within an idealized secular state, where religious expression is seemingly at odds with separation of church and state, as well as potentially detrimental to liberalism. Here, veiling took on hyperbolic meaning, indicating not only one's commitment to religion and inversely her inability to modernize, assimilate, or otherwise progress but also her (and by proxy, "her people's") belonging within the civilized world. Similar controversies and bans on veiling have developed in the United States, where representations of the veil have been the cornerstone of U.S. popular cultural distinctions between the West, Europe, and America and "Orientals," "the East," Arabs, or Muslims (McCloud 2000; Hatem 2011; Jarmakani 2008; Abu-Lughod 2002; Saliba 1994; Shaheen 2001; Street 2000). Veiling has been a crucial point of contention and debate in the fictive formulations of East and West, Islam and democracy, and Muslims and America. Accordingly, and sometimes begrudgingly, many Muslim feminists and their allies have spoken directly to the problematic of veiling. One strand of Muslim feminist critique contends that Muslim women do not seem to be terribly conflicted about veiling, and that many have already decided what veiling means to them. Muslim women, Abu-Lughod argues, don't prioritize veiling as an equality or rights issue, so perhaps neither ought the "West." What would be more beneficial, Abu-Lughod argues, would be addressing those concerns Muslim women self-articulate as impinging or pressing on their lives. In the everyday lives of young Muslim women activists, their *hijab* drew them into totalizing discourses about the veil, Muslims, and America. This small sampling from interviews with women who wear the *hijab* illustrates how the Orientalist symbol of the veiled woman takes on local form in the Bay Area:

Maya: Because I wear *hijab*, people are surprised to discover that I speak English. If you're wearing a scarf, people think you're an immigrant, and they think you have an accent. If you're wearing this, you're not an American, until you speak. Then you throw them off.

Tala: I was standing at the Muslim Student Association's table on my college campus. A student approached the table and asked me if women cover their faces from the bruises they get after their husbands beat them.

Randa: We were in the exhibit of modern art and everybody thought we were part of an exhibit! We were talking and then asked the people next to us, "Why are you staring at us?" and they were like, "You foreigners, go back to your country."

Hala: Some friends asked me if I could go to the mall with them. I said no and she said, "That's so unfair—your parents are forcing you to stay home!" My friend works in a police station. She set me up with a job interview there. When I went to visit her one day, she heard the boss say, "I would be afraid to give her a job because she would never speak up." I went, got the job, and said, "I don't want the job anymore." Now his image changed.

In the stories above, the *hijab* signifies a range of meanings. It renders women who wear the *hijab* not as agents but as extensions of violent, misogynist Muslim men. Muslim women are transformed into the "property," "the harmonious extension" (Shohat and Stam 1994) of the enemy of the nation within, or symbols that connect others to the "real actors" or "the violent Muslim men" but who do not stand on their own (and lack agency). In this sense, dominant U.S. discourses on the veil condemn Muslim women for veiling. They reify the logic of nation-based racism that constructs a binary through gender of us versus them and good, or moral, Americans versus bad Muslims. They reduce Muslim women's possibilities to unveiling or allying with foreignness, backwardness, or violence: Muslim women are either unveiled/with us, or veiled/with the foreign, backward, potentially violent, Muslim Others. Here, the veil serves as a boundary marker between "us" and "them" (Abu-Lughod 1986; Razack 2008; Jarmakani 2008).

Becoming an Activist

Everyday exposure to Islamophobia contributed to an affiliation with a distinctly Muslim identity among Muslim student activists. Some young adults were inspired to become actively engaged in countering dominant discourses in public spaces in everyday life. In January 2000, I attended a Muslim Student Association (MSA) meeting at the University of California in San Diego. MSA members developed a plan for *daawa* (invitation to Islam) that incorporated strategies for assisting non-Muslim students in overcoming negative assumptions about Islam. A discussion that took place at the meeting resembled those I often heard in the Bay Area. Rana, who prayed in public on her college campus, supported this plan. She said, "I know that when I pray on campus, they're looking at me with hate." Several young adults I worked with in the Bay Area told me that they are often "forced to become activists" in the classroom.

Tala: I felt forced by my circumstances to challenge the status quo, even at a minimal level, only to reflect that what is being talked about does not reflect who I am, or my culture, civilization, religion, or history. I learned that if I do not confront, then I would be silenced.

Hatem: I see the students feeling comfortable wearing a head cover or Muslim beards. They care less that they might appear to be wearing the most bizarre outfit. The way they present themselves is a way that they force others to deal with them as Muslims.

For some women, this entailed redefining the negative meanings associated with the *hijab* and bringing new meanings to U.S. publics, a process that some women related to with ambivalence. Hannan, a twenty-year-old college student, felt burdened by the ways her teachers discussed Islam in the classroom and felt responsible for responding to Orientalist representations of backward, oppressed Muslim women. She told me, "Arab women are forced to represent the entire situation of Muslim women. The teacher has an anti-Muslim position, so even if I don't have the tools, it becomes the class versus me and I have to answer for Afghanistan, Saudi Arabia, and other places I don't even know much about." This reflects the way structures of gendered racism contribute to the constitution of Muslim identity. As youth define Muslim identity, they also constitute forms of sociability. In addition to alternative forms of dress, Muslim students adopt a specifically Muslim form of English. Many students greet each other with "*assalamu alaikum*" (Peace be upon you), speak Arabic on their answering machines, and weave terms such as "*alhamdulillah*" (thank God), "*inshallah*" (God willing) and "*astaghfirullah al azeem*" (I ask for pardon from the Great One) into their everyday English language.

In addition to actively asserting Muslim identity in public, most of my interlocutors were involved in organized forms of political dissent, illustrating the significance of geopolitics to local articulations of Muslim identity. Many community leaders highlighted perspectives on the significance of social justice activism in their everyday lives in their speeches, which circulated in debates, discussions, and classes, and informed student activism.[18] The following quotations are from two community leaders who influenced my interlocutors and other Muslim student activists.

Hamza Yusuf, in a speech, remarked, "Islam is about compassion and about going out and speaking the truth. . . . We have to ask ourselves what are we doing with our lives?"

Hatem's words reflect a view that several community leaders upheld that tremendously influenced my young adult subjects:

Islam is about rendering divine manifestation in the world. Divine manifestation is how to be Godlike in conduct and how to manifest prophet-like
qualities. Feeding people is one of the highest values. The prophet (Peace Be
Upon Him) said, "Feed people or spread salutation, feed people then get up
and pray at night if you want." Meaning faith and belief is about serving people. Really, it is a sense of responsibility that you have to make a difference in
people's lives and to leave the world in a better position or a better condition
than how you entered it. . . . You have to move within the world with that
eye—that you could make a difference even if that difference is not complete
in this life but if you are able to bring about a tangential benefit while there is
overwhelming calamity and harm, you are obligated to seek bringing about
the tangential benefit. So, you actually, from a legal perspective, are obligated
to make a difference. Asking questions like: Well, how is helping this homeless [person] going to make a difference in the whole homelessness . . . in the
bigger issue . . . if it is within your ability, you are obligated to do that. And
you need to measure it accordingly. That for me is a central issue.

These quotations reflect a tacit knowledge among student activists that
emerged throughout much of their public discourse, a sense that being Muslim entails a responsibility to advocate for social justice and to take up political and ethical issues. Not all students who shared this sense of commitment were political activists or involved in public politics of dissent. Yet as
we will see, the protests and activities of student activists provide a platform
for exploring the politically constituted religious discourse that emerged in
Muslim spaces in the Bay Area at the turn of the twenty-first century, and
reflect the significance of global politics to local concepts of self, affiliation,
community, and belonging.

The Global

In Muslim spaces, perspectives on global politics reflected a shared sense
of membership in a transnational moral religious community, the *umma*; a
belief that Muslims are under attack on a global scale; and a shared sense
of coresponsibility to Muslims living under conditions of war and oppression. The Bosnian war significantly sparked the mobilization of this narrative among Muslims. Osama, a leader of a Muslim social justice organization
in the Bay Area, tells me, "It was Bosnia that broke the hearts of Muslims
and awakened the dead among Muslims worldwide. It brought Muslims to
their knees." Indeed, many people told me that Bosnia was the culmination
of decades of increasing anti-Muslim violence on a global scale.[19]

Henna, a cofounder of an organization that raises awareness about Islam in U.S. society, tells me,

> It wasn't one hundred people who died, it was three hundred thousand. There were rape camps and concentration camps. Bosnia made people realize that you can be Muslim and white in Europe and still be killed on the basis of your Islam. They're blonde, blue-eyed, they live in Europe, and they were still mutilated, slaughtered, and thrown into mass graves because they're Muslim. That's when it's not just about Arabs anymore. And you have Algeria, Asia, the Philippines—they're being persecuted because they're Muslim. It's going on all over the world.

Henna's view reflects U.S. and bay area progressive discourses that feature particular definitions of racism in making claims about oppression, assuming that only forms of racism that invoke assumptions about phenotype or biology qualify as oppression. Appealing to this sensibility, Henna asserts that a different framework is needed. For her, people in Bosnia were targeted because of their religion, not because they were assumed to belong to a racial group defined in biological terms. Bosnia, she implies, illustrates that anti-Muslim violence requires an analysis of religious, civilizational, and spiritually based violence and racism. More specifically, she points out the conflation of the categories "Arab" and "Muslim," a dominant conceptualization in U.S. popular discourses, which assumes that all Arabs are Muslim and all Muslims are Arabs. She asserts a different politics, one that articulates Muslims through a concept of community that transcends conventional racial or national boundaries. It involves Muslims from diverse countries who share a similar history of oppression that cannot be explained in terms of racial or national oppression. According to Osama and Henna, Bosnia revitalized a global communal consciousness and enabled a particular image of a Muslim community under attack on a global scale.[20]

Crucial to this critique—and a strand of this that many young adults took up—was the idea that while global violence against Muslims is growing, it is simultaneously obscured, ignored, or deemed acceptable. This perspective expands the conceptualization of global anti-Muslim violence toward a focus on the relationship between the dehumanization that occurs through racial discourses (Islamaphobia, Orientalism, discourses about terrorism, Muslim violence, Muslim women's oppression) and "the likelihood of premature death" (Gilmore 2006). Muslim student activists expressed this critique of global anti-Muslim violence and racism in their actions of political dissent. One day in 1994 at the University of California–Davis, I witnessed an instance in which the Bosnian genocide inspired a Muslim student activist to bring this discussion to a campus audience. As I walked onto campus that day, I noticed people gathering in front of the art building a few hundred feet away from me. People were walking exceptionally slowly and peering down with shock and confusion on their faces. As I neared the area, I saw that someone had placed a great deal of dirt on the ground. Surrounding the dirt was a "No Trespassing" sign and yellow "Do Not Cross" tape that students had had to knock down or break to get to their classes. Walking on the dirt was unavoidable, and as more people crossed the area and pushed away the dirt with their steps, a hidden collage began to emerge from under the soil. I overheard a group of students saying it was about Bosnia. Later that day, as I walked past the art building again, I saw the full collage: it was Bosnian rape survivors' faces along with their personal testimonies.

The artist was Khadija, a Pakistani woman actively engaged with the Muslim Student Association on campus. Several years later, I asked her about it. She called the piece "The Battle Ground" and she used the dirt as a metaphor for how Bosnian women's bodies had been treated. Khadija obtained the collage materials from news magazines and her personal experience with Bosnian rape survivors while she was working in refugee camps. She told me, "The treading on the dirt signified the rape of Bosnian women and we [students] were the rapists due to our apathetic attitudes. Students were clueless as to what the purpose of the project was until the next morning, when the dirt was completely cleared and they could see the collage in full."

Khadija's artwork reflected what many scholars and activists, Muslim and non-Muslim, have described since Bosnia. Her art asserts that while there were media reports of camps, mass killings, rape, the destruction of mosques, the more than two hundred thousand Muslim civilians systematically murdered, the more than twenty thousand missing and feared dead, and the two million who had become refugees, the world community remained indifferent. This appraisal took issue with the U.N.'s prohibiting its troops from interfering militarily against the Serbs and remaining neutral no matter how bad the situation became. It also contended that Serbs in Bosnia freely committed genocide against Muslims on the basis of their confidence that the United Nations, the United States, and the European Community would not take military action—that "they knew about it but chose to look away." The most severe forms of violence—the slaughter of eight thousand men and boys and mass rapes of Muslim women—took place after President Clinton issued an ultimatum through NATO, reinforcing the sense that "intervention" was only stopping the genocide in the abstract rather than in reality.[21] Overall, Khadija's artwork was a response to the few Americans who were pressing for intervention while genocide proceeded unimpeded and often emboldened by U.S. inaction. In this analysis, the inaction reflected a systematic anti-Muslim stance by global powers, which had taken on local form in the silence among U.S. publics.

Ruthie Gilmore defines racism as the likely promotion of the premature death of those individuals and groups subjected to the debilitating terms and conditions of racist configurations and exclusions (2006). Here, accumulated racism in the media, everyday racisms, and global violence against Muslims render Muslims "targets of legitimated violence and ultimately unnoticed or overlooked death" (Goldberg 2009, 27). By the late 1990s, while crises such as Bosnia, Kosovo, Kashmir, and Chechnya remained central to Muslim student activism in the Bay Area, U.S.-led economic sanctions on Iraq and the Israeli occupation of Palestine revitalized communal consciousness that a global Muslim community is the target of a global war, a war legitimized through a racist discourse that devalues Muslim lives and renders the killing of Muslims acceptable.[22]

Iraq

In the Bay Area, activism over Iraq took the form of teach-ins, film showings, benefit concerts, tabling, public protests, and the publication of advertisements, articles, and letters to the editor in campus newspapers. Muslim student activists, in collaboration with a range of Muslim community-based organizations, played critical roles in the peace and justice movement that was working to end sanctions on Iraq. On April 27, 1999, which antiwar activists refer to as the National Day of Action to End Economic Sanctions Against Iraq, a coalition of fourteen organizations coordinated a public protest that included a funeral procession in which activists held coffins of more than five thousand children under the age of five to represent those who die each month as a result of the sanctions. The coalition included socialist organizations, student groups, civil rights groups, and Muslim peace and justice organizations. To this coalition, Muslim activists brought a collective narrative about Iraq that proliferated in Bay Area mosques, at Muslim student conferences, on e-mail lists and websites shared by Muslim activists, in the speeches of the imams presenting at public protests, and in the literature of Muslim social justice–oriented organizations. They contended that Iraqi people were suffering as a result of eight years of economic sanctions supported primarily by the United States. Mosques and Muslim leaders throughout the Bay Area, in a pattern that has also been documented worldwide, played important roles in mobilizing this effort and galvanizing people to act (Werbner 2002a, 176).

Several events in 2000 at which leaders and students came together reflect the perspectives that Muslim activists circulated about Iraq. A Muslim community organization distributed a publication at a rally against U.S. sanctions on Iraq in April that provided statistics on the impact of the sanctions on Iraqi people and said, "The silent genocide of the Iraqi civilian population by the deadly United Nations sanctions is the grimmest tragedy affecting the Muslim world today."[23]

In May 2000, the University of California–Berkeley administration invited Secretary of State Madeleine Albright to be their commencement speaker. The ceremony took place in the open-air Greek Theatre. Muslim activists co-organized an action with hundreds of protesters to challenge Albright as a representative of the State Department's enforcement of U.S.-led sanctions on Iraq. They repeated over and over her statement on *60 Minutes,* in which she claimed that the price of killing a million Iraqi children is "worth it" ("Punishing Saddam," *60 Minutes*). Hundreds of activists entered the graduation ceremony and dispersed themselves throughout the theater to disrupt Albright's speech, charge her with genocide, and name her a war criminal in order to bring the matter to the awareness of the large audience who would attend the graduation. They chanted antiwar statements, dropped banners

Demonstration against the sanctions on Iraq, San Francisco.

from the bleachers, and resisted arrest to distract from Albright's speech. A Muslim organization contributed an aerial advertisement featuring a banner that read: "1.7 Million Dead. End the Sanctions Now!" After the ceremony, protesters who had entered the theater joined those who were outside for a rally in front of UC–Berkeley's Boalt Hall. Between public presentations, speakers turned to the audience for their participation in a series of chants. Adding to those chants, Muslim activists called out *"takbir"* and their counterparts responded, *"allahu akbar."*[24]

Muslim activists' perspectives on Iraq reflect a sense of belonging to a global community that is under attack in Iraq, among other places, as well as the distinct position of Muslims living in the United States and the Bay Area, specifically. Their response to Albright was indicative of the fact that they lived in the country responsible for the attacks, which mobilized them to address Iraq in a particular way. They expressed this not from a position of "Muslim outsiders" or "foreigners," or an "anti-local" position (Werbner 2002a), but as Muslims sharing in this struggle with a wide spectrum of Bay Area peace and justice activists in a diverse antisanctions movement based on a shared analysis that the sanctions were a form of genocide, that the U.S. role was unjust and racist, and that the U.S. media and government were hiding the war from the U.S. public (2002a).

They fused their general dissent with U.S. politics in Iraq with their perspective on their relationship to a global Muslim community and with their interpretation of their responsibility to ethics and morality as Muslims. Hamza Yousef, for example, calls for a deeper questioning of life that entails a coresponsibility and connection to others that cannot be captured by liberal progressive concepts of individual rights. This reflects what Kevin Dwyer found among Muslims in Morocco. There, he explains, Islamic resurgence is "a response to contemporary problems," including the desire to construct societies free from the ills of modern Western society: its materials, lack of social cohesion, lack of common purpose, absence of a sense of community" (Dwyer 1991, 41). Hamza Yousef evaluates capitalism and consumerism while grappling with questions about community and how Muslims might reimagine new forms of living beyond capitalism and oppression.

What Muslim students are engaged in cannot be reduced to an abstract sense of religious identity or an Islamic tradition understood in opposition to Western modernity. Race and global politics contribute to their concept of being Muslim, and they grapple with being Muslim while contemplating ways of imagining the world beyond contemporary U.S.-led geopolitics, war, and oppression (Majid 2000, 61). The Muslim student movement is not an isolated, separatist movement envisioned through a call to the past but is in constant dialogue with other contemporary, local kinds of affiliations—Muslim and non-Muslim. It cannot be explained with theories of Islamic fundamentalism, migrant nostalgia, or conventional analyses of culture, ethnicity, or morality. Here, affiliating with a Muslim identity is just as much of a critique of capitalism, imperialism, militarism, racism, and war as it is a matter of ethics, morality, and religiosity.[25]

Palestine

Muslim student organizations participated in a range of Bay Area political events that scrutinized Israeli occupation of Palestine through a discourse framing Palestine solidarity as a unifying issue for Muslims globally. The global spread of technology, including satellite television and the internet—what one activist calls "the era of Al Jazeera and the internet"—has directly exposed Muslims from multiple racial/ethnic communities to events in Palestine on a daily basis, and has inspired an intensified attachment to the Palestinian cause and people, concretizing transnational links among a multiracial constituency of Muslim student activists.

In the Bay Area, Iranians, Pakistanis, Indians, Afghans, Malaysians, Filipinos, Africans, and African Americans united as "Muslim" with their "brothers and sisters in Palestine." Maha, a Muslim student activist of Palestinian descent, says, "What makes this *intifada* different from the *intifada* of the 1980s is that not just Arabs—but Muslims throughout the world, like Pakistanis—see the images of murdered children on TV." The internet enhanced such alliances among Arab students who identify as practicing Muslims within and beyond local and national borders.

The second Palestinian *intifada* began in October 2000. Massive political mobilizations in solidarity with Palestinians broke out on a global scale. A grave sense of urgency circulated within networks of Arab and Muslim activists as well as antiwar and racial-justice organizers in the Bay Area. Activists tended to turn to alternative media outlets, websites, and e-mail lists for news from Palestine. Political activists committed to Palestinian self-determination, particularly people with loved ones in Palestine, seemed more captivated by cell phones, satellite television, and the internet than ever before. Personal stories from Palestine circulated through local constellations of family and friends, religious, cultural, and political networks, and alternative television and internet outlets. Within the first six days of the uprising, people connected to Palestine in the Bay Area were hearing news from the ground such as the Israeli army killing of sixty-one and injuring of three thousand Palestinians. A collective sense of connection to Palestinians

Prayer in front of San Francisco City Hall.

living under a military invasion brought Arab and Muslim people together in a communal state of crisis.

A new development came out of this moment: the centrality of religion as an organizing framework for Palestine-solidarity activism in the Bay Area. Within the framework of global Muslim social justice, the movement for Palestine solidarity in the Bay Area became more expansive than it had been in the past. Bay Area Arab and Muslim political organizations, along with a range of antiwar activist networks, organized mass marches that coincided with similar events worldwide. These efforts rallied around the shared objective of urging "peace-loving people to protest the ongoing massacres and to demand that the United States government immediately stop providing the weapons to Israel which are used to massacre civilians."[26] One call for action included a march and rally on a Friday afternoon that was to begin in front of San Francisco's City Hall and end in front of the Israeli Consulate. A coalition of Muslim organizations added a call for a public Friday prayer before the march. Over five thousand Muslim worshippers—men, women, and children—were lined up in several hundred rows facing the *Kaba* (the most sacred site in Islam, located in Mecca) in *Sujud* (prostration for prayer) position, with their foreheads touching the ground, in the largest political mobilization of Muslims in San Francisco's history. This event marked an important shift in Bay Area activism related to the Arab region. The public

Prayer in front of San Francisco City Hall.

prayer signified an intensification of religious displays of political alliance and solidarity with Palestinians. Muslim student activists from various college campuses were among several constituents who organized and participated in the event.[27]

Overall, Muslim student activists were engaged in crafting a counternormative narrative on Iraq and Palestine. They were committed to rearticulating Islam in a manner different from U.S. Islamophobic discourses that mark Muslims as potential terrorists and inherently backwards, uncivilized, and violent. They linked Israeli policies against Palestinians to U.S. support for Israel. They also linked their critique to local U.S. and Bay Area racial justice issues through the deployment of rap music and by making connections to the criminalization of youth of color in Oakland. They engaged liberal U.S. discourses about life, liberty, and happiness as a strategy to humanize Muslims to a generalized American public. They simultaneously articulated social justice through distinctly Muslim concepts of resistance and struggle. The internet and satellite TV helped to inspire a transnational, coalitional concept of Islam that connected people from various Muslim-majority countries and connected Muslims to local subaltern communities.

A filmmaker interviewed several of the organizers before and after the rally and conference. In one of these interviews, a conference organizer explained, "The rally will take a public stance against oppression and imperialism and the conference is to unite Muslims. It will be about our brothers and sisters everywhere—Palestine, Chechnya, Bosnia, and here. We'll have sisters in *hijab* [head covering] and brothers in *kufis* [short, rounded caps] holding signs" (Berkeley Ihsan Conference 2000).

Mazen, an Arab American student, told me something similar, that the purpose of their actions was to "expose Israel's use of aggression and both Republican and Democratic candidates' pro-Israeli bias. We also want to expose the U.S.'s excessive military aid to Israel and the media's pro-Israeli bias."

A graduate student and central leader of this movement told a journalist,

> Israel continues to occupy lands and there is no reconciliation between us. The peace process is fundamentally flawed. It doesn't give Palestinians self-determination or sovereignty over their land. The rally is to educate people about what is taking place and to express our views—that Israel is committing injustices. It is to begin telling people that Islam is one of the largest religions in the world and can no longer be unaccepted as a non-Western religion. (Berkeley Ihsan Conference 2000)

Another speaker explained what was a consistent theme throughout the day—that it is the duty of all Muslims to resist oppression. In general, the speakers grounded their call to resistance as a duty in Islam to the diverse Muslim populations around the world who were bearing the brunt of U.S. militarism and war. They also critiqued what they perceived as a relationship between the United States and corrupt regimes in Muslim-majority countries.

Local Muslim institutions were crucial to the success of the mobilization for Palestine that took place in front of City Hall, a mobilization that brought together secular forces with people affiliated with Bay Area mosques. Muslim activists who co-organized this mobilization told me that they had asked local mosques, such as the Jones Street mosque of San Francisco and Mesjid Al Islam in Oakland, to relocate their Friday prayer to San Francisco's civic center. The idea that mosques would close their doors that Friday was a political strategy that used Friday afternoon as a strategic organizing time, a time to bring people out into the civic center. Some of the largest Muslim institutions of the Bay Area, located in Santa Clara, also participated and mobilized their constituencies. When Muslim organizers successfully mobilized a large crowd who represented the majority of political participants in front of City Hall that day, secular forces recognized the Muslim community as a political force that they would need to contend with when it came to Palestine-related organizing. This shift comes in the context of the collapse

of the generally secular Palestinian movement post-Oslo and the context of
the late 1990s and early twenty-first century. New coalitions between religious and secular forces, reflected in the events above, gave new shape to the
Palestinian movement in the Bay Area. It was the first time mosques participated in significant ways and illustrated their capacity to mobilize their
grassroots, a Muslim grassroots that is greater in size than an Arab or Palestinian constituency.

Racial Justice and Coalition Politics

In the 1990s, local and national Muslim organizations with diverse membership were established. Hatem summarizes this period as one in which "Muslim politics shifted to thinking beyond immediate needs or distinct needs of
distinct Muslim racial/ethnic communities and towards civic engagement."
In the Bay Area, some activists were heavily committed to maintaining multiracial alliances among Muslims, which specifically improved relationships
between migrant Muslims and African American Muslims. While there are
histories of connections in the Bay Area, such alliances have existed primarily on the leadership level. Since the early 1990s, Hatem had been researching
relationships between African Americans and immigrant Muslims for a book
he is writing on Muslim Americans in the Bay Area. He tells me that there
was a stronger alliance between diverse immigrant Muslims than between
immigrants and African Americans:

> Multiracial alliances have not yet reached the various levels of the commu-
> nity. In the Bay Area, there was the African American group, the Nation
> of Islam, that by 1976 moved to Orthodox Islam. However, relationships
> between primarily migrant Muslim communities and this group are very
> minimal. Pakistanis and Arabs have struck alliances way back. They view
> themselves from historical lands and both came into this country as Mus-
> lims. They came from an experience in the Indian subcontinent with polit-
> ical activism from Islam in an early period. The Indo-Pakistanis have a
> very strong commitment to Palestine. The first item they tackled in the
> foundational principles in the Pakistani state was in support of Palestine.
> They came of age and the independence of Pakistan was intertwined at
> the core, intertwined to Palestine. When Pakistan obtained independence
> and Kashmir was cut out of Pakistan into India, that was compared imme-
> diately to the 1948 War and the cutting of Palestine. That alliance was
> already there. But I think one of the most powerful periods will emerge
> if the immigrant communities can strike a real alliance with the African

American Muslim community and the resources of the immigrants are wedded into the resources for the African Americans.

Hatem had been working among several Muslim American leaders in the Bay Area on multiracial alliance building. He was part of a political current that was articulating a racial-justice politics among Muslims and striving to strengthen relations between immigrant and African American Muslims. He argues that these groupings are connected through their shared relationship to neoliberal economic structures that target poor African Americans locally and people living in countries targeted by U.S. war globally.

In my class on Islam and America, I examine the external imperial to the internal imperial. We can comprehend what is occurring with U.S. policies in the external imperial, if we take a look at Oakland, California. African Americans are the subject of empire internally, and the political, social, economic, security structure that is set up on them is reflective of the external imperial. The development zone has been given to a developer that has no connection to the community. The developer gets a tax break and all kinds of incentives from the city. Police are protecting that one developer, pushing the bad drug dealers, prostitutes away, moving the poor and low class away. So you concentrate poverty and drug dealing, and crime. As a result, you need more security, so you hire more police and the military infrastructure is increased and those police are often hired from outside the community so they live in the rich suburbs of Walnut Creek and Lafayette where they take the resources of the city to the external community. They get to keep up with the lifestyle of Walnut Creek and Lafayette and do not have to be accountable to Oakland. You bring corporations and set them up in the downtown area in the development zone where they are not paying taxes because they have a tax break, their returns are for their investors.

Hatem contends that the external empire works in similar ways:

You add it and multiply it and this is what the external imperial looks like. This is instrumental in thinking local and acting global—drawing the paradigm locally and then taking it to the globe. An empire thinks and articulates its machinery in an internal structure before it is exported and used in other territories and other places.

Hatem, along with both immigrant and African American student and community leaders, spearheaded a political event at the University of

California–Berkeley in 2000. This event entailed a political rally and a conference and was based upon a similar analysis as Hatem's above that centered upon connections between racial and imperialist forms of oppression within and outside of the United States. Yet event organizers framed the imperial "external" and "internal" in a way that could foster coalition building between African American Muslims and immigrant Muslims living in the United States. The event centered upon their shared struggles with U.S.-state policies within the United States. Organizers decided to raise awareness about U.S.-state violence against African American Muslims and U.S.-state violence against Muslim immigrant communities living in the United States. Their understanding of the U.S. state was that it increasingly criminalized Muslim immigrants through a logic that associated them with potential enemies of the U.S. nation within the war on terror. Event organizers were equally outraged about this problem as well as the persistent criminalization of African Americans in general and African American Muslims specifically. Event organizers named the event *Ihsan* (the Muslim responsibility to obtain perfection or excellence) and explained that its purpose was to bring awareness to "the U.S. government's injustices against its citizens."

As the *Ihsan* event began, a young man stood in front of a table set up by the Muslim Student Association and explained, "The rally today is about . . . U.S. domestic policy . . . the case of Amadou Diallo and police brutality, Proposition 21, the antiterrorism bill, and the FBI's harassment of Iman Jamil Al-Amin."[28] Unlike conventional Bay Area racial justice discourses, this event centered on anti-Muslim racism, specifically attacks against Muslim migrants and African American Muslims, and framed Muslim activism within a coalitional, multiracial parameter that brought together different communities who were similarly outraged over their experiences with racial violence. It interpreted these problems as the unjust criminalization of youth and people of color. Amadou Bailo Diallo, a 23-year-old Guinean immigrant, was shot and killed in the Bronx, New York, in February 1999 by four plainclothes police officers who fired a total of forty-one rounds. He was unarmed. His killing inspired outrage and massive uprisings that centered on racial profiling, police brutality, and contagious shooting. California Proposition 21, which increased a variety of criminal penalties for crimes committed by youth and incorporated many youth offenders into the adult criminal justice system, passed in 2000 and similarly inspired massive uprisings. Among other provisions, it requires an adult trial for youth fourteen or older who are charged with murder or particular sex offenses.

The event also highlighted the case of African American Imam Jamil Al-Amin, who was arrested in connection with the shootings of two Atlanta sheriff's deputies. His case created great controversy since critics argued that the initial police reports suggested that he was innocent. Critics read the case as an example of the rise in national attacks against Muslims in the United States, particularly those with political activist histories. Imam Jamil Al-Amin was a member of the Black Panther Party and the Student Non-Violent Coordinating Committee (SNCC) before he converted to Islam and became an imam who worked as an antidrug activist.

The first speaker explained how race played a role in the murder of Diallo and how similar practices are being sanctioned by Proposition 21. He said, "If someone walks a certain way, dresses a certain way, they could be rendered a violent gang member. We're not just protesting the murder of Amadou Diallo, we're protesting laws that allow abuse and sanction harassment against citizens! And then there is the antiterrorism bill." In 1995, President Clinton passed the Omnibus Counterterrorism Act of 1995, which many human rights and immigrant rights leaders refer to as an unconstitutional attack on the Bill of Rights. It grants sweeping powers to the executive branch and grants law enforcement much broader wiretapping authority with less judicial oversight and access to personal and financial records without a warrant. Since a majority of persons targeted by this bill are Muslims, a major conflict is that authorities deploy this act as a form of racial profiling (Saalakhan 1999).

These speakers' arguments are part of a political current that took shape in the 1990s that theorized anti-Muslim violence or targeting through the framework of race and racism (Omi and Winant 1994). In the 1990s, a new body of scholarly literature contended that because anti-Muslim policies within the United States had a great deal to do with U.S. imperialism outside the United States, they reflected forms of racism that are transnational in scope. Asian Americans have faced similar transnational forms of racism at times when the United States has been at war with Japan or China, for instance. In the context of anti-Muslim racism, targets of racism are not always linked to a particular country or nation of origin, but are associated with the arbitrary, deterritorialized category of the new empire: the terrorist (Rana 2007). At the *Ihsan* event, activists argued that the new racism against Muslim immigrants was bleeding into anti-Black racism, particularly in cases involving earlier forms of anti-Black racism by U.S. law enforcement that was directed specifically at African American Muslims. In this overlap, they found possibilities for new multiracial immigrant and African American Muslim alliances.

The global, transnational Muslim consciousness that was articulated through these young adults' political activism related to Iraq can be located in the history of a general post–Gulf War consciousness that proliferated among Arab American and Muslim American young adults in the 1990s. In the 1990s, a new Arab American and Muslim American political conscious-ness was underway that responded to the intensification of U.S. militarism in the Arab and Muslim region with a sense that it is far more immediate to recognize that which unites us than that which separates us. In the Bay Area, the political organizing that took place contributed to the growth of this consciousness. The political organizing around the first Gulf War in the early 1990s was rooted in a transnational analysis that conceptualized impe-rialism as a political formation that had global and local implications and assumed that the global and local are interconnected, not mutually exclusive. For instance, interlocutors who were involved in Gulf War–related activism connected U.S. policy in Iraq to U.S. state violence against people of color in the United States. This analysis came forth within political work that con-nected Gulf War violence and police violence against Rodney King and the anti-immigration legislation of the 1990s.

* * *

This chapter has focused on young adults affiliated with the politics of Mus-lim First and a global Muslim consciousness. I have located Muslim First politics within the post-1980s context of the increased movement of people within and beyond the Arab and Muslim worlds and intensified migration of Muslims to the Bay Area. In addition, the expansion of U.S. empire in Muslim-majority countries, Islamophobia, and the rise of Muslim global political movements has shaped the articulation of Muslim First as a frame-work for organizing identity, community, and belonging. Among my inter-locutors, Muslim First works as a mechanism for challenging the gender and racial hierarchies underpinning their immigrant parents' concepts of cul-tural identity in ways that cannot be explained through conventional immi-gration studies frameworks that focus on apparent tensions between immi-grant traditions and second-generation assimilation. Muslim First restores a sense of rootedness in Arab and Muslim histories while it transcends what young adults perceive as the limitations of their immigrant parents' politics of Arab cultural authenticity. Muslim First provides my interlocutors with a framework for surviving various power struggles and envisioning a new world beyond the varied constraints they face. The limitations of Muslim First are beyond the scope of this chapter. Rather than evaluating whether or not Muslim social justice politics is progressive or conservative, oppres-sive or liberatory, "American" or "anti-American," I have taken interest in the conceptual frameworks through which my interlocutors understand the terms of debate, the way they approach the question of being Arab, Muslim, and American, and the multiple transnational discourses and historical circumstances they draw upon.

Indeed, Muslim First emerges through an interplay among global politics, U.S. racial politics, and local Bay Area progressive racial justice and antiwar politics. Concepts and practices of gender permeate each of these domains and generate a range of perspectives about gender in Muslim spaces. The stories I analyze open up new possibilities for thinking beyond popular assumptions that divide Muslim Americans into two seemingly separate groups: good Muslim citizens who participate in the American melting pot versus bad Muslims who are actively involved in homeland politics (Alsultany 2007; Mamdani 2005). Similar binary frameworks that distinguish between the politics of "immigrant Muslims" and "American Muslims," "Muslims focused on domestic issues" and "Muslims focused on international issues," cannot explain the politics of Muslim First (Khan 2000). Here, Muslim First, as a transnational political discourse, emerges not in nostalgic, or simply traditionalist terms, but in an open-ended conversation with a range of discourses of social justice among Muslims and non-Muslims that are local and global in scope. In this respect, I draw upon Anouar Majid's critique that leftist intellectuals cannot accept and are not willing to learn about Islam beyond culturalist/civilizational analyses (2000, 31-32) and the general Eurocentric assumption that Muslims have to be secular to believe in the virtues of social justice and the inviolability of human dignity (2, 7, 21, 41; Mandaville 2007). As we have seen, in some moments, the politics of Muslim First reifies essentialist concepts of religious or cultural identity. Yet in other moments, my interlocutors transcend the politics of Arab cultural authenticity, U.S. Orientalism, Islamophobia, and rigid self-representations of Islam. My interlocutors' concepts of culture, religion, family, gender, and sexuality are mediated through their engagements with and understandings of race, immigration, and imperialism.

4

Dirty Laundry

Aisha: When I graduated from college, I worked for Global Exchange, a soft-left human rights organization in San Francisco, but constantly bumped into limitations with the American liberal line on Palestine. They wanted to focus only on oversimplified human rights abuses but not about the colonial devastation in the Middle East and the larger political forces at hand. I didn't feel as if we were building the organization together. Someone was always discrediting my legitimacy. I felt a desperate desire to find people who felt the same way as me and wanted to create an alternative space where we didn't have to be constantly fighting alone.

That was when I met the activists from LAM [the Leftist Arab Movement]. Many of the women I met were like me—completely exhausted by their political work and needing a safe sanctuary. In most other organizing spaces, even those for queer women and feminists of color, our support of Palestinian rights created tensions and isolated us. We were asserting a politics that wasn't asserted in the larger movements we were part of. When you're vocal and active on Palestine, you are alienated from all of humanity. The political becomes intensely personal. In LAM, for the first time, I sensed that other people had my back politically—even if it didn't always play out like that. It was a romantic idea of a community of people who shared the same politics, came from the same background, and understood that crazy feeling that comes from questioning, "What is going on? My people are being murdered and no one cares?" The fact that they understood that . . . made them family.[1]

Aisha, twenty-two years old during the period of my research, is Egyptian but grew up both in Saudi Arabia and the United States. In the quoted passage, she details her involvement in the Leftist Arab Movement (LAM) in the late 1990s. The activists in LAM during this time period were primarily middle-class college students and graduates between the ages of eighteen and thirty, but represented a range of subject positions and histories of displacement within the United States. They were Iraqis, Egyptians, Palestinians, Jordanians, Lebanese; men, women, queers; Christians, Muslims, agnostics, and atheists; recent immigrants and exiles, and individuals born or raised predominantly in the United States; computer engineers, nonprofit workers, service workers, artists, and students. Although this diversity contributed to a varied and often contentious set of political visions, certain matters brought these activists together. LAM activists' ideas harmonized around a feeling of political urgency about U.S. global power—in terms of its military, economic, and cultural hegemony in the Arab world, particularly in Palestine and Iraq. LAM activists were outraged over the dominant U.S. government and media strategies and contended that they contribute to a general state of apathy in the United States over the massive loss of Arab lives and land caused by U.S.-led war. Through their political alliance, LAM activists developed two campaigns, one that entailed launching a "divest from Israel movement" in the United States modeled after the international movement opposing South African apartheid and another that aimed at ending U.S.-led sanctions on Iraq.[2] Through their involvement in LAM these activists rearticulated Arabness, replacing what we have seen as a politics of middle-class Arab cultural authenticity with a politics of diasporic anti-imperialism. Like Aisha, many LAM activists described LAM with words like "family," "home," and "belonging" precisely because it provided them with a collective domain for enacting political commitments that are deeply intertwined with their life histories, who they are as individuals, and their concepts of self and being in the world but are generally censored, misunderstood, and delegitimized in U.S. public space. Yet like any social movement or political alliance, LAM was internally fraught with tensions, contradictions, and power relations, which explains why Aisha later clarified that the sense of family she found in LAM was romantic, inconsistent, and even short-lived.

This chapter takes up these intra-communal tensions through the perspectives of six women activists who dedicated much of their lives to LAM at the turn of the twenty-first century. What brought them to LAM were multiple, irreducible experiences of displacement and their plural engagements with U.S. empire—all of which coalesced into a shared feeling of outrage and an urgent sense that they could not sit back and watch the destruction of the region of their homelands.[3] Over time, through their involvement in LAM, and their political alliance with other LAM activists, these women began articulating emergent feminist and queer anti-imperialist politics. I map these politics as an archive of a diasporic feminist and queer anti-imperialism even though at the time, these women did not formally articulate their critiques as a collective political vision or strategy.

Taken together, my interlocutors' stories provide us with a language and a framework for conceptualizing the way heteropatriarchy, co-constituted with multiple, interlocking power structures, such as immigration and class, contributes to the intra-communal tensions that often ensnare our movements. It is intra-communal hierarchies, such as those related to gender, that we often fear discussing in public because they might be used to reify the very Orientalist discourses that rely on notions of "Arab patriarchy" to justify imperial violence, war, and racism. As the work of these six women in LAM progressed, they increasingly raised critiques of heteropatriarchy in LAM with one another and with their LAM counterparts and, in the process, developed a distinctly feminist and queer approach to anti-imperialist Arab activism. Yet theories about whether and to what extent feminism is compatible with national liberation fall short in explaining what transpired in LAM. In fact, the political tensions and possibilities that these six women narrate must be conceptualized in terms of the collision of feminism, queer politics, and national liberation *and* a set of power dynamics that were distinct to the diasporic context of the Arab Bay Area. As we have seen, the Arab Bay Area can be thought of as an assemblage of people, history, and ideas that is constantly reshaped and redefined in the context of global flux and turmoil. These same complexities ensnared LAM, creating obstacles when it came to addressing intra-communal hierarchies in the movement. Hierarchies of gender and sexuality were enmeshed within a multitude of power relations, such as those of socioeconomic status, country of origin, immigration status, immigration histories, and histories of political activism, producing a collision of subjectivities, political visions, and strategies. The flux and fluidity that define Arab diasporas in the Bay Area produced a situation in which multiple lines of political alliance were constantly drawn and redrawn among LAM activists. While this group of women activists shared a critique of sexism and some of them also challenged the pressure for compulsory heterosexuality in LAM, they did not always cohere as a group with shared interests across the board as women or as feminists, and power struggles related to immigration, history of activism, country of origin, and class took place among them. Similarly, uneven power structures characterized relations among their male counterparts in LAM, producing dynamics in which the interests of LAM's men activists also cohered as much as they diverged. The multiple criss-crossing of alliances and interests among LAM activists allowed for an apathetic stance on sexism and homophobia to cohere in LAM. Women's critiques were often met with a sense that it was too difficult to determine whether and to what extent particular power struggles could be attributed to sexism or homophobia at all and whether they could in fact warrant a feminist or queer critique. These complexities became an obstacle to the possibilities for a feminist or queer critique to cohere and often diluted or delegitimized conversations about sexism and homophobia among LAM activists.

Besides the multiple subject positions that constituted LAM's internal membership, another set of diasporic conditions obstructed the possibilities for feminist and queer critique even further. First, the brutality of U.S.-led imperial violence that they were fighting from the distance of diaspora created a movement logic that privileged the region of Arab homelands over the diaspora, rendering any intra-communal diasporic matters such as heteropatriarchy in the movement secondary at best. Second, the position of Arabs in the United States in a post–Cold War context—as "diasporas of empire"—produced a sense of fear among LAM activists that airing problems related to heteropatriarchy in LAM would reinforce Orientalism and further justify anti-Arab/anti-Muslim violence.

In LAM, heteropatriarchy was shaped and reshaped within the dual contexts of empire and diaspora—and co-constituted with socioeconomic class; the transnational experiences of forced migration and displacement; and the collision of multiple histories and subjectivities in the diaspora. I read the stories of six women activists in LAM as an archive of feminist and queer critique that emerges within and beyond a diasporic national liberation framework, a critique that can account for the multiple entanglements of power that ensnare intra-communal politics among Arab diasporas and for the urgency of ending imperial violence and war. This chapter sets the stage for the following chapter, where I discuss distinct moments in LAM's work in which these same six women more explicitly brought diasporic feminist and queer visions to LAM's public audiences.

Methods

Between January 1998 and August 2000, I actively participated in LAM during a period of its revival, when a new group of activists who came together in 1998 revived an earlier incarnation of LAM that thrived in the 1970s, 1980s, and early 1990s but became dormant after the Oslo Peace Accords of 1993. In the late 1990s incarnation, six women activists came together around a shared critique of sexism and, for some, compulsory heterosexuality in LAM. This chapter focuses on their stories. I could have just as well centered a different critique, such as that of immigrants or refugees who argued that U.S.-born activists in LAM had leverage over others due to the exacerbated forms of racism newcomers encountered and their disadvantaged access to education and the English language. I decided to focus on these six women's stories because I took interest in how critiques of patriarchy and homophobia unfolded within a movement organized by and for diasporic subjects aimed at dismantling U.S. empire. These six women do not represent all the women active in LAM during this period, and there were indeed other women and men who disagreed with these six women's charge that LAM's dominant movement structure reinforced patriarchy and compulsory heterosexuality.

Four of these six women were actively involved in the feminist collective, the Arab Women's Solidarity Association, San Francisco Chapter, which worked closely with LAM during this period. This chapter draws on my involvement in LAM between 1998 and 2000 and on extensive, repeated interviews and participant observation with these six women between 1998 and 2010: Mai, Dahlia, Aisha, Camelia, Yara, and Raya. Our conversations centered upon the gender politics at play in the late 1990s. Early on, when still deeply immersed in the adrenaline rush of this period, we shared similar interpretations of the interactions between us and many of our counterparts who were men, and tended to rely on feminist narratives about the secondary position of women's concerns within national liberation or racial justice movements (Jayawardena 1986; Johnson and Kuttab 2001). Upon further and shared reflection, however, we came to similar conclusions that sexism and homophobia in the movement were entangled within a complex set of diasporic conditions that required us to think beyond a narrow analysis of heteropatriarchy within national liberation movements. The interviews provided us with the opportunity to reflect on our experiences and to develop a language for speaking about what we experienced. Each interview probed points of unity and tension, identification and disidentification among LAM activists that in some instances mapped onto stereotypical gender lines and in others did not. We were unpacking the forces at play that complicated a simplistic gender analysis. Our conversations illuminated the possibilities and foreclosures related to articulating a feminist critique in the context of a diasporic Arab anti-imperialist movement in the San Francisco Bay Area at the turn of the twenty-first century. Conducting the interviews over a twelve-year period offered us the opportunity to reexamine a past that we were not equipped to conceptualize through a collective feminist vision at the time. Over the years, we talked about what brought each woman to LAM, the connections LAM inspired for us, the tensions we faced, and why some of us left. Our conversations revealed the centrality of feminist and queer politics to our anti-imperialist political activism of the late 1990s.

In the beginning of the chapter, I present life story narratives of each woman. To compile these narratives, I relied upon the words of the women I interviewed, with light editorial modifications. I edited the interview material into a chronologically accessible format. I relied upon what I call "documenting activist stories" because I compiled a specific kind of "life story," a life story that I situate within broad transnational historical and political contexts. I also situate each woman's story in relationship to one another's, to the other activists with whom they worked, to the communities to whom they claimed to be accountable, and to general trends in Arab feminist discourse in the United States during this period. I composed these narratives with a focus on the aspects of their life stories that help us understand how they became political activists and what they desire, believe, and experience as activists. I thus present fragmented and partial stories rather than composite life histories.

To historically contextualize the women's stories in this chapter, I conducted additional interviews with seven activists: five men and two women who were actively involved in LAM's earlier period (between 1980 and the early 1990s). LAM's work during the late 1990s must be understood in continuity with an earlier period in LAM's history spanning the 1980s and the early 1990s. Yet, LAM's composition in the late '90s drastically differed from the earlier period. In the earlier period, LAM was comprised primarily of men and women who were Palestinian immigrants, refugees, and exiles. At the turn of the twenty-first century, LAM activists were primarily Palestinian men who were for the most part immigrants, refugees, and exiles and women who were from various Arab countries. All but one woman of this later period was either born or raised in the United States. These periods often bled into each other as three of the Palestinian men interviewed from the earlier period remained active in LAM during the period that is the focus of this chapter. Two of the Palestinian men from the earlier period remained loosely connected to LAM in the later period but were not actively involved. The two women I interviewed from the earlier period were born and raised in Palestine and shared their stories and analysis about how gender intersected with leftist Arab national liberation in the earlier period, before the diversification of LAM in terms of country of origin and increasing numbers of members being born or raised in the United States. These additional interviews, as well as unpublished community-based documents, allowed the coalescence of LAM's earlier histories contained here. These differences in the two periods and the ways they often mapped onto gender underscore the stories and interpretations that follow.

Biographies: Experience, Subjectivity, and Action

The following vignettes narrate plural histories that led Mai, Dahlia, Aisha, Camelia, Yara, and Raya to similar conclusions, analyses, and indignation about U.S. empire. Their stories illustrate how their different histories of displacement and engagements with U.S. empire and its discourses about the Middle East and their shared sense of political urgency and outrage about these issues form the bases of their affiliation and alliance with one another and with their counterparts in LAM.

Mai was a nineteen-year-old college student when we began our discussions. She was born into a Muslim family from Palestine, her parents having come to the United States in the 1970s, but Mai was born and raised primarily in the United States.

My father is from Abu Dis, just outside of Jerusalem. He came to San Francisco in 1970. He went home, married my mama in 1975, and returned to San Francisco with her. I started going to Palestine regularly when I was seven. In the third grade, I knew that the U.S. didn't go to war to oust Saddam, but for oil. Every Friday we went to an Arabic school. The leaders and founders were secular nationalists who got kids to do cultural programming [within nationalist dance troupes, for instance]. We learned songs and plays and *debkah*.[4] I grew up incredibly proud of my identity. At school, I participated in cultural programs and made it a point to discuss these issues at every turn. What made my life difficult, if not miserable, were my mama's rules demarcating what it meant to be an Arab versus an American. She created a conflict in my identity that made it so that I could not simultaneously embrace my culture and heritage while taking a lead role in school activities like government, theater, volunteer work, and sports. For those reasons I yearned to be in Palestine where I would not be presented with those conflicts and later I yearned to have an Arab social group outside my family because I never had one. When I was in high school, I couldn't wait to get to college to meet like-minded Arab friends. I always felt like I knew a reality that was not shared by my peers at school. There was no awareness outside of my immediate family and the Arabic school about Palestine. It made it difficult to be able to feel whole—unless I talked to other minorities I could relate to on issues like displacement, refugees, or marginalization. People around me didn't own up to the impunity of [the United States as a colonial power]. I felt disconnected. If I spoke about these things, I had to take several steps, build trust, before I felt they could hear me. I couldn't just say, "This shit is f——ed up." [Keeping things quiet] affects your identity. You are the repository and the messenger on this issue. I also didn't feel like I could be completely myself with my family.

During my freshman year at the University of California, Berkeley, in 1998, I was trying to do things on campus about the sanctions on Iraq. My cousin introduced me to the activists in LAM and it became a home, and not only politically. It was about feeling that I could relate to people outside my family and create a social network with them—especially the women. That was the best part of all of it. I always embraced my Arab and Palestinian identity and never felt a sense of loss or shame. I wasn't searching for a space where I could meet Arabs to feel safe. What I found in LAM was a political refuge, a place where I can be at once both radical and Arab because in the other radical spaces I was in, there were never any Arabs. Issues of homelessness, health care, affirmative action, or immigration all mattered to me, but none of them mattered as much as working on the Middle East. Palestine is at the center of LAM, and I didn't have to deal with a major controversy just because I was talking about Palestine. It was a safe space to grow and be active.

LAM was also a refuge from difficulties I faced within the Arab community. As a young, strong-willed, sharp-tongued, outspoken woman I did not fit neatly within my family. Unlike the other girls who were all courted multiple times over, I was told repeatedly that men came to see me but after witnessing me at a protest or learning of my late-night organizing [concluded] that I was "too much" or "too strong." Relatives often made me feel guilty for not being a caretaker of the family, calm, more rooted and less restless. They didn't chastise me but told me, for example, "rather than volunteer in the public sphere, you should spend more time with your grandparents at home to care for them." Today I continue to experience this although to a much, much lesser degree as I am constantly told to settle down, to sit still, to stop traveling, and in the worst cases those calls for me to be more home-bound are connected with a desire that I be well enough to have children.

Dahlia is Iraqi. She was born into a Shi'ite Muslim family and came to the United States in the 1990s during the first Gulf War. She was in her late twenties when we began our discussions.

My immediate family comes from Iraq and escaped to Kuwait after members of my father's family were deported from Iraq to the Iranian border. Two of my cousins were arrested and executed in 1982 and 1983. My mother, sister, and I returned to Iraq in the late 1980s, toward the end of the Iraq-Iran war; it was a remarkable risk since my father's name could have been on the *mukhabarat* [red list]. In 1990, my family and I came to the U.S. for two weeks to uphold the requirements of our green cards, obtained through relatives already in the U.S., just a few days before the Iraqi invasion of Kuwait. We arrived on August 2, 1990, and learned about it, and realized we would not be able to return.

The invasion, the sanctions, the Gulf War in 1991, the second *intifada,* the events of September 11 and its aftermath in Afghanistan, Iraq, Palestine, and Lebanon, were all experiences of violence that splintered my ability to belong in the U.S. and magnified my alienation. For our first seven months in the U.S., we lived the war in our living room, glued to the TV coverage that glorified the obliteration of my peoples and country. Once several neighbors came to my parents' house during the war (none of them had any contact with my parents before then, and they purposefully avoided my parents' greetings on the streets of the neighborhood). They asked to inspect our house. I remember the rage I felt as one of them audaciously made his way through the house, inspecting room by room as if we were hiding something in our bedrooms. I painfully watched the tall white man who supposedly was sent as a representative of the local church and neighborhood; he scavenged through our most sacred inner worlds. Every moment of my existence in the U.S. affirmed that I did not belong, that my brother and father (as constructed in the U.S.) could be enemies, violent, and criminal; that my sister, my mother, and I were seen as backward, oppressed, and silent; that my peoples were savages, uncivilized, and dispensable; that I did not belong and will never belong.

The streets in the Bay Area became the new "war zone," where other activists and myself utilized public spaces to demonstrate, educate, and organize; I could bear the occasional spitting, cursing, and assault since I was now actively engaging. But in most progressive organizations, my support for Palestine was a divisive issue. Organizations like San Francisco Women Against Rape (SF War) attempted to bring a critical perspective on Israel to their work.[5] In response, they were met with severe threats, attacks, and budget cuts, and were systematically marginalized and silenced. SF War became an example to any other organization that dared speak up against Israel.

In the mid- to late 1990s I worked on antisanction and antiwar campaigns with the International Action Center (IAC) against the war in Iraq.[6] I was drawn to the IAC because it was the only organization in the Bay Area that continued to engage assertively and publicly in antiwar and antisanction campaigns long after the first Gulf War began. Iraq continued to be sanctioned and bombed throughout the 1990s under the Clinton administration, though this fact did not receive the attention and outrage it deserved by most in the United States. The IAC, on the other hand, continued to be steadfast in its activism, tactics, and public activities, such as mass demonstrations. I was also attracted to working with the IAC because of its progressive and leftist internationalist political orientation and its mobilizing strategies. My active involvement and politicization with the IAC and other organizations in the Bay Area, as well as my own lived experiences, gave me access to exploring the links among class, race, indigenous people's struggles, and immigrant and third world struggles with U.S. imperialism and hegemony. It was a critical time since I was exposed to political and ideological analysis that resonated with my own lived experiences.

Yet at times within the antiwar and progressive movements, I felt that I was the token representative of a diverse Iraqi community. Since I was the only Iraqi organizing in a predominantly white leftist progressive space, I found the need to organize among other Iraqis, Arabs, and other West Asian/North Africans. I realized that I also needed to organize with others who also shared similar lived experiences as myself, including racism. After many years of experiencing institutional marginalization [as an Arab woman in white-leftist organizations], I also came to realize that there was a need to organize as an Arab community. It was a turning point for me and for Arab organizing in the Bay Area, as our efforts culminated in the creation of a grassroots movement [LAM] that addressed and dealt with our systematic institutional marginalization as well as united and empowered our community to work toward justice and self-determination.

In 1999, I returned to Iraq with my mother and two fellow Iraqis from the U.S. In collaboration with LAM SF, before the trip we organized an antisanction community event. We outreached to community members and were able to fundraise and elicit donations of toys, medical journals, and medicine. It was inspiring to witness the collective energy of our community. The trip and the community work were an attempt to create solidarity, to engender consciousness about the political situation, and to mobilize the resistance needed to fuel our dreams and the potential for a more just reality.

Aisha was in her early twenties when we began talking. She is Egyptian, born into a Muslim family. She grew up in the United States, Egypt, and Saudi Arabia.

My parents moved from Egypt to Chicago, where I was born in 1978. We moved to Saudi Arabia for my dad's job and lived there for seven years. We left because of the Gulf War and moved to upstate New York. I lived in Georgia for tenth and eleventh grades. Then the INS denied my dad permanent legal residency, so we moved back to Egypt. I was there for my last years of high school. I went to Santa Cruz, California, for college. I learned about Palestine in Saudi from my best friend, who was Palestinian. Our American teacher in Saudi told her that there is no such thing as Palestine. My friend was in so much pain. As part of my community studies major, I went to Palestine with a friend in 1998 to give something back to my people. It shook my life. I came back with so much anger and rage, and I channeled it into campus activism. My friend and I brought speakers to campus, and had film, art nights, and spoken-word nights related to Palestine. When I graduated, I started working with a soft-left human rights organization in San Francisco but constantly bumped into limitations with the American liberal line on Palestine. My labor doubled and tripled there because I had to spend so much time explaining Palestine to people. There was always someone cornering me to give a ten-minute sound bite of education on the issue, or I had to explain why I didn't agree with someone's politics. I was the spokesperson. This created a belonging issue where I didn't feel at home anywhere. In LAM, there was a romantic idea of a community of people who shared the same politics, came from the same background, and understood what you were feeling—that crazy feeling that comes from questioning, "What is going on? My people are being murdered and no one cares?" The fact that they understood that made them family.

Raya is Palestinian. She was in her late twenties when we began talking. She was born in the United States to an Antiochian Orthodox Christian family.

My mom is from Ramallah and my dad is a refugee from Lydda. My mom came to San Francisco in 1952 and my dad came later. I grew up in Beaumont, Texas. My mom went to SF City College. My dad was illiterate. He dropped out of school in the third grade and was working as a child to help his family survive. There were deep class tensions when I grew up. I grew up living and working with Blacks in the South in Kentucky thirty minutes away from the KKK's main headquarters. We made our living from a male clothing store called the Soul Dude Shop. I was a saleslady at age five. There was a lot of injustice around—a lot of good relations with Black folks and a lot of treating Blacks as undesirable. I was so hurt watching it play out—especially when we talked in Arabic about the customers after they left. There were three racial groups there—whites, Blacks, and Mexicans. We never had Arab friends and didn't mingle with other people either because my parents worried about the influence of American people on us. We had relatives from a refugee camp in Jordan move in with us for a while—nine of them. My parents divorced and I moved to SF with my brother, sisters, and mom in 1984 and connected with the Ramallah club. We relocated to Oakland, California, where our new men's clothing store was. We were supposed to go to school according to where we were living, to a primarily Black high school, but my mom heard about a shooting there so she freaked out. She rented a house in Piedmont so we could go to the Piedmont school—a fancy school that was mostly white and Jewish. I joined a sorority and it further confirmed that I didn't fit into their box or their worlds. We didn't act like them or dress like them. After high school, I traveled overseas by myself, for the first time. I traveled to different parts of Europe, Gambia, West Africa, and Palestine, gaining more awareness of myself as a young woman, my ethnic identity, and the global world we live in. Then I returned to the Bay Area and went to SF City College. I met Arab activists there, immigrant men who were organizing protests. It affected me to learn that there is all this horrible stuff going on in Palestine and no one knows about it here. It put a spark in me. My parents talked about Palestine but never explained it to us clearly. There were no real conversations because they were always busy with work or because it was too painful to share these sad stories where many Palestinians feel like they shouldn't have left their massacred towns and villages or that we weren't strong enough to defend ourselves. People who felt that way didn't know how this was a story about us that came from the Zionists with the help of many others, especially Britain and Germany.

I went to Palestine in 1990. When I left the airport in London, I was heavily interrogated for two hours by three different groups of security people and the head security person was working really hard to break me down. When I arrived in Tel Aviv, I was strip-searched. I was in the West Bank for six days and four of them were under curfew. The tanks would come and tell everyone to go inside and I would say, "I'm going out! I'm an American!" My aunt would say, "You can't! No one cares if you're American!" I felt like we were in prison. People lived in locked-up homes. My aunt would sneak me out the back door to run to the neighbor's house just to see other people. It was the first time I got to experience my family's origins and roots, in real time on the ground with their horrible realities. I came back with a lot of questions and then all the dots started to connect—about why my mom told me to say we were white during the Iran-Contra scandal, about why my mom never told us much about Palestine, about why I felt shame for being Palestinian in the U.S. I came back from Palestine when the Gulf War started. It then hit me—Iraq is an Arab country and it's connected to Palestine and the U.S. is supporting this, spear-heading another occupation!

I was working at my cousin's deli in Berkeley and started reading the progressive papers and figured out that there's something wrong, but this information [of the strategic relationship between the United States and Israel] is kept secret. I went to more events—including a Palestinian women's event at San Francisco State University. I still have the poetry by Fadwa Touqan they handed out. Then I got involved with an Arab women's collective in the mid-1990s. I started understanding why I felt so alienated in the U.S., why my mom would tell us no one likes us, that the U.S. doesn't like Palestine; why people have no reaction or an unpleasant reaction when I say I'm Palestinian; why my fitness trainer stopped talking to me once I said I was Palestinian; why people have assumptions about how Palestinian women are treated. I realized that we can't defend our Palestinianness if there aren't organized spaces that can provide the tools we need.

When I joined LAM, there was a familiarity, being around other Arabs who are leftists and activists. Everyone understood each other. We could be ourselves. We had a commitment to Palestine. I felt closer to the women, even though we also had dysfunctional dynamics. It wasn't always

clear what we were trying to accomplish exactly, but we wanted social justice in Palestine and for Iraq. We wanted visibility in the Bay Area and the
U.S.—visibility for the invisibles and connecting with other larger activist
communities and movements.

*Yara is Lebanese. She came to the United States with her family when she was
eleven. She was in her midtwenties when we began talking. She was born into a
Maronite and Greek Orthodox family.*

During my time at the university when I spoke, people were in shock, as if
they had never heard an Arab woman speak before—as if it was something
they could never imagine or conceptualize. When no one else identifies
with what you're saying and you don't have a support system, then you're
going to start to question your views. When you're always forced to challenge stereotypes or respond to someone's critique, your issues get watered
down. When I was younger, this made me feel silenced, less valid, but I
didn't understand the depth of the politics.

I took a women-of-color feminism class and then everything started
making more sense. I was finally able to use a language—it wasn't my own
language—to advocate for myself. I decided that everything I did was going
to go back to the Arab community. Only when I moved to San Francisco
did I find a broader Arab community to work with through LAM. LAM
was so important to me because, finally, I was able to apply all the things
that I knew without having to react to other people's worlds. Even if someone didn't have the same experiences, I didn't have to explain where I was
coming from. I also worked with mainstream human rights groups during
that time. There, I had to constantly assert myself as an Arab woman. A
progressive person might feel comfortable saying that the Zapatistas are
doing amazing work, but they have a much more difficult time saying the
same about Arab liberation movements.

*Camelia is Egyptian. She was born into a Coptic Christian family. She was in
her late twenties when we began talking.*

I was born in Canada and we moved to the U.S. when I was seven. I grew
up going to Egypt all the time. I became aware at a young age about things
you don't see in the U.S. I learned about Iraq from my aunt, who was
an activist against sanctions on Iraq and in the movement against using
depleted uranium in Iraq. Palestine was always there—my family talked
about it, and about the 1967 war, when everyone was getting drafted in

Egypt; it was part of the reason my father left Egypt. But I didn't know much about the intricacies of it. In high school in Los Angeles in the 1980s, there was a lot of Central American activism around. I went to my first march around the federal building calling for the U.S. to get out of El Salvador. In college, I was active around the Rodney King beating. I marched. We closed down the bridge between San Francisco and Oakland. I went to some meetings on racial justice and immigrant rights and I got my feet wet with an Arab students' movement on Palestine.[7]

In college, I volunteered with homeless women at a daytime shelter and worked with special education youth. I started working in an empowerment and education program in public schools within a middle school in Berkeley. It gave me a different perspective on what youth are going through. I got more involved with issues in El Salvador. The first political movement I worked with was the FMLN's youth organization chapter in San Francisco.[8] I did my thesis on public health and underserved communities based on the women-of-color movement's work on AIDS. When I finished college in 1995, I went to Cuba, which was a big part of my political development. I went there again in 1997 to a youth festival and met Palestinian students, people from West Sahara, and all over the world. I came back and was doing health education and street outreach work at a community clinic in Oakland and started working at a housing development organization in the Mission District in San Francisco. From 1997 to 2001, when my daughter was born, I lived and breathed the struggles in the Mission and Oakland, and the antigentrification movement, and I went to Cuba with the Venceremos Brigade. It was during that time that I joined LAM.

I've always felt alienated in the U.S. It started in kindergarten when I was completely shut out, and then in grammar school, and it continued. I was seen as weird and different and so were my parents all through my schooling. I always felt I wasn't white and whatever it meant. My thoughts were always different than white people's, than my teachers', about political issues, about what was going on in the world. My mom heard from other white moms that a sorority is a good thing for a girl to go to. I went to one in college and it was the worst thing ever. Most were Republicans. That was when all kinds of events took place—Rodney King, the Iraq war. I was fighting all the time and angry with people all the time. That was when my class, race, and political consciousness woke up—especially because I had all these white privileged people around me.

I found a home in LAM on a political level around my beliefs about Palestine and the history of U.S. colonialism and domination, and what social justice could look like in those places. It was where I did not have to explain my convictions and my beliefs all the time. It was a place to work on justice in Palestine, Egypt, Iraq. . . . It was the only place where I could do that. It sat right with my vision that justice means self-determination, freedom from violence, war, and colonial domination, freedom to be able to provide for yourself and eat, and live without the constant threat of out- side intervention that is bombing people to smithereens. As an organiza- tion it felt like a relief and a home. With the women, it felt like a home, that feeling of us being together and totally feeling each other. It was amazing. But I didn't find home on a soul level; there was so much of me that wasn't understood there. My identity is much more complex than just an Arab identity. I also identify with being African and being a person of color in the U.S. The cornerstone of LAM was a strong Arab nationalism.

The stories above help explain some of the factors that brought Mai, Dahlia, Aisha, Raya, Yara, and Camelia to the United States, to a shared sense of outrage about U.S. global politics, and, ultimately, to a leftist anti-impe- rialist Arab movement. Their sense of self and being in the world was intri- cately wrapped up in the interconnected conditions of empire and diaspora. Indeed, each narrative contains common themes that scholars of diaspora studies have theorized: distinct moments of becoming scattered from a par- ticular place or multiple places, such as Palestine, Iraq, Egypt, Kuwait, Leba- non; an emotive connection to people living "over there," including family, friends, and people from similar ethno-national or geographic places facing occupation and war; and a range of moments in which it becomes necessary to challenge the structures that shape their lives "over here," in the United States. By theorizing diaspora as a state of consciousness that comes with living "here" and "there" simultaneously, diaspora studies calls for a rethink- ing of narratives of assimilation and a challenging of binaries between tradi- tion (the "third world"/over there) and modernity (America/Americaniza- tion/over here). Further, diasporic subjectivities are complicated by their engagements with various manifestations of U.S. expansion and militarism and push us to think beyond theorizations of diaspora as "making it between multiple worlds" (Manalansan 2003, 3, 150) or "mediat[ing], in a lived ten- sion, the experience of separation and entanglement, of living here and remembering/desiring another place" (Clifford 1997). Yet their stories reveal a distinct diasporic subjectivity in which these women, in different ways and to different extents, became recipients of U.S. policy "over there" while they were living "over here," which I theorize as a sense of belonging to a "dias- pora of empire." Each story describes a different experience of how their concepts of self and their political work became inextricably wrapped up in events and discourses that were shaped within the logics of U.S. imperialism taking place on the world stage.

For Mai, Dahlia, Camelia, and Raya a sense of belonging to a diaspora of empire shaped their conceptualizations about the U.S. state and dominant U.S. discourses, such as the moments in which their understanding of U.S. involvement in Palestine and Iraq disrupted the possibility of feeling a sense of affiliation with America. Alternately, "America" was the nation at war with their homelands. In most of their stories, an understanding of the perceptions of themselves by others in the United States shaped a shared sense that dominant U.S. discourses associated them with people perceived to be potential "enemies of the nation." For Camelia, Raya, and Dahlia, their earlier exposure to the Palestinian struggle in their extended families initially propelled their engagement with activism. Such transnational connections to the Arab world, coupled with household satellite TV and their access to alternative media from and about the Middle East, regularly exposed them to stories from the ground—of war, violence, militarism, occupation, and death—in the region of their homelands. Out of these transnational connections, affiliations, and understandings, Aisha, Dahlia, Mai, Yara, and Raya recalled feeling a sense of alienation during their formative years. Thus, attending college, joining people with shared views, and traveling to Palestine constituted watershed experiences for many of them. Raya's trip to Palestine, a visceral experience of the occupation with her own eyes and via the loss of bodily integrity through being strip-searched, illustrates the immense influence travel to her parents' country of origin had on her sense of self, as well as her sense of being and belonging in the world. It helped crystallize her understanding of why she felt at being Palestinian in the United States. Her trip to Palestine constituted what James Clifford theorizes as a diasporic "connection (elsewhere) that made a difference (here)" (1997, 269). Her story also depicts the historically specific and subjective conditions that emerge among diasporas residing in a nation (the United States) at war with their homelands. These six women experienced their lives between the Bay Area and other places—through travel, transnational relationships, and political affiliations—in a situation of living "home away from home" or "here and there" (Gilroy 1993), criss-crossing regional and national borders (Shohat 2001, 2006), or "dwelling here with solidarity and connection there" (Clifford 1997, 255).

While the devastation caused by the war on Iraq and the colonization of Palestine fueled a sense of political urgency among each of them, the looming presence of U.S. empire in their own lives in the United States was a compounding force of outrage and frustration. Mai, Raya, and Camelia shared stories about the dominant U.S. discourse about the Middle East they encountered on the TV screen, or via their teachers and peers, as a discourse of U.S. empire, or a discourse that supports and legitimizes the imperialist interests of the U.S. state and operates to garner support for U.S. imperial interventions. As young adults, their attempts to articulate Arabness entailed a negotiation with dominant U.S. discourses and totalizing debates about their communities. Perhaps most importantly, they realized that in order to be able to articulate Arabness, they would need to grapple with the ways in which Arabness is conceived within the United States in dominant Arab and U.S. discourses. Mai shared stories about tensions between her political beliefs and those of others from the Arab families she grew up with. Aisha, Raya, and Mai shared feelings of alienation and frustration over the way their Arabness was viewed in U.S. public spaces. Both Yara and Camelia described having to constantly explain their positions on Palestine while they were active in political organizations across the Bay Area. Dahlia recalled a neighbor seeing her family as potential terrorists. Yara explained the sense of people's shock and curiosity when she spoke—as if they had never before heard an Arab women speak—as an experience of being seen and heard primarily through dominant U.S. Orientalist discourses about Arab women.

Their stories as a collection illustrate shared engagements and analyses of a three-fold rhetorical strategy that is proliferated by the U.S. corporate media, U.S. government discourse, and the discourses of many U.S. residents. This strategy figures the Arabs and Muslims through gendered Orientalist discourses; silences Palestinian narratives or informed critique of the Israeli state; and hides from public view the material consequences of U.S.-led militarism and war in the Arab region. Their critique is explicit in the ways several women reflected upon dominant U.S. discourses that reduce the complex political struggles of Israel and the Palestinians to a reductive binary: Israeli self-defense and Palestinian violence and terrorism. For Raya, Yara, Carmelia, Mai, and Dahlia, the drive behind their political commitments stemmed from their analysis that dominant U.S. discourse excludes Arab and Palestinian narratives from U.S. public debates and obscures the human realities and costs of U.S.-led war.

Dahlia's narrative reveals the frustrations she encountered due to these "blocking strategies" (Said 1981, 39) when she referred to the organization SF War, an organization that received public funding and found itself in the midst of a contentious battle with pro-Israeli activists, the state of California, and the city of San Francisco after referring to Israel as a colonialist and racist state. Her narrative references the kind of events that inspire interlocutors' shared analysis regarding the difficulty in voicing critiques of Israel in the United States. A shared understanding coalesces among these women that pro-Israeli political currents and pro-Israeli government discourses and policies in the United States have established a deeply silencing discursive strategy pervading U.S. public debate about Palestine and Israel: the conflation of criticism of the Israeli state with antisemitism that operates to discredit criticism of the Israeli state. They, along with their counterparts in LAM, brought their disapproval of this conflation into public view, arguing that their critique focused on the Israeli nation-state rather than the Jewish people; thus, it did not constitute antisemitism. LAM's critiques must be understood within the context of long-standing critques developed by a range of scholars and activists. These scholars argue that the deliberate conflation of criticism against Isreal with hatred of Jewish people is a strategy used to stigmatize any substantive critique of the Israeli state and its treatment of Palestinians.[9]

The consequences of this silencing strategy are profound. In particular, those who assert a Palestinian or Arab perspective on Palestine-Israel, especially Arabs and Palestinians, become open to a disturbingly racialized rhetoric about Palestinian or Arab violence or the charge of antisemitism. Aisha and Yara both analyzed a dominant trend among less radical progressive political organizations—that Aisha calls "soft-leftist"—who became hesitant to work with them out of fear that they too might be seen as antisemitic. Aisha remembered her employment in a human rights organization in which her critique of Israeli occupation was delegitimized, inspiring her critique of "the American liberal line on Palestine." The American liberal line on Palestine, in Aisha's view, remains silent on the Israeli occupation of Palestine, rendering critiques of Israel too politically charged to engage. This made it difficult for them to speak about Palestine without getting drawn into contentious, difficult debates or leading other activists to avoid identification with them. One theme woven throughout many of their narratives is a yearning for a space not only where their viewpoints would be heard and considered but also where self-proclaimed progressives, radicals, or leftists would stand up against injustices in Palestine in ways that were consistent with their stances on other social justice issues.

In the stories these women told to me, relationships to the Arab world and their understanding of empire and its discourses intersect with another profoundly meaningful set of relationships: those built with U.S. people of color, women of color, immigrant rights activists, and antiwar activists. In particular, Camelia's, Yara's, and Dahlia's activism was mediated by their exposure to the struggles and histories of oppression of other immigrant and people of color communities—Salvadorians, women of color, Rodney King, and Latino immigrants. Raya's race and class consciousness came out of both her work-ing-class sensibility and her family's potentially exploitative relationship to their African American customers. Camelia, Yara, Aisha, and Dahlia became politicized through a spectrum of interconnected movements—racial justice, immigrant rights, antiwar, feminist, and queer. Mai, a freshman in college at the time, worked closely with Latino student movements. Yet, despite the connections they developed within these movements, a sense of disconnec-tion tended to remain. Dahlia worked with the International Action Center (IAC), an organization committed to ending U.S. imperialism in the Middle East, yet she felt tokenized as the only Iraqi in the group and felt a need to organize with people who could more deeply understand the problem of anti-Arab racism. While her peers in IAC shared her outrage over the war in Iraq, they did not share her understanding of anti-Arab racism, which came out of her lived experiences. The lack of a firm stance supporting Palestin-ian rights in the human rights organizations where they worked prevented Yara and Aisha from fully identifying with these organizations. Perhaps worse, few of my interlocutors encountered substantive commitment to or understanding of Palestine and Iraq in the activist movements of other peo-ple of color, immigrant rights, and racial justice movements in which they worked. Camelia, for instance, traveled to Cuba through her involvement in anti-imperialist people of color–based politics. The centrality of Cuba within anti-imperialist movements of the Bay Area is rooted in a particular history of third world liberation politics in the United States generally and the Bay Area specifically. As anti-imperialist movements in the third world radicalized leftist anti-imperialist politics in the United States in the 1960s and 1970s, Cuba became central to a particular Marxist trend among the U.S. Left, resulting in the creation of organizations such as the Venceremos Bri-gade, in which young activists of color traveled to Cuba for the opportunity to "interact with Cuban communists" and participate in "political education programs" centered around "socialism and Marxism" (Elbaum 2002, 85). Camelia's grounding in Bay Area leftist people of color and anti-imperialist politics led her not to Palestine but to Cuba and participation in the Vencer-emos Brigade, "which served as the main bridge leading from vague radical-ism or nationalism to Marxism for many activists of color" (ibid., 85).

Clearly, Mai's, Dahlia's, Camelia's, Raya's, Yara's, and Aisha's stories cannot be understood through Orientalist frameworks that explain Arab women's lives through abstract concepts of "culture" or "religion." Moreover, liberal multicultural frameworks that reduce nuanced histories and experiences to coherent categories such as "Arab identity" or "Arab American women's identity" fall short. As we have seen, there is no unified or singular identity

that ties these stories together. Rather, it was the "multiplicity of reterritori-
alization" and what happened when their distinct experiences coalesced that
inspired their solidarity and alliance with one another and with their counterparts in the leftist Arab movement. In this sense, their alliance must be
thought of beyond identitarian politics. Perhaps "it is 'the communication of
singularities' that must be the new thought of solidarity where the 'singular
emergence' of struggles creates alliances through 'the intensity that characterizes them one by one'" (Puar and Rai 2004, 88, quoting Hardt and Negri
2001, 58).[10]

Between local engagements with the discourses of empire, Bay Area progressive politics, and global engagements with the Arab world that illuminated the realities of war and occupation, these women activists narrated
themselves in terms of what Gilroy calls a "duality of consciousness," or
decentered attachments (1993). Their political consciousness was constituted
by a sense of disconnection between their understanding of U.S. politics
and the dominant U.S. discourses of their political milieu. A similar discord
emerges via the narratives in which they sought to make sense of the world
and the limits on the possibilities for those same narratives to be legitimized
in U.S. public space. For Dahlia, Aisha, Mai, Raya, Yara, and Camelia, their
understanding of U.S. imperialism in the Arab world and elsewhere politicized them and inspired a desire for new forms of collectivity and action.
They wanted the opportunity to tell their stories, to expand the possibilities
for telling them in the United States, and to participate in collective actions
and coalitions that take Palestine and Iraq seriously. They sought to find others who shared their vision of bringing counternarratives on Palestine and
Iraq to U.S. public spaces from behind the shadows. These desires coalesced
in the late 1990s when they found LAM and each other. LAM provided a
space for becoming actively involved in two campaigns aimed at dismantling
U.S.-led militarism and war in Palestine and Iraq and a space where they
would no longer have to explain or justify their outrage.

Finding Home: LAM's Revival in a New Moment of Empire

In the late 1990s, Mai, Dahlia, Aisha, Camelia, Raya, and Yara began working
among a group of like-minded Arab activists in LAM. While they came to
LAM through different means and at different times in their lives, the LAM
activists with whom they worked had a similar analysis about Iraq and Palestine, as well as a critique of the contribution that dominant U.S. discourses
on Palestine, Israel, and Iraq made in creating support for U.S. policy in Palestine and Iraq in the United States. What this movement stood for in the

late 1990s both drew upon and departed from a previous period in which LAM thrived in the Bay Area between the 1970s and the early 1990s. In the earlier period, LAM focused primarily on Palestinian national liberation and was primarily composed of Palestinian immigrants, exiles, and refugees. During this time period the Bay Area was a hotbed for revolutionary activity, which allowed LAM to develop relationships with a wide array of Bay Area–based Third World liberation organizations. Such movements demanded liberation from colonial and imperial powers that threatened to destroy the heritage, identity, self-sufficiency, and well-being of its colonized populations in places such as the Arab region, China, North Vietnam, Ghana, and Cuba (Chang and Chung 1998). The U.S. antiwar movement related to the Vietnam War engendered an environment that supported leftist anti-imperialist politics among students, youth, G.I.'s, veterans, and communities of color, among others. In the Bay Area, LAM emerged in continuity with the varying leftist movements of the Arab world and internationally, most of which have united around Palestinian liberation.[11] Within this combination of political mobilizations, left-leaning Arab activists developed leftist national liberation movements in the United States. In its earlier and later iteration in the Bay Area, LAM has theorized the Israeli state through the ideological and political framework of settler-colonialism, a framework that has similarly informed the work of social justice–based scholars, Palestinian, Jewish, and beyond. The framework of settler-colonialism classifies the Zionist movement, the movement that founded the state of Israel, as a settler colonial project and the Israeli state as its manifestation. This classification is not merely a critique of the historical origins of Israel but an analysis of "Zionism's structural continuities and the ideology which informs Israeli policies and practices in Palestine and toward Palestinians everywhere" (Jadaliyya 2011). In this analysis, in Israel, "like other settler colonial projects such as the British colonization of Ireland or European settlement of North America, South Africa, or Australia, the imperative is to control the land and its resources—and to displace the original inhabitants" (Jadaliyya 2011). LAM's work has thus contended with the exclusionary nature of the Israeli state as a state for Jews only that denies a majority of Palestinians access to their land; the creation of the Palestinian refugee problem and continued Israeli expansion and displacement of Palestinians (Morris 2004);[12] the denial of Palestinians living within Israel of equal rights and access to land and resources; and the harsh Israeli military rule forced upon disenfranchised Palestinians of the West Bank and Gaza since 1967.[13]

In the Bay Area, the 1967 Arab-Israeli War that led to Israeli occupation of the West Bank and Gaza and consolidated the United States' alliance with

Israel spurred LAM activists to call for an end to U.S. support for the intensification of Israeli encroachment into the West Bank and Gaza and the increasing human rights violations against Palestinians in the aftermath of 1967. The stalemate in any attempt for an equitable solution to the Palestinian struggle also spurred LAM's analysis that U.S. support for Israel is an extension of U.S. imperialism in the Arab region.[14] By the 1980s, LAM established coalitions with Bay Area progressives and anti-interventionist movements and envisioned building a movement similar to the Vietnam-era antiwar movement.[15] Concurrently in the 1980s and early '90s, a feminist collective within LAM addressed matters of sexism within the group and connected with other feminists in the United States. In 1981, a group of women founded the General Union of Palestinian Women's Associations (GUPWA), an umbrella for the diverse Palestinian women's associations in the United States working in the context of the broader Palestinian movement. In Palestine, the first *intifada*, lasting from 1987 to 1991, was a spontaneous, primarily grassroots movement that involved the majority of Palestinian civil society. The Palestine Liberation Organization and various primarily left-leaning organizations within it led this uprising. This was the period in which the left-leaning Palestinian liberation movement peaked in Palestine and its diaspora. This period also entailed a cultural revival in Palestine—of music, dance, and theater—all of which trickled down to the Bay Area. Cultural revival was seen as crucial to challenging the Zionist narrative and providing unifying symbols of collective Palestinian national identity. The 1993 Oslo Accords, however, extinguished the feeling of urgency surrounding this political work, and Bay Area activists of this time period argue that the Oslo Accords crushed the Palestinian movement in Palestine, eventually leading to a similar diminution in the United States and the Bay Area. Following Oslo, disillusionment led many Bay Area activists to focus on other matters, such as daily survival, for the economic and social networks the movement provided to them and their families collapsed. Similar to what transpired on a global scale with Palestinian liberation and Palestine solidarity movements, LAM became dormant in the Bay Area in the years after Oslo in the mid-1990s.

LAM's revitalization in the late 1990s came as a response to a worsening series of changes taking place in Palestine, as well as increasing U.S. warfare in Iraq. In the United States, U.S. interventions in Palestine-Israel and Iraq generated highly charged political debates. LAM activists' perspectives contested much of the standard U.S. discourse prevalent in the corporate media and supported by the state. LAM activists of the 1990s shared a concern over the doubling of the Israeli settler population of occupied Palestine between the signing of the first Oslo Peace Accord in 1993 and 1999 (Farsoun and

Aruri 2006, 292), a reflection of policies through which Israel gained control over 78 percent of Palestinian land (Johnson and Kuttab 2001). Ominously, new Israeli policies divided Palestinian territory into noncontiguous areas and increased physical separation through the establishment of checkpoints, road closures, and Israeli-only bypass roads. These measures, in addition to the expansion of Israel's border control and military occupation in the mid-1990s, challenged Palestinian political leadership as the territories lost physical and political sovereignty at the same time that U.S. mediators adopted less ambitious objectives for peace.[16] Activists analyzed these conditions as the catalyst of the second *intifada* in Palestine. The dominant U.S. and Israeli narratives of these issues was paltry at best, and most often sadly distorted the portrayal of the United States' role in the crisis—in these situations, LAM activists felt a deep dissonance not only with U.S. actions but also with U.S. narratives.

Reframing LAM's historical analysis in light of these new conditions, LAM launched a divestment campaign in the Bay Area in 2000 as a strategy for demanding justice for Palestinians from the location of the United States. The divestment campaign developed in continuity with similar efforts worldwide that relied on divestment from Israel as an awareness-building strategy aimed at creating an environment that is historically aware of Israeli injustices. LAM's divestment campaign demanded that businesses

Demonstration against the sanctions on Iraq.

and institutions pull their funds out of Israeli private and public investments until these demands were met: (1) the recognition and implementation of the right of return for Palestinian refugees; (2) the decolonization of land occupied after 1967 of Jewish-only settlement colonies; (3) the end of the Israeli military occupation of the Gaza Strip and the West Bank, including East Jerusalem; and (4) an end to the Israeli system of apartheid and discrimination against the indigenous Palestinian population within Israel, in the 1967 territories, and in exile. During the same time period, LAM activists were outraged over U.S.-led sanctions on Iraq and the ongoing U.S. bombing of Iraq in the 1990s. This led LAM activists to launch an end-the-sanctions-on-Iraq campaign, also in 2000, as we will see.[17] Working around the clock for several years, LAM activists inserted these campaigns into Bay Area progressive politics, into social movements of all sorts, campuses, and alternative media outlets. Their work was taking on a life of its own.

Since the late 1990s, nearly every LAM activist I spoke with shared the sense that their involvement in LAM represented the most momentous period in their life. Reflecting on the late '90s in 2009 and 2010, activists remember this period as one that "institutionalized a new Arab discourse" and "moved the streets." Even a decade after this period, LAM activists felt that it continues to have a profound impact on Bay Area progressive politics. Experiencing this period together, with all of its intensity and with little sleep, contributed to the profound sense of connection and alliance these activists shared with one another.

Externally Focused Anti-Imperialist Feminism

In the late 1990s and at the turn of the twenty-first century, during my closest period of affiliation with LAM, activists agreed that dominant U.S. discourses were crucial in garnering support for U.S. policy in Iraq and Palestine and creating a generalized sense of apathy in the United States regarding the impact of U.S. policy on Arab land and life. As part of their Iraq and Palestine campaigns, LAM activists dedicated a great deal of their effort to replacing dominant U.S. discourses with Arab counternarratives or bringing Arab narratives to U.S. publics, to different institutions, across all sectors of society in order to shift the consensus and, thereby, to shift the balance of powers.[18] They understood the process of articulating Arab counternarratives as a crucial strategy, particularly since the group was active in the United States, where the empire-sustaining discourses circulated. Paul Gilroy's concept of the "countercultures of modernity" helps describe the political strategy of counternarrative as used by LAM activists during this time period, to counter the material conditions of war and occupation (1993). LAM's counternarratives sought to recover effaced stories shaped within "hybrid historical conjunctures" (Gilroy 1993, 16)—specifically grounded in anticolonial Arab histories and new conditions of the diaspora. And while part of this counternarrative vision included a feminist critique generally supported by all in LAM, this critique was limited to an externally focused anti-imperialist feminism. Virtually no obstacles existed in bringing this externally focused anti-imperialist feminist critique to the center of LAM's work, since it converged with LAM's dominant anti-imperialist framework. As a result, an externally focused anti-imperialist feminism, while not always the primary analysis underscoring LAM's official movement discourse, became the privileged form of feminist critique within LAM. Indeed, several women activists were the most vocal in articulating this externally focused anti-imperialist feminism, and when they expressed it, they met little resistance from their counterparts in LAM. Three arguments underscore the anti-imperialist feminism that coalesced with LAM's dominant movement discourse. First, LAM's official movement discourse contended that U.S. and Israeli state violence is gendered and sexualized, and LAM activists often highlighted the way U.S. and Israeli state violence relies on sexist and sexualized violence in their public discourse.[19] Second, LAM's official movement discourse assumed that women and children are disproportionately impacted by imperial war. Dahlia, Raya, Yara, Aisha, and I were involved in the feminist collective Arab Women's Solidarity Association, San Francisco Chapter (AWSA SF), a collective that worked closely with LAM. AWSA SF members, along with AWSA members throughout the United States, distributed a position paper in 2000 at a nationwide Feminist Expo that illustrates this critique that permeated LAM's work. In this paper, AWSA activists asserted, "A genocide, waged by the U.S. government, is taking place in Iraq. Millions of Iraqis are dying, the Iraqi infrastructure is destroyed, and the U.S. bombs Iraq on a regular basis. These policies disproportionately impact women. Women's oppression in Iraq cannot be separated from U.S. imperialism." Third, LAM's dominant movement logic assumed that U.S. media and governmental representations of Arabness through the figure of the "male terrorist" and the "oppressed woman" are crucial to the justification of imperial war. This third critique focused on the gender- and sexuality-reliant discourses that operate to legitimize war and imperialism. This critique finds parallels between U.S. media representations about the Middle East and U.S. imperial interests, arguing that (a) U.S. corporate media representations of Arabs and Muslims as backwards and uncivilized rely heavily

Puppet of Palestinian woman.

on images of gender and sexuality; and (b) these gendered and sexualized media images work to support and legitimize U.S.-led imperialist ambitions in the Middle East.

Women activists in LAM, along with their male counterparts, tended to critique such popular culture representations as well as similar ones in the news media. Aisha's reference to images of "Muslim women covered from head to toe [in] long black garb walking ten feet behind their men" signals what my interlocutors argued as a pervasive need to counter these tropes. This anti-imperialist feminist critique in LAM reflects a political current in Arab American feminist critiques of the 1990s, grown from the soil of various Arab American feminist networks in which Raya, Yara, Dahlia, Aisha, and I actively participated.[20] In LAM, initially, this view generated a commitment to replacing representations of "oppressed" Arab women with representations of "powerful" Arab women. Consider, for instance, a puppet several of LAM's women activists brought to a political demonstration in Washington, DC, on behalf of Palestinian refugees' right of return. The puppet was fifteen feet tall and held a baby in one hand and a Palestinian flag in another. Aisha, who spearheaded the effort to create the puppet, argued that "she represented that women, specifically Palestinian women, are a huge part of the resistance work—whether it is through raising families or through their leadership." The puppet allowed Aisha and the other women involved to bring positive images of Arab women into the public domain.

The visual and performative logic of the puppet signifies not only that women participate significantly in anti-imperialist activism but also that these women became involved on particular terms. And though the puppet could indeed be construed as complying with normative Arab nationalist and U.S. imperialist assumptions about Arab women as mothers, more meaningfully it reflects a creative impulse to make a profound public statement about women's centrality to formal, public politics in addition to their significant work within intra-communal spheres. Overall, there was little to no opposition in LAM to an externally focused anti-imperialist feminism, a feminism that conceptualized imperialism and sexism as mutually constitutive.

"You Can't Blame Everything on Sexism"

While the members of the new LAM of the late 1990s shared a great deal, the membership also fractured. Members of the old iteration of LAM who continued working with the new group significantly shaped the political vision and strategies of the new formation of the leftist Arab movement in the late 1990s. They joined Arabs from Iraq, Palestine, Jordan, Lebanon, and Egypt, among other Arab countries, and young adults like Mai, Dahlia, Raya, Aisha, Camelia, and Yara claimed a seat at the table. This created a new demography of membership within the organization. While a core group of men from the earlier LAM were part of the revival, earlier women activists were no longer present. LAM was now comprised of primarily Palestinian immigrant, refugee, and exile men who had been active in the previous era and women born or raised primarily in the United States, a group that included Mai, Dahlia, Raya, Aisha, Camelia, and Yara. The women who are the focus of this chapter felt challenged by heteropatriarchal structures in LAM. These structures were not simply upheld by men who took power over women. Sometimes, women activists argued that other women activists reinforced heteropatriarchy and at times, men activists actively worked against heteropatriarchy.

At first, when I began speaking with Mai, Aisha, Dahlia, Camelia, Yara, and Raya, many of our discussions entailed recollecting experiences in which we shared both a deep sense of alliance and belonging in LAM and intensely personal and structural struggles with patriarchy and, for some, compulsory heterosexuality. These women shared the general sense that these struggles undermined their sense of belonging and contributed to a sense of disidentification with LAM to different extents. They also shared the sense that at the time, they had virtually no collective language and few opportunities to discuss these issues among their counterparts in LAM.

Subsequent conversations with these women and with several men active in LAM elucidate that the complicated diasporic conditions that brought LAM activists together also complicated the ways in which sexism and the pressure for compulsory heterosexuality operated in LAM. Our conversations also elucidate the factors that foreclosed the opportunities to address matters of heteropatriarchy internal to LAM. These conversations allow for the illumination of these conditions and what an internally focused feminist critique looks like. As we talked, it became more and more clear that patriarchy and compulsory heterosexuality were deeply entangled in an assemblage of power relations related to immigration history and status, socioeconomic class, country of origin, and history of political activism that ensnared LAM's membership during this period. Through our ongoing conversations, these women activists articulated an internally focused feminist critique, one that could account for the nuanced power relations and historical conditions that constituted our lives and our work among each other.

As they spoke with me about their experiences in LAM over the years, these six women shared the critique that at times, it seemed as though heteropatriarchy was a normative structure through which LAM activists worked with one another. Mai remembers

> a general dynamic of men *thinking* and women *working*. I would be working on a strategy and some men decided on a different strategy and didn't tell me about it. Then there was the time that Samia came out. That brought out a contradiction between being politically radical but not on certain things. Women got swept up in a tide of not getting to envision our own activism.

Dahlia remembers that "[t]he leadership qualities of women activists were marginalized even though women were incredible facilitators and organizers. Men would take center stage." Aisha observes,

> There were key men setting the agenda. If anyone tried to critique it they would get patronizing condescension. Dynamics emerged in the meetings where women were not allowed to have the floor when they had things to say. It was indirectly delegitimizing of them. Certain women that toed the LAM line were allowed the floor more than women who may not have been as articulate.

Raya remembered that such dynamics resulted in both structural and personal silencing: "Once at a meeting, I said something and one guy totally

shut me down. Then there were men changing our decisions without anyone's consent."

There was indeed a gendered hierarchy in terms of decision making, leadership, and political strategy and a dynamic that did not allow people whose
lives did not conform to the normative demand for heterosexuality to feel
welcome. Yet there were many factors that complicated heteropatriarchy. The
people who were most outspoken about heteropatriarchy were women, and
most of the women in LAM had been born or raised primarily in the United
States. Dahlia was an exception. She was an Iraqi refugee who came to the
United States as a young adult. The people who were the implied targets of
my interlocutors' critiques of heteropatriarchy were predominantly Palestinian male immigrants, exiles, or refugees.

A set of transnational circumstances explains the diverse migration histories among LAM activists and the ways they mapped onto an asymmetrical
gender structure in LAM. As we saw in chapter 1, complex local and global
conditions brought diverse histories of Arab migration together in the Bay
Area, producing a diaspora constantly in flux. In the 1990s, the expanding
U.S. empire intensified conflict in Arab regions, and as neoliberal economic
structures influenced particular forms of labor migration, long-standing
Arab communities in the Bay Area came into contact with more recent Arab
migrants, exiles, and refugees from countries facing war and economic hard-
ship. LAM's membership reflects the ways in which the demographic realities of this diaspora were gendered. As suggested by Kuumba (2001), who
argues that gendered structures of social movements reflect the gendered
structures within the broader society, an examination of the gendered demographics of LAM—specifically, the relative absence of migrant Arab women
and U.S-born or -raised Arab men—reflects broader gender patterns among
the Bay Area's Arab diasporas. Most LAM members were unmarried college
students or graduates, and the Bay Area drew substantially more unmarried single Arab men migrants than single women migrants. The political
economy of migration also brought more middle-class migrant Arab men
to the Bay Area compared to migrant Arab women—a result of gendered
economic structures in which more opportunities existed for middle-class
men migrants in one of the most crucial sites for migrant technical workers
in the 1980s and 1990s. This imbalance was compounded by cultural praxes
of family and marriage that supported the migration of unmarried men over
the migration of unmarried women from Arab countries.[21] Generally speaking, Arab men who were born and/or raised in the United States tended to be
less accountable, concerned, or committed to Arab community affairs than
U.S.-born/raised women.[22] Conditions specific to the history of LAM in the

Bay Area and its location between empire and diaspora also explain the virtual absence of women migrants compared to the Palestinian men migrants.

A shifting relationship between gender and migration during the first and second period of LAM sheds some light upon this difference. Women activists, primarily Palestinian migrants, held significant leadership positions in the leftist Arab movement of the 1980s and early 1990s in the Bay Area. The aftermath of Oslo, however, significantly disrupted these women's continued activism. Some Bay Area families returned to Palestine, including some of the most active women leaders who co-led the Palestinian women's association that worked with LAM in the Bay Area in the previous era. It must also be stated that more Arab men than women participated in LAM in the Bay Area, and so the small number of people who stayed active after LAM folded were, by default, primarily men. Perhaps most importantly, however, activists from LAM's earlier period spoke about the movement of the 1980s and 1990s as a social world to which they gave everything. When it dissolved, many were faced with a disruption in their life conditions and demoralization. Some felt they had invested their entire lives in a cause that had led to nothing. And since many began as student activists, by the late 1990s they were middle-aged. The movement was a large collectivity that people relied upon for a support system, even jobs. Without it, many felt they had nothing. Several people active during LAM's earlier period (1980s and early 1990s) spoke of the aftermath of the Oslo Peace Accords, the period leading up to LAM's revival, as a time of personal and political crises. In particular, many women—always disproportionately responsible for the invisible labor of community survival and parenting—turned to raising children and other forms of community survival after what Maysa, a Palestinian activist from the earlier period, called "giving everything to the movement." In this sense, normative gender structures contributed to immigrant women's withdrawal from the movement. These factors contributed to the lopsided gender structure of the late 1990s in which LAM's membership was comprised primarily of Palestinian immigrant, refugee, and exile men and women who were primarily born and/or raised in the United States. In a sense, these diasporic conditions foreclosed the possibilities for continuity between the previous generation of women activists, who had developed an infrastructure to address women's concerns in LAM, and the newer generation of women, and for the previous generation to pass on their legacies of a women-based national liberation politics.

My interlocutors' narratives imply that a dynamic ensued in LAM in which the movement generally granted more political authority to men activists—not simply because they were men but because they were primarily

Palestinian and had come to the United States more recently than all of the women (except for Dahlia). The lopsided gender structure in LAM in the late 1990s and the beginning of the twenty-first century contributed to a process in which most men's status as recent exiles, refugees, or migrants positioned them as more authentically Arab or Palestinian, and therefore more legitimate as political leaders. Differences of migration history and class mapped onto stereotypical gender lines and resulted in significant implications for the privileging of men's leadership within the organization. Women's leadership, particularly since most of them were born and/or raised in the United States, became less authentic and less legitimate. Overall, LAM activists participated to various degrees in a process that granted hegemonic status to the political narratives of a cohort of men activists. The women I worked with narrated this dynamic as a tension that manifested most clearly in LAM's Palestine-related initiatives in which the voices of this male cohort were reified on the basis of unproblematized notions of territorial national authenticity and suffering. Aisha recalled,

> Men like Sami were here because of political asylum so it was like his voice has to be upheld first and foremost. They are still connected to the communities we're fighting for so they are the authentic voice. I didn't have experience . . . so I can understand that I may have needed guidance, but it was hard for me to feel I was fully part of the organization.

Camelia agreed on the gendered dynamics of activist experiences, for when she joined LAM,

> There was this whole kind of political argumentative, intellectual word battle that would happen between men. Women were excluded from these kinds of conversations. Men would take political stances and make comments that had hidden political meanings that we weren't always in on. It wasn't clear what would come up in these conversations—they would discuss political stuff that was important—and use language that we were not familiar with—like saying "one secular democratic state" to talk about Palestine. Many of the men grew up in Palestine and were closer to the issues. For me, social justice was about self-determination, but beyond that . . . I don't live there, I'm not from Palestine or Iraq—that was what the difference was. People who were from Palestine and Iraq had a very specific vision of what they want to see there. I didn't have that. I grew up without one specific country. It was like that for almost all the women. For many of the men, it was about what was happening in their country and how they

wanted to change it and their vision of what that would look like. If we were all from the same place, I would have spent a lot more time telling the men to shut up and would have taken my place as a woman in that group, but because there was that dynamic. . . . It wasn't because they were men per se but that it was the country they were exiled from. It wasn't always male/female—some women were also Palestinian from there but even the Palestinian women were born and raised here.

Raya's experiences resemble those of Aisha and Camelia, in which a greater authenticity and thus a greater voice were attributed to immigrant male activists.

These guys are from the *blad* [homeland] so it was always like they know more. It was like we were the ground army and they can tell us what to do. We have a lot less contact with Palestine and we wanted to know more about what's happening there and they knew it. They are heroic because they are the real Palestinians.

Aisha, Camelia, and Raya grew into their activism through a wide range of social movements, including the women of color, racial justice, immigrant rights, antigentrification, students of color, and antiwar movements. They advocated for Palestinians but were not actively involved in a distinctly Palestinian or Arab movement until they joined LAM in the late 1990s. The foundation of their political action privileged many histories of violence and oppression that were global and local: Palestine, Iraq, El Salvador, gentrification of Latino neighborhoods in the United States, anti-Black violence in the United States, women of color and queer of color issues, and so on. Meanwhile, several of the key men crucial to crafting LAM's official movement politics brought a specific leftist Arab national liberation politics to LAM, politics loosely connected to leftist movements in Arab countries. These men, displaced Palestinians who came to the United States after living in various Arab nations, were predominantly migrants, refugees, or exiles who had been active in the Palestinian movement in the Arab world or were socialized in the Arab world during the height of the first *intifada* (1987–1991).

Socioeconomic class complicated the tensions that mapped onto gender in LAM. There were indeed class hierarchies among women activists, and women with greater access to higher education were often the same few women who were granted the privilege of representing LAM as spokespersons at public events. Since a select group of men had more power in deciding the structure of LAM's events, several women argued that these men chose these more highly educated women to speak, reflecting a situation in which class and gender intersectionally produced hierarchies among women.

In my discussions with her, Raya reminded me that

> [t]here were some divisions among us around class—work and educa-tion—although we never talked about it. Most women were in the process of receiving college degrees from prominent institutions and most of them came from families with parents who were married, and not divorced. This played into producing favorites in the group, especially favorites that some of the men hand selected to speak over and over at our events.

Raya, arguing that several women were disproportionately marginal-ized from leadership, told me that by accepting these invitations to speak, some women played into or reinforced the patriarchy. Socioeconomic class complicated the difference in immigration histories between the dominant cohort of men in LAM and the majority of LAM's women activists and con-tributed to the process by which this cohort of men made decisions when women were not present. Many LAM activists recall that the assemblage of class, gender, and immigration history brought a particular cohort of men together in friendship or in shared social spaces, where they shared meals, listened to music, or smoked *shisha*. In the moment contemporary to the height of the second wave of LAM activism and the post-Oslo period lead-ing up to the beginning of the second Palestinian *intifada*, most of the men worked or studied in technical fields. Waseem, a Palestinian man I worked with, recalls, "There were men who had their own homes and could invite their buddies over to dinner to stay up late and cook in the dark." Within social spaces such as these, as a cohort of immigrant men developed what several activists called "clickishness," social gatherings merged with politi-cal decision making and strategizing. The interests and affiliations among the women who were born and/or raised primarily in the United States also aligned with each other on the basis of factors that cannot be reduced to gender. While LAM's men activists were primarily employed in or study-ing science or engineering, most of the women who were raised primarily in the United States were employed in the nonprofit industry or the art world or were students of law, social sciences, or humanities. In fact, the ways in which immigration history merged with socioeconomic class and profession complicated differences related to gender and also complicated the possibili-ties for addressing heteropatriarchy in LAM. In some instances, the women I worked with argued that men generally marginalized or excluded them. Yet several men responded by arguing that the women who are the focus of this chapter developed their own "clickishness" on the basis of their similar socialization in the United States and upheld privileges over many of the men activists such as proficiency in the English language, the ability to speak in more sophisticated ways, or the ability to relate to LAM's U.S. audiences.

Differences among LAM activists in terms of history of political activism and country of origin often mapped onto differences in political vision and contributed to further hierarchies among LAM activists. A dominant movement logic consistent with histories of Arab nationalist movements prioritized Palestine over other Arab struggles. In LAM, the fact that most men were Palestinian immigrants, exiles, and refugees compounded this dynamic. Overall, there was a dynamic in which men, as primarily Palestinian male immigrants, refugees, and exiles, came to LAM disproportionately invested in Palestine and women came to LAM committed to multiple struggles, as we will see in chapter 5. Yet women also came to LAM with different political histories that positioned them differently in relation to this dominant movement logic. Camelia is Egyptian and argued that LAM privileged a particular Arab nationalist vision that privileged Palestine over other matters and the Levant over other parts of the Arab region, a pattern in Arab activism we saw in chapter 1. Camelia was more committed to an internationalist leftist perspective than a leftist Arab national liberation framework. In addition, her involvement in LAM reflected the first time she had ever been actively involved in specifically Arab- or Palestine-related activism. As a result, she argued, her counterparts in LAM seemed to value her views less than those of other LAM activists. As we will see in chapter 5, Dahlia argued that because she was Iraqi and Shi'i, she was "doubly marginalized."

This combination of factors that emerged from the activists' different past and present life circumstances produced criss-crossing hierarchies in LAM and differences in political visions. Although people came to the movement with a general anti-imperialist politics, not everyone shared the same vision of what the movement should prioritize or exclude—or the specific framework through which LAM should engage with imperial power, occupation, violence, and war. Raya told me, "We had different mindsets about things and why we were in the movement. People were in it for different reasons."

Reflecting back on the late 1990s, several women activists say their critiques of heteropatriarchy were often met with the response that it is necessary to distinguish between when sexism or homophobia were at play or when different migration or political histories or socioeconomic class dynamics were at play. For instance, LAM activists have different analyses about when and to what extent patriarchy, different migration histories, or both were involved when men and women differed on whether to center

artwork or not, and when men's insistence on politicized speech over artwork dominated LAM. While these six women maintained that distinct gender hierarchies were at play, they were entangled in the different geographic,
socioeconomic, political, and cultural contexts in which women and men
were socialized and politicized and operated simultaneously. This complexity
had various implications for feminist critique in LAM, especially when the
men I spoke with as well as several women shared statements such as Adel's:
"You can't blame everything on sexism."

Complicating matters, some women activists upheld a hypersensitivity
about their privileges as individuals who had lived in the United States for
longer periods of time compared to their male counterparts. LAM activists
were keenly aware of the power imbalances in the United States between citizens and immigrants and people perceived to be "Americans" and people
perceived to be "foreign." They shared an analysis that dominant U.S. discourses portray people perceived to be "immigrant Arab men" as violent
and misogynist. This sensitivity fueled responses to the charge of sexism that
asserted that "the dynamics they encounter are not a consequence of sexism
alone." It also contributed at the time to a shared reaction that several men
had toward women who critiqued heteropatriarchy. In interviews, men who
felt troubled that some women blamed everything on sexism argued that
these women were reducing immigrant men's behaviors to "sexism" and that
this was an example of the women acting as Orientalists. Waseem recalls,

> There was a lot of internalized Orientalism. You would hear things like,
> "Well, Middle Eastern men are so and so . . . as if each Arab man is a sexist
> pig, trying to act like their counterpart sexist pigs . . . as if Arab men are a
> uniform group. This is no different than how we are perceived by the lib-
> eral U.S. establishment.

Waseem is referring to a larger dilemma that plagued LAM. Over the
years, several immigrant men raised the critique that an Orientalist discourses about Arab men circulated in LAM, particularly among women
activists. In response to the charge of heteropatriarchy among LAM's men
activists, Ibrahim told me, "not all men see eye to eye with each other on gender or sexuality. In fact, there were divisions between men over whether and
to what extent certain men supported the feminist current in LAM." There
were also hierarchies among men related to class and experience in political activism. These differences complicated discussions about patriarchy.
The fact that nearly all of LAM's women activists were born and/or raised
in the United States and nearly all of LAM's men activists were immigrants

fueled this problem. In a movement where members shared a critique that "America" perceives "Arabs" in Orientalist terms, LAM's women activists, most of them U.S. born or raised, could also be perceived as potential Orientalists, particularly when Orientalism often depicts "American women" as both victims of and superiors to "Arab men." While some activists contended that internalized Orientalism led other activists to misconstrue patriarchy in LAM, others, as we will see, add that the charge of being a potential Orientalist obstructed the possibility of discussing patriarchy in LAM altogether.

Airing Our Dirty Laundry in the Belly of the Beast

While Orientalism is the discourse that reifies the imperial wars LAM was working against, LAM's reactions to Orientalism often obstructed their work. Reactions to Orientalism foreclosed the possibilities of addressing internal movement hierarchies, particularly as related to gender and sexuality. Women and men, to different extents, were similarly invested in a "common culture" that emerged in LAM, a "common culture" that assumed that discussing matters of sexism and homophobia among Arab communities in public could endanger the goals activists were fighting for. Members shared the belief that U.S. Orientalist representations of Arabs and Muslims, specifically images of hyper-oppressed Arab and Muslim women and Arab Muslim sexual savagery, were among the most common images Americans saw—especially from the news media and Hollywood. In their analysis, Orientalist representations were a key reason why so many Americans supported U.S. military interventions in the Middle East, and why many Americans, particularly liberals, expressed profound empathy for Arab and Muslim women—perceived to be victims of their culture and religion—but little concern over the impact of U.S. policies on Arab and Muslim communities (Jarmakani 2008; Abu-Lughod 2002; Razack 2005). In response, LAM activists operated according to a tacit knowledge that discussing sexism and compulsory heterosexuality within Arab communities would reinforce Orientalism.[23] LAM activists, women and men alike, wittingly or unwittingly developed an anti-Orientalist politics that reinforced the relegation of gender and sexuality to the margins. Looking back on the late 1990s several years later, women discussed the ways in which the movement had accommodated an externally focused anti-imperialism/anti-Orientalism and foreclosed the possibility of tackling intra-communal matters of sexism and homophobia, at times engendering its own forms of coercion and repression. This should come as no surprise; many scholars have explored the dynamic in which colonized women often become "ideological pawns between the colonizer and the colonized" (Lazreg 1994, 140). Lazreg's research shows how French discourses constructing Algerian women as backwards and inferior worked to justify French colonization. Mai, Aisha, Yara, Raya, Dahlia, and Camelia all grappled with and remembered a tacit issue circulating in LAM: each was cautious about speaking about intra-community issues in public, perhaps reflecting the ways in which third world and women of color feminists face the potential charge of being "Western" or "Westernized" (Shohat 2001; Suárez-Orozco and Suárez-Orozco 1995; Moghissi 1999). A significant danger of this accusation for activist women lies in the assumption that one might occupy a "suspect location, and that her perspective is a suspiciously tainted and problematic product of her 'Westernization'" (Narayan 1997, 3).

Aisha explained,

We were operating with the mindset that we are always under attack—by feminists, soft leftists, racists. . . . If I was going to come out and say this person was sexist, I would be giving fuel to the fire, or legitimizing the attacks against our communities. . . . How can I bring up sexism when Zionists are waiting for any moment that we would falter to dismantle our work? I felt like I had to shut up and deal with the sexism.

Dahlia echoed these concerns during her interview, stating,

If I were to come out publicly and say this person is sexist. . . . I can hear it now—even from other progressive activists. . . . "Even progressive Arab women are oppressed by progressive Arab men!" That would just legitimize further violence, colonization, and oppression against us. If we were to talk about homophobia . . . people would say, "Oh my God! LAM is homophobic!" So there was never a place to talk about what was going on in our organizations or internally.

This strong feeling of being under attack from all sides engendered a commitment to, at times, muting feminist concerns. In Camelia's view,

I would see myself as a traitor if I said LAM was sexist publicly. Our countries are under attack and anything that can be used against us will be. Some people were sexist but a lot of us were not politically mature enough to deal with it. It wasn't just when it came to sexism. . . . We also had a hard time discussing whether or how to critique Saddam Hussein in public. Some people felt strongly that we should not hold back and others were more hesitant. Many of us internalized this idea that we could only criticize what the U.S. does. Our internal stuff was not for the public—untouchable. It was kind of naïve.

Underneath the tacit agreement to mute feminist critiques within the Arab Left was a visceral fear of betraying one's home community. For example, Raya noted, "It was so hard to talk about our gender issues. It felt like we were betraying our own kind. It was never the right time. It was like there was a consensus that it would look bad when people already think we're bad. It was really uncomfortable."

In this set of passionate—and at times confusing—multiple activist loyalties, LAM critiques of U.S. imperial discourses such as Orientalism, Zionism, and imperial racism pressured group members to remain united. At times, this unity created a shell against opportunities for women's critiques of sexism in the movement. Women of color throughout the United States and Canada continue to analyze similar relationships between racism and racial justice–based resistance movements. African American feminist scholarship, for example, sheds light on the deployment of assumptions about Black women within U.S. racist discourses in order to justify the oppression of Black people; further, scholars have noted that African American institutions at times reinforce the objectification of Black women through a "culture of resistance." Several scholars of U.S immigrant communities and communities of color document similar scenarios in which racism produces "the converse of discrimination's distancing role" (Gutierrez 1995, 33). As Moghissi writes, "any community whose sense of identity is collectively denigrated by the structural racism of the larger society feels the need to mute dissenting voices which challenge its sense of homogeneity, common fate and common cause" (1999, 216). She adds, "living in the territory of not-belonging can shift social and political priorities and individual aspirations in favor of maintaining communal dignity and cultural identity at the expense of gender equality" and that the "pain and anger that racism causes encourage members of diaspora . . . to stick together and to suppress disharmony . . . no matter what form it takes" (ibid., 207–9).

Women's perspectives in LAM reflect what many feminists of color and third world feminists referred to as the difficulties of "airing our dirty laundry in public." Although one of LAM's platforms against militarized violence rested upon critiquing its deployment of gender and sexuality, concerns about gender and sexuality *within* the movement were deprioritized due to a shared urgency concerning the need to challenge the discourses of empire. The suppression of discussions of sexism was deployed as a tactic to avoid the reification of Orientalist/racist assumptions, and was seen as a necessary component of resisting empire *from within empire* or, as one LAM activist put it, "living among our oppressors." Underlying these heartbreaking choices was the very real—if tacit—fear that at any moment nonactivists would use any articulations of sexism against the activist collective and their goals. Such equations of power and voice help explain the regulation of feminist critique in LAM, including the privileging of anti-imperialist feminism as its only acceptable form.

LAM activists fell prey to a common power dynamic. Leila Ahmed explains a similar dynamic in the case of Egyptian nationalist resistance against British colonialism in Egypt, in which women's issues, such as veiling, became trapped within the colonialist and nationalist imaginary (1992). Moghissi studies a situation among Iranian immigrants in which "voices that critique sexism in community are branded westernized or corrupt or as personifications of a dominant racist culture—or the enemy who threatens group harmony" (1999, 136). Narayan addresses a similar situation in which "third world feminists" are marked as "outside" influences and labeled traitors, suspect, or suspiciously tainted (1997). Lazreg, writing on French colonialism in Algeria, explains that with or without the veil, Algerian women have been objects of a debate between Algerian and French men (1994, 137). The widespread nature of these experiences, combined with the confidence built by increasing activist praxis, have led to incisive critique within activist and academic communities—but these developments may never erase the sting of gendered and sexualized marginalization within one's home community.

Imperial Violence and Political Activism in a State of Crisis

Operating in a state of crisis exacerbated the foreclosure of feminist critique. LAM's revival took place in the period leading up to the second Palestinian *intifada* and the height of the U.S. sanctions on Iraq. Regarding Palestine, no moment better captures the sense of urgency that mobilized LAM activists, along with social justice advocates all over the world, than an event that took place on September 30, 2000, one week before the start of the second Palestinian *intifada*. Twelve-year old Mohammad al-Durrah and his father, filmed by Talal Abu Rahma, a Palestinian cameraman freelancing for France 2, sought cover from Israeli gunfire behind a concrete cylinder. The footage, which lasts just over a minute, shows the pair holding onto each other, the boy crying and the father waving, then a burst of gunfire and dust, after which the boy is seen slumped across his father's legs. Since then, Mohammed al-Durrah has been hailed as a martyr of the Palestinian struggle. For

LAM activists, Palestinians, and social justice advocates all over the world, this incident confirmed their view of the apparently limitless nature of Israel's brutality toward Palestinians. Regarding Iraq, LAM activists were responding to international human rights reports that documented the number of deaths caused by U.S.-led sanctions on Iraq. They were mobilized by news from sources such as the Red Crescent, Red Cross, and various UN agencies that repeatedly and graphically reported tens of thousands of deaths resulting annually from the sanctions and by the statements of U.S. officials such as Madeline Albright who argued on a 1995 *60 Minutes* TV program that the deaths of more than five hundred thousand children in Iraq caused by U.S.-forced sanctions was "worth it" (Clark 1998a; Gordon 2010).

As LAM activists vied to respond to such events, they were mobilized by a logic of emergency. The women I worked with found it difficult to find a language to account for anything other than the brutal violence taking place in Palestine and Iraq, a dynamic that produced an official movement discourse that resembled the narrow, one-dimensional focus of conventional nationalisms and foreclosed the possibilities for addressing sexism and homophobia among LAM activists. This dynamic resembles what Gayatri Gopinath has theorized as conventional nationalist logics that render the diaspora inauthentic by naming the diaspora as the nation's queer Other. Within this conventional nationalist logic, diaspora is impure and inauthentic, an impoverished imitation of the originary national culture (Gopinath 2005). Yet for LAM activists, the hierarchy between nation and diaspora took on distinct form in the context of the specific conditions of imperial violence in Palestine and Iraq at the turn of the twenty-first century. The adrenaline was running high and LAM activists threw intense energy into mobilizing people and sparking resistance to the United States and Israel. The urgency of this mobilization complicated interpersonal relations in the group. As Camelia explained, "It was as though . . . once we dealt with all the immediate problems of death, starvation, bombing, political prisoners, then we can look at women's rights." Mai's experiences resonated with Camelia:

It was hard to make interventions about what we were experiencing because we were always responding to attacks against our communities. To be "a good Arab activist" you have to respond to violence, to racism. You have to be on the front lines. You have to be able to get our work on these issues done. Mentioning anything else seemed superfluous. That played out on the organizational level because it made anything else feel not important—like it wasn't going to contribute to our victory. There was a hierarchy that the immediate political issues were more important than anything. I never felt that we could talk about sexism or homophobia. It was like an implicit agreement we made with each other.

Aisha remembers not only moments in which her concerns about heteropatriarchy were silenced but also the problem of, as she put it,

> not even having a language to talk about sexism—especially since our people are dying . . . they're being killed! And then here I am trying to talk about sexism and homophobia! So there would be times in the meetings where I or another woman would say . . . "Dynamics emerging are not comfortable for me." . . . "Don't you guys see." . . . I would be shot down if I called out the sexism and homophobia, or that LAM was not welcoming to queers. I ended up leaving because of the homophobia . . . . It was as if gender and sexuality issues were personal processing moments and not relevant to the organization's work as a whole. It was a way to instantly delegitimize what we saw as sexist or homophobic.

Dahlia remembers a theoretical spatialization and compartmentalization of activist agendas, as if fellow activists had agreed, "This is a space to work on Palestine and Iraq, and sexism is outside of this. If you try to bring it up . . . you're seen as diverting . . . fragmenting the movement . . . causing problems . . . *mushkeljiya* [a problem maker]."

Here, the dominant movement logic in LAM assumed that since the violence in Palestine and Iraq is extreme—the authentic site of political resistance is "over there"—diasporic matters—sexism and homophobia among LAM activists, as well as other issues taking place among and around LAM activists in the United States in which many of these women were involved, such as gentrification, abolition, native land struggles, and immigrant rights, for instance—were an illegitimate site of politics. The disappearing of sexism and homophobia among LAM activists must be understood within the state of consciousness I theorize as a sense of belonging to a "diaspora of empire." Here, empire inscribes itself on the diasporic subject within the domestic (national) borders of empire, producing a narrow nationalist movement logic that privileged the territorial homeland over the diaspora.

The official movement discourse affirmed this perspective in response to the barrage of news and information about the violence, bodily harm, and death in Palestine and Iraq, as well as the general sense of nonbelonging and political outrage that LAM members shared. The following e-mail exchange reflects the general dismissal of feminist critiques that these women had been objecting to all along. In an e-mail exchange in early June 2001, Aisha, an Egyptian woman activist, forwarded an e-mail announcement about a conference organized by and about queer Muslims to her fellow board members of the American Arab Anti-Discrimination Committee, San Francisco Chapter (LAM SF). In response to her e-mail, Ali, a Palestinian man, replied, "What is the relevance of this e-mail to LAM?" Camelia, president of LAM SF, wrote that his question reflects a form of censorship. Following Camelia's response, a heated e-mail debate ensued about the term "queer Muslim." Women and men tended to take opposing stances on the relevance of sexuality to LAM's work. The debate took place simultaneously with another e-mail exchange regarding LAM's upcoming fundraising banquet dinner that aimed to raise awareness of and mobilize the Arab community around the group's Palestine and Iraq campaigns. In one of the most contentious postings of this period, Riad, a Palestinian exile who came to the United States when he was eighteen, contributed to the general exchange with a message in two parts. In the first part, he jokingly wrote, "Hey Guys, I just heard about this conference: MUSLIM WOMEN: HOW THEY SHOULD STAY IN THE HOME. We should all go to this. . . . I have the flier if you need more information." In the second part he added, "Just as many of you were offended by what I just wrote, Ali was offended by the posting about queer Muslims. And now, instead of arguing, why don't we concentrate on selling our banquet tickets? Ali sold seven, how many did you guys sell?" Riad's fictive conference and flier equated Ali's offense over the possibility that queer Muslims existed with the offense he assumed LAM activists shared about the idea that "Muslim women should stay at home." He assumed that LAM activists, particularly the women who had been exceptionally outspoken in criticizing representations of "Muslim women" that reify Orientalism, would take offense to the idea of a conference about "Muslim women staying home." Riad's fictive conference used relativism to dismiss queer issues as secondary or irrelevant to the organization's primary objective—to sell the banquet tickets.

Many activists understood Riad's sarcasm, and he later admitted he was well aware his e-mail would provoke a reaction, particularly from some of the women. But while Riad's aim was to point to his perception of the absurdity of the debates taking place on the list-serve, his e-mails revealed the disempowering homophobic and sexist assumptions women activists had been critiquing all along. They felt as though Riad's e-mail positioned queers and women as fictive entities to be swept away with a sarcastic missive; a mere joke is all it takes to make them disappear.

Indeed, the above exchange can be interpreted in terms of a heteropatriarchal logic that disappears sexism and homophobia in the movement, assumes a "common culture" (let's sell the tickets), and "has the power to

authorize an impersonal holistic or universal discourse that naturalizes difference, turns sexism into a second nature argument," and renders queerness impossible (Bhabha 1992). Compounding matters, one male activist
wrote that "Queer Muslim is an oxymoron," rendering queerness in the context of LAM an impossibility such that LAM activists "need not speak its
name" (Bhabha 1992).[24] While Aisha, like the women with whom I worked,
recalled this exchange as an example of the ways in which LAM's dominant
movement logic disappeared gender and sexuality from its anti-imperialist
frame, there were other interpretations of this exchange among LAM activists. Waseem, for instance, argued that the response to her e-mail reflected
a political trend that indeed supports nonnormative sexualities and is committed to challenging the pressure for compulsory heterosexuality in LAM
yet contends that one cannot reconcile Islam and homosexuality. He told me,
"the e-mail response was saying 'we need to stop grappling with trying to be
accepted within a Muslim framework.' It was stated with a spirit of support
and solidarity rather than saying 'we don't want to deal with you or your
issues.'" As such exchanges took place, so did others, in which women themselves said it was difficult to prioritize anything other than the brutal violence of imperial war in Iraq and Palestine. For Aisha,

> Because we were under attack on so many levels and don't belong any-
> where it was like the only belonging any of us felt was back home. Arab
> American activists have such deep issues over belonging in this country. It
> makes sense that so much work was directed to the homeland. We didn't
> feel like we are citizens of this country called America. The leftist Arab
> anti-imperialism rhetoric was so easily digested by us because it played
> into that dynamic. We didn't see ourselves as part of the fabric of this
> nation so the homeland was a place where we belonged.

The urgency of the violence in Palestine and Iraq produced a situation in
which the women I worked with "didn't even have a language to talk about
the sexism and homophobia." Yet they *were* articulating a critique, a critique
of how a logic of emergency that privileged immediate matters underscored
the hierarchy between war on the one hand and sexism and homophobia in
LAM on the other. They understood that the wars in Palestine and Iraq must
stop immediately, but they also did not want a logic of emergency to define
their politics. Their critiques raise important questions about the meaning of
human life—particularly when Palestinians and Iraqis have been reduced to
targets of war in public discourse and are thought of in terms of their bare
life or death. These women conceptualized "life" in a more comprehensive

way. They were centering bodily harm, death, and killing while refusing to give up other forms of human dignity and what it means to live a full life—forms that don't appear in a temporality of crisis. They were articulating an emergent analysis of different forms of life that take place in different time frames—so that one cannot let the urgency of Palestine and Iraq disappear everything else, to the detriment of women and the erasure of queers. This does not mean that they attributed the same urgency to every issue but that they were imagining a politics in which countering military violence and heteropatriarchy are both part of a struggle aimed at keeping people alive. They put the heteropatriarchy that exists in their Arab families and communities in the United States—and in LAM—in the same frame as what was happening in Palestine and Iraq, thereby bringing various regimes that people have had to live with to the center. In continuity with scholars and activists who have analyzed the masculinity of war and the feminization of the colonized—and how sexuality permeates the regimes of war and empire—these women were enlarging the frame in which we understand empire; they were struggling to imagine radical responses that can expand the future that one imagines.

* * *

Early on, my interlocutors did not have a language for defining the complicated histories that constituted the assemblage of power relations that operated in LAM. Immersed in a state of crisis and two massive campaigns, they found little space to begin contemplating this complexity. Yet stories narrated over several years provide an archive of what a diasporic anti-imperialist feminist critique might look like: a critique that can account for these complexities without losing sight of the larger picture, the empire and imperial war—a critique that succumbs neither to the privileging of homeland over diaspora nor to a privileging of anti-imperialism over feminism. In this sense, a feminist narrative about heteropatriarchy and nationalism that focuses solely on the problem of privileging national unity over heteropatriarchy cannot fully explain the gendered structures in LAM, and must constitute only a first step toward understanding the organizational activist dynamics.

While Dahlia, May, Raya, Aisha, Yara, and Camelia participated in LAM for profound reasons, they felt constrained by LAM in different ways, and these constraints help elucidate limitations and tensions that ensnared LAM at large. In fact, their stories show that LAM's work was constrained when a singular definition of power, politics, or oppression dominated activists' analyses. They elucidate the multiplicity and variation that the movement would need to account for in order for its members to participate fully, in order for the movement to thrive. Any attempt to articulate a feminist critique that could not account for variation and the criss-crossing of power relations that intersected with gender and sexuality fell short. My interlocutors also felt constrained when the dominant movement logic assumed that success could only be achieved through a simplistic sense of unity or agreement, or when political success could only be achieved when everyone prioritized one political site, such as the homeland, to the marginalization of other sites of violence or oppression.

The experiences recognized and given voice and an equal claim to authenticity in this chapter call attention to the need for an analysis that can conceptualize the relationship between Arab feminism and Arab national liberation within the dual contexts of empire and diaspora. In particular, the predominantly immigrant men came to LAM and the second *intifada* out of their history within the first *intifada*. The predominantly U.S. women came to LAM and the second *intifada* out of their involvement in primarily "American" social movements. This dynamic raises the central paradox underscoring this chapter—between the constant flux and multiple migration histories constituting this Arab diaspora and the articulation of a historically and territorially rooted leftist Arab anti-imperialism movement. At the nexus of this paradox, Mai, Aisha, Camelia, Dahlia, Raya, and Yara struggled over the ways in which patriarchy and homophobia merged with the realities of a diaspora in flux and the possibilities for articulating a feminist and queer politics within a new diasporic Arab collectivity in the late 1990s. In the following chapter, we will continue to see how a political vision that accounts for such multiplicity could move us beyond a singular, anti-Orientalist, externally focused feminist politics that obscures the interconnections between our internal and external problems and perpetuates the placement of apparently "internal" issues on the back burner.

5

Diasporic Feminist Anti-Imperialism

In 2000, Raya, Dahlia, Yara, Aisha, and I were involved in the Arab Women's Solidarity Association, San Francisco chapter (AWSA SF), which was working closely with LAM. During this time, AWSA SF activists made a postcard to distribute at various political events. One side included information about the U.S. sanctions on Iraq. The other side had an artistic image with the words "the Arab Women's Solidarity Association," in Arabic and English. The artistic image included a background colored with the black and white print of the *kuffiya* scarf, the long-time symbol of Palestinian resistance. Over the background print was a fist, resembling the symbol used by the Black Power movement of the 1960s. Yet this fist had a brightly colored bracelet around the wrist, signifying the centrality of women's labor and leadership to Palestinian and Arab social justice struggles. The postcard represented an alternative to both the masculinist politics that dominate national liberation movements and the U.S. imperialist discourses that operate through representations of passive, victimized Arab-Muslim women. The image on the postcard captures the focus of this chapter: moments in which a group of women activists rearticulated Arabness beyond masculinist nationalisms and patriarchal imperial racism in LAM. In chapter 4, we saw that the leftist Arab movement's (LAM's) dominant discourse had implications for women's leadership and the possibilities for feminist critique. LAM's official movement discourse operated through a rigid distinction between the movement's intra-communal and external-political domains and the repression of intra-Arab differences and hierarchies, including those related to sexism and homophobia. In this chapter, I continue my analysis of leftist anti-imperialism and the emergence of a diasporic Arab feminist critique. On several occasions, when LAM was putting its counternarrative into praxis through its campaigns, women activists generally gained more opportunities to work at the forefront of LAM's leadership. These occasions opened up new possibilities for articulating a diasporic Arab feminist politics that transcends the bifurcation of Arabness into an intra-communal and an external-political domain. In the pages to come, I map and analyze occasions in which Mai, Dahlia, Aisha, Raya, Yara, and Camelia put forth distinctly feminist and queer diasporic anti-imperialist visions while working with LAM. Taken together, these occasions represent collective political visions that underpinned these six women's work and came about specifically through two political strategies they prioritized: grassroots work and artwork. Through these strategies, they temporarily reframed the politics of gender and sexuality in LAM and expanded the possibilities for articulating anti-imperialist activism in feminist and queer terms.

In our conversations, Mai, Camelia, Raya, Yara, Aisha, and Dahlia shared a similar sentiment with me. They contended that early on, before the Palestine and Iraq campaigns were in full swing, LAM generally promoted public speech over other kinds of political work as mechanisms for implementing LAM's anti-imperialist counternarrative. LAM had been pushing its counternarrative through public speech, in printed or oral form, at demonstrations, rallies, and teach-ins; through faxes, e-mails, or websites; and on TV or radio.

As LAM's Palestine and Iraq campaigns expanded, the gap between the growing needs of the campaigns and LAM's actual labor force opened up space for women's enhanced leadership. The campaigns could use as much labor power as they could get, and the door was wide open to anyone who stepped up and made the campaigns happen. On several occasions, women activists spearheaded and implemented grassroots work and artwork as strategies for political action. Grassroots work brought a new articulation of Arabness that accounts for multiple Arab histories, heterogeneous stories, and contentious, competing political standpoints. Artwork opened up

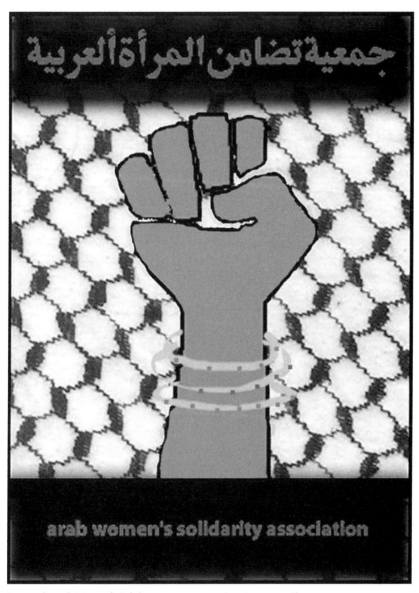

Postcard, Arab Women's Solidarity Association, San Francisco Chapter.

possibilities for more explicitly defining power as an intersection of imperialism, race, class, gender, and sexuality. In what became a strategy for
intersectional political work, artwork expanded LAM's capacity for coalition
building with multiple Bay Area–based struggles and social movements.

Another set of power parameters related to the plural migration histories, and the gendered underpinnings that constituted LAM, contributed
to the expanded possibilities for these women to deploy these strategies. As
we saw in chapter 4, LAM had a lopsided gender structure. Most women
were raised in the United States, and most men were immigrants, refugees,
or exiles. Most women had a longer history working in a range of social justice movements and organizations before they joined LAM. Most men came
to LAM out of a history of involvement in Palestine liberation–based social
movements. As a result, women were generally positioned at an advantage,
compared to their male counterparts, when it came to building relationships
with many of the U.S.-based progressive organizations LAM activists imagined as their potential allies and audiences. Through grassroots work and
artwork, women's labor was crucial to putting into practice an objective to
which everyone in LAM had committed: building alliances with people and
social movements beyond Arab communities and bringing LAM's message
to broader U.S. public audiences.

This chapter focuses primarily on six women activists' stories and analyses of these moments, and maps the debates and tensions, lived experiences,
and visions that surrounded the emergence of grassroots work and artwork
in LAM's Palestine and Iraq campaigns. As we saw in chapter 4, these six
women did not always have a language for naming their political vision at
the time and did not always share the same political vision with one another,
and there were differences and tensions among them. For instance, feminist
visions often operated at the exclusion of queer visions. Yet, I interpret their
work together during these moments as an archive of diasporic feminist and
queer anti-imperialism and politics. Beyond these moments, their visions
were not always realized in practice. At the same time, this *was* a period in
which a feminist and a queer politics—to different degrees—were set into
motion in LAM.[1]

Grassroots Work
A Gendered Form of Labor

LAM's dominant movement strategy that elevated public speech over a grassroots strategy is not unique to LAM. Feminist scholars have noted a similar dynamic in which dominant social movement discourses, by conflating

manhood and the public-political domain, privilege strategies that represent the community to the public through politicized speech (Stall and Stoeker 1998; The Latina Feminist Group 2001). Feminist scholars of nationalist and civil rights movements have documented a masculinist distinction between the private and public domains that works through a prioritizing of seemingly exterior political over interior cultural, familial, or communal domains (Blackwell 2009; Denetdale 2008; Williams and Pierce 1996; Robnett 1997; Radcliffe and Westwood, 1993). LAM's strategy was geared toward its external domain, its perceived public audience. The grassroots strategy sought to incorporate what several LAM activists referred to as "the community" into its externally focused campaign.

The gendered tensions related to LAM's grassroots strategy could be seen in a general gendered division of labor in LAM. Several women and men activists agreed that, more often than not, during this period LAM disproportionately positioned men activists (as compared to women) as representatives of LAM in LAM's exterior-public domain. Women activists disproportionately conducted the set-up and clean-up for LAM's events; they ordered and brought the food and printed event flyers, programs, and educational materials. Here are memories in the activists' words:

Ibrahim: Men wanted to be in those highlighted public spots. It was a dynamic where the legwork and preparation happens with women in the group and men end up speaking or getting in the limelight.

Aisha: I can barely remember one man involved in the groundwork.

Dahlia: For the November 29th Palestine solidarity event, it was mostly women who arranged the room. Raya made the room look beautiful. She brought the food and tables and decorated the space with candles, flowers, food, incense, artwork, cloth. . . . [S]he set up embroidery work from Palestine that we exhibited. She went to different Arab-owned coffee shops and got the food donated.

In general, the women activists I worked with shared the analysis that they were often excluded from positions as public speakers and comment on the way LAM tended to deploy the mechanism of politicized speech as follows: a few men activists determined which women would speak and how they would frame their analysis. Yet at the same time, this masculinist strategy did not neatly map onto gender categories among LAM members. In fact, some women in LAM upheld it like their counterparts who were men and some men resisted it. Several women, for instance, recalled events in which their women counterparts accepted superior positions as spokes-persons, positions that were primarily assigned by men. Women critical of this dynamic argued that socioeconomic class and access to language and education heavily informed which women were granted positions as spokespersons. Women like myself, who had advanced university degrees or were students at high-ranking universities, were almost always asked to speak in LAM's public-political domain. Some women argued that even when women had a public role, some men would diminish it by policing their speech or what they were going to say. Among LAM activists, crit-ics of this strategy argued that it reified a masculinist movement strategy by failing to challenge the hierarchical gendered binary between public speech and secondary forms of labor within LAM's seemingly private, communal, or invisible domain. At the same time, there were men who shared women's critiques of gender and grassroots labor and allied with women on this issue.

Feminist critics have argued that a gendered division of labor in social movements reflects gender structures that underlie the larger social and political environment in which social movements operate (Robnett 1997; Kuumba 2001). The gendered division of labor in LAM resembled similar distinctions between public and private domains that shape dominant lib-eral U.S. discourses and institutions (Pateman 1983). While such critiques of liberal theory vary, particularly in terms of the way feminists should respond to them, a general consensus exists that the separation and opposition of pri-vate and public domains is based on patriarchy. Feminist scholars have also contended that the consequences of liberalism relegate women to informal, private, less valued positions and men to formal, public, official positions (Scott and Keates 2005).

Generally, feminist scholars of social movements have theorized the way similar distinctions have operated within social movements. Some have shown that national liberation movements rely on modernist European dis-tinctions of public-private and inner-outer (Chatterjee 1993; Kaplan, Alar-cón, and Moallem 1999). In chapter 2, we saw how the middle-class Arab immigrant politics of cultural authenticity distinguishes between an inner Arab private domain and an external American domain, and dispropor-tionately supports the movement of men (as compared to women) beyond an inner-familial-communal domain. I argue that the politics of cultural authenticity draws upon dominant U.S. liberal and masculinist third world nationalist logics in demarcating community boundaries in gendered terms. Similarly, LAM's dominant movement logic tended to define LAM's political

strategy as directed toward an exterior-public domain that men disproportionately represented.

Most women activists' disproportionate commitment to grassroots work
grew out of their experiences in grassroots forms of activism before they
joined LAM. Most male activists were not previously involved in grassroots
forms of activism. Camelia, for instance, had worked for Mission Housing
Development Corporation, an organization that provides housing options
primarily to low-income immigrant residents of San Francisco. Dahlia had
volunteered translation services to local Iraqi refugees while she was active
with the media and with the International Action Center as an organizer and
public speaker. Yara had founded a creative arts organization that served the
needs of young immigrant girls and girls of color. Overall, as LAM revived
in the late 1990s, a gendered structure was in place that disproportionately
located men within LAM's external, outward domain and women within
LAM's internal, communal, and, in some cases, invisible domain.

Grassroots and Diaspora in Flux

Discussions about whether and to what extent LAM should incorporate
grassroots work into its Iraq campaign took place in a transnational political context that was in constant flux. At first, LAM activists developed their
campaign through a conceptual framework that focused on U.S. politics
"over there"—in Iraq, seemingly far away from the United States. This is the
mindset of many antiwar/peace-and-justice movements and anti-imperialist
activists who assume responsibility—as people living in the United States
and benefiting from U.S. global economic and military policies—to put
pressure on their own government and to mobilize others to do the same in
order to stop U.S.-led war. This approach makes it difficult to relate the activism to the actual people living the war and directly impacted by the military
violence at hand, or to work toward making political strategies and visions
accountable to them (Hyndman 2008).

Yet, an unanticipated change was happening in the San Francisco area that
raised the significance of grassroots work for LAM and disrupted the framework of an antiwar campaign disconnected from the people of Iraq. In the
mid-1990s, several thousand Iraqi refugees moved to San Francisco. The identities and journeys of these refugees is crucial to the story of LAM's grassroots
work, particularly in light of LAM's campaign against sanctions on Iraq. The
refugees' arrival was a result of decades of U.S. involvement in Iraq. In January 1991, President George W. Bush led a United Nations coalition force into
the region to expel Iraqi troops from Kuwait in an operation officially named

"Desert Storm." Led by American troops on the ground and in the air, they pushed the Iraqi army back almost to Baghdad, devastating both the Iraqi infrastructure and its political morale. In light of Saddam's weakened leadership, he turned to internal military repression to secure political order and power. In March 1991, uprisings against a hated regime broke out in Shi'i cities. Saddam's regime inflicted massive harm upon them, killing tens of thousands of people.[2] Approximately fifty thousand Iraqi refugees poured into Saudi Arabia, and thousands sought sanctuary in Iran. Many who fled to marshes in the south were killed by Iraqi armed forces; thousands perished in Iraqi prisons during coming years (Tripp 2002, 247-58). In 1996, a policy under the administration of President Clinton allowed approximately seven thousand Iraqi Shi'i, who opposed Saddam Hussein and faced military attack by his regime, to enter the United States (Myers 1996; Gedda 1996). Several thousand were resettled in the Tenderloin, one of San Francisco's most diverse but most economically devastated neighborhoods. It is home to young people, families, artists, and recent immigrants, as well as homeless individuals, people living in extreme poverty, and many nonprofit social service agencies, soup kitchens, religious rescue missions, homeless shelters, and single room occupancy (SRO) hotels. These Iraqi refugees had few resources for coping with the conditions they faced there; they had limited English-language skills and they dealt with challenges related to housing, employment, and personal safety. Nor did they have support networks or financial resources. They could not return to Iraq and were living on the margins in the United States. Several Bay Area activists who worked with these refugees have argued that the manner in which the Clinton administration purported to save them, but then turned its back on them after they arrived, suggested that they had been used as a political tool in the war with Saddam.[3]

The call for an explicit grassroots strategy in LAM took place within this context. Until that time, the established Arab communities in the Bay Area were largely middle-class, and from the Levant and Egypt. A majority of them had moved to the suburbs over the years. The arrival of poor migrants to the city mapped the growing class distinction onto geographic space. By the 1990s most middle- to upper-class Arabs now lived in the suburbs, and most recent immigrants lived downtown, in poverty. According to one Arab community leader who worked with the Tenderloin community, "Poor Arabs believed that rich Arabs abandoned them and acted like they didn't exist."

LAM activists who called for a grassroots strategy during that time often framed their claim as a call for LAM to uphold its commitment to a politics of socioeconomic justice that could contend with these demographic shifts. Yet the process of agreeing upon a grassroots strategy was not so easy. Dahlia recalls that some LAM activists "were concerned that the Iraqi refugees might be sympathetic to the U.S. administration since the U.S. administration brought them here. I remember arguing that we must be accountable to this community by asking them to be included before making assumptions about them."

While LAM developed the Iraq campaign, discussions about grassroots work and building relationships with local Iraqis involved a conceptual framework of community accountability. Activists grappled with questions like this: "How can we talk about the Iraq war without the presence of the Iraqi refugees who now live among us?" "Are we going to join forces with elitist Arabs and ignore the refugees' existence?" "How can we make our campaign accountable to them?" LAM activists were contending with the changing realities of political activism among a diaspora in flux, in which its constituents were constantly changing in light of the ebbs and flows of U.S. empire. At that time, the targets of the devastation in Iraq were no longer people "over there" whom LAM supported from a distance; they were over here, right in San Francisco. While it often seemed as though there was a clear distinction between the two groups, Iraqi refugees living in the Tenderloin on the one hand and LAM activists on the other, even the lines between these groups was not so easily drawn. Indeed, there were general distinctions related to socioeconomic class and these refugees' particular history of displacement. However, in reality, Dahlia, who was actively involved in LAM, was an Iraqi refugee herself and in addition, despite the geographic distances between nation-states and ideals about citizenship, everyone involved in LAM had directly or indirectly experienced displacement, and their lives were shaped in constant relationship to both the local and the global, "here" and "there."

Camelia and Dahlia were among the LAM activists who felt strongly about a grassroots strategy. Dahlia said, "The campaign didn't make sense reaching out to the same kind of people over and over, to other activists who are already questioning U.S. policies." According to Camelia,

Making the campaign sustainable means asking whether the people most impacted by our work have their basic human rights met—not just getting them involved politically. How can they get involved if they don't have food, health care, or housing? We need to work with youth and families. We need to take people's needs seriously in the campaign.

Camelia and Dahlia speak about the grassroots through the language of social movement principles of community accountability: activists are to be held accountable to the people their work represents and to their ongoing safety (Naples 1998; Kuumba 2001; Visweswaran 1994; Smith 1999). Community accountability entails a commitment to create opportunities for the people most impacted by the issues at hand to define the political stands and strategies as well as the visions for self-determination. Regarding LAM's Iraq campaign, the strategy Camelia and Dahlia advocated prioritized building relationships with the Iraqi refugees, involving them in the campaign, and working to ensure that LAM's campaign was relevant to their needs and circumstances.

Grassroots: From Unofficial to Official Movement Strategy

As LAM was increasingly presented with information and stories about local Iraqi refugees in San Francisco, LAM activists' visions harmonized around the necessity for a grassroots strategy, within the larger campaign, reflecting LAM's general commitment to principles of justice related to socioeconomic class and community accountability. Yet it also was very much in line with LAM's larger goal—to bring an Arab counternarrative to U.S. publics and to craft a counternarrative about the Iraq war. This explains why LAM reached out not only to the Iraqi refugees of the Tenderloin but also to other exiled Iraqis across ethnic, religious, and class divides. As we saw in chapter 4, in order to shift the balance of powers, LAM prioritized the strategy of producing counternarratives that could bring to U.S. publics histories that dominant discourses have tended to disregard, obscure, or erase. Regarding LAM's Iraq campaign, the perspectives of Iraqi refugees could strongly enhance the articulation of an Arab counternarrative about the realities of U.S. war on Iraq.

The grassroots strategy took off through a series of relationship-building activities. The first was a picnic at Coyote Point, a state park overlooking San Francisco. The next event was a walk-a-thon at Tilden Park in Berkeley that brought together a diverse crowd: people from all walks of life who supported LAM's campaign, LAM activists, and Iraqi refugees, primarily women and children. These events, too, served as community-building activities that offered Iraqi refugees a way to meet new people, overcome their isolation, and learn about the campaign. As Dahlia described the event, "It brought [Iraqi] youth and families together with all kinds of other people: men, women, lots of people from other Arab organizations. The youth loved it. It was an incredible event."

LAM activists continued to develop this grassroots strategy. While they raised funds for a project in which they planned to put up a billboard about

Image of the billboard placed on Highway 101.

the Iraq war on highways and continued to work with other antiwar groups, they consolidated relationships with local Iraqi refugees. LAM's Iraq campaign culminated on August 28, 2000, when LAM's billboard went up on Highway 101. The same day, LAM organized a press conference at a local Iraqi refugee organization, where a panel of speakers represented LAM activists and Iraqi refugees. Most guests commended LAM for their work and for educating them about the new Iraqi community.

I arrived early and joined LAM activists in reconnecting with Azzar, Sumaya, Malik, Manar, and other Iraqis we had spent time with over the preceding several months. We shared strategies for presenting the campaign to the public. An unexpectedly large crowd showed up. The room was packed. A national Arab American civil rights leader, two women activists from LAM (myself and Dahlia), and several Iraqi refugee children spoke, calling for an end to sanctions on Iraq.

Yet this event was unique. While the audience included LAM's typical supporters—activists from the antigentrification movement, the immigrant rights movement, and the antiwar movement and people from the Arab communities, among others—the location brought out new audiences and allowed for bringing new stories to LAM's publics. The event was held at the location of an Iraqi organization in the poverty-stricken Tenderloin neighborhood. As Iraqi refugees spoke at the event, thereby bringing the realities of real Iraqi people to life, the event brought reporters from mainstream and alternative media outlets. In line with LAM's aim of crafting an Arab

Press conference in support of the End the Sanctions campaign.

counternarrative and ensuring that Arab people narrate their own histories, it brought new public knowledge through a grassroots strategy that aimed to be accountable and involve Iraqi people living locally, in the Bay Area.

Writing on the post-2003 U.S. war on Iraq, Hyndman refers to grass-roots strategies that she recommends for countering the U.S. war on Iraq as "feminist geopolitics" (2008, 193). She argues that putting forth account-able visions and versions of war can work to combat people's ambivalence toward violence and war and spur political change. Here, LAM placed the people most impacted by the issue within a broader strategy of legitimizing Arab experiences that dominant U.S. discourses erase from history. Hynd-man argues that personal accounts present a political strategy for moving beyond masculinist practices of a disembodied epistemology of omniscient knowledge production (2008). Personal accounts recast war as a field of live human subjects with names, families, and hometowns. This establishes the moral proximity necessary to link people in the United States to U.S. poli-cies "over there." Iraqi stories, or "peopling" the campaign, enhanced LAM's strategy of countering U.S. geopolitical scripts. Reflecting on this and other consequences of the press conference, Yara recalls,

> Our grassroots work did more than just legitimize our project. This press conference created a shift in our internal leadership and our strat-egy of community accountability. Also, it created visibility not of U.S.

involvement in Iraq but of the Iraqi and Arab communities in San Franc-sico—and the city itself began accounting for their needs through policy changes and integration in social/economic/health-based support.

Yet, as Dahlia put it, "I also had the impression that LAM tokenized the Iraqi refugees, including myself, since my public role was marginalized except when I was asked to speak to the media during the media campaign at the refugee center." There were indeed times in which some LAM activists expressed concern that the strategy could have the effect of tokenizing Iraqi people.

Women's Invisible Labor

In fact, these events only tell part of the story of the incorporation of grass-roots work into LAM's Iraq campaign. What structured LAM's work behind the scenes leading up to the picnic, the walk-a-thon, and the press conference was a gendered division of labor, and women's invisible labor was crucial to the unprecedented interaction between LAM's audiences and Iraqi refugees. Before LAM defined grassroots as an official movement strategy, Dahlia and her friend Nadia, an activist loosely connected to LAM, were working with Iraqi refugees in the Tenderloin as translators for lawyers. They had been working closely with Iraqi community leaders and another Iraqi woman activist who were establishing the local Iraqi social service organization where LAM held its press conference. Through this work, Dahlia and Nadia learned about the refugees' needs. Many Iraqi mothers told them that the isolation their children were experiencing was among their most immediate concerns. Dahlia and Nadia brought these concerns to LAM. This knowl-edge informed LAM's outreach strategy and shaped the kinds of events LAM organized—which they geared specifically toward children and focused on fun, outdoor activities such as games and hiking, and social interaction. The labor of many of LAM's men activists was also critical to the success of the picnic and the walk-a-thon. Women conducted a significant portion of the work that involved aligning closely with local communities, such as serv-ing as translators, organizing events for women and children, and teaching classes in local communities.

Feminist scholars have theorized that often women activists' preexist-ing ties to grassroots constituencies and the relationships women already have set in place make achieving grassroots objectives possible (Kuumba 2001, 45-46; Robnett 1997, 45-46; Naples 1998, 182; The Latina Feminist Group 2001). Several scholars refer to this as women's invisible labor in social movements. This was the case with Dahlia and Nadia, whose invisible labor helped LAM achieve a relationship with the Iraqi community and provided the stepping stones for their grassroots constituency to interact with the movement. Feminist scholars have also theorized women's work as "bridge work" between activists or social movements and people not actively engaged in politics. They challenge the idea that grassroots efforts are merely private, invisible, unofficial political work and contend that grassroots labor, often conducted by women, dissolves the boundaries between private and public, invisible or visible, and unofficial or official politics. Scholars writing about communities of color and people living with war, colonization, and occupation have theorized "activist mothering" to refer to situations that expand the definition of mothering beyond the scope of "family" to a public domain (Stall and Stoecker 1998; Collins 2000; Stack 1997; Johnson and Kuttab 2001; Baca Zinn 2000). "Activist mothering" emerges out of collective experiences of marginality, violence, or exclusion that lead to a politicization of the labor of "motherhood" in which women become accountable to a host of needs beyond the domain of family (Rodriguez 1994). Regarding LAM's Iraq campaign, women's disproportionate commitment to grassroots work bridged distances between LAM and its constituency, Iraqi refugees. At the same time, like activist mothering, women's labor contributed to a revaluing of the intra-communal domain as fundamental to LAM's official, public, political work.[4]

Plural Arab Histories and Relations to Empire

Women's "invisible" labor was a key catalyst that brought the communal to the public and made connections between the "grassroots/communal" and "political activists." It also brought middle-class Arabs from Palestine and its neighboring countries (Jordan, Egypt, Lebanon, and Syria) and recent Iraqi refugees into relations with one another. These new connections transformed LAM's public discourse from a singular narrative about Arabs and U.S.-led war to a plural narrative encompassing multiple Arab histories and experiences.

At LAM's largest fundraiser for the Iraq campaign, Artists for Iraq, the participation of Iraqi refugees brought to light aspects about Iraq that were different than what most LAM activists seemed to have planned for, envisioned, or anticipated. This disrupted LAM's dominant singular anti-imperialist narrative, which had framed much of its work to this point. The Iraqi refugees who participated in the event, like Dahlia and Nadia, were predominantly Shi'i from southern Iraq. Their family members and communities had recently been brutalized, tortured, killed, or displaced by Saddam Hussein and his regime. This was the position from which these Iraqis engaged in geopolitics—as direct targets of a dictator whose power the United States and its global allies enabled. In addition, these Iraqis, as refugees, lived in fear of losing their refugee status. Nadia, after working closely with the refugees of the Tenderloin, told me that a tacit understanding among the Iraqis of the Tenderloin was that publicly criticizing U.S. policy in Iraq could endanger their status. Nadia told me, "U.S. government officials strongly encouraged anti-Saddam perspectives among the refugees, but discouraged them from critiquing the sanctions. It was never official, just an underlying understanding they shared." What took place at Artists for Iraq, when these refugees joined LAM's public event, reflects this distinct historical context and positioning through which Dahlia, Nadia, and the Iraqi refugees with whom they worked viewed U.S.-led war and militarism and the overall devastation in Iraq. LAM now had to contend with U.S. empire from a different vantage point—that of people who encountered U.S. power first through their direct relationship to Saddam and from the geographic location of Iraq, before their arrival in the United States, and, second, as recent refugees living in poverty. At Artists for Iraq, the Iraqi refugees who spoke to LAM's public audience told different stories than did LAM activists, and had crafted their views about Iraq from a different vantage point.

Out of the strategy that invited Iraqi refugees to Artists for Iraq, a set of contradictions unfolded. Nadia and Dahlia, with assistance from several of LAM's women activists, had spearheaded an effort to invite two Iraqi refugee women, Elham and Ghada, to give testimonials as part of the program at Artists for Iraq. At the event, Elham's testimony came as a great surprise to many LAM members. Rather than addressing what LAM envisioned as the focus of their event (U.S.-led sanctions or U.S. policy on Iraq), she gave a heart-wrenching personal account of her experiences living under the regime of Saddam Hussein. The following is from Elham's presentation, which I have edited for readability:

I lived in Baghdad for sixteen years, and then we moved to southern Iraq where I learned Saddam killed many people. When Saddam took Kuwait, I was in Baghdad visiting my family. When the war started, we spent two months in terrible conditions and many people were killed. Some Iraqi people said we don't want Saddam anymore and he sent an airplane to kill Iraqi people. We left Iraq in 1991 and couldn't go back. They took everything—our house and all our stuff in it. I was pregnant. The UN brought us to Saudi Arabia for two years. I lost my baby after six months. We lived in tents. The UN helped us go to either the U.S. or Canada. I felt lonely here. My English wasn't strong. I didn't understand anybody. I wanted to go back to my country. I have been here for nine years. I haven't seen my parents since then. I hope in the future Iraq will change.

After the event, Elham's testimony inspired a heated debate in LAM that centered on whether and to what extent LAM should criticize Arab leaders in its public discourse. The dilemma that emerged was whether the act of publicizing corrupt Arab regimes would reinforce support for the sanctions on Iraq, which was precisely what the movement was working against. In Camelia's view of the debate,

> Many people in our group had an anti-imperialist stance and did not want anything to be said at the event about Saddam that would appear as if our movement was on the same side as the U.S. A lot of times, what the Iraqis we worked with wanted to talk about was what Saddam was doing. It was not until later that we developed an analysis that Saddam committed war crimes and that the U.S. had supported his war crimes for years. There was a lot of . . . "No, no. . . . Let's not focus on what Saddam is doing." When we invited Iraqi women to speak at the event, there was this struggle. Some of us felt that if we are going to invite them, we have to support what they want to talk about. What pained Elham is what Saddam had done to her people and that was the story she wanted to tell.

LAM activists who shared this critique said they confronted a dominant perspective in LAM that the campaign should only critique the United States. Looking back on this period several years later, Dahlia says,

> It was as if we were supposed to use the local Iraqi community only for the messages that we want to expose while dismissing other parts of their voices because we were afraid of how their voices would be used. I had always pushed for a critical analysis of the link between U.S. imperial expansion and interest in the region and its relationship to dictators like Saddam Hussein, but again there was much resistance in LAM.

Camelia and Dahlia are referring to an iteration of the tension we saw in the previous chapter. LAM's official movement discourse, which developed within a state of emergency and the context of living within the empire, led some activists to suppress discussions about the "internal" issue of sexism in the movement and to repress anything that resembled "airing our dirty laundry in public," whether it was the distinct issue of sexism or homophobia among Arabs, on the one hand, or the issue of violence of Arab dictators on the other (for different reasons and to different degrees). The attempt to silence these critiques reflects the pitfalls of nationalist consciousness, which often operates through a rigid concept of cultural identity (Saliba 2003; Fanon 1963). A tacit knowledge existed in LAM that the United States enabled Saddam's political power. Yet as LAM activists developed their Iraq campaign, LAM's official movement discourse did not yet incorporate a language for articulating this dimension into their critique of U.S. power and the impact of U.S. power on Iraqi people. It was as if LAM's dominant anti-imperialist narrative, generated in a state of emergency, could only account for a one-dimensional power relation between two parties: oppressed (Iraqis) and oppressor (the United States).

The concern that any critique about forms of oppression within Arab communities (from sexism to state repression) could be used to reinforce support for the sanctions complicated the possibilities for LAM activists to incorporate into their counternarrative a more complex analysis of intra-Arab power relations and violence enacted by Arabs upon other Arabs, and many Arab leaders' complicity in U.S. imperialism. Some LAM activists said that working in a state of emergency created the sense that they did not have the time to develop this critique. Instead, they were working to inspire other people living in the United States to take a stance against U.S. state violence, an objective most easily articulated through a campaign against U.S. sanctions on Iraq. Anything that could possibly disrupt this objective was met with resistance as it could apparently disrupt the end-the-sanctions campaign. Yet Elham, like Dahlia and other Iraqis who directly encountered Saddam's violence, could not remain silent. Many Iraqi Shi'i looked at geopolitics from a distinct geographic and political location and saw Saddam Hussein as an immediate problem. LAM's dominant movement discourse was created from the location of the United States for a U.S. audience, with the aim of ending the direct impact of militarism and war. First and foremost, LAM activists wanted their U.S. audiences to know about what the U.S. government and their tax dollars were doing in Iraq. Yet by revaluing the intra-communal, "private" domain, grassroots activism brought together multiple histories and engagements with geopolitics. This expanded LAM's focus and forced LAM activists to generate an anti-imperialist politics that could account for the complex dimensions of U.S. imperialism, including both a critique of Saddam and the United States and the United States' earlier support for Saddam Hussein and the ways in which previous U.S. policy enabled his dictatorship. The idea to bring Elham and Ghada to the event opened up the possibility of sharing personal stories of loss, pain, and destruction and of expressing Arab perspectives on Iraq that were not static or frozen in time but contextual and diverse, depending on who someone was and where he or she stood in relationship to global and local regimes of power. Grassroots work, spearheaded primarily by women activists, opened up possibilities for challenging LAM's dominant movement logic, which relied upon a singular, unified concept of both Arabness and U.S. imperialism.

The challenge to singular articulations of Arabness and imperialism had further implications for the emergence of a feminist and queer politics in LAM. Singular visions of Arabness, as we have seen, operate through rigid nation-based concepts of community, concepts that rely on compulsory heterosexuality, patriarchy, and idealized concepts of biological reproduction within kin relations. By tackling outward-focused issues such as imperialism and war and the internal power relations that ensnared LAM, grassroots work with Iraqi refugees reflects a multisited feminist vision that opens up possibilities for grappling with intra-communal power relations, tensions, and contradictions. Through this politics, intra-communal power relations—whether related to gender, and sexual orientation, or class, immigration history, and political perspective—are revalued to be as urgent as external power structures. Moreover, these intra-communal differences were constantly changing and taking shape in relationship to external forces such as war and displacement. For instance, the tensions that developed over airing critiques of Saddam in public were produced out of a particular U.S. imperial moment. Thus even the boundaries between the internal and external are not fixed but historically specific and changing. Thus, grassroots labor enhanced the possibilities for imagining Arabness beyond the rigid dichotomy between private and public that underscores LAM's dominant anti-imperialist national liberation framework. In fact, this grassroots work women disproportionately advocated parallels a theoretical current in feminist discourses and practices that commit to struggling on multiple fronts, both the larger society and structures and practices within the community (Burnham, Tatnall, and Women of Color Resource Center 2006; Jayawardena 1986; Blackwell 2011; Smith and Kauanui 2008). In the United States, third world and women of color movements of the 1960s and 1970s developed theories and methods for articulating a multisited feminist politics that was vibrant in the context of the Vietnam War (Mohanty, Pratt, and Riley 2008; Burnham, Tatnall, and Women of Color Resource Center 2006). Frances Beal, an active member of the Black Women's Alliance and Third World Women's Alliance, used the term "double jeopardy" to explain the position of being Black and female and to present a theory of "multiple and simultaneous oppressions" in which "racism and sexism operated together in the lives of black women to create a particular set of experiences, concerns, and problems" (2008). Out of this history came the Third World Women's Alliance in the 1970s.

They "pioneered the concept of 'triple jeopardy,'" which signaled "the organization's view that women of color faced the combined and intersecting burdens of capitalism, racism, and sexism." Their analysis of capitalism, racism, and sexism centered on a critique of imperialism, particularly since the Vietnam War had a tremendous impact on their political consciousness and reflected their view of "exploitation at home and imperial wars abroad." The Third World Women's Alliance's theory of multiple oppressions came out of their members' attempts to make sense of U.S. state–based oppression and the internal limitations of the racial justice and national liberation movements to which they belonged.

Working in a different historical context, my interlocutors' politics operated on multiple fronts and insisted on the interconnections between LAM's private and public domains. Their work transformed the group's dominant definition of the "Arab community" from within and in the process articulated a feminist vision that revalued the "internal" as a crucial domain for politics.

R. Radhakrishnan writes that, "[o]bsessively concerned with the West, nationalism fails to speak for its people . . . suppresses the politics of subalternity . . . and fails to historicize this inner reality in its own multifarious forms." He calls for alternative visions in which the inner self becomes a protagonist or agent of its own history (1992, 89-90). The strategy of testimonials that women's work brought to Artists for Iraq liberated "those many spaces foreclosed within nationalism" and enabled "a non-reactive, non-paranoid mode of subjectivity and agency in touch with its own historically constituted interiority . . . a prey neither to the difference of the western subject nor to the mystique of its own indigenous identity" (1992, 91-92). The debates that ensued after Elham's testimony forced LAM to contend with multiple Arab histories. Indeed, this Arab diaspora inhabits many locales. Enhanced by a grassroots strategy driven primarily by women, LAM exposed a tacit knowledge many LAM activists already shared but did not yet collectively make explicit—that Arab subjectivities can occupy positions of both oppressor and oppressed and that the relationship among Arab people, Arab dictators, and U.S. empire is crucial to an anti-imperialist politics. Elham's testimony illustrated that persisting with a singular anti-imperialist narrative can lead to the exclusion of certain narratives and can cover up the complex ways U.S. power has manifested itself. Through grassroots work, a new anti-imperialist vision came to the fore, even if only temporarily, that did not require sameness or coherence, and accounted for the complex relationship between the United States and Arab dictators.

Artistic Alliances
Complementing Speech

Throughout this period, these six women complemented their insistence on the significance of grassroots work by asserting that LAM had been prioritizing politicized speech over artwork. They argued that by coupling political speech with artwork, LAM would enhance its capacity for reaching a broader audience. Artistic expressions, they contended, would humanize the people targeted by occupation and war to public audiences; inspire more and more people to take interest in LAM's Palestine and Iraq campaigns; and enhance LAM's capacity for building connections with a wider range of people and movements. In addition, these six women found more room to express themselves through art than through political speech. The art forms they brought to LAM deployed alternative forms of communication that, they argued, were less hierarchical. Music and dance, for instance, displaced the charismatic style of political leadership that addressed a passive audience with a collective style of performance in which the audience is more involved. Several women also spoke of politics in a way that conceptualized emotional well-being, human relationships, and social transformation as interconnected. Accordingly, they were committed to expanding the possibilities for creative expression in LAM in order to center both political rhetoric and emotional expression as interconnected mechanisms of political discourse. Most importantly, women activists found it easier to put forth an intersectional, multisited feminist analysis through artwork than through political speech. Artwork allowed them to represent complex, interconnected ideas that were difficult to express in words.

> Dahlia: As a cultural worker, I saw art as a political statement. But art wasn't considered valid or legitimate political work so I never included it in the movement. A lot of the women were doing that work on the side— work that would have given the movement more power, more legitimacy, more visibility and access to more places. Yara used to write and paint. Raya had been making all kinds of art and art exhibits. . . .

> Aisha: I felt like our work was too one-dimensional—not fresh, not exciting, not visibly beautiful to look at. It didn't seem like men were that interested in cultural work. Women spearheaded that kind of work. Anytime

we prepared for a march, it was women leading the effort to make the signs creative—to make it have a broader appeal to reach different kinds of people. Women were committed to not have it be talking heads all the time and to create ways to express not just ideas but pain and sadness—and art and culture are important. Once, we made an altar for victims of Palestine and Iraq. Only two of the men helped out. Raya, Dahlia, and I did most of the work. It was a way of healing and moving forward, a way to deal with emotions within the movement.

Mai: Some of our brothers didn't see art as a legitimate thing to do. When some of us organized a music concert to fundraise for supplies for Palestinians, this same member said that "we are wasting our time" and that this was "a weak strategy for building a movement."

Dahlia, Aisha, and Mai confronted a dominant movement logic that considered art and culture secondary to "real politics." It was not that LAM's earlier iteration of leftist Arab politics did not belong to a legacy that valued art. Those who were politically active in the Arab world or in the Bay Area in the 1970s and '80s told me that leftist Arab movements used a range of art forms, such as dancing, singing, and poetry, extensively in their resistance work. Yet, the dominant approach to art and politics, they told me, was that art is important but secondary to politicized speech and direct confrontations with power structures.

This distinction persisted in LAM's movement logic during the early period of LAM's revival in the 1990s. During LAM's revival, Dahlia, Aisha, and Mai were arguing for a more central place for artwork as a movement strategy. Early on, at events related to the Arab world, LAM indeed relied on artwork, such as the *debkah* dance or Palestinian embroidery. LAM, in continuity with leftist Arab movements historically, presented art separately from official political discourse or practice. A typical LAM event from this period featured a speaker as the center of the event and then a group that performed the *debkah* dance. Palestinian embroidery would be featured on tables near the door or in the lobby. Here, artwork operated as a symbol of a culture or cultural tradition that exists in a separate domain of it own, or as a symbol of an authentic culture that is to be expressed and reproduced. This resembles what Lisa Lowe and David Lloyd refer to as the modernist separation between a static concept of culture, on the one hand, and dynamic, constantly changing politics and economics on the other (1997). Lowe and Lloyd argue that leftist and conservative thinkers similarly rely on this separation.[5] Ella Shohat notes that a similar binary between modernity and tradition underpins

European modernist discourses. She argues that "both bourgeois nationalists and Marxist anticolonialists" reinforce this demarcation by conceptualizing 'tradition' as dead weight" (Shohat 2001, 20). Partha Chatterjee makes a similar statement that anticolonialist nationalist discourse constructs culture as a manifestation of the existence of an essentialist difference between us and them and a reflection of the colonized people's essential identity (Chatterjee 1993).[6] Along these same lines, during the period of LAM's revival, *debkah* and embroidery would stand in as symbols of an authentic, static, unchanging Arab or Palestinian tradition that the resistance movement was fighting to keep alive.

Art as Politics

As LAM developed its Palestine and Iraq campaigns, women had more opportunities to take on leadership positions and spearhead events and activities. During this period, women activists generated a series of events that featured artwork as a central mechanism for communicating political discourse alongside LAM's speeches and lectures. At two events in particular, centralizing artwork had three distinct effects on LAM's work. Artwork opened up new possibilities for women's leadership. It also transformed the meaning of culture as "dead weight." Furthermore, artwork enabled a new kind of political analysis in LAM that was intersectional and coalitional. The first event was Artists for Iraq in April 2000 at which Elham and Ghada spoke. Artists for Iraq was the launching pad for LAM's Iraq campaign. The second event was a commemoration of *al-Nakba* (the catastrophe), or the creation of the state of Israel and the dispossession, displacement, and uprooting of Palestinians in 1948. The second event was a launching pad for LAM's divestment campaign.

Artists for Iraq took place at the Mission Cultural Center in San Francisco's Mission District. As the doors opened, the audience packed the aisles and stood across the back of the room. The security guard turned away the remaining crowd on the street. LAM members directed guests upstairs to a gallery displaying Iraqi women artists' sculptures, women activists' paintings, and Palestinian women's embroidery. As the crowd settled into their seats, a Latina dance troupe, Azteca, opened the event. Next, the audience danced at their seats to the beat of the Company of Prophets, an African American hip-hop duo. I was one of the emcees with Mai. We opened up the event performing a spoken-word jam that critiqued the U.S. media, cultural appropriation, and war. Art Concordia, a spoken-word artist active with the League of Filipino Students and the

Committee for Human Rights in the Philippines addressed connections between Filipino and Arab decolonization struggles. After Elham and Ghada's testimonies, Sima Shaksari, an Iranian spoken-word artist, performed a poem where she interconnected what she saw as the problems of the Clinton administration's attack on Iraq in 1998, California's criminalization of youth of color, and the institutionalization of homophobia in California state law. The performers represented distinct social movements—anti-interventionist/anti-imperialist, decolonizing, immigrant rights, racial justice, women of color, and queer of color—and beyond. Egyptian feminist Nawal El Saadawi closed the event, framing the end of sanctions on Iraq as a feminist cause. Indeed, there were tensions and power imbalances that bringing these performers and speakers together brought about. Some participants and attendees charged Nawal El Saadawi for reifying homophobia and Islamophobia. Yet taken together, the performances asserted a politics that held the United States accountable for violence, oppression, and marginality.

Afterward, LAM members celebrated what they agreed was the most successful and well-attended event to date. Over five hundred people attended and LAM met its fundraising goals. Artists for Iraq marked a key shift in LAM's efforts to bring an Arab counternarrative to U.S. publics during this period. Until this time, LAM's work had taken place primarily among leftist antiwar activists—people already committed to an antiwar agenda. This event brought LAM's message to a much broader crowd that extended far beyond the middle-class Arab community who supported LAM's work, and beyond those LAM referred to as "the already converted"—leftist activists who were already committed to antiwar activism.

A range of people who do not frequent Bay Area antiwar events attended, including Iraqi refugees and people from the less politicized Arab American community–based institutions. The range of artists brought out various people connected to other left-leaning Bay Area social justice movements related to the struggles of immigrants, working-class people, and people of color in the Bay Area. A feminist crowd from nearby colleges and universities came for Nawal El Saadawi. This was the first time since LAM's revival that LAM's work was not operating on the margins of Bay Area progressive politics. At Artists for Iraq, LAM asserted its Iraq campaign in connection with multiple struggles located in the Bay Area, allowing them to circulate their counternarrative within a constellation of people and movements. LAM's campaign was on stage amid multiple, distinct struggles, which seemed to intensify the sense of urgency that LAM had previously been able to invoke among its audiences related to ending the sanctions on Iraq. In chapter 4 we saw how LAM's dominant movement logic, which focused on a singular, unified political issue, suppressed a multisited political platform based on a sense that such a platform could fracture the movement. Artists for Iraq brought about an alternative politics in which a multisited political platform moved the cause forward, rather than fractured it.

Art as a Mechanism of Feminist Discourse

Similar to what Elham's testimonial did at Artists for Iraq, artwork provided a mechanism to position women as coleaders within LAM and cocreators of LAM's political discourse. In my conversations with Mai and Aisha, they told me they felt marginalized from LAM's leadership since they found it difficult to participate in the main political debates and forms of public political speech that LAM favored. They attributed this partly to gender and partly to the fact that they were younger than most of the organization's activists or less knowledgeable about the region. Yet through art, they found new possibilities for political expression. While she was active in LAM, Mai took poetry classes with June Jordan at the University of California–Berkeley and found her voice through spoken-word poetry and performance. Aisha was also writing political poetry around this time. They felt alienated from the political discourse and terminology that circulated in LAM and found that artwork allowed them to highlight human experiences, which seemed to have an important impact on audiences and allowed LAM to bring a multiplicity of experiences with imperialism and racism that grandiose political speech obscures.

Another moment in which primarily women activists brought artwork to LAM's audiences happened in November 2000 when LAM organized an event to commemorate *al-Nakba* at San Francisco's Women's Building. The *al-Nakba* event featured theatrical and dance performances coupled with a panel discussion and a fundraising pitch. Aisha and Mai reflected upon women's artistic contributions to the event.

Aisha: The event featured a *debkah* dance group—a few men played important roles in the performance, but it was an important part of the event where women were really central.

Mai: I was one of the people who insisted that we do *debkah* as part of the event. . . . [I]t was an art form that afforded us room to redefine ourselves. It was as if the door was swung open and how far we were going to swing it after that was up to us. . . . It was much easier to be able to speak . . . for and by women . . . in an art form than it was in speeches. We didn't have many forms of resistance . . . so we couldn't address gender issues . . . but art made it more possible.

The idea to create a puppet of the fifteen-foot-tall Palestinian woman that Aisha featured for the Palestinian right to return rally in Washington, DC, in 2000 developed out of a similar conceptual framework. Aisha told me, "Creating puppets was a way to bring art to our movement. I wanted to make a contribution to an agenda that is being pushed forward by men in a positive cultural way." The puppet depicted the often obscured histories of Palestinian women and their active involvement in resistance against colonization. The puppet drew on Palestinian feminist imagery of powerful Palestinian women activists to make an intervention into the leftist Arab movement in the United States, where women were negotiating similar yet distinct struggles over feminism and national liberation.

At the rally, LAM activists discussed who was going to hold the puppet up at the rally. A few women came up with the idea that it was the men's job to carry it. Aisha told me, "She was really heavy and someone had to give support to this huge beautiful Palestinian woman." Carrying the puppet entailed standing inside it and becoming invisible, except for one's eyes and nose. In Aisha's analysis, the puppet was a representation of women's agency as actors and leaders in the movement. The men who held her stood as invisible supporters of women's leadership. While this was indeed an important moment for women activists who saw this as a symbolic act in challenging patriarchy, it was also one that reveals the persistence of patriarchal movement logics. As we saw earlier, women involved in "invisible" labor argued that their work was rarely recognized or acknowledged in LAM. Yet here, to LAM activists, men's "invisible" labor becomes an accolade. The men were proud to take part, and the women who felt shorted by their roles in comparison to men saw men's positioning as subservient, at least to onlookers, in a positive light.

As we saw in chapter 4, these six women brought to LAM an analysis that broadened LAM's definition of violence and suffering beyond a logic of emergency and its focus on bodily pain, life, and death. And in the first part of this chapter, we saw that these women's work opened up new possibilities for articulating Arabness in terms of multiple histories and internal-communal difference and contestation. In the previous section, I mapped the ways artwork opened up new possibilities for women's participation in LAM's work. In the following pages, I elaborate upon the distinct political visions that their work brought to LAM's public audiences. As we will see, together, the visions they put forth constitute an intersectional, transnational, coalitional feminist and queer politics that is firmly grounded in anti-imperialism.

Intersectional Feminist Anti-Imperialism

Mai wrote a one-woman show from the perspective of a fictional Palestinian woman prisoner. Although she began performing it in 2004, after the period I discuss here, Mai developed her artistic voice during the period of my research, and the play reflects the kind of art that women activists were developing in LAM during that time. Here is an excerpt from this piece, in the voice of a Palestinian woman prisoner:

> That night was so intense, even I believed it was going to be my liberation day. . . . [T]he women were singing, the men followed, I was going to be free. . . . They say that I am so *uncivilized*, so *savage* that I send my babies out to the front line to blow themselves up for me—look, I may be poor, and sick of these damned concrete walls, but I would never turn my babies into bombs. . . . I wasn't the one who killed Inas. I wasn't the one who drove a bulldozer into the home she was studying in. I wasn't the one who made the roof fall in and crush her and her books.

Mai's performance offered a feminist analysis of Israeli state discourses and practices. She brought into focus the existence of Palestinian women political prisoners, thus intervening in Israeli, Arab, and international discourses that either prioritize discussions about Palestinian male prisoners or address prisoners in gender-neutral terms, which assume a male subject (Bayour 2005). Mai challenged imperialist tropes that portray Palestinian women as savage mothers who raise terrorists or as passive victims of a backwards culture or religion and provided an alternative perspective. In this excerpt, the woman prisoner is constrained, not simply by family or patriarchy, but by the Israeli state. Yet she is also an agent of her destiny. She sings, while men follow. Mai articulated Palestinian women's lives beyond an Orientalist focus on their "culture" or "religion" but in the context of the material realities of Israeli expansion. She narrated an experience many Palestinian women and men have encountered in one way or another: an Israeli bulldozer crushing one's home. Mai humanized Palestinian girlhood as the audience soon learns that it is a Palestinian girl reading a book who faces the bulldozer. Mai located Palestinian girlhood within the conditions of militarization and colonial expansion.

Mai's performance portrayed Palestinianness beyond a singular (male) national subject, reflecting the intersectional vision underpinning women activists' work. Imperialist imagery relies on gender and Mai countered it through a focus on the gendered realities of Israeli state violence and Palestinian women's resistance to violence. Nearly all of the artwork women brought to LAM similarly counters imperial acts of military violence and expansion and the U.S. and Israeli discourses that justify them. Their critiques center the analysis that gender permeates imperialism. Their work presents imperialism as an intersection of oppressions and Arab engagements with imperialism as heterogeneous. Here, an intersectional anti-imperialist feminist critique transcends the idea of an internally coherent Arab identity, culture, or nation, without giving up on the commitment to liberation (Shohat 2001).

Transnational Feminist Anti-Imperialism

In U.S. women's studies, the theory of feminist intersectionality has become short-hand for a wide range of analyses that view race, class, and gender as interconnected.[7] Yet it is important to distinguish the continuity between my interlocutors' visions and a particular strand of feminist intersectionality that was born out of third world women's and women of color's struggles and was consolidated in the 1960s and '70s. At the same time, the moments in which intersectional anti-imperialist feminist visions emerged in LAM's public discourses in the late 1990s reveal that my interlocutors, like many Arab woman scholars and activists of this period, were authoring a distinct anti-imperialist politics in the midst of the general silence in the United States, even among most U.S. feminist movements, about U.S. imperialism in the Arab and Muslim region at the turn of the millennium. At Artists for Iraq, a transnational anti-imperialist feminism framed the event that brought onto the same stage struggles for decolonization and self-determination taking place outside the United States with struggles for decolonization and self-determination taking place within the boundaries of the United States. Mai remembered this event as one that "ruptured the nationalist bubble by fighting not only for the homeland, but also here in this home." The vision these six women put forth constitutes a diasporic anti-imperialist feminism that accounts for organizing beyond rigid nationalist boundaries and enhances the possibilities for coalition building, as we saw at Artists for Iraq. It differs from the conventional long-distance nationalist narratives of diaspora communities that focus on the decolonization of the homeland over decolonization here in the United States, and it also differs from progressive U.S. politics that fails to interrogate the interconnectedness between U.S.-state violence within and beyond the geographic boundaries of the United States. The vision that these six women's work brought to LAM's audiences articulates Iraqi and Palestinian liberation with and through a U.S. racial justice and decolonizing framework that connects the Palestinian struggle and U.S. imperialism in Iraq with the racial and colonial situation here in the United States.

Of course diasporic Arab feminists of the 1990s were not the first to articulate a transnational anti-imperialist feminist vision of U.S. empire in the Middle East. A few feminist publications on post–Cold War U.S.-led wars exist (Chaudhuri and Strobel 1992; Eisenstein 1996; Enloe 1993). More substantially, native and indigenous Pacific Islander feminists have been historicizing the local and global implications of U.S. empire long before the 1990s, through a post-1492 framework (Smith 2005; Kauanui 2008). Also, in the '60s and '70s and in the context of the Vietnam War, transnational anti-imperialist feminisms were at their height (Burnham, Tatnall, and Women of Color Resource Center 2006). Yet such analyses were less prominent in feminist scholarship and activism in the '80s and '90s and tended to more systematically take up such analyses of U.S. empire in the Middle East only after the attacks of September 11, 2001. Consider, for example, the plethora of feminist writings published after September 11 on the local and global impacts of the U.S.-led war on terror compared to the virtually nonexistent publications on similar subjects beforehand (Hawthorne and Winter 2003; Mohanty, Pratt, and Riley 2008; Alexander and Hawkesworth 2008; Reed and Pollitt 2002; Bhattacharyya 2008; Enloe 2007; Puar 2007). This dynamic parallels a pattern in U.S. progressive politics more generally. The antiwar movement arose during the Vietnam War and then fell and peaked again after the attacks of September 11, 2001. Patricia McFadden's argument exemplifies this feminist anti-imperialism of the post-9/11 era: "For U.S. feminism, the ability to see the world beyond parochial white nationalistic anxieties that inform daily life with such persistence and repetition, pushing boundaries of our understanding of war is crucial in crafting an alternative ideology—to change ways in which U.S. communities exist in relation to the rest of the world—today and into the future" (2008, 64). My interlocutors' political work of the late '90s anticipates this critique. Mai's performance, for instance, frames her story of the Palestinian woman prisoner in reaction to what she had been perceiving as dominant U.S. and Israeli discourses that paint Palestinian women as bad mothers who send their children out to the streets where Israeli soldiers can kill them (Marcus and Zilberdik 2010; Amireh 2011). Like Mai, my interlocutors' transnational feminist vision is born out of a sense of belonging to a diaspora of empire, of residing in the United States as people affiliated with a region where the U.S. empire had intervened long before the events of September 11, 2001.

At the turn of the twenty-first century, these six women activists articulate a vision that transcends LAM's tendency to prioritize Arab struggles over other histories and struggles or to craft solidarity with predominantly white, leftist antiwar movements that were already working in support of Palestine and Iraq. Consider the Artists for Iraq event, an event organized primarily by women. At Artists for Iraq, women's work conjoined a multiplicity of struggles, struggles of people whose lives had been shaped by centuries of settler-colonialism and racism in the United States in relationship to the struggles of people from countries the United States was invading. Through their work, along with their counterparts in LAM, these women brought a new vision of community to LAM's public audience. On stage were not only Arab activists calling on audiences to be in solidarity with Palestinians or Iraqis but multiple struggles, each with its distinct histories, claims, and visions joined together.

LAM activists reflected on the new forms of solidarity that the Artists for Iraq event mobilized.

> Camelia: At the time, most of the men did not seem to think that solidarity work was as important as other kinds of work. They were not as interested in being involved in other communities' struggles. It was women who would bring up how our work was related to other stuff that's happening locally. Men would say, we need to focus on Palestine, we need to focus on Iraq. They would think it was taking away from the work we were doing instead of seeing it as a longer, larger movement and that it would make all of our movements stronger. Maybe it's partly because women have a unifying approach . . . or maybe because more of the women were raised in the U.S. and had affinities with other communities. Before that event, I had mostly seen the typical march or speaking event. This was different. I was seeing lots of different people of color. It wasn't just about art or culture, but about having different people coming together. Usually our events had been broken down along the lines of Arab activists and white leftists talking about the Middle East but we are not as used to seeing other people of color getting in touch with these issues. It was important to have these voices against the sanctions also representing concerns like the call for the U.S. out of Puerto Rico, and other anti-imperialist demands against interventionism in the Philippines . . . and in the Black community locally. The event tied together all these different issues as part of a struggle with different fronts. It was about expressing similar hopes.

Dahlia: In the past we struggled so much over how to bring different kinds of people into our movement. The art and cultural work brought these folks in. They didn't have to know everything about the sanctions or Iraq because we invited them to collaborate through cultural work. We gave them a way to access our movement. We invited them to our home without it being boring or top down.

Mai: We wanted to try and make links between different communities while we were raising money for the billboards. We made links around issues that stem from the same place . . . imperialism, racism, and what the U.S. is doing all over the world and to communities of color here, which has a different character. The idea was to show solidarity with other communities of color and bring people to the end-the-sanctions campaign. Iraqi women were there sharing a stage with Filipinos and Latinos. We focused on Iraq but said we should not be ghettoized.

People expressed a desire for liberation in ways that transcended nationalist divisions—not just with words, but with culture. To see people express struggles through dance was to fulfill something that couldn't be fulfilled in words. It was lived and dynamic. We usually talk a lot. However much you talk, it is not the same as expressing lived experiences. We were able to do that through art forms. As a new Arab American community, we were trying to create a different kind of organizing—not just a political party or platform. We were bringing a type of resistance that included who we are as Arab Americans . . . and brought these to other struggles. Bringing these artists together allowed us to slash the nationalist bubble. It made it clear that we were not just fighting for liberation in our homeland but here in this home.

Some of the men active in LAM with whom I spoke in 2007 came to similar conclusions about LAM's deployment of artistic expression during this period.

Ibrahim: Something that was different happened. It didn't attract the same audience but new people and new crowds. I now see how those events were beneficial to the movement and were a means to achieve that. We got more people involved because we outreached to them through different means even though it's hard to quantify how it affected our movement.

Obeid: Poetry provided a language people understood. It's a mechanism, a language that resonates with folks here. We were able to address communities that we were never ever before able to speak to. The audience can't negate cultural expression in the same way they can negate interviews or lectures. They can't say art is wrong . . . it's an expression. It's an important proactive tool.

The vision that came out of women's commitment to artwork as a strategy for coalition disrupts the dominant logic that had been fueling LAM. As Obeid expresses above, this dominant logic appreciates the art but considers it a tool, a means to an end rather than an end in itself. By conceptualizing art and politics as an interwoven relationality, women's work challenges conventional nationalist hierarchies between "art" or "culture" and "politics." In their vision, artwork is a mechanism that mobilizes Iraqi, Filipino, Puerto Rican, Native American, and other decolonizing struggles to share the stage and to speak to and with one another. The success of this event was not in the unification of these movements on stage or their resemblances, but the "communication of singularities" (Hardt and Negri 2000, 57, cited in Puar and Rai 2004, 88) that emerges where the "singular emergence" of struggles creates alliances through "the intensity that characterizes them one by one'" (Hardt and Negri 2000, 58, cited in Puar and Rai 2004, 88).

This vision transcends the dynamic in which conventional nationalisms articulate national identity in rigid terms and community boundaries as sealed-off entities. As we saw in chapter 4, these six women activists articulated Arabness beyond the conventional nationalist and diasporic logics oriented primarily toward homeland, exile, and return and the "traditionally hierarchical relation between nation and diaspora, where the former is seen as merely an impoverished imitation of an originary national culture" (Gopinath 2005, 7). This vision was consolidated at Artists for Iraq when they staged a diasporic anti-imperialism that works for the liberation of Arab countries from imperial and colonial domination while bringing multiple concerns that are based "here" (in the United States) and "there" (in the Arab world and beyond). Here, a transnational feminist vision releases my interlocutors from the burdens of masculinist nationalisms (Saliba 2003) by transcending the limitations of singular national liberation logics without giving up the focus on self-determination and ending imperial violence. It can be captured by what Ella Shohat explains as "a skepticism towards metanarratives of liberation" that does not necessarily "abandon the notion that emancipation is worth fighting for" (2006; Shohat and Stam 1994, 288).[8] At Artists for Iraq and the *al-Nakba* event, they transformed the place of art and cultural forms such as music and dance in LAM from a secondary to a central mechanism of political discourse, and simultaneously changed LAM's political stance at large. They articulated a diasporic anti-imperialist feminist vision driven by a coalitional politics that centers a multiplicity of struggles "there" and "here."

Emergent Transnational Queer Anti-Imperialism

The coalitional vision driving women's work presents an alternative to heteropatriarchal meanings of culture in conventional national liberation discourses. The coalitional politics at Artists for Iraq and the November 29 event rearticulates culture from the dominant nationalist notion that conceptualizes cultural reproduction in biological, kinship-based terms. A national culture, in this analysis, is pure and is transmitted through blood, through the vertical transmission from one generation to the next, and through heteropatriarchal marriage and reproduction. Women's work reimagines cultural reproduction through the possibility of horizontal cultural exchange, or moving from the ideal of blood-based cultural transmission to the notion of culture as an ongoing production. This vision is best reflected in what transpired after the right to return rally in Washington DC, before LAM activists prepared to return to the Bay Area of California. At the end of the rally, women activists passed the puppet on to another group of activists from Canada, who committed to continue carrying it in their own actions where they lived. Aisha explained that she had always envisioned that "it was going to be shared and would travel." Like the multiplicity of struggles that conjoined at Artists for Iraq, the act of creating an articulation of Arabness (the puppet of the Palestinian woman activists) that would travel (to unknown Canadian activists) is an act that rearticulates Arabness beyond the heteronormative structures of nationalism. As we have seen, conventional nationalisms rely on a patrilineal, heternormative reproductive logic that maintains community boundaries through the ideal of heterosexual marriage and reproduction. By rearticulating culture across rigid national boundaries, Aisha, through the puppet, put forth a vision for national liberation that was not reliant on the ideal of a unified nation, connected together through concepts of cultural purity, genealogy, and, by implication, heternormativity. Here, Aisha dislodged "diaspora from adherence to a conventional nationalist ideology" and set into motion an emergent queer diasporic anti-imperialism, an anti-imperialism that brings into focus "the non-reproductive potential of diaspora," thus "troubl[ing] the relationship between diasporic nationalism and heterosexuality" (Gopinath 2005, 7).

No moment better represents the coalescence of diasporic feminist and queer anti-imperialism that emerged during this period than the moment at Artists for Iraq when Sima Shaksari, an Iranian spoken-word artist, performed an antiwar poem on the stage of the Mission Cultural Center. Here are excerpts from Sima's poem:

> why do I write about war
> when the freedom to choose
> keeps the fire going . . .
>
> and no . . .
> the statute of liberty
> doesn't have to wear a veil . . .
>
> maybe this is not a dream or a tale of love . . .
> and no,
> bellies stuck to the bone
> cannot belly dance . . .
>
> tell me in your dreams
> do you see anything
> but bombs
> in the black eyes of the children
> you once captured in snapshots
> for your *National Geographic*?
> the children you feel sorry for
> and to whom you offer
> hunger and death? . . .
>
> I still write about war . . .
> I still yearn to write poems
> between your bullets and blood
> between detention and welfare cuts
> between the sanctions and Props. 21 and 22 . . .
>
> I still yearn to write love poems
> I still
> love
> love
> love
> beyond your hate

and is that my 3rd strike
america?

Sima calls out contradictions in hegemonic U.S. feminist discourses that celebrate liberal feminist concepts of "choice" while failing to challenge U.S.-led war and its impact on women and children in the countries the United States is invading. Sima calls into question the contradictions between U.S. liberal multicultural discourses that celebrate "the East" in Orientalist terms (belly dancing and *National Geographic* photos) and acts of U.S.-state violence against the same apparently "Eastern" people. The children U.S. popular culture once captured in *National Geographic* snapshots, she contends, are the same as the Iraqi children the United States is now offering hunger and death. Yet her poem goes beyond feminist critique of U.S. imperialism and war. Sima brings together her critique of U.S.-led war, racist policies such as the three strikes proposition (Proposition 21), and attacks on gay marriage (Proposition 22), political problems that progressive and U.S.-state discourses often address separately. Her poetry critiques the patriarchy and homophobia that structure the U.S. nation-state. Bringing these critiques into conversation with each other, she ends her poem with the words "I still / love / love / love / beyond your hate" and "is that my 3rd strike / america?"

One could interpret her words "I still love, love, love beyond your hate" as an assertion that queer love can overcome militarism, war, and racism. Yet a simplistic gay-rights framework cannot explain Sima's vision. The queer critique she articulates is not simply correlated with her queer self-identification, concepts of homosexual love or desire, or outrage at antigay marriage policies. In fact, the queer anti-imperialist vision, as Sima's poem illustrates, is rooted in a queer vision that transcends conventional heteronormative nationalist and diasporic logics. Consider, for instance, that Sima affiliated herself with queer Iranian and Southwest Asian collectives, among other groups, at the time she wrote this poem. One collective was organized by and for queer people from Southwest Asia and North Africa (SWANA), a framework that committed to alliances that are regional rather than nationalist. To a certain extent, the regional framework of SWANA affirms a commitment to political alliances that transcend nationalist concepts of affiliation that predominate in the Middle East, concepts that, its advocates argue, were brought to the region through European colonial domination. Activists who advocate for affiliations with the concept of SWANA argue that this term refers to people from a region with shared histories of domination in relation to European and U.S. empire, including people from the Arab region and Iran, for instance. It is not coincidental that queer activists have been among the most persistent advocates of this framework, especially since this regional concept opens up possibilities for affiliations that are not based in the triangulation of patriarchy, heterosexual marriage, and biological repro- duction that is fundamental to nation-based concepts of community.

Also, Sima's poem puts forth a transnational anti-imperialist vision that brings a critique of U.S.-led sanctions on Iraq into the same frame of critique as forms of racism and homophobia existent within the geographic bound- aries of the United States (in terms of Propositions 21 and 22). When Sima states, "I still love beyond your hate, and is that my third strike, America?" she asks if her nonnormative sexuality will bring her into the criminaliza- tion system of the three strikes policy, and by referring to her potential oppressor as "America," she brings three sites of oppression to the center: queerness, criminalization of U.S. people of color, and the "America" at war abroad. Here, she expands conventional queer analyses that argue for "gay rights" into a larger analysis of U.S.-led racism and imperialism. By bringing U.S. militarism and war into the same frame as problems typically defined as "domestic-U.S.-national," this vision contests U.S.-based gay rights and racial justice narratives that ignore the global implications of U.S. power structures. In Sima's poem, the racist, classist three strikes proposition is not entirely separate from American empire globally. This vision thus articulates a multiplicity of struggles not hierarchically but simultaneously and rejects the rigid structures of U.S. politics that force her to choose between a gay or queer rights framework, on the one hand, and anti-imperialism and anti- racism on the other.

By putting forth an intersectional, transnational queer critique, this vision transcends the liberal single-issue-based gay rights politics and the conven- tional nationalist logics that require heteropatriarchy and privilege the home- land over the diaspora. In this diasporic, queer, anti-imperialist vision, crim- inalization must be understood beyond progressive critiques that explain the three strikes proposition in terms of institutionalized racism and classism while ignoring the ways institutionalized racism takes on different forms in the lives of women and queer people. Moreover, it demands "reject[ing] the ethnic and religious absolutism at the heart of nationalist projects" (Gopinath 2005). As we have seen, conventional nationalisms are based upon an ideal of ethnic purity and origins and rely on the ideal of heterosexual reproduction as a primary structure of collectivity, culture, and belonging. Sima's poem, interweaving the struggles of people of color, queers in the United States, and Iraqis living under U.S. sanctions, puts forth an alternative rendering of diasporic national liberation and anti-imperialism. By articulating concepts of affiliation, solidarity, and belonging through a multiplicity of communities

238 << DIASPORIC FEMINIST ANTI-IMPERIALISM

of political struggle and activism, this vision dislodges diasporic nationalist notions of community and alliance from a loyalty to genealogy, or an implicitly heternormative reproductive logic; troubles the relationship between nationalism and heterosexuality; and restores the nonreproductive potential of diaspora (Gopinath 2005).

I shared my interpretation of this poem with Sima. After reading it, she wrote this to me:

> The poem is not just about my subjectivity as a queer person, but also the way that my contestation to U.S. imperialism goes beyond the liberal logic, which I have expressed in the beginning of the poem as a form of seemingly harmonious multiculturalism that was/is quite prevalent in the area I lived at the time (Mission district of SF, right around the time it was being gentrified . . . the rush of liberal folks who loved tasting "ethnic" food and discussing new-age forms of peace, while we lived in a time of war that tore Iraqi lives apart). And of course, the criminalization of youth—particularly immigrant youth, people of color, and queer youth, along with the discrimination against queers that props 21 and 22 signified were not separate from the war in Iraq. So the "queer loving" beyond the American hate and violence in this poem refers to loving beyond the heteronormative (and homonormative) forms of desire and belonging—a form of love that makes one subjected to laws that criminalize those who refuse to be complicit with the violence of war and neoliberal multiculturalism. Of course, there are queers who are complicit with homophobic nationalism and imperialism. I guess the poem represents a particular queer politics that is critical of complicities with U.S. nationalism and imperialism.

The emergence of a queer anti-imperialist vision within LAM's public discourse at Artists for Iraq reflects a distinct moment in which feminist and queer visions coalesced in the context of LAM's work and beyond in the Bay Area. Sima, reflecting on this moment, told me,

> Well, I came to the event because I liked AWSA [the feminist collective working with LAM] and I believed in alliance-building beyond the rigid identity politics that are exclusionary and problematic. It was always a struggle to build bridges between Iranian/Arab, straight/queer, Middle Eastern/non-Middle Eastern American communities. Yet I did not feel any tension in that event at all . . . in fact, all I felt was a feeling of collaboration and solidarity.

Reflecting on the late 1990s, Lana, who was also active in queer SWANA politics, told me, "So much organizing was happening—I felt more connection with a larger Arab community than before. Before that I didn't have a lot of experience with a larger Arab community. I didn't feel I could bring my whole self. That was when I didn't feel that I had to desexualize myself."

There were also reminders at events like Artists for Iraq of the ongoing tensions and hierarchies that persist in the process of alliance building. For instance, after the event some attendees recognized the featured speaker, Nawal El Saadawi, as someone who has made invaluable contributions to feminist critiques of patriarchy and U.S. empire but who has also reified homophobic concepts that "gay and lesbian Arabs do not exist" in previous public lectures in San Francisco. These activists were referring to a public lecture in 1994 in which I shared the stage with Saadawi. As Laura recalls, "she was denying that homosexuality in the Arab world exists even though the room was filled with Arab dykes." Also after Artists for Iraq, several Muslim women activists confronted Saadawi for reinforcing in her lecture Islamophobic concepts that define women who wear the *hijab* as passive victims of their religion. In fact, several years later, Sima told me that she would not have accepted the invitation to read her poem on stage if she had been expected to share the stage with Saadawi alone.

You Can't Blame Everything on Sexism: Contextualizing Women's Artwork

The terminology women activists used to refer to politicized artwork helps elucidate the difficulties LAM activists faced when they discussed the gender tensions over artwork and politicized speech. Women activists tended to use the term "cultural work" to refer to the artwork they brought to LAM. Their concept of artwork as "cultural work" assumes a particular analysis about the relationship between art and politics. When Mai said that the performances at Artists for Iraq were "not for entertainment or exposition," she clarified a vision in which political work takes place through culture. For women activists, art as cultural work is not meant to symbolize an abstract, authentic culture fixed in time, but to define culture in varying forms that are shaped within distinct political and historical contexts and are open to production, reproduction, and transformation (Lowe and Lloyd 1997, 21-26).

Moreover, women activists' deployment of artwork as cultural work has drawn upon an understanding of art and culture that has been crucial to U.S. leftist politics and Bay Area progressive social movements for decades. African American scholar and civil rights activist Angela Davis used the same term to refer to works that are "concerned not only with the creation of progressive art, but must be actively involved in the organization of people's political movements" (1998, 245). Davis has also argued that the Bay Area has been a hotbed of politicized art and that in recent years, conscious political art has become increasingly evident (1998). In the late 1990s in the Bay Area, I observed activists from various leftist social movements using this term to refer to a particular concept of art and politics that Lisa Lowe and David Lloyd have theorized in terms of the mobilization of art forms for contesting "the incessant violence of the new transnational order with its reconstituted patriarchies and racisms" (Lowe and Lloyd 1997, 26). Lowe and Lloyd argue that the idea of cultural work entails "redefining the political" and centering the idea that politics is "always braided with culture" (ibid.).

Most of the performances at Artists for Iraq drew upon forms of cultural work that peaked in the Bay Area in the 1990s and relied specifically upon art forms developed within the histories of rap music and hip-hop. In the 1990s, a great deal of California progressive politics came to rely upon hip-hop music and hip-hop–based spoken-word performances as crucial mechanisms of political discourse (Fusco 1999; Davis 1998). Hip-hop as a mechanism of political discourse has been particularly significant for inner-city youth in California. George Lipsitz contends that African American hip-hop artists have raised awareness about "residential and educational segregation, police brutality, discrimination in employment, and cultural suppression in the lives of inner-city dwellers" (2000, 165).

Scholars have also argued that hip-hop has given rise to new coalition politics (Lipsitz 2000; de Leon 2004). Paul Gilroy argues that hip-hop extends beyond the idea of an organic, natural, racial family (Gilroy 1992). Lipsitz analyzes hip-hop as a new historicity that seeks strategies for living with difference and building on the hybrid qualities of the form itself (2000, 91). Lipsitz alleges that hip-hop overrides what conventional concepts of nation and family provide. Lipsitz, writing about the 1990s, suggests that hip-hop provides an entry point into understanding the cultural complexity of the present moment in California (2000). LAM's women activists' commitment to cultural work emerged out of the hip-hop culture of the 1990s in California, a moment when hip-hop came to serve as a crucial mechanism of political expression, mobilization, and coalition building and when political activism centered on cultural syncretism and bringing diverse cultural forms together (de Leon 2004).

Women activists' commitment to cultural work also reflects a specific U.S. feminist strategy for challenging power and revealing multiple oppressions that has circulated in feminist and feminist of color politics in the United States generally and the Bay Area specifically. This feminist strategy has relied on representations of women's bodies and bodily performances to articulate political subjectivities that have been previously silenced or ignored. Mai's one-woman performance and the spoken-word poetry at Artists for Iraq drew specifically on the ways this feminist strategy has been deployed among politicized women of color in Bay Area progressive politics. These political strategies of left-leaning women of color have centralized one-woman performances, spoken word, and hip-hop as mechanisms for reawakening monolithic nationalist or racial justice narratives and putting forth an intersectional analysis of power.

Spoken-word poetry, a popular mechanism of political discourse in Bay Area women of color politics, draws heavily on hip-hop and rap cultural forms. Performance art also was a highly consistent genre in this 1990s milieu. Cultural workers from Cherrie Moraga to Margaret Cho used racialized and sexualized bodies as metaphors to intervene in dominant systems of representation. Women of color have found performance art a viable medium for expressing multiple oppressions simultaneously (Arrizón 1999). Writing in the 1990s, during the same period LAM launched its Palestine and Iraq campaigns, Arrizón stated that the feminist deployment of theater and performance for redefining patriarchy, colonialism, and sexual oppression culminated in this generation (1999). Sandoval-Sánchez and Sternbach similarly explain that Latina playwrights dismantle representations and revise and rearticulate new ways of seeing through a new genre called Latina theater and solo performance (2001, 4). Lisa Lowe analyzes the significance of cultural work to multi-axial analyses of power, arguing that it offers an alternative kind of political discourse for linking multiple oppressions (1996, 157-58). The cultural work that emerged from the labor of the six women I worked with promoted similar kinds of awareness. It opened up new possibilities for distinctly intersectional, multi-axial feminist perspectives, critiques, and vision. Women activists' use of cultural work to express a feminist viewpoint of war and occupation resembles a specific mode of feminist culture that has been in the making for decades in the United States, which relies on performance art or theater as a strategy for speaking through bodily representation. This strategy entails centering a woman's body on stage for the audience to see and letting her speak in public through this highly visible physical presentation. Bringing women's bodies into public forums in this way makes the seemingly private or invisible domain of women and women's stories and perspectives public. It is a strategy that crosses boundaries and dismantles the concept of private/communal/secondary and public/political/official.

More general than hip-hop, spoken-word, and women of color–based performances, women activists' commitment to cultural work drew upon a long-standing reliance on concepts of cultural exchange and travel in Bay Area progressive politics. Aisha's involvement in syncretic forms of cultural work in the Bay Area before and during her involvement in LAM informed her stance we saw earlier—that men did not help out with the altar that she and other LAM women developed to honor the lives of people killed in Palestine and Iraq. The altar is a Latino art form that has been a long-standing part of the cultural fabric of San Francisco's Mission District, a historically Latino neighborhood. Altars are made as a way to honor and remember the deceased, and are linked to Mexican histories and to the Day of the Dead. I have observed altar making as a widespread activity among Bay Area progressive political circles, particularly among activists connected to Latino people and histories. Aisha's observation that men did not help with the altar is a commentary on the movement's patriarchal structures in which women did a great deal of set-up and clean-up for LAM's events, as well as a commentary on women's and men's different relationships to the kinds of cultural work that women prioritized.

Forms of cultural work that have circulated in Bay Area progressive politics also informed the puppet-making project that women activists spearheaded. Puppets have been used throughout the Americas to create alternative forms of resistance among the Mexican Zapatistas, in Argentina and Guatemala, and in the United States—notably in demonstrations against the Democratic Convention in Chicago in 1996, at Toronto's Active Resistance gathering in 1998, and at the mass protests against the World Trade Organization in Seattle. Puppets represent a syncretic form of organizing that comes out of Latin America, and they have reemerged in Seattle-style acts of resistance. Growing up in the San Francisco Bay Area, I learned that Bay Area activists have long borrowed the idea of puppet making as a strategy for public protest. Women activists' disproportionate involvement in Bay Area social justice movements, specifically those related to racial justice and immigration, where cultural work proliferated in the 1990s, helps explain their commitment to particular art forms.

Complicating "Sexism in the Movement"

Most women activists' experiences among Bay Area progressive politics provided them with access to political networks where cultural work was already a crucial mechanism of political discourse. By gaining literacy in the vernacular of "cultural work," women activists enhanced LAM's ability to entice new people to LAM's events. In November 2000, when LAM organized the first major event of its Palestine campaign, women were primarily responsible for set-up and clean-up. They also played a key role in outreach and advertising before the event and made key decisions about the event's program. Dahlia and Aisha reflected on the connections between LAM's political connections and its impact on women's contributions to this event.

Dahlia: Women brought so much to this event because we were working on other kinds of projects at the time. Mai had gone to Palestine . . . and she was on her own, writing and doing workshops and a performance piece about it. She did a slide show and a performance about her trip. Yara had been organizing a youth art workshop where people made these murals. We brought their murals over to the event and hung them there. Other artists heard about the workshops and donated their art to LAM.

Aisha: Women were making connections with other movements and struggles and were responsible for a lot of the solidarity work that came out of the event. You [the author] worked at the Center for Political Education. That linked us to a number of progressive organizations who brought members to the event, like the Institute for Multiracial Justice and Asian Pacific Islanders for Community Empowerment and the folks from the Freedom Archives and the Committees of Correspondence. I worked with Global Exchange, Lillian with Mission Housing. . . . A lot of the Arab women organizers worked in the larger progressive movement. Men worked in the corporate world and their official jobs did not involve organizing.

Women's affiliations with Bay Area–based progressive movements enabled crucial connections that facilitated the coalitions that LAM developed throughout this period. For instance, women's political alliances explain why LAM held Artists for Iraq at the Mission Cultural Center for Latino Arts (MCCLA). Several women activists knew the directors of MCCLA, and holding the event in their space allowed LAM to publicize and sell tickets through MCCLA's networks, including artists and community-based activists, which was crucial to turnout and to reaching audiences previously inaccessible to LAM.

One evening when Mai was performing at the Ashkenaz in Berkeley, she met one of the members of the hip-hop group Company of Prophets. Camelia was also in touch with the group through Just Cause, a housing rights movement in Oakland at whose events they had performed. Camelia said, "We knew they would be willing to perform at our event because of their lyrics." Camelia's work within the Mission District's Latino/a community and Mai's work among Latino/a activists on her campus opened up possibilities for LAM to connect with the Azteca dancers, a group that performed at Artists for Iraq. For several years, Camelia had worked on various antigentrification and antidisplacement projects that the Azteca dancers were also involved in:

> They would open up a march, a community meeting or workshop that was going on. I worked with some of the dancers in different community organizations that I was involved in. They were integrated in my social life and work at the time. They gave a feeling of grounding to a lot of community events . . . and gave it a cultural and spiritual vibe that I thought would bring something different to our regular politics and words, which is what it usually is.

These experiences set the conditions through which LAM's women activists envisioned the art-based events they spearheaded. According to Dahlia,

> It was the first time we did an event like that. Each one of us brought something different. Camelia brought folks from the Mission; Mai brought East Bay people of color; you brought Center for Political Education folks; Iraqi refugee women and folks from the Iraqi refugee community came out of the work that Nadia and I were doing in the Tenderloin; women brought Nawal Saadawi and she brought the women's studies crowd from San Francisco State and Berkeley; Sima brought in the Queer West Asian crowd.

Several men activists I spoke with several years later helped me nuance my analysis of the gendered mechanisms of political work in LAM. Some men attributed women activists' disproportionate access to Bay Area progressive politics to their history of socialization in the United States and their greater access to the English language compared to their male counterparts. Osman, a Palestinian man who grew up primarily in Jordan, told me that because of his training and work in computer engineering, he had limited skills in and access to forms such as performance and art. He said that while he thought art was an important mechanism, he felt inadequate participating. Some men contended that women's access to cultural work provided them with leverage over their male counterparts because it gave them access to the privileged discourses and networks of Bay Area progressive politics, as well as the opportunity to critique the United States alongside what Bay Area progressive politics articulates as the most central political struggle in the United States—the fight for racial justice. Women's efforts to revalue the subordination of artwork to politicized speech was the result of a complex dynamic in which gender intersected with plural migration histories, histories of politicization, and women's and men's different relationships to the localness of the Bay Area.

*   *   *

Mapping the movement strategies these six women prioritized elucidates the collective political visions they brought to LAM, visions that brought multiple struggles—antigentrification, prison abolition, decolonization, and anti-imperialism—into the same political frame. Their vision allowed for multiple subjectivities within and beyond "the Arab community" to take the stage. While their visions were indeed rooted in Arab histories and cultural sensibilities, they were also reenvisioning masculinist nationalist concepts that assume that Arabness can only be transmitted or reproduced vertically. Indeed, their work enabled the transmission of Arab identity within and across multiple communities.

The fact that most of LAM's women activists were raised in the United States provided them with a proximity to new stories and languages distinct to the Bay Area, even as they maintained ties to the stories of people in the Arab region. Their entanglement in the narrative of pan-Arab leftist politics, an intersectional feminist critique of patriarchy, homophobia, racism, and imperialism, and a politics of coalition building constitutes the political visions they brought to LAM. Women's labor and what these women activists experience as gendered differences in political vision and strategies cannot be explained solely through feminist or queer critiques of heteropatriarchal social movements or heteropatriarchal nationalisms, but require a situated analysis of the way plural migration histories in diaspora and socioeconomic class can complicate gender tensions within social movements.

This chapter also troubles approaches that view diaspora as a coherent space in which a unified nationalist story meets up with various new stories in the diaspora (Boyle 2001, 434-39). Indeed, the stories I have mapped elucidate what diaspora studies scholars have theorized as the multiple senses of place and locale that come together (in tension and unison) within diaspora (Brah 1996). Yet, LAM was already an internally heterogeneous and contradictory diasporic space constituted by plural and contending migration histories and political visions. LAM's multiple intra-communal histories met up with a host of others—from dominant U.S. imperial discourses about Arabs to radical people of color and women of color discourses and practices of the

Bay Area. This helps explain why some women activists were marginalized along some modalities of power (i.e., sexism) but privileged along others (immigration history and access to local politics). From these multiple positions, they redefined diasporic leftist Arab anti-imperialism as multi-axial and brought diasporic feminist and queer anti-imperialist visions to Bay Area progressive politics. At the same time, redefining LAM momentarily did not fully resolve the complex and often ambiguous power struggles internal to LAM, power struggles shaped by the realities of a diaspora in flux living in empire, and the fragility of life in a time of imperial violence and war.

Toward a Diasporic Feminist Critique

Throughout this book we have witnessed what young adults are saying about the predicaments of Arab diasporas in the United States at the turn of the twenty-first century. We have seen the continuities and discontinuities between what takes place within themselves, their families, and their communities and the ways they engage with the United States at large. Like so many diasporic communities, Arab Americans live life on these multiple tracks, and our days are built upon the divide between the internal and the external, the communal and the wider world, the cultural and the political. Sometimes these tracks exist side by side, and we can navigate them in tandem. Sometimes the gulf between the two seems impossible to bridge. Navigating the multiplicity can be maddening, and yet, I believe, it can also be liberating.

We have seen, throughout my interlocutors' journeys, the dynamic interplay between the cultural forms projected upon them by the new Orientalism and those that they project upon themselves. My analysis of the significance of religion, family, gender, and sexuality to the ways my interlocutors negotiate the interplay shows how middle-class Arab American concepts of "cultural authenticity" are entangled in dominant U.S. Orientalist concepts of Arabnes. Women's bodies and idealized concepts of family values, familial connectivity, and heterosexuality are the battlegrounds upon which young adults negotiate their immigrant parents' and dominant U.S. society's meanings of Arabness and Americanness. We also have seen how some young adults are rearticulating Arabness through their active involvement in anti-imperialist social justice movements, transforming dominant concepts of Arabness and Americanness, and putting forth new visions for the future.

One of my investments in this project comes out of my personal history as an Arab American feminist born and raised in the San Francisco Bay Area. This book is indeed self-reflexive and auto-ethnographic: it maps and critiques the very power structures that I and my Arab American peers have grappled with, and participated in, for much of our lives. From the hairdresser several years ago who asked, "What is it like to be from a culture that oppresses women?" to the repeated invitations to give lectures on sensationalist topics such as female circumcision or the veil (coupled with a lack of interest in other issues that matter in Arab women's lives), I am often seen as one-dimensional. It seems that everyone, from hairdressers to newscasters, has a very good idea of what it means to be Arab and a woman. As I study gender and sexuality among Arab communities within the U.S. academy, I am often forced to engage contemporary U.S. Orientalist academic analyses of "Arab culture" and "Islam" that argue that Arab and Muslim traditions, particularly as related to gender and sexuality, are merely backwards and uncivilized. The power of this idea requires Arabs and Muslims to defend themselves before it. This has contributd to the problem among many feminists like myself of remaining silent about intra-communal matters for fear that there is no way to do so that will not reify Arab-bashing, Orientalism, or Islamaphobia.

As part of my work in Arab American studies for the last fifteen years, this book is also an internal critique of my own field and much of my own previous scholarshship. Most Arab American studies research—important and necessary as it is—has taken one of two approaches. First and foremost, there are analyses that interrogate the historically specific and changing effect of U.S. government and media discourses about the Middle East on Arab American lives. This mode of analysis—perhaps conducted in resistance to the sensationalist Orientalist focus on "backward," "uncivilized" Arab and Muslim "culture"—remains all but silent on intra-Arab American relationships and differences, most critically those associated with gender and sexuality, as well as on any other issue falling under the rubric of "culture." A second and less prevalent approach emphasizes "cultural" analyses and is built upon the same assimilationist frame as the dominant middle-class Arab American discourses. From this perspective, Americanization appears as a struggle between an essentialized "Arab culture and tradition" that immigrants brought with them and the dynamic "modern" culture they encountered in the United States.

This book has been driven by my dissatisfaction with both approaches and, more broadly, by a commitment to answering the question, How can Arab American studies scholars respond to Orientalism in ways that do not reinforce it or encourage Arab-bashing? I have aimed to create an alternative model of Arab American identity, one that does not rely on the bifurcated and ultimately false options of the "effeminate cultural" self and the "masculinist political" self. While the former depends on and deploys an Orientalist logic, the latter claims to counter that logic through its critique of politics, war, and racism. But neither approach is sufficient for the study of gender and sexuality as lived relations of difference, power, and belonging in Arab American lives. But as all of us know, these problems are not merely academic ones; as we have seen, they are shaping the lives of people around the world, every day. My work both as an academic and as an activist ultimately seeks not just to alter the perspective of Arab American studies but also to alter the way we understand sensationalized topics such as "Islamic revival" and "Arab patriarchy," since these are the same topics that reify and legitimize imperial racism, military violence, and war.

The result of nearly a lifetime of thinking about the world of Arab America, as well as the potent insights of so many people within the Arab American community, is what I call a diasporic Arab feminist critique. This approach has provided me with a resolution to the difficulties of critiquing issues such as patriarchy and the pressure for compulsory heterosexuality among Arab communities without reifying Orientalism. More generally, diasporic Arab feminist critique opens up new opportunities for dislodging the themes of religion, family, gender, and sexuality from the domain of "culture" (read ahistorical and unchanging). How do we do this? We can utilize the techniques of ethnography, in order to simply sit with the people that we seek to understand, to observe and to ask questions, to enable their own narratives—rather than our preconceived ideologies—to structure our thinking. We can utilize the insights of feminism, particularly as crafted by women of color (Crenshaw 1994; Smith and Kauanui 2008) and queer of color theorists (Gopinath 2005; Muñoz 1999; La Fountain-Stokes 2009), to analyze the intersections of race, class, gender, and sexuality. We can utilize the methodology of transnational feminism to "view the impact of war and internal repression in a larger context of global histories of displacement, forced migrations, and expulsions" (Bacchetta et al. 2002; Shohat 2006; Grewal and Kaplan 1994; Mohanty 2003). The result, I believe, is a new way of looking, seeing, and telling.

I completed most of my research about Arab Americans in the Bay Area in August 2001. I packed up my bags and prepared for my new job as an assistant professor of anthropology at the American University in Cairo, Egypt. I made one stop on my way—at the United Nations World Conference against Racism (UNWCAR) in Durban, South Africa. The conference took place between August 31 and September 7, 2001. I participated in WCAR as a member of a national delegation of community-based activists and scholars organized by the Women of Color Resource Center (WCRC) in Berkeley, California. Also attending WCAR were several Arab and Arab American activists with whom I had worked during the period of my research. They were attending WCAR as members of Muslim social justice and Palestinian solidarity movements that were gathering from various parts of the world. They had gone to Durban to bring their work to a broader, global audience and to connect with other activists from various parts of the world with shared interests.

Contrary to the virtual U.S. media blackout about this conference, the general sentiment that circulated among the tens of thousands of people who gathered in Durban was that WCAR was a historic meeting of the global antiracism movement in all of its diverse manifestations. The conference dealt with themes such as colonialism, hate crimes and violence, ethnic cleansing, migration/refugees, slavery and slave trade, poverty and social exclusion, institutionalized racism, anti-Semitism, caste-based discrimination, gender, sexual orientation, youth, foreign occupation, environmental racism, religious intolerance, reparations, labor, trafficking, and globalization. During and after Durban, I had the opportunity to talk informally with my interlocutors who attended, as well as other people they worked with. They shared the view that Durban was a historical moment for their own movements. For many, Durban was the first time they were among large groups of activists from the global south, where there is much greater support for Arab and Muslim political concerns than in the United States. Local South African Muslim and Palestine solidarity activists had played a crucial role in organizing the conference itself and the massive mobilizations that South Africans organized in the streets of South Africa throughout the period of the conference.[1]

The environment at WCAR allowed for people coming from the United States to have their voices heard on a world stage. As we have seen, debating and discussing the United States and the Middle East can be politically explosive. This was precisely what happened at Durban. At the core of what transpired at WCAR was a discursive struggle, or a struggle over representation and the power to define narratives—not unlike what my interlocutors, and my peers, and so many other ethnic groups encounter in the Bay Area and around the world. The U.S. government, for instance, threatened to boycott WCAR after a proposed resolution to define slavery as a crime against humanity and to criticize Israeli violations of Palestinian rights. I observed pro-Israeli conference participants, angered by discussions at Durban that criticized Israeli state racism, picket Palestine solidarity workshops and argue to the media that Palestinians hijacked the conference.

Amidst these battles, a secondary fight was taking place at WCAR over gender and "related intolerance." Durban was the first UN-sponsored conference against racism to include "related intolerance"—that is, to address the way racism intersects with poverty, gender discrimination, and homophobia. In response, there were debates among many activists at Durban over whether "related" issues were watering down the struggle against racism or whether gender should be secondary to the struggle to end racism. This same viewpoint seemed to have played out when conference organizers scheduled nearly all of the major sessions organized by or about women in venues away from the central conference rooms. Despite these tensions and other problems, the general sentiment among my interlocutors was that Durban felt like the beginning of a new era.

On September 9, 2001, I moved to Cairo, Egypt. A few days later, I was sitting in a café near my apartment where a TV screen hung on the wall in front of me. My dazed eyes watched in disbelief. Footage of two airplanes flying into the World Trade Center was played over and over and over again, in between clips of Palestinian children dancing and celebrating in the streets. On e-mail list-serves and in the alternative media, a flurry of counternarratives circulated—that CNN used old footage to fake images of Palestinians dancing in the streets to celebrate 9/11, or that reporters distributed candy and paid the children to dance for the camera.[2] As the counternarratives were refuted, new ones unfolded: namely, that this was an isolated incident magnified by the news media, and not reflective of Palestinians or the Arab or Muslim world more broadly. I felt that this repetition on television was an attempt to slander the Arab world in general. At the same time, I saw the counternarrative of the images as an "isolated incident" as an example of hopefulness, an example that the mainstream media could correct its biases. That day, the promise of Durban lay buried under the rubble and the massive loss of life at the World Trade Center, at the Pentagon, in Pennsylvania, and, days later, in the U.S. bombing campaign against Afghanistan. It felt nearly impossible to remember a time before September 11, before the ugliness of cable news commentary about Islam, before the perpetual images of a smoking New York City, before the gut-stabbing feeling that people who looked like my brothers had attacked my own country.

There were enormous continuities in the daily reality of our lives, but in the emotional turmoil and ideological hysteria of 9/11's aftermath, nobody could see those continuities—everything felt different. Yet as we have seen, there *are* immense continuities between the preceding decades of U.S. interventions in the Middle East and the aftermath of September 11, 2001. As my interlocutors' stories have shown, U.S. imperial discourses about its Arab-Muslim Others have been decades in the making (Moallem 2005). Despite these continuities, it was now a pre- and post–September 11th world. Activists and organizers returned home from Durban to find that political terrain had shifted beneath our feet in ways we will probably be measuring for decades to come.

We have seen how the aftermath of September 11th brought about the consolidation of a new and terribly broad racial category, which can only be described along the lines of "Arab-Middle Eastern-South Asian-Muslim." Anyone perceived to belong to this group—read: brown men and even women—might now be seen as a potential terrorist. The administration of George W. Bush consolidated a great many legitimate fears and a great many illegitimate biases into a new, simplified discourse of U.S. empire. Either you stood with the United States, and everything it stood for in our increasingly ugly age, or you stood with the terrorists. With our new, endlessly elastic racial category, anyone from Palestinians to Al Qaeda could be lumped in with the latter, which inspired a similar arbitrary category on the streets of the United States, where Sikhs mistaken for Arabs or Muslims were harassed by other Americans and even killed.

* * *

Before September 11th, Arab American feminist scholars had been arguing that U.S. government and corporate media images portrayed Arab women through colonialist tropes—oppressed Arab-Muslim women compared to liberated American women—and that these tropes were emerging alongside expanding U.S. economic and military interventions in the Middle East (Saliba 1994; Amireh 2000; Majaj 1994; Kahf 2000; Elia 2002). After September 11th, it became clear: not only did these images emerge alongside U.S. government discourse but in fact the notion that oppressed Arab and Muslim women needed to be saved by American heroes became a lynchpin of U.S. foreign policy (Razack 2005; Mohanty, Pratt, and Riley 2008; Abu-Lughod 2002). Five weeks after the United States began its bombing campaign on Afghanistan, despite glaring evidence that the situation had worsened, Laura Bush stated, "Because of our recent military gains in much of Afghanistan, women are no longer imprisoned in their homes. The fight against terrorism is also a fight for the rights and dignity of women."[3] After September 11th, the gendered discourse of Arabs versus Americans, Islam versus the West was now forged in an intensified, globalized context of imperial violence and war. I have tried to show that these totalizing categories in the 1990s had massive ramifications for the communities perceived to be related to "the terrorists"—for their concepts and practices of gender and sexuality, their religious affiliations, and their relationships with one another. Since September 11th, these ramifications have only become more potent. If the "war on terror" can justify itself as a means of saving oppressed women—and, by definition, thus decide who exactly is oppressed—then the stakes for regulating the boundaries of acceptable Arab and Muslim feminist speech are higher than ever before (Razack 2005; Kahf 2000).

There exists an urgent need for a broader analysis of Arabs and Arab Americans. America's visions of the Arab and Muslim regions have been supplanted by the devastating acts of September 11, 2001. At the core of America's new totalizing vision is the "woman question" and sensationalized representations of gender and sexuality in the Middle East. Feminist ethnography is an essential tool that we can use to move forward. By contextualizing the complex stories, messages, and lessons of Arab Americans long before September 11th, we can move beyond the tired push-pull of Orientalism and anti-Orientalism and can open up new possibilities for the expansion of internal Arab political critiques that take up urgent, yet often unspoken internal dynamics of oppression. An ethnographically grounded analysis also brings about new visions for the future, for ending violence, oppression, and war. Times of crisis tend to inspire radical new visions. In the years since September 11th, crisis has for many of us become the norm. But simultaneously, there are signs across the globe that we are also finding the creative manifestations of that crisis.

After the tenth anniversary of September 11th, movements aimed at creating a world without violence and war are as vital as ever. While the U.S. military has expanded its reach more than ever before, and much of the United States remains mired in imperial wars and an us versus them mentality, I take hope in the Arab revolutions and the fact that the Boycott, Divestment, and Sanctions Movement (BDS) and feminist movements such as

INCITE! Women of Color against Violence, the Global Fund for Women, and Nasawiya continue to thrive. When I started my research more than a decade ago, I rarely encountered public debate about U.S. global hegemony. Now, despite the deteriorating conditions in much of the Arab-Muslim-majority countries, the United States, and the world at large, there is more and more public debate on such matters. It remains to be seen what new alternatives might emerge. Ideally, new generations of Arabs in the United States will continue to work toward social justice and nonhierarchical ways of being in the world and will continue to keep the ever-changing possibilities of the Arab revolution alive—in Egypt, Tunisia, Iraq, Palestine, Yemen, Libya, Bahrain, and beyond.

NOTES

INTRODUCTION

1. My parents' families are from Al-Salt Jordan. They were living in
   Amman, Jordan, before they immigrated to the United States. In 1954,
   my father immigrated to San Francisco, where he lived and worked for
   ten years before he returned to Jordan to marry my mother. They came
   to the United States together after they were married.
2. To some extent, working-class Arab kids we knew from church or
   school faced similar struggles. Yet the stakes seemed to be different, as
   the reputation of one's father's family name was very much tied up in
   socioeconomic class status. Working-class families had less at stake, at
   least in terms of tarnishing their class status, when their children transgressed their parents' demands.
3. See Kent Ono's analysis of the racial formation of the "Potential Terrorist" (2005).
4. Feminist scholars like Chandra Mohanty, Minnie Bruce Pratt, and
   Robin Riley (2008) and Mohanty (2006) contribute an invaluable
   assessment of how the new Orientalism operates in relationship to
   imperial feminisms. The justification for imperial expansion rests on
   the idea of the West saving Muslim women from gendered and sexualized oppression (Razack 2008; Mohanty, Pratt, and Riley 2008; Abu-
   Lughod 2002; Sudbury 2000). Jasbir Puar (2007) contributes an analysis
   of how the idea of a "failed heterosexuality" serves as a crucial justification for violence and war (Puar 2007).
5. For analyses of intensified xenophobia and racism in California, see
   Gibbs and Bankhead (2001) and Almaguer (1994). The theorization of
   the United States as empire contends that U.S. empire works through
   covert and overt mechanisms and through economic, military, and
   cultural hegemony, which continues to take on new forms in different historical contexts inside and outside the United States (Smith and
   Kauanui 2008; Steinmetz 2005; Stoler 2006; Kaplan 2003; Kim 2010;
   Kim 2008; Diaz and Kauanui 2001; Harvey 2003; Hammami and Rieker
   1988; and Mann 2005).

6. Drawing upon Stuart Hall's theory of "articulation," Native Pacific cultural studies seeks to "avoid the pitfalls of anti-essentialist critiques that, in privileging hybridity, contingency, and syncretism, can relinquish the grounding of indigenous politics and identity" (Diaz and Kauanui 2001, 315-16; Teaiwa 2001). James Clifford, writing within this intellectual current, argues that "articulation . . . evokes a deeper sense of the 'political'—productive processes of consensus, exclusion, alliance, and antagonisms that are inherent in the transformative life of all societies" (2001, 472–73). I draw upon his theory of "articulation" as a "nonreductive way to think about cultural transformation and the apparent comings and goings of 'traditional' forms" (Clifford 2001, 478).

7. For instance, LAM and Muslim student activists often came together as co-organizers of Bay Area antiwar or immigrant rights political rallies or demonstrations among a wide range of Bay Area social justice organizations.

8. See Diaz and Kehaulani 2001; Smith 2008; Smith 1999; Simpson 2007; Blackwell 2010; Mohanty 2003;Visweswaran 1994.

9. This analytic brings Shohat and Stam's (1994) pioneering methods for reading Middle Eastern media representations through a transnational feminist lens to an ethnographic study about lived cultural forms among Arab Americans. My methodology draws upon my active participation in transnational Middle East feminist studies networks and scholarship that explores the significance of relationships to "homelands" in the formation of concepts of family, gender, and sexuality in the diaspora (Saliba 2003; Tsoffar 2006; Gualtieri 2009; Kadi 1994; Shakir 1997). Transnational Middle East feminist studies also considers how multiple relationships of power—imperialism, race, class, gender, and sexuality—shift and change shape in relationship to local and global politics and histories of displacement and migration (Abdulhadi 2010; Moallem 2005; and Bachetta et al. 2002). Queer critiques have questioned binary gender categories and the disenfranchising of queerness and transgender people in Arab American studies and community politics (Jadallah 2010). Other concerns have included engagements with Orientalist and imperial feminist definitions of Arab and Muslim women through the symbols of the veil, clitorodectomy, and victimhood (Ahmed 1992; Amireh 2000; Abu-Lughod 2002; Shohat and Stam 1994; and Elia 2002).

10. Starting with the earliest publications in the field, Arab American studies scholars have documented and examined the phenomenon of transnationalism, ranging from the study of the relation between

global politics and Arab migration to the impact of U.S. imperial interests in the Middle East on Arab American lives (Howell and Shryock 2003; Naff 1985; Joseph 1999; Suleiman 1999; Cainkar 2009; Khater 2001; Abraham 1994; Davidson 1999; and Terry 1999). Much of Arab American studies scholarship thus precedes the shift toward an emphasis on the transnational in the fields of American studies and ethnic studies.

11. Organizations connected to this network included the American Arab Anti-Discrimination Committee, San Francisco Chapter; Aswat (an Arabic Choir); the Arab Cultural Center; the Arabic language program at the College of San Mateo, San Francisco State University, and the University of California–Berkeley; the Arab Women's Solidarity Association, San Francisco Chapter; the General Union of Palestinian Students (San Francisco State University); St. Anne's Arab Catholic Church's Arab American Youth Group; St. George's Church; Students for Justice in Palestine (University of California–Berkeley); and St. Nicholas's Greek Orthodox Church's Youth Group.

12. See Lata Mani and Ruth Frankenber, cited in Visweswaran (1994, 11-12).

13. See Sabeel (http://www.sabeel.org/).

14. See Behar and Gordon's discussion of the anthropological imperative (1995).

15. For further discussion on the difficulties in overcoming the violence of representation in anthropology, see Minh-Ha 1989; Simpson 2007; Spivak 1994; Smith 1999.

CHAPTER 1

1. I borrow from Sarah Gualtieri's theorization of a "proximity to whiteness" (2009).

2. The following studies analyze the racialization of Arabs and Muslims in the context of U.S. expansion: Alsultany 2012; Moallem 2005; Balibar 1991; Little 2008; Maira 2009; Rana 2007. A key argument in this critique is that the "clash of civilizations" thesis, developed by Samuel Huntington in 1993 and adopted into U.S. government policy and rhetoric, has shaped the new U.S. racial discourses about Arabs and Muslims. Scholars also argue that the "clash of civilizations" thesis has its roots in European Orientalism (Said 2003; Moallem 2005).

3. I draw on these theories of diaspora in terms of local and global attachments (see, e.g., Brah 2003; Dayal 1996; Bhabha 1994; Hall 1994; Vertovec 1997; Braziel and Mannur 2003; Appadurai 1996; Shohat 2006; Gilroy 1993; Clifford 1994; Lavie and Swedenberg 1996).

4. I depart from conventional trends in diaspora studies critiques that celebrate deterritorialization. Articulations of Arabness are very much wrapped up in claims and life and death struggles over land, place, and territory and a significant sense of historical continuity between people and their land.

5. Black British cultural studies writers coined phrases such as "we are here because you were there" (Mercer 1994). Emergent perspectives in Asian Pacific Islander studies have drawn up the idea "we are here because you were there" to analyze the relationship between Asian Pacific Islander Americans and U.S. empire (Bascara 2006; Kim 2010; See 2009; Balibar 1991). For further analyses of diaspora and empire, see, e.g., Ho (2006); Maira (2009); and Cainkar (2009).

6. Existing documentation includes the following: Laffrey et al. 1991; Rafidi, Howell, and Elkarra 1999. For other mention of Arabs in San Francisco see, e.g., Marschner (2003) and Lopez, Snipp, and Camarillo (2002).

7. Gualtieri (2004), Khater (2001), Naff (1985), and Suleiman (1999) have further studied Arab migration to the United States.

8. Although Arab immigration to the United States predates the nineteenth century, the first significant group came to the United States in the late 1880s. Kayyali (2006) studies Arab immigration to the United States before 1880.

9. This resembles general patterns in immigrant business entrepreneurship (see, e.g., Light and Bonacich 1988; Park 1997; Mahler 1995; Chu 2000; and Moallem 1991).

10. I collected many stories about the early Arab immigrants from the publications of community-based institutions. These institutions provided a linear, singular story of Arab immigration and assimilation in the Bay Area, heralding the story of a Syrian man, Khalil Khouri, for example, as the first Arab to the Bay Area. A document from a church office reads that during the time of the Gold Rush, instead of "digging for gold," Khouri became a merchant "selling expensive linens" and "after accumulating wealth from linen sales, he moved to San Francisco." It also focuses on stories of single males who came to the Bay Area primarily from present-day Syria and Lebanon and "peddled goods from door to door" or those from Jordan or Palestine who worked in mining or the auto industry or as peddlers.

11. Many historians have shown that the turn of the twentieth century brought about the first significant influx of people from the Arab region to the United States. Early migrants were primarily Christian and were

from the Ottoman provinces of Syria, Mount Lebanon, and Palestine (Shakir 1997; Naff 1985; Khater 2001; Hooglund 1985). At the time, the Ottoman Empire comprised Turkey, the Balkans, much of North Africa, Egypt, and most of the rest of the Arab world (Khalidi 2004, 11). In Mount Lebanon, two economic setbacks of the mid-1800s contributed to early migration, coupled with the demographic pressures of an exploding population: the opening of the Suez Canal, which sidetracked world traffic from Syria to Egypt so that Japanese silk became a major competitor to the Lebanese silk industry, and the invasion of Lebanese vineyards by the phylloxera pest, which nearly destroyed the vineyards (Khater 2001, 59; Suleiman 1999, 2).

12. Mai Ngai's work (2005) provides proof of the Immigration Act of 1965 and how it increased the possibility of immigration for people from Asia.

13. There are many different forms of anti-imperialist Arab nationalism and heated debates among anti-imperialist Arab nationalists. Some, for instance, have focused on external forces—Europeans, for example. Others have contended that Arab nationalism must also challenge corrupt Arab regimes (Choueiri 2000).

14. There were, for instance, numerous official and unofficial projects and attempts to unite Arab states from Morocco to Iraq between 1950 and 1978 (Choueiri 2000).

15. Contributing to the growing relationship between Israel and the United States, the Zionist movement decided upon the United States as their main center of diplomatic and fundraising work as early as 1942 (Choueiri 2000). It is important to note that there is not one single Zionist movement or Zionist narrative. See, for instance, Silberstein (1999). In addition, there are contending viewpoints about when and why the United States established its support for Israel. Many scholars have argued that the United States based its early relationship with Israel on the idea that this relationship would further U.S. economic interests in the Middle East. Others have contended that before the 1967 Arab-Israeli War, Israel was an invaluable ally to the United States only against the "dangerous" Arab clients of the Soviet Union (Khalidi 1997).

16. For further discussion on 1970s representations of Arabs in U.S. popular culture, education, and media, see, e.g., Griswold 1975; Abu-Laban 1975.

17. For further discussion on U.S. empire in the Middle East see, e.g., Ho 2004; Mamdani 2005; Maira 2009; Khalidi 2004; and McAlister 2001.

18. They were never deported because a federal appeals court declared the anticommunist law unconstitutional (D. Cole 2003).

19. This created a socioeconomic division between those small business owners who invested in real estate and those who did not—those whose children become professionals and those whose children take over family businesses—and often played out in social networks such as marriage.

20. Some Arab Americans participated in religious institutions that were not based on ethnicity.

21. Among the Palestinian village-based clubs formed in the 1980s were the Sahil, Beir Zeit, Beit Lahim, and Dair Dibuwan clubs. The Jordanian American Association was founded in 1985. The Lebanese American Association was founded in 1989 and the Syrian American Association in 1992.

22. There have also been exceptions. For instance, during the height of the civil war in Lebanon, Christians were divided. Some preferred sectarian over nationalist politics. Also, Christians in Egypt revered Abdel Nasser because of his secular nationalist politics. Yet when sectarianism arose in Egypt, some conservative Christians tended to turn to the church as their primary community and become sectarian.

23. U.S. officials, academics, and media spokespersons have mouthed this discourse in quotations such as this from news clips provided by the Media Foundation: "Neither the best intention of the Saudis nor the power of the Israelis could stop another young zealot willing to die so he could kill Jews on Passover" (*Peace, Propaganda, and the Promised Land* 2004)

24. In an Arab Cultural Center newsletter, Dudum and Saliba reported that Arab Americans have been limited to operating small retail establishments in disadvantaged neighborhoods. This has created ethnic hostility and has been documented in local neighborhoods and public housing projects. They stated that Arab Americans have limited access to networking or affluent individuals and remained in the small retail sector because of stereotypes and were underrepresented in terms of statistical availability for city contracts. They quoted many business owners who expressed a need to conceal their Arab ancestry. In this report, they called for a need to expand opportunities to integrate Arab Americans at all levels of business and civic life in San Francisco to prevent increasing prejudice. The SF Affirmative Action ordinance became law on Nov. 4, 1998. Businesses can now obtain certification under the ordinance.

25. In the late 1990s, three initiatives were placed on the ballot. In 1994, Proposition 187 prohibited undocumented immigrants from receiving

state-provided health care and education. It required government employees to report the immigration status of their clients. Proposition 184 (the Three Strikes Initiative) (1994) increased sentences for convicted felons who have previous convictions for certain serious or violent felonies. It includes as prior convictions certain felonies committed by older juveniles. In 1996, Proposition 209 prevented the state of California from implementing affirmative action programs in public education, public employment, and public contracting. In 1998, Proposition 227 limited the ability of school districts in California to use bilingual education programs lasting more than one year. California voters supported each of these initiatives (Baldassare 2000; Chavez 1998; Ono and Sloop 2002). For more information on the L.A. riots, see, e.g., Song (2005) and Wall (1992).

CHAPTER 2

1. These groups included the American-Arab Anti-Discrimination Committee, San Francisco Chapter; Aswat (an Arabic Choir); the Arab Cultural Center; Arabic language courses at the College of San Mateo, San Francisco State University, and the University of California–Berkeley; the Arab Women's Solidarity Association, San Francisco Chapter; the General Union of Palestinian Students (San Francisco State University); Muslims for Global Peace and Justice; the Muslim Student's Association (University of California–Berkeley); St. Anne's Arab Catholic Church's Arab American Youth Group; St. George's Church; Students for Justice in Palestine (University of California–Berkeley); St. Nicholas's Greek Orthodox Church's Youth Group; and the Zaytuna Institute for the Dissemination of Traditional Islam.

2. I draw on Avtar Brah's theorization that "the entanglement of a multiplicity of biographies in diaspora spaces needs to be conceptualized as simultaneously being mediated by different modalities of power: class, race, gender, ethnicity, nationalism, generation, and sexuality" (1996).

3. Suad Joseph argues that idealized notions of relationality in Lebanon are inscribed in national institutions and that these ideals are sanctified by the state and by religion (2000, 108).

4. It is beyond the scope of my research to compare the differences between the policing of male-male and the policing of female-female sexualities (see e.g., Mosse 1988; Edelman 1999; Parker et al. 1992; de Lauretis 1998; Habib 2010; Babayan and Najmabadi 2008).

5. In a November 17, 2001, radio address, First Lady Laura Bush argued that one of the benefits of the United States' bombing of Afghanistan

was that women would now be freer in their own homes and nation. Lila Abu-Lughod argues that this is an example of the rhetorics of liberal feminism being used to justify the military ambitions of the United States (2002). During the Abu Ghraib prison scandal, prisoners were put into same-sex sexual positions, as it was assumed that they would be even more traumatized by this because Arab culture is particularly homophobic. Trishala Deb and Rafael Mutis argue that this is an example of the United States government positioning Arab cultures as more homophobic than U.S. culture to justify operations against them (2004).

6. Deeb, writing on Lebanon, argues that the United States is taken as the center of the West. "No doubt, this is related to multiple factors, including the military presence of the United States in the Middle East, directly in Iraq or indirectly through Israel (which is viewed by many Lebanese as a U.S. proxy in the region); U.S. involvement during the Lebanese civil war; and U.S. cultural imperialism and economic power" (2006, 25).

7. See, e.g. Rowsen 2008; Amer 2008; and Luongo 2010.

8. Abdulhadi (2010) argues that the Caliphates (623-624) ordered the burning of homosexuals; Omar Ibn Al-Khattab (634-644) had lax attitudes regarding sexuality; Ali Ibn Abi Talib (656-661) was not fond of homosexuals, but he, in turn, was not favored by the Muslim people nor the prophet's wife, Aisha. The Umayyad rulers (661-680) did not exercise state control over sexual practice, and at least one was reputed to enjoy sex with other men.

9. Stiffler (2010) provides anlaysis of Lebanese Orthodox communities in the United States and their identification with the term "Arab."

10. A range of scholars have documented the permeable and shifting history of the categories Arab and Muslim (see, e.g., Eickelman 1998; Hitti 1968; Dawisha 2005; and Majid 2000).

CHAPTER 3

1. Major provisions of the proposition are increased punishment for gang-related felonies; death penalty for gang-related murder; creating a new crime of recruiting for gang activities; and the requirement of adult trial for juveniles fourteen or older charged with murder or specified sex offenses. It designates additional crimes as violent and serious felonies, thereby making offenders subject to longer sentences (SOSC 2000).

2. I worked with community leaders who worked with these Muslim institutions: Al Qalam Institute of Islamic Sciences; Zaytuna Institute;

Muslim student organizations; political social justice or advocacy groups, including the Islamic Networks Group and Muslim Institute for Global Peace and Justice; and various mosques.

3. Several scholars have critiqued modernist logics of the nation-state for delegitimizing the possibility for religiously constituted identities to operate as a site for political participation and critique (Majid 2000; Asad 1995).

4. Hatem Bazian, a community activist who has been documenting the history of Muslims in the Bay Area, told me, "This is not counting all Muslim student organizations in every university." Bazian explains that this growth continued up until the year 2000, when the information technology industry collapsed. Currently, he says, there are more than 150 Islamic schools operating on a full-time basis, as well as dozens of organizations. As reported by Bukhari et al., "over 16,000 Muslim community organizations and Islamic centers dot the American landscape" (2004).

5. Two foundational Muslim organizations were established as early as the 1950s and 1960s, when in 1952 Syrian and Lebanese Muslim immigrants formed the International Muslim Society, which was later renamed the Federation of Islamic Associations of U.S. and Canada (FIA), and in when in 1963 the Muslim Student Associations was formed. By the 1980s and 1990s, as in the Bay Area, there was a massive growth in national advocacy organizations such as the Arab Muslim Council (AMC) and the Council on American Islamic Relations (CAIR) (Bukhari et al. 2004).

6. See Bagader's analysis of the factors explaining the growth of an Islamist presence in Muslim-majority countries (1994, 118-19).

7. The Muslim Community Association of the San Francisco Bay Area, a religious, nonprofit, and nonpolitical organization established in 1983, is the largest Islamic center in Northern California, offering Qur'an classes, Arabic classes, *halaqas* (religious gatherings), and a full-time school, among other activities.

8. Ray Baker uses the term "new Islamists" to refer to similar intellectual currents among Muslims in the Middle East, including former leftists who adopted a more Islamist orientation; people whose social consciousness was formed through participation in civic and charitable associations; and religious scholars emphasizing the relevance of traditional Islamic knowledge to contemporary issues and problems and seeking to provide nonauthoritarian guidance for their solution (2003). This trend within the Islamic mainstream contends that the Qur'an is

a source of general principles and that religion needs to be regarded in conjunction with national interests, economic realities, and cultural traditions, which include non-Muslims and those with different political tendencies as equal partners (2007, 114, 316-19).

9. There is a vast range of intellectual opinion on these issues, depending on the person and school of thought.

10. This term is not employed widely because of its weighted connation.

11. It is crucial to note that specific issues, terminologies, and ideas involved in gender activism differ from place to place and from region to region, and depend in part on the national, legal, and cultural contexts in which people are working (Deeb 2006). Amina Wadud refers to gender activism among Muslim women as "Qu'ranic hermeneutics from a gender perspective" (Wadud 2006). Barazangi explains that the active participation in the ongoing "reading" and interpreting of the Qur'an provides a foundational means for a woman to become a spiritually and intellectually autonomous person mandated in the Qu'ranic views of the individual, male or female, as a trustee of God (2000). For Muslim feminists, the aim is to transform areas of Islamic law, a system they perceive to have been conceived in the midst of past patriarchal structures that affect women's lives (Al-Hibri 2000, 51-71).

12. There is a growing body of literature on the deployment of Islam by second-generation young adults within intergenerational tensions (see, e.g., Haddad and Esposito 1998; Khan 2000; Cainkar 2005).

13. Many scholars have argued that the inseparability of Islam and Arab culture is rooted in sixth-century Arabia, since the early forms of Muslim culture were predominantly Arab. Marshall Hodgson notes the above difficulty of religious versus secular academic usage of the words "Islamic" and "Muslim" in his three-volume work, *The Venture of Islam*. Early Muslim literature is in Arabic, as that was the language of Mohammed's communities in Mecca and Medina. People can track the pan-Arab movements all the way back to the founding of Islam by the Prophet Mohammed. Also, signs of pan-Arabism can be located in the collectivization of the Arab World through the Ottoman Empire.

14. For further analysis on the reworking of gender norms through Islam, see Abu-Lughod 1998.

15. Wadud's critique of the "personal is political" standpoint is centered on marriage, and women's domestic roles have enabled masculine privilege in public arenas of intellectual and philosophical discourse (2006, 190).

16. According to Wadud, this approach views Islamic texts as utterances *in progress*. The central idea posited is the development of a

methodological practice of talking back to texts, which through similar interpretive projects have enabled a textual intervention in Islamic studies (Wadud 2006, 192).

17. For further analysis of cultural racism and the relationship between antisemitism and Islamophobia, see Moallem 2005; Rana and Rosas 2006; and Stockton 1994.

18. For further discussion on the role of activism in the lives of Muslims and the idea of a progressive Islamic ethical theory, see Wadud 2006 (23-24) and Majid (2000).

19. Indeed, the developments that took place in Bosnia became complicated for Muslim activists over time. Eventually, the United States did go to war against Milosevic in the name of defending Kosovo. The Clinton administration then bombed Serbia and the Chinese embassy in the process. A debate then developed among Muslim activists on how to respond to the U.S. intervention. One activist with whom I spoke stated that Muslims tended to care more about the lifting of the U.S.- and European-backed arms embargo against Bosnia so that Muslims could defend themselves than about the U.S. and NATO intervention. He argued that most saw the U.S./NATO attack as an "intersection" of interest and not an example of the United States supporting Muslims or of a Muslim lobbying success story. He argued, "no one was 'fooled' as to what the U.S./NATO's real interests were."

20. For further analysis of the significance of the first Gulf War to Muslim politics, see Werbner's writings on the Gulf Crisis for Pakistanis in Britain (2002a, 164).

21. Power's analysis parallels that of Muslim activists, who expressed such profound outrage over Bosnia:

> Many knew what was going on but few Americans pressed for intervention, and genocide proceeded unimpeded by U.S. action and often emboldened by U.S. inaction. . . . The media insisted that any proposed U.S. response would be futile, potentially increasing harm to the victims and jeopardizing other precious American moral or strategic interests. There is an explicit avoidance of the use of the word "genocide." Thus, they can in good conscience favor stopping genocide in the abstract, while simultaneously opposing American involvement, (2002, xviii)

22. Enseng Ho argues that "at some point after the Gulf War, a choice was made to enlarge the terrain of Muslim activism from anti-colonial to anti-imperial" (2004, 241).

23. The longer quotation from this publication states,

In Iraq, the nine-year sanctions have accomplished the following: (1) 1.5 million citizens dead and climbing, (2) five thousand children die every month, (3) the price of basic necessities such as rice, wheat, and barley has gone up by 30,000 percent (4) a 90 percent decrease in vitamin, protein, calcium and mineral intake over the period, (5) medicine and medicinal supplies meet only 30 percent of the people's need, and (6) the oil for food program meets only 1/3 of the need of the people. . . . It's a crime committed in silence as there is no media coverage. . . . The drumbeat of war must stop and sanity must prevail. . . . Stand up for peace and justice! Millions of lives are at stake!

24. To perform *takbir* is to call others to say *Allahu Akbar* (God is the greatest). It is followed by the response, *Allahu Akbar* (God is great).

25. Werbner and Modood found a similar dynamic among Pakistanis in Britain. They argue, "Constituted by a global discourse, we see here a fusing of global discourses of liberation, anti-racism, and feminism with Muslim religious love for the Prophet. These discourses render America as a source of corruption within global dissent" (1997).

26. This reference is from one of the most circulated press releases on the internet during this time.

27. In addition to a plethora of historical information, maps, and articles, Muslim students distributed a publication that correlated Palestine with the oppression of Native Americans and injustices in Honduras, South Africa, Guatemala, Mozambique, and Panama. The staffs of *al Talib* (the Muslim students' news magazine at the University of California–Los Angeles) and *al Kalima* (a news magazine produced by Muslim students at the University of California–Irvine) published this document.

28. Imam Jamil Al-Amin, formerly known as H. Rap Brown, was a leader of the Student Nonviolent Coordinating Committee and a member of the Black Panthers who later converted to Islam. In 2000, Al-Amin was arrested and convicted on charges of murder and given life imprisonment. Government officials asserted that Al-Amin engaged in gunfire with two police officers and murdered one of them (CNN.com 2002). Al-Amin's supporters counter that government officials framed him and that his conviction is another attempt to attack Muslims in the United States (Wexler 2002). California Proposition 21 increased a number of penalties for criminal offenses committed by juveniles and placed many juvenile offenders within the realm of the adult legal system (SOSC 2000). Several organizations were opposed to the passage of Proposition 21, including the Ella Baker Center for Human Rights, Californians for Justice, and the Critical Resistance Youth Force Coalition.

CHAPTER 4

1. In the late 1990s, LAM temporarily manifested as the San Francisco Chapter of the American-Arab Anti-Discrimination Committee. ADC's official mission is to defend Arab American rights within an assimilationist civil rights framework. LAM's emphasis on anti-imperialism and self-determination for Arab people never fully aligned with ADC's mission. This disjuncture culminated in 2004, when this movement in the Bay Area manifested in the organization Arab Resources for Organizing and Community (AROC)—operating out of the former ADC SF office. To avoid confusion over organizational names, I use the term "leftist Arab movement" (LAM), even though activists did not use this term.

2. See LAM activist Eyad Kishawi's essay, "Divestment from Israel in Its Fourth Year" (2006), for an analysis of LAM's divestment strategy.

3. I draw upon Puar and Rai's analysis of coalition politics beyond liberal multiculturalist (2004).

4. *Debka* is an Arab folk dance in Palestine, Jordan, Syria, and Lebanon.

5. The organization SF War receives public funding. After including language critical of Israel, SF War received pressure from pro-Israeli constituencies in the San Francisco Bay Area, and officials from the state Office of Criminal Justice Planning and the San Francisco Department on the Status of Women required the organization to remove this language from their training manual. Examples of the responses SF War received are published online (Cohn 2003).

6. International Action Center is the Worker's World–sponsored political group that transformed into the ANSWER coalition after September 11, 2001 (Act Now to Stop War and Racism).

7. California Proposition 187 was a ballot proposal in 1994 that sought to make undocumented immigrants ineligible for public benefits (Ono and Sloop 2002).

8. FMLN is an El Salvadorian political party that fought as a guerilla movement during that country's civil war. Youth FMLN was the youth component of the FMLN and had support chapters in the United States, including a branch in San Francisco.

9. For analyses that reflect their critique of the exclusion of Palestinian perspectives from being heard, see Said 1984; Butler 2006; and Wistrich 2004. Also, see the debate over the U.S. government stance in boycotting the United Nations World Conference against Racism in response to apparent criticism of Israel that was to take place at the conference. In addition, see the U.S. government's Global Anti-Semitism Review Act of 2004; line ten reads, "Anti-Semitism has at times taken the form

of vilification of Zionism, the Jewish national movement, and incitement against Israel" (Pub.L.108-332).

10. Citing Hardt and Negri 2001.

11. British and French domination in the Arab world, coupled with the Zionist settlement of Palestine in early the 1930s, gave rise throughout the region to anticolonial Arab nationalism (Choueiri 2000, 92). A number of scholars have written on varying perspectives of the 1948 war (see, e.g., Pappe 2006; Tal 2003; and Silberstein 1999). Israeli and Palestinian narratives on the creation of the state of Israel and the events that transpired since then are almost entirely opposing. The Palestinian narrative remembers the creation of the state of Israel in terms of the destruction of four hundred villages and the displacement of over seven hundred thousand Palestinians; considers the creation of the state of Israel as *al-Nakbah* (the catastrophe); and understands Zionist policy as a systematic, state-sponsored program to replace Palestinians and their land with Jews and Jewish villages (Pappe 2006). Israeli narratives disavow the process of colonization that underpinned the creation of the state of Israel, place the responsibility on Arabs for starting the Arab-Israeli War, and remember 1948 as the war of independence, the moment Jews finally obtained their homeland (Rabinovich 2004). There is tremendous variation within Israel, among Palestinians and Arabs, and among observers throughout the world who read and understand this history according to a multitude of contending perspectives. Even among Arabs who advocate for Palestinian liberation, there are differences. Palestinian national liberation groups are diverse, and different political trends and factions constituted the Palestinian movement of the 1960s, some of which privileged a Palestinian focus while others articulated the Palestinian struggle within an Arab national liberation framework. There are also ideological divides among Israelis. There are revisionists, religious right perspectives, and anti-Zionist perspectives.

12. LAM's analysis of Palestinian refugees lines up with international law, such as United Nations Resolution 194 calling for Palestinian refugees' right to return. Arguments in support of Palestinian refugees contend that they possess the inalienable and basic human right protected under international law, the right to return to their homes or villages. The United Nations General Assembly passed Resolution 194 on December 11, 1948. The Israeli government has not viewed the admission of Palestinian refugees to their former homes in Israel as a right, but rather as a political claim to be resolved as part of a final peace settlement.

13. LAM has been driven by the contention that Israel, as a state for Jews only, in law and in policy, has been based upon an exclusionary logic that denies the majority of Palestinians indigenous to the land of present-day Israel access to their land and resources. Tony Judt, exemplifying this stance, refers to Israel as "a state in which Jews and the Jewish religion have exclusive privileges from which non-Jewish citizens are forever excluded" (2003). The dominant Israeli stance generally is concerned with Jewish settlers on a land believed to be either previously uninhabited or tenanted by a miscellaneous group of people without nationhood or national aspirations (Peters 2001; Avineri 1981). LAM activists draw on the Fourth Geneva Convention, which prohibits the removal of people from their land and the demographic alteration of occupied land by an occupier. Leftist Arab movements generally contend that by legally categorizing people in Israel as Jewish nationals against those who are not; by holding Palestinians in the West Bank and Gaza under military dominance and continuing to displace them and confiscate their land for the construction of Jewish-only colonies; and by denying Palestinian refugees the right to return, Israel remains a settler-colonial state.

14. See Naseer Aruri's analysis of U.S. diplomatic history in relation to the Middle East (2003). Aruri argues that a special relationship has formed between the United States and Israel that, at one point, sought to protect U.S. interests in the Middle East in the context of the Cold War, and today promotes the War on Terror that has arguably lasted beyond the Bush II administration.

15. The period of the first Palestinian *intifada* (uprising) (1987-1994) was a period of massive growth for LAM in the Bay Area in light of the massive growth in the Palestinian movement during this time on a global scale. LAM developed relationships with various anti-imperialist revolutionary political currents that similarly identified links between the Israeli state and imperialism. In addition to working with anti-interventionist movements in Nicaragua and El Salvador, the Palestinian movement generally has had some minimal connections to the Black Power and South African anti-apartheid movements (Azikwe 2009; Nadelmann 1981).

16. LAM activists perceived the impact of Oslo as safeguarding Israeli security, opening up more possibilities for Israeli expansion, and controlling Palestinian opposition. Post-Oslo, Israel expanded its border control and military occupation to a majority of Palestinian territory and the new Palestine. In the first two months of the *intifada*, Israel responded

with what some of its critics have called brutal force and excessively punitive measures: attack helicopters and tank fire against a largely unarmed population; incursions and occupation of Palestinian cities and refugee camps; closures and sieges of residential areas; travel bans on roads, especially for Palestinian men; the disemployment (or shutdown of work places) of 110,000 Palestinian workers; and a 50 percent increase in the poverty rate (Johnson and Kuttab 2001).

17. The United States established a no-fly zone across the country to prevent the use of Iraqi aircraft and placed economic sanctions on Iraq to force the regime to disarm. From the end of the first Gulf War in 1991 to the beginning of the invasion of Iraq in 2003, the United States and the United Kingdom, in violation of international law and sometimes with the help of countries such as Turkey and Kuwait, carried out continuous bombing campaigns against Iraq. Many of these bombings hit civilian installations and communities instead of military targets, which resulted in massive civilian casualties (Simons 2002). U.S.-led United Nations sanctions were placed on Iraq from August 6, 1990, until June 2003. Sanctions on Iraq were the most comprehensive in modern history, directly targeting water treatment plants and electrical infrastructure. In June 1991 UNICEF reported "an alarming and rising incidence of severe and moderate malnutrition" among Iraqi children. According to a Harvard-based international study team, there were forty-seven thousand excess deaths among children under five years of age during the first eight months of 1991 and child mortality rates in southern and central Iraq had more than doubled since 1989 (Garfield 1999). Prior to the imposition of sanctions, the Iraqi welfare state was among the most comprehensive in the Arab world (Economist Intelligence Unit 1995; United Nations Children's Fund 1990).

18. I borrow from Kishawi's analysis of the divestment campaign (2006).

19. For examples of the kinds of arguments LAM activists articulated, see Bayour (2005) and Khoury (2004).

20. Several women in LAM were part of a cyber network, "Arab Women's Solidarity Association," an e-mail list-serve where many of these same critiques were developed and circulated. For further discussion, see the Arab American feminist anthology *Food for Our Grandmothers* (Kadi 1994).

21. Several scholars have analyzed differences in the migration of unmarried men and women (see, e.g., Hoodfar 1997; Joseph 1993).

22. In 2010, I returned to the Bay Area's Arab Cultural and Community Center as a guest speaker for an event about Arab Americans and civic

engagement. Out of the approximately sixty people who attended the event, a large majority were Arab women who were either born in the United States or socialized primarily in the United States. This pattern was repeated over and over through the period of my research. Perhaps this was an outcome of the politics of cultural authenticity I explore in chapter 2, which provided Arab American men with more room for movement beyond an intra-communal cultural Arab domain compared to Arab American women.

23. The battle between Orientalist and anti-Orientalist politics has haunted a great deal of Arab American feminist scholarship and political discourses (Saliba 1994; Amireh 2000).

24. Shohat suggests an alternative to this when she states that in the Middle East or North Africa, "a kind of informal bisexuality had sometimes been tacitly accepted" (2001, 20). Babayan and Najmabadi (2008) further discuss histories of sexualities in the Middle East that do not map onto European modernist binarisms.

CHAPTER 5

1. The politics these women brought to LAM has paralleled similar trends across the United States in which Arab feminist and queer politics have converged. This dynamic culminated in the 2006 gathering in Chicago, Arab Movement of Women Arising for Justice (AMWAJ) (https://www.facebook.com/group.php?gid=7217393370).

2. During the few weeks of unrest, tens of thousands of people were killed. Many more died during the following months, while nearly two million Iraqis fled for their lives. In the aftermath, the government intensified the forced relocation of Marsh Arabs and the draining of the Iraqi marshlands, while the Allies established the Iraqi no-fly zones (Tripp 2002).

3. The activists' critique was that the Clinton administration painted itself as helping the refugees but placed them in an economically devastated neighborhood without resources. The activists' outrage was based on what they witnessed in terms of the impact of the refugees' living conditions on the refugee families. The resettlement program placed the refugees in one of San Francisco's harshest neighborhood, the Tenderloin. One activist told me, "Kids walked out of the house to see people shooting up and sex work. People were scared to go outside. Of course all the kids in the Tenderloin saw this—so the larger problem was the U.S.' failed economic policies and how they became imposed on recent refugees."

4. In some ways, one could argue that women's commitment to "the grass-roots," despite its potential to be a site of women's agency, could also reify patriarchy. Several feminists have made such a critique against the trend among some feminists to celebrate "activist mothering" (McFadden 2008).

5. Lowe and Lloyd argue that Orientalist and classical anthropological discourses rely on a similar modernist bifurcation in constructing the culture of colonized people as a form of tradition that is fixed and unchanging and a sign of backwardness and primitivism (1997, 24). Leftist definitions of culture as commodified or conservative concepts of culture as merely aesthetic similarly assume that culture is a manifestation of the existence of difference (1997, 26). Coco Fusco contends that cultural nationalisms demand aesthetic products that are devoid of outside influence and become the hallmark of an authentic national or ethnic culture. Performance art, he contends, is critical of this and presents cultural identity as ever evolving (1999, 5-7).

6. Paul Gilroy argues for rereading and rethinking expressive countercultures as a "philosophical discourse that refuses the modern, occidental separation of ethics and aesthetics, culture and politics" (1993, 39).

7. This includes liberal multicultural notions that call for a recognition or tolerance of women's diverse experiences.

8. See, for example, Kuumba 2001; Bobo 1995; and Arrizón 1999. See the following analysis of African American women redefining themselves through hip-hop: Bobo 1995; Forman and Neal 2004; and Rose 1994.

CONCLUSION

1. Here I am referring to the activities that emerged in the streets of Durban, ignited by a two-day general strike with mass marches led by the Congress of South African Trade Unions (COSATU) and an estimated one million workers marching in Johannesburg.

2. The following reference documents that the images were real: Mikkelson and Mikkelson 2011. At the same time, an alternative viewpoint argued that this was an isolated incident: Barrett 2002.

3. A 2005 Amnesty International report detailed and analyzed the worsening situation in Afghanistan for women. Rawi (2004) provides analysis of Laura Bush's remark about women's rights in Afghanistan. Also see Abu-Lughod 2002.

BIBLIOGRAPHY

Abdo, Nahla. 2010. "Imperialism, the State, and NGOs: Middle Eastern Contexts and Contestations." *Comparative Studies of South Asia* 30, no. 2: 238-49.

Abdulhadi, Rabab. 2010. "Sexualities and the Social Order in Arab and Muslim Communities." In *Islam and Homosexuality*, edited by Samar Habib, 463-88. Santa Barbara, CA: Praeger.

Abdulhadi, Rabab, Evelyn Alsultany, and Nadine Naber. 2011a. "Arab and Arab American Feminisms: An Introduction." In *Arab and Arab American Feminisms: Gender, Violence, and Belonging*, edited by Rabab Abdulhadi, Evelyn Alsultany and Nadine Naber, xix-xxxix. Syracuse, NY: Syracuse University Press.

———, eds. 2011b. Arab and Arab American Feminisms: Gender, Violence, and Belonging. Syracuse, NY: Syracuse University Press.

Abraham, Nabeel. 1994. "Anti-Arab Racism and Violence in the United States." In *The Development of Arab American Identity*, edited by Ernest McCarus, 204-26. Ann Arbor: University of Michigan Press.

———. 1992. "The Gulf Crisis and Anti-Arab Racism in America." In *Collateral Damage: "The New World Order" at Home and Abroad*, edited by Cynthia Peters, 255-78. Boston: South End Press.

Abu-Laban, Baha. 1975. *Arabs in America: Myths and Realities*. Wilmette, IL: Medina University Press International.

Abu-Lughod, Lila. 2002. "Do Muslim Women Really Need Saving? Anthropological Reflections on Cultural Relativism and Its Others." *American Anthropologist* 104, no. 3.

———. 1998. "The Marriage of Feminism and Islamism in Egypt: Selective Repudiation as a Dynamic of Postcolonial Cultural Politics." *Remaking Women: Feminism and Modernity in the Middle East*, edited by Lila Abu-Lughod, 243-69. Princeton, NJ: Princeton University Press.

———. 1986. *Veiled Sentiments: Honor and Poetry in Bedouin Society*. Berkeley: University of California Press.

———. 1991. "Writing against Culture." *Recapturing Anthropology: Working in the Present*, edited by Richard Fox, 139-61. Santa Fe, NM: SAR Press.

———. 1993. *Writing Women's Worlds: Bedouin Stories*. Berkeley: University of California Press.

Abu-Nimah, Ali. 2007. *One Country: A Bold Proposal to End the Israeli-Palestinian Impasse*. New York: Picador.

Ahmed, Leila. 1992. *Women and Gender in Islam: Historical Roots of a Modern Debate*. New Haven, CT: Yale University Press.

Ahuja, Sarita, Pronita Gupta, and Daranee Petsod. 2004. *Arab Middle Eastern and South Asian Communities in the San Francisco Bay Area*. San Francisco: Grantmakers Concerned with Immigrants and Refugees and Asian Americans/Pacific Islanders in Philanthropy.

Akram, Susan. 2002. "The Aftermath of September 11, 2001: The Targeting of Arabs and Muslims in America." *Arab Studies Quarterly* 24, nos. 2/3 (Spring).

Aladdin. 1992. Directed by Ron Clements and John Musker. Walt Disney Pictures.

Al-Ali, Nadje, and Nicole Pratt. 2009. *What Kind of Liberation? Women and the Occupation of Iraq.* Berkeley: University of California Press.

Alarcón, Norma. 1999. "Chicana Feminism: In the Tracks of 'the' Native Woman." *Between Woman and Nation: Nationalisms, Transnational Feminism, and the State,* edited by Caren Kaplan, Norma Alarcón, and Minoo Moallem, 63-71. Durham, NC: Duke University Press.

———. 1991. "The Theoretical Subject(s) of *This Bridge Called My Back* and Anglo-American Feminism." In *Criticism in the Borderlands: Studies in Chicano Literature, Culture, and Ideology,* edited by Hector Calderon and Jose Davod Saldivar. Durham, NC: Duke University Press.

Alexander, Karen, and Mary E. Hawkesworth. 2008. *War and Terror: Feminist Perspectives.* Chicago: University of Chicago Press.

Al-Hibri, Azizah. 2000. "An Introduction to Muslim Women's Rights." In *Windows of Faith: Muslim Women Scholar-Activists in North America,* edited by Gisela Webb, 51-71. Syracuse, NY: Syracuse University Press.

Almaguer, Tomás. 2004. *Racial Fault Lines: The Historical Origins of White Supremacy in California.* Berkeley: University of California Press.

Al-Sayyad, Ayisha A. 2010. "'You're What?' Engaging Narratives from Diasporic Muslim Women on Identity and Gay Liberation." In *Islam and Homosexuality,* edited by Samar Habib. Santa Barbara, CA: Praeger.

Alsultany, Evelyn. 2012. *Arabs and Muslims in the U.S. Media Post-9/11.* New York: New York University Press.

———. 2007. "Selling American Diversity and Muslim American Identity through Nonprofit Advertising Post-9/11." *American Quarterly* 59, no. 3: 593-622.

Amar, Paul. 2010. "Queer Arab Studies." Guest lecture in Introduction to Arab American Studies, University of Michigan, Ann Arbor, October 23.

Amer, Sahar. 2008. "Cross-Dressing and Female Same-Sex Marriage in Medieval French and Arabic Literatures." In *Islamicate Sexualities: Translations across Temporal Geographies of Desire,* edited by Kathryn Babayan and Afsaneh Najmabadi, 72-113. Cambridge, MA: Harvard Center for Middle Eastern Studies.

American-Arab Anti-Discrimination Committee. 1991. *1991 Report on Anti-Arab Hate Crimes: Political and Hate Violence against Arab-Americans.* Washington, DC: ADC Research Institute.

Amireh, Amal. 2011. "Palestinian Women's Disappearing Act: The Suicide Bomber through Western Feminist Eyes." In *Arab and Arab American Feminisms,* edited by Rbab Abdulhadi, Evelyn Alsultany, and Nadine Naber, 29-45. Syracuse, NY: Syracuse University Press.

———. 2000. "Viewpoint—Framing Nawal El Saadawi: Arab Feminism in a Transnational World." *Signs* 26, no. 1: 215.

Amnesty International. 2005. *Afghanistan: Women Still under Attack—A Systematic Failure to Protect.* London: Amnesty International.

Anderson, Benedict. 1983. *Imagined Communities: Reflections on the Origin and Spread of Nationalism.* London: Verso.

Appadurai, Arjun. 1990. "Disjuncture and Difference in the Global Cultural Economy." *Public Culture* 2, no. 2: 1-24.

———. 1996. *Modernity at Large: Cultural Dimensions of Globalization.* Minneapolis: University of Minnesota Press.

Arrizón, Alicia. 1999. *Latina Performance: Traversing the Stage*. Bloomington: Indiana University Press.

Aruri, Naseer. 2003. *Dishonest Broker: The U.S. Role in Israel and Palestine*. Cambridge, MA: South End Press.

———. 2001. *Palestinian Refugees: The Right of Return*. London: Pluto Press.

Asad, Talal. 1973. "Introduction." In *Anthropology and the Colonial Encounter*, ed. Talal Asad, 9-19. London: Ithaca Press.

———.1995. "Modern Power and the Reconfiguration of Religious Traditions. Interview with Saba Mahmood." *Stanford Humanities Review* (Special Issue: *Contested Polities*) 5, no. 1: 1-18.

Aswad, Barbara. 1974. *Arabic Speaking Communities in American Cities*. New York: Center for Migration Studies of New York and Association Arab-American University Graduates.

Avineri, Shlomo. 1981. *The Making of Modern Zionism: Intellectual Origins of the Jewish State*. New York: Basic Books.

Awad, Gary. 1981. "The Arab Americans: An Invisible Minority Awakens." *New Circle* (March): 31-32.

Axel, Brian Keith. 2001. *The Nation's Tortured Body: Violence, Representation, and the Formation of a Sikh "Diaspora."* Durham, NC: Duke University Press.

Azikwe, Abayomi. 2009. "Pan-Africanism and Palestine Solidarity: A History of Anti-Imperialist Struggle." *Pambazuka News*, February 12.

Babayan, Kathryn, and Afsaneh Najmabadi, eds. 2008. *Islamicate Sexualities: Translations across Temporal Geographies of Desire*. Cambridge, MA: Harvard University Press.

Baca Zinn, Maxine. 2000. "Feminism and Family Studies for a New Century." *Annals of the American Academy of Political and Social Science* 571: 42-56.

Bachetta, Paola, Tina Campt, Inderpal Grewal, Caren Kaplan, Minoo Moallem, and Jennifer Terry. 2002. "Transnational Feminist Practices against War."*Meridians: Feminism, Race, Transnationalism* 2, no. 2: 302-8.

Bagader, Abubaker A. 1994. "Contemporary Islamic Movements in the Arab World." In *Islam, Globalization, and Postmodernity*, edited by Akbar S. Ahmed and Hastings Donnan, 111-22. New York: Routledge.

Baker, Raymond William. 2003. *Islam without Fear: Egypt and the New Islamists*. Cambridge, MA: Harvard University Press.

Baldassare, Mark. 2000. *California in the New Millennium: The Changing Social and Political Landscape*. Berkeley: University of California Press.

Balibar, Etienne. 1991. "Is There a 'Neo-Racism'?" In *Race, Nation, Class: Ambiguous Identities*, edited by Etienne Balibar and Immanual Wallterstein, 17-28. Brooklyn, NY: Verso.

Barakat, Halim. 1985. "The Arab Family and the Challenge of Social Transformation." *Women and the Family in the Middle East*, edited by Elizabeth Warnock Fernea, 27-48. Austin: University of Texas Press.

———. 1993. *The Arab World: Society, Culture, and State*. Berkeley: University of California Press.

Barazangi, Nimat Hafez. 2000. "Muslim Women's Islamic Higher Learning as a Human Right: Theory and Practice." In *Windows of Faith: Muslim Women Scholar-Activists in North America*, edited by Gisela Webb, 22-50. Syracuse, NY: Syracuse University Press.

Barrett, Greg. 2002. "Strength of Its Culture Makes U.S. Loved, Hated on Arab Street." *Gannett News Service*.

Bascara, Victor. 2006. *Model-Minority Imperialism*. Minneapolis: University of Minnesota Press.

Bayour, Elham. 2005. "Occupied Terri-
tories, Resisting Women: Palestinian
Women Political Prisoners." *Global
Lockdown: Race, Gender, and the
Prison-Industrial Complex*, edited
by Julia Sudbury, 201-14. New York:
Routledge.

Beal, Frances. 2008. "Double Jeopardy:
To Be Black and Female." *Meridians:
Feminism, Race, Transnationalism* 8, no.
2: 166-76.

Becker, Brian. 2010. *Will Sanctions on Iraq
Be Lifted? International Action Center
Urges Movement to Stay Vigilant.* New
York: Workers World Service.

Behar, Ruth, and Deborah A. Gordon.
1995. *Women Writing Culture.* Berkeley:
University of California Press.

Berkeley Ihsan Conference. 2000. Organized by University of California–
Berkeley Muslim Student Association.

Bernal, Dolores Delgado. 1998. "Grassroots
Leadership Reconceptualized: Chicana
Oral Histories and the 1968 East Los
Angeles School Blowouts." *Frontiers* 19,
no. 2: 113-42.

Bernal, Victoria. 1994. "Gender, Culture,
and Capitalism: Women and the
Remaking of Islamic "Tradition" in a
Sudanese Village." *Comparative Studies
in Society and History* 36, no. 1: 36-67.

Bhabha, Homi K. 1992. "A Good Judge
of Character: Men, Metaphors, and
the Common Culture." In *Race-ing
Justice, En-Gendering Power: Essays on
Anita Hill, Clarence Thomas, and the
Construction of Social Reality*, edited
by Toni Morrison, 232-50. New York:
Pantheon Books.

———. 1994. *The Location of Culture.* London: Routledge.

Bhattacharjee, Anannya. 1992. "The Habit
of Ex-Nomination: Nation, Woman,
and the Indian Immigrant Bourgeosie."
Public Culture 5, no. 1: 19-44.

Bhattacharyya, Gargi. 2008. *Dangerous
Brown Men: Exploiting Sex, Violence,*
and Feminism in the War on Terror.
London: Zed Books.

Blackwell, Maylei. 2011. *Chicana Power!*
Austin: University of Texas Press.

———. 2010. "Líderes Campesinas:
Nepantla Strategies and Grassroots
Organizing at the Intersection of Gender and Globalization." *Aztlán: A Journal of Chicano Studies* 35, no. 1: 13-47.

———. 2009. "Zones of Autonomy: Gendered Cultural Citizenship and Indigenous Women's Organizing in Mexico."
In *Gender and Cultural Citizenship:
Rethinking Knowledge Production, Political Activism, and Culture*, edited by Citizenship, the Working Group on Gender
and Cultural. New York: Palgrave Press.

Bobo, Jacqueline. 1995. *Black Women as
Cultural Readers.* Film and Culture
Series. New York: Columbia University
Press.

Boyle, Mark. 2001. "Towards a (Re)Theo-
risation of the Historical Geography
of Nationalism in Diasporas: The Irish
Diaspora as an Exemplar." *International
Journal of Population Geography* 7, no. 6
(November/December): 426-46.

Brah, A. 1996. *Cartographies of Diaspora: Contesting Identities.* New York:
Routledge.

———. 2003. "'Diaspora, Border, and
Transnational Identities.'" In *Feminist
Postcolonial Theory: A Reader*, edited
by Reina Lewis and Sara Mills, 613-34.
New York: Routledge.

Braziel, Jana Evans, and Anita Mannur,
eds. 2003. *Theorizing Diaspora: A
Reader.* Malden, MA: Blackwell.

Brodkin, Karen. 2002. *How Jews Became
White and What That Says about Race
in America.* New Brunswick, NJ: Rut-
gers University Press.

Bukhari, Zahid H., Sulayman S. Nyang,
Mumtaz Ahmad, and John L. Esposito.
2004. "Introduction: Hope, Fears, and
Aspirations: Muslims in the American
Public Square." In *Muslims' Place in the*

American Public Square: Hope, Fears, and Aspirations, edited by Zahid H. Bukhari, Sulayman S. Nyang, Mumtaz Ahmad, and John L. Esposito, xiv-xlii. Walnut Creek, CA: Alta Mira Press.

Burnham, Linda, Erika Tatnall, and Women of Color Resource Center. 2006. "Paving the Way: A Teaching Guide to the Third World Women's Alliance." CD-ROM. Available at http://coloredgirls.live.radicaldesigns.org/article.php?id=241 (accessed September 17, 2011).

Bush, Laura. 2001. *Radio Address by Mrs. Bush*. George W. Bush White House Archives. Crawford, TX.

Butler, Judith. 2006. "Academic Norms, Contemporary Challenges: A Reply to Robert Post on Academic Freedom." In *Academic Freedom after September 11*, edited by Beshara Doumani,107-42. Cambridge, MA: Zone Books/MIT Press.

Cainkar, Louise. 2009. *Homeland Insecurity: The Arab American and Muslim American Experience after 9/11*. New York: Russell Sage Foundation Publications.

———. 1996. "Immigrant Palestinian Women Evaluate Their Lives." In *Family and Gender among American Muslims: Issues Facing Middle Eastern Immigrants and Their Descendents*, edited by Barbara Aswad and Barbara Bilgé, 41-59. Philadelphia: Temple University Press.

———. 2004. "Islamic Revival among Second-Generation Arab Muslims in Chicago: The American Experience and Globalization Intersect." *Bulletin of the Royal Institute for Interfaith Studies* 6.2 (Autumn/Winter): 99-120.

Carr, Jesse. 2010. "Gender, Imperialism, and Militarized Violence." Unpublished essay.

Central Intelligence Agency. 2010. *C.I.A. World Factbook*. Washington, DC: Central Intelligence Agency.

Chang, Edward Taehan, and Angela Y.Chung. 1998. "From Third World Liberation to Multiple Oppression Politics: A Contemporary Approach to Interethnic Coalitions." *Social Justice* 25, no. 3: 80-100.

Chatterjee, Partha. 1993. *The Nation and Its Fragments: Colonial and Postcolonial History*. Princeton, NJ: Princeton University Press.

Chaudhuri, Nupur, and Margaret Strobel. 1992. *Western Women and Imperialism: Complicity and Resistance*. Bloomington: Indiana University Press.

Chavez, Lydia. 1998. *The Color Blind: California's Battle to End Affirmative Action*. Berkeley: University of California Press.

Choueiri, Youssef M. 2000. *Arab Nationalism: A History*. Oxford: Blackwell.

Chu, Patricia P. 2000. *Assimilating Asians: Gendered Strategies of Authorship in Asian America*. Durham, NC: Duke University Press.

Clark, Ramsey. 1998a. "Fire and Ice." In *Challenge to Genocide: Let Iraq Live*, 3-32. New York: International Action Center.

———. 1998b. *The Impact of Sanctions on Iraq: The Children Are Dying*. New York: International Action Center.

Clarke, Kamari Maxine. 2004. *Mapping Yoruba Networks: Power and Agency in the Making of Transnational Communities*. Durham, NC: Duke University Press.

Clifford, James. "Diasporas." 1994. *Cultural Anthropology* 9, no. 3 (Aug.): 302-38.

———. 2001. "Indigenous Articulations." *The Contemporary Pacific* 13.2 (Fall): 468-90.

———. 1997. *Routes: Travel and Translation in the Late Twentieth Century*. Cambridge, MA: Harvard University Press.

Clifford, James, and George E. Marcus. 1986. *Writing Culture: The Poetics and Politics of Ethnography*. Berkeley: University of California Press.

CNN.com. 2009. "Ex-Black Panther Convicted of Murder." *CNN.Com,* March 9, Law Center.

Cohen, Cathy J. 1999. *The Boundaries of Blackness: AIDS and the Breakdown of Black Politics*. Chicago: University of Chicago Press.

———. 2004. "Deviance as Resistance: A New Research Agenda for the Study of Black Politics." *Du Bois Review* 1, no. 1: 27-45.

———. 1997. "Punks, Bulldaggers, and Welfare Queens." *GLQ: A Journal of Lesbian and Gay Studies* 3, no. 4: 437-65.

Cohn, Abby. 2003. "S.F. WAR Lifts Anti-Israel Language As It Faces City, State Probes." *J. Weekly*, Friday, July 18, http://www.jweekly.com/article/full/20211/sfwar-lifts-anti-israel-language-as-it-faces-city-state-probes/.

Cole, David. 2003. *Enemy Aliens: Double Standards and Constitutional Freedoms in the War on Terrorism*. New York: Norton.

Cole, Juan. 2003. "The Iraqi Shiites: On the History of America's Would-Be Allies." *Boston Review*, October/November.

Collins, Patricia Hill. 2000. "It's All in the Family: Intersection of Gender, Race, and Nation." *Decentering the Center: Philosophy for a Multicultural, Postcolonial, and Feminist World*, edited by Uma Narayan and Sandra Harding, 156-76. Bloomington: Indiana University Press.

Cotera, María Eugenia. 2008. *Native Speakers: Ella Deloria, Zora Neale Hurston, Jovita González, and the Poetics of Culture*. Austin: University of Texas Press.

Crenshaw, Kimberlé Williams. 1994. "Mapping the Margins." In *The Public Nature of Private Violence: The Discovery of Domestic Abuse*, edited by Martha Albertson Fineman and Roxanne Mykitiuk, 93-118. New York: Routledge.

Darity, William A. 2008. "Arabs." In *International Encyclopedia of the Social Sciences*. Vol. 1, 159-61. Detroit: Macmillan Reference.

Davidson, Lawrence. 1999. "Debating Palestine: Arab-American Challenges to Zionism, 1917-1932." In *Arabs in America: Building a New Future*, ed. Michael Suleiman. Philadelphia, PA: Temple University Press.

Davis, Angela Y. 1998. "Art on the Frontline." In *The Angela Y. Davis Reader*, edited by Angela Y. Davis and Joy James, 235-47. Malden, MA: Blackwell.

———. 1989. *Women, Culture, and Politics*. New York: Random House.

Dawisha, Adeed. 2005. *Arab Nationalism in the Twentieth Century: From Triumph to Despair*. Princeton, NJ: Princeton University Press.

Dayal, Samir. 1996. "Diaspora and Double Consciousness." *Journal of the Midwest Modern Language Association* 29, no. 1: 46.

De Lauretis, Teresa. 1998. "Sexual Indifference and Lesbian Representation." *Theater Journal* 40, no. 2 (May): 151-77.

de Leon, Lakandiwa M. 2004. "Filipinotown and the DJ Scene: Cultural Expression and Identity Affirmation of Filipino American Youth in Los Angeles." In *Asian American Youth: Culture, Identity, and Ethnicity*, edited by Min Zhou and Jennifer Lee, 191-206. New York: Routledge.

Deb, Trishala, and Rafael Mutis. 2004. "Smoke and Mirrors: Abu Ghraib and the Myth of Liberation." *Colorlife! Magazine*, Summer.

Deeb, Lara. 2006. *An Enchanted Modern: Gender and Public Piety in Shi'i Lebanon*. Princeton, NJ: Princeton University Press.

Denetdale, Jennifer. 2008. "Carving Navajo National Boundaries: Patriotism, Tradition, and the Diné Marriage Act of 2005." *American Quarterly* 60, no. 2: 289-94.

Denzin, Norman K. 1997. *Interpretive Ethnography: Ethnographic Practices for the 21st Century*. Thousand Oaks, CA: Sage.

Diaz, Vicente M., and J. Kehaulani Kauanui. 2001. "Native Pacific Cultural

Studies on the Edge." *Contemporary Pacific* 13, no. 2 (Fall): 315-41.

Duggan, Lisa. 2004. "Holy Matrimony!" *The Nation*, March 14.

———. 2003. *The Twilight of Equality? Neoliberalism, Cultural Politics, and the Attack on Democracy*. Boston: Beacon.

Dwyer, Kevin. 1991. *Arab Voices: The Human Rights Debate in the Middle East*. Berkeley: University of California Press, 1991.

Economist Intelligence Unit. 1995. "Iraq: Country Report." *Economist Intelligence Unit*.

Edelman, Lee. 1999. "Rear Window's Glasshole." In *Out Takes: Eassys on Queer Theory and Film*, edited by Ellis Hanson, 72-96. Durham, NC: Duke University Press.

Eickelman, Dale. 1998. *The Middle and Central Asia: An Anthropological Approach*. Upper Saddle River, NJ: Prentice Hall.

Eisenstein, Zillah R. 1996. *Hatreds: Racialized and Sexualized Conflicts in the 21st Century*. New York: Routledge.

El-Badry, Samia. 1994. "The Arab-American Market." *American Demography* no. 16: 22-30.

Elbaum, Max. 2002. *Revolution in the Air: Sixties Radicals Turn to Lenin, Mao, and Che*. London: Verso.

Elia, Nada. 2010. "The Burden of Representation: When Palestinians Speak Out." In *Arab and Arab American Feminisms: Gender, Violence, Belonging*, edited by Rabab Abdulhadi, Evelyn Alsultany, and Nadine Naber. Syracuse, NY: Syracus University Press.

———. 2006. "Islamophobia and the 'Privileging' of Arab American Women." *National Women Studies Association Journal* 18, no. 3: 155-61.

———. 2002. "The 'White Sheep' of the Family: But Bleaching Is Like Starvation." *This Bridge We Call Home*, edited by Gloria Anzaldúa and AnaLouise Keating, 223-32.

Elits, Hermann F. 1982. *The "Fresh Start" Initiative: Media and U.S. Perceptions of the Middle East*. Washington, DC: American-Arab Anti-Discrimination Committee.

Elyachar, Julia. 2005. *Markets of Dispossesions: NGOs, Economic Development, and the State in Cairo*. Politics, History, and Culture Series. Durham, NC: Duke University Press.

Enloe, Cynthia. 2004. *The Curious Feminist: Searching for Women in a New Age of Empire*. Berkeley: University of California Press.

———. 2007. *Globalization and Militarism: Feminists Make the Link*. Lanham, MD: Rowman and Littlefield.

———. 1993. *The Morning After: Sexual Politics at the End of the Cold War*. Berkeley: University of California Press.

Espiritu, Yen Le. 2003. Home Bound: Filipino American Lives across Cultures, Communities, and Countries. Berkeley: University of California Press.

Fanon, Frantz. 1963. *The Wretched of the Earth*. New York: Grove.

Farsoun, Samih K., and Naseer H. Aruri. 2006. *Palestine and the Palestinians: A Social and Political History*. Boulder, CO: Westview.

Food and Agriculture Organization of the United Nations. 1995. *Technical Cooperation Programme: Evaluation of Food and Nutrition Situation in Iraq*. Rome: United National Food and Agricultural Organization.

Forman, Murray, and Mark Anthony Neal. 2004. *That's the Joint! The Hip-Hop Studies Reader*. New York: Routledge.

Foster, John Bellamy. 2005. "Naked Imperialism." *Monthly Review* 57, no. 4.

Foucault, Michel. 1979. *Discipline and Punish: The Birth of the Prison*. New York: Vintage.

———. 1978. *The History of Sexuality*. New York: Vintage.

Frontline World. 2001. *The Debate over U.N. Sanctions.* Iraq: Truth and Lies in Baghdad, edited by Frontline World. Corporation for Public Broadcasting, 2002.

Fusco, Coco. 1999. "Introduction: Latin American Performance and the Reconquista of Civil Space." In *Corpus Delecti: Performance Art of the Americas,* edited by Coco Fusco, 1-20. New York: Routledge.

Gaines, Kevin. 1996. *Uplifting the Race: Black Leadership, Politics, and Culture in the Twentieth Century.* Chapel Hill: University of North Carolina Press.

Garfield, Richard. 1999. "Morbidity and Mortality among Iraqi Children from 1990 through 1998: Assessing the Impact of the Gulf War and Economic Sanctions." *CASI Internet:* July, http://www.casi.org.uk/info/garfield/dr-garfield.html.

Gedda, George. 1996. "U.S. Fields More Iraq Refugees." *Associated Press,* September 17.

George, Marcus. 2009. "Multi-Sited Ethnography: Notes and Queries." In *Multi-Sited Ethnography,* edited by Mark-Anthony Falzon, 181-96. Burlington, VT: Ashgate.

G.I. Jane. 1997. Directed by Ridley Scott. Hollywood Pictures.

Giacaman, Rita, and Penny Johnson. 1989. "Building Barricades and Breaking Barriers." In *Intifada: The Palestinian Uprising against Israeli Occupation,* edited by Zachary Lockman and Joel Beinin, 155-70. Boston: South End Press.

Gibbs, Jewelle Taylor, and Teiahsha Bankhead. 2001. *Preserving Privilege: California Politics, Propositions, and People of Color.* Westport, CT: Praeger.

Gilmore, Ruth Wilson. 2006. *Golden Gulag: Prisons, Surplus, Crisis, and Opposition in Globalizing California.* Berkeley: University of California Press.

Gilroy, Paul. 1993. *The Black Atlantic: Modernity and Double Consciousness.*

Cambridge, MA: Harvard University Press.

———. 1992. "Cultural Studies and Ethnic Absolutism." In *Cultural Studies,* edited by Lawrence Grossberg, Cary Nelson, and Paula Treichler, 187-98. New York: Routledge.

Glick Schiller, Nina, Linda Basch, and Cristina Szanton Blanc. 1995. "From Immigrant to Transmigrant: Theorizing Transnational Migration." *Anthropological Quarterly* 68, no. 1 (January): 48-63.

Gökariksel, Banu, and Katharyne Mitchell. 2005. "Veiling, Secularism, and the Neoliberal Subject: National Narratives and Supranational Desires in Turkey and France." *Global Networks* 5, no. 2: 147-65.

Goldberg, David Theo. 1993. *Racist Culture.* Oxford: Blackwell.

———. 2009. *The Threat of Race: Reflections on Racial Neoliberalism.* Malden, MA: Blackwell.

Gopinath, Gayatri. 2005. *Impossible Desires: Queer Diasporas and South Asian Public Cultures.* Durham, NC: Duke University Press.

Gordon, Joy. 2010. *Invisible War: The United States and the Iraq Sanctions.* Cambridge, MA: Harvard University Press.

Gorkin, Michael, and Rafiqa Othman. 1996. *Three Mothers, Three Daughters: Palestinian Women's Stories.* Literature of the Middle East. Berkeley: University of California Press.

Greenhill, Kelly M. 2010. *Weapons of Mass Migration: Forced Displacement, Coercion, and Foreign Policy.* Ithaca, NY: Cornell University Press.

Grewal, Inderpal, and Caren Kaplan. 1994. *Scattered Hegemonies: Postmodernity and Transnational Feminist Practices.* Minneapolis: University of Minnesota Press.

Griswold, William J. 1975. *The Image of the Middle East in Secondary School*

Textbooks. New York: Middle East Studies Association of North America.

Gualtieri, Sarah M. A. 2009. *Between Arab and White: Race and Ethnicity in the Early Syrian American Diaspora.* Berkeley: University of California Press.

———. 2004. "Strange Fruit? Syrian Immigrants, Extralegal Violence, and Racial Formation in the Jim Crow South." *Arab Studies Quarterly* 26, no. 3.

Gupta, Akhil, and James Ferguson. 1997. "Discipline and Practice: 'The Field' as Site, Method, and Location in Anthropology." In *Anthropological Locations: Boundaries and Grounds of a Field Science*, edited by Akhil Gupta and James Ferguson, 1-47. Los Angeles: University of California Press.

Gutierrez, David. 1995. *Walls and Mirrors: Mexican Americans, Mexican Immigrants, and the Politics of Ethnicity.* Berkeley: University of California Press.

Habib, Samar. 2010. *Islam and Homosexuality.* Santa Barbara, CA: Praeger.

Haddad, Yvonne Yazbeck, and John L. Esposito. 1998. *Muslims on the Americanization Path?* Atlanta: Scholars Press.

Hall, Stuart. 1994. "Cultural Identity and Diaspora." *Colonial Discourse and Post-Colonial Theory: A Reader,* edited by Patrick Williams and Laura Chrisman, 392-403. New York: Columbia University Press.

———. 1996. "Race, Articulation, and Societies Structured in Dominance." In *Black British Cultural Studies: A Reader,* edited by Houston A. Baker, Manthia Diawara, and Ruth H. Lindeborg, 16-60. Chicago: University of Chicago Press.

Hammami, Reza, and Martina Rieker. 1988. "Feminist Orientalism and Orientalist Marxism." *New Left Review* 1.170 (July–August).

Haraway, Donna. 1988. "Situated Knowledges." *Feminist Studies* 14, no. 3: 575-99.

Hardt, Michael, and Antonio Negri. 2001. *Empire.* Cambridge, MA: Harvard University Press.

Harum Scarum. 2004. Directed by Gene Nelson. Turner Entertainment.

Harvey, David. 2003. *The New Imperialism.* Clarendon Lectures in Geography and Environmental Studies. Oxford: Oxford University Press.

Hassan, Riffat. 2000. "Human Rights in the Qur'anic Perspective." In *Windows of Faith,* edited by Gisela Webb, 241-48. Syracuse, NY: Syracuse University Press.

Hasso, Frances. Forthcoming. *"Family Crisis," Governmentality, and Neo-Liberal Desire: The United Arab Emirates and Egypt.* Palo Alto, CA: Stanford University Press.

———. 1998. "The 'Women's Front': Nationalism, Feminism, and Modernity in Contemporary Palestine." *Gender and Society* 12.4 (August): 441-65.

Hatem, Mervat F. 2001. "How the Gulf War Changed the A.A.U.G.'s Discourse on Arab Nationalism and Gender Politics." *Middle East Journal* 55, no. 2: 277.

———. 2011. "The Political and Cultural Representations of Arabs, Arab Americans, and Arab American Feminisms after September 11, 2001." In *Arab and Arab American Feminisms: Gender, Violence, and Belonging,* edited by Rabab Abdulhadi, Evelyn Alsultany, and Nadine Naber, 10-28. Syracuse, NY: Syracuse University Press.

Hawthorne, Susan, and Bronwyn Winter. 2003. *After Shock: September 11, 2001; Global Feminist Perspectives.* Vancouver, BC: Raincoast Books.

Hayes, Jarrod. 2001. "Queer Resistance to (Neo-)Colonialism in Algeria." In *Postcolonial, Queer,* edited by John C. Hawley, 79-97. Albany: State University of New York Press.

Hirschkind, Charles, and Saba Mahmood. 2002. "Feminism, the Taliban,

and Politics of Counter-Insurgency."
Anthropological Quarterly 75, no. 2:
339-54.

Hitti, Phillip. 1968. *The Arabs in History*.
London: Macmillan.

Ho, Engseng. 2004. "Empire through
Diasporic Eyes: A View from the Other
Boat." *Comparative Studies in Society
and History* 46, no. 2: 210-46.

———. 2006. *The Graves of Tarim: Genealogy and Mobility across the Indian
Ocean*. Berkeley: University of California Press.

Hoodfar, Homa. 1997. *Between Marriage
and the Market: Intimate Politics and
Survival in Cairo*. Berkeley: University
of California Press.

Hooglund, Eric. 1985. *Taking Root: Arab-
American Community Studies*. Washington, DC: ADC Research Institute.

Howell, Sally, and Andrew Shryock. 2003.
"Cracking Down on Diaspora: Arab
Detroit and America's 'War on Terror.'"
Anthropological Quarterly 76, no. 3:
443-62.

Hudson, Michael C. 1980. *The American
Media and the Arabs*. Washington, DC:
Center for Contemporary Arab Studies,
Georgetown University.

Hussaini, Hatem. 1974. "The Impact of the
Arab-Israeli Conflict on Arab Ameri-
can Communities in the United States."
In *Settle Regimes in Africa and the Arab
World: The Illusion of Endurance*, edited
by Ibrahim Abu-Lughod, Abdu'l-
Baha, and Baha Abu-Laban. Wilmette:
Medina University Press International.

Hyndman, Jennifer. 2008. "Whose Bodies
Count? Feminist Geopolitics and Lessons from Iraq." In *Feminism and War:
Confronting U.S. Imperialism*, edited
by Robin L. Riley, Chandra Talpade
Mohanty, and Minnie Bruce Pratt, 194-
206. New York: Zed Books.

Incite! Women of Color against Violence. 2007. *The Revolution Will Not
Be Funded: Beyond the Non-Profit

Industrial Complex*. Cambridge, MA:
South End Press.

Isseroff, Ami. 2011. *Right of Return of Palestinian Refugees: International Law and
Humanitarian Considerations*. Zionism
and Israeli Information Center. http://
www.zionism-israel.com/issues/return_
detail.html.

Jadaliyya . 2011. *Past Is Present: Settler Colonialism Matters!* http://www.jadaliyya.
com/pages/index/661/past-is-present_
settler-colonialism-matters. Accessed
December 9.

Jadallah, Huda. 2003. "Arab Americans." In
*Encyclopedia of Lesbian, Gay, Bisexual,
and Transgender History in America*,
edited by Marc Stein: Scribner's Books.

———. 2010. "Reflections on a Gender-
queer Palestinian American Lesbian."
In *Arab and Arab American Feminisms:
Gender, Violence, and Belonging*, edited
by Rabab Abdulhadi, Evelyn Alsultany,
and Nadine Naber, 276-82. Syracuse,
NY: Syracuse University Press.

Jamal, Amaney, and Nadine Naber. 2008.
"Introduction: Arab Americans and
U.S. Racial Formations." In *Race
and Arab Americans before and after
9/11: From Invisible Citizens to Visible
Subjects*, 1-45. Syracuse, NY: Syracuse
University Press.

Jameson, Fredric. 1998. *The Cultural Turn:
Selected Writings on the Postmodern,
1983-1998*. London: Verso.

Jarmakani, Amira. 2008. *Imagining Arab
Womanhood: The Cultural Mythology
of Veils, Harems, and Belly Dancers
in the U.S.* 1st ed. New York: Palgrave
Macmillan.

Jayawardena, Kumari. 1986. *Feminism
and Nationalism in the Third World*.
London: Zed Books.

Johnson, Penny, and Eileen Kuttab. 2001.
"Where Have All the Women (and
Men) Gone? Reflections on Gender
and the Second Palestinian Intifada."
Feminist Review 69: 21-43.

Joseph, Suad. 1999. "Against the Grain of the Nation: The Arab." In *Arabs in America: Building a New Future*, edited by Michael W. Suleiman, 257-72. Philadelphia: Temple University Press.

———. 2000. "Civic Myths, Citizenship, and Gender in Lebanon." *Gender and Citizenship in the Middle East*: 107-36.

———. 1994. "Gender and Family in the Arab World." In *Arab Women: Between Defiance and Restraint*, edited by Suha Sabbagh, 194-202. Washington, DC: Olive Branch Press.

———. 1993. "Gender and Relationality among Arab Families in Lebanon." *Feminist Studies* 19, no. 3 (Fall): 465.

Judt, Tony. 2003. "Israel: The Alternative." *New York Review of Books*, October 23.

Kadi, Joanna. 1994. "Introduction." In *Food for Our Grandmothers: Writings by Arab American and Arab Canadian Feminists*, edited by Joanna Kadi, xiii-xix. Boston: South End Press.

Kahf, Mohja. 2000. "Packaging 'Huda': Sha'Rawi's Memoirs in the United States Reception Environment." In *Going Global: The Transnational Reception of Third World Women Writers*, edited by Amal Amireh and Lisa Suhair Majaj, 148-72. New York: Garland.

Kamalipour, Yahya. 1995. *The U.S. Media and the Middle East*. Westport, CT: Greenwood Press.

Kaplan, Amy. 2003. *The Anarchy of Empire in the Making of U.S. Culture*. Cambridge, MA: Harvard University Press.

Kaplan, Caren, Norma Alarcón, and Minoo Moallem. 1999. "Introduction: Between Woman and Nation." In *Between Woman and Nation: Nationalism, Transnational Feminism, and the State*, edited by Caren Kaplan, Norma Alarcón, and Minoo Moallem, 1-18. Durham, NC: Duke University Press.

Kastoryano, Riva. 1999. "Muslim Diaspora(s) in Western Europe." *South Atlantic Quarterly* 98, no. 1-2: 191-202.

Kauanui, J. Kehaulani. 2008. "Native Hawaiian Decolonization and the Politics of Gender." *American Quarterly* 60, no. 2: 281-87.

Kayyali, Randa A. 2006. *The Arab Americans*. Westport, CT: Greenwood.

Khalidi, Rashid. 1997. *Palestinian Identity: The Construction of Modern National Consciousness*. New York: Columbia University Press.

———. 2004. *Resurrecting Empire: Western Footprints and America's Perilous Path in the Middle East*. Boston: Beacon.

Khalidi, Rashid, Lisa Anderson, Muhammad Muslih, and Reeva Simon. 1991. *The Origins of Arab Nationalism*. New York: Columbia University Press.

Khan, Shahnaz. 2000. *Muslim Women: Crafting a North American Identity*. Gainesville: University Press of Florida.

Khater, Akram F. 2001. *Inventing Home: Immigration, Gender, and the Middle Class in Lebanon, 1870-1920*. Berkeley: University of California Press.

Khoury, Buthina Canaan, ed. 2004. *Women in Struggle*. Palestine: Majd Production.

Kim, Jodi. 2010. *Ends of Empire: Asian American Critique and the Cold War (Critical American Studies)*. Minneapolis: University of Minnesota Press.

Kim, Nadia. 2008. *Imperial Citizens: Koreans and Race from Seoul to LA*. Stanford, CA: Stanford University Press.

King, Peter. 2005. "18 Years Waiting for a Gavel to Fall." *Los Angeles Times*, June 29, sec. A1.

Kishawi, Eyad. 2006. "Divestment from Israel in Its Fifth Year: A History and Method for U.S. and European Activists." Al-Jazeerah online. www.aljazeerah.info. Accessed Dec. 9, 2011.

Kobti, Father Labib. 2006. *Webpages, Panels, Interviews, and Articles by Father Labib Kobti*. http://www.al-bushra.org/LabibKobti/labib.htm. Last visited September 18, 2011.

Kurashige, Scott. 2010. *The Shifting Grounds of Race: Black and Japanese Americans in the Making of Multiethnic Los Angeles*. Princeton, NJ: Princeton University Press.

Kuumba, M. Bahati. 2001. *Gender and Social Movements*. Walnut Creek, CA: AltaMira Press.

Labelle, Deborah. 2008. "Bringing Human Rights Home to the World of Detention." *Columbia Human Rights Law Review* 40, no. 79: 79-83.

Laffrey, S. C., A. I. Meleis, J. G. Lipson, M. Solomon, and P. A. Omidian. 1989. "Assessing Arab-American Health Care Needs." *Social Science & Medicine* 29.7: 877-83.

La Fountain-Stokes, Lawrence M. 2009. *Queer Ricans: Cultures and Sexualities in the Diaspora*. Minneapolis: University of Minnesota Press.

Latina Feminist Group, The. 2001. *Telling to Live: Latina Feminist Testimonios*, edited by The Latina Feminist Group. Durham, NC: Duke University Press.

Lavie, Smadar, and Ted Swedenburg. 1996. "Introduction." In *Displacment, Diaspora, and Geographies*, edited by Smadar Lavie and Ted Swedenburg, 1-27. Durham, NC: Duke University Press.

Lawrence of Arabia. 2003. Directed by David Lean. Columbia Tristar Home Entertainment.

Lazreg, Marnia. 1994. *The Eloquence of Silence: Algerian Women in Question*. New York: Routledge.

Light, Ivan, and Edna Bonacich. 1988. *Immigrant Entrepreneurs: Koreans in Los Angeles, 1965-1982*. Berkeley: University of California Press.

Lipsitz, George. 2000. "Music, Migration, and Myth: The California Connection." In *Reading California: Art, Image, and Identity, 1900-2000*, edited by Stephanie Barron, Sheri Bernstein and Ilene Susan Fort, 153-70. Los Angeles: University of California Press.

Little, Douglas. 2008. *American Orientalism: The United States and the Middle East since 1945*. Chapel Hill: University of North Carolina Press.

Lockman, Zachary. 2010. *Contending Visions of the Middle East: The History and Politics of Orientalism*. Cambridge, UK: Cambridge University Press.

Lopez, Alejandra Marcella, Matthew Snipp, and Al Camarillo. 2002. *Middle Eastern Populations in California: Estimates from the Census 2000 Supplementary Survey*. Stanford, CA: Center for Comparative Studies in Race and Ethnicity.

Lopez, Ian Haney. 1996. *White by Law: The Legal Construction of Race*. New York: New York University Press.

Lowe, Lisa. 1996. *Immigrant Acts: On Asian American Cultural Politics*. Durham, NC: Duke University Press.

Lowe, Lisa, and David Lloyd. 1997. "Introduction." In *The Politics of Culture in the Shadow of Capitol*, edited by Lisa Lowe and David Lloyd. 1-33. Durham, NC: Duke Universtiy Press.

Luongo, Michael. 2010. "Gays under Occupation: Interviews with Gay Iraqis." In *Islam and Homosexuality*, edited by Samar Habib, Vol. 1, 99-110. Santa Barbara, CA: Praeger.

Lyon-Callo, Vincent, and Susan Brin Hyatt. 2003. "The Neoliberal State and the Depoliticization of Poverty: Activist Anthropology and 'Ethnography from Below.'" *Urban Anthropology & Studies of Cultural Systems & World Economic Development* 32, no. 2 (Summer): 175.

Mahalingam, Ramaswami, and Janxin Leu. 2005. "Culture, Essentialism, Immigration, and Representations of Gender." *Theory & Psychology* 15, no. 5: 839-60.

Maharidge, Dale. 1996. *The Coming White Minority: California's Eruptions and America's Future*. New York: Times Books.

Mahler, Sarah J. 1995. *American Dreaming: Immigrant Life on the Margins*.

Princeton, NJ: Princeton University Press.

Mahmood, Saba. 2005. *Politics of Piety: The Islamic Revival and the Feminist Subject.* Princeton, NJ: Princeton University Press.

Maira, Sunaina. 2008. "Belly Dancing: Arab-Face, Orientalist Feminism, and U.S. Empire." *American Quarterly* 60, no. 2: 317-45.

———. 2002. *Desis in the House: Indian American Youth Culture in New York City.* Asian American History and Culture. Philadelphia: Temple University Press.

———. 2009. *Missing: Youth, Citizenship, and Empire after 9/11.* Durham, NC: Duke University Press.

Maira, Sunaina, and Magid Shihade. 2006. "Meeting Asian/Arab American Studies: Thinking Race, Empire, and Zionism in the United States." *Journal of Asian American Studies* 9, no. 2: 117-40.

Maira, Sunaina, and Elisabeth Soep. 2005. *Youthscapes: The Popular, the National, the Global.* Philadelphia: University of Pennsylvania.

Majaj, Lisa Suhair. 2000. "Arab-Americans and the Meaning of Race." In *Postcolonial Theory and the United States: Race, Ethnicity, and Literature*, edited by Amritjit Singh and Peter Schmidt, 320-37. Jackson: University Press of Mississippi.

———. 1994. "Boundaries: Arab/ American." In *Food for Our Grandmothers: Writings by Arab American and Arab Canadian Feminists*, edited by Joanna Kadi, 65-86. Boston: South End Press.

Majid, Anouar. 2000. *Unveiling Traditions: Postcolonial Islam in a Polycentric World.* Durham, NC: Duke University Press.

Mamdani, Mahmood. 2005. *Good Muslim, Bad Muslim: America, the Cold War, and the Roots of Terror.* New York: Three Leave Press/Doubleday.

Manalansan, Martin F. 2003. *Global Divas: Filipino Gay Men in the Diaspora.* Perverse Modernities. Durham, NC: Duke University Press.

Mandaville, Peter. 2007. *Global Political Islam.* New York: Routledge.

Mann, Michael. 2005. *Incoherent Empire.* New York: Verso.

Marcus, George, and James D. Faubion, eds. *Fieldwork Is Not What It Used to Be: Learning Anthropology's Method in a Time of Transition.* Ithaca, NY: Cornell University Press, 2009.

Marcus, Itamar, and Nan Jacques Zilberdik. 2010. "Mother Celebrates Son's Martyrdom Death." Palestine Media Watch online. http://palwatch.org/main.aspx?fi=1578doc_id=1662. February 21. Accessed Dec. 9, 2011.

Marr, Phebe. 2004. *The Modern History of Iraq.* Boulder, CO: Westview.

Marschner, Janice. 2003. *California's Arab Americans.* Sacramento, CA: Coleman Ranch Press.

Massad, Joseph. 1995. "Conceiving the Masculine: Gender and Palestinian Nationalism." *Middle East Journal* 49, no. 3: 467.

———. 2007. *Desiring Arabs.* Chicago: University of Chicago Press.

———. 2010. "How Surrendering Palestinian Rights Became the Language of 'Peace.'" *The Electronic Intifada.* http://electronicintifada.net/news.

McAlister, M. 2001. *Epic Encounters: Culture, Media, and U.S. Interests in the Middle East, 1945-2000.* Berkeley: University of California Press.

McClintock, Anne. 1993. "Family Feuds: Gender, Nationalism, and the Family." *Feminist Review* no. 44 (Summer): 61-80.

McCloud, Aminah Beverly. 2000. "The Scholar and the Fatwa: Legal Issues Facing African American and Immigrant Muslim Communities in the United States." In *Windows of Faith: Muslim*

Women Scholar-Activists in North America, edited by Gisela Webb, 136-44. Syracuse, NY: Syracuse University Press.

McFadden, Patricia. 2008. "Interrogating Americana: An African Feminist Critique." In *Feminism and War: Confronting U.S. Imperialism*, edited by Chandra Talpade Mohanty, Minnie Bruce Pratt, and Robin L. Riley, 56-67. New York: Zed Books.

Melamed, Jodi. 2006. "The Spirit of Neoliberalism: From Racial Liberalism to Neoliberal Multiculturalism." *Social Text* 24, no. 4 (Winter): 1-24.

Mercer, Kobena. 1994. *Welcome to the Jungle: New Positions in Black Cultural Studies*. New York: Routledge.

Metcalf, Barbara Daly. 1996. *Making Muslim Space in North America and Europe*. Comparative Studies on Muslim Societies. Berkeley: University of California Press.

Mikkelson, Barbara, and David Mikkelson. 2011. "False Footaging." http://www.snopes.com/rumors/cnn.asp. March 8. Accessed December 9, 2011.

Minh-Ha, Trinh T. 1989. *Women, Native, Other: Writing Postcoloniality and Feminism*. Bloomington: Indiana University Press.

Mitchell, Timothy. 1991. *Colonising Egypt*. Berkeley: University of California Press.

Moallem, Minoo. 2005. *Between Warrior Brother and Veiled Sister: Islamic Fundamentalism and the Politics of Patriarchy in Iran*. Berkeley: University of California Press.

———. "Ethnic Entrepreneurship and Gender Relations among Iranians in Montreal, Quebec, Canada." In *Iranian Refugees and Exiles since Khomeini*, edited by Asghar Fathi, 43-69. Costa Mesa, CA: Mazda.

Moallem, Minoo, and Iain A. Boal. 1999. "Multicultural Nationalism and the Poetics of Inauguration." In *Between Woman and Nation: Nationalism,*

Transnationalism Feminism and the State, edited by Caren Kaplan, Norma Alarcón, and Minoo Moallem, 243-64. Durham, NC: Duke University Press.

Moghissi, Haideh. 1999. "Away from Home: Iranian Women, Displacement, Cultural Resistance, and Change." *Journal of Comparative Family Studies* 30, no. 2: 207-18.

Mohanty, Chandra Talpade. 2003. *Feminism without Borders: Decolonizing Theory, Practicing Solidarity*. Durham, NC: Duke University Press.

———. 2006. "U.S. Empire and the Project of Women's Studies: Stories of Citizenship, Complicity, and Dissent." *Gender, Place, and Culture* 13, no. 1: 7-20.

Mohanty, Chandra Talpade, Minnie Bruce Pratt, and Robin L. Riley. 2008. "Introduction: Feminism and U.S. Wars—Mapping the Ground." In *Feminism and War: Confronting U.S. Imperialism*, edited by Chandra Talpade Mohanty, Minnie Bruce Pratt, and Robin L. Riley, 1-19. London: Zed.

Moore, Henrietta L. 1999. "Anthropological Theory at the Turn of the Century." In *Anthropological Theory Today*, edited by Henrietta L. Moore, 1-23. Malden, MA: Blackwell.

Moraga, Cherrie, and Gloria Anzaldúa. 1981. *This Bridge Called My Back: Writings by Radical Women of Color*. Watertown, MA: Persephone Press.

Morris, Benny. 2004. *Birth of the Palestinian Refugee Problem Revisited*. Cambridge: Cambridge University Press.

Mosse, George L. 1988. *Nationalism and Sexuality: Middle-Class Morality and Sexual Norms in Modern Europe*. Madison: University of Wisconsin Press.

Mousa, Issam Suleiman. 1984. *The Arab Image in the U.S. Press*. New York: Peter Lang.

Muñoz, Jose Esteban. 1999. *Disidentifications: Queers of Color and the*

Performance of Politics. Minneapolis: University of Minnesota Press.

Myers, Lee Steven. 1996. "U.S. to Help Free Refugees in Iraq." *New York Times,* September 13, sec. A1.

Naber, Nadine. 2000. "Ambiguous Insiders: An Investigation of Arab Invisibility." *Ethnic and Racial Studies* 23, no. 1: 37-61.

———. 2006. "The Rules of Forced Engagement: Race, Gender, and the Culture of Fear among Arab Immigrants in San Francisco Post-9/11." *Cultural Dynamics* 18, no. 3: 235-67.

Nadelmann, Ethan. 1981. "Israel and Black Africa: A Rapprochement?" *Journal of Modern Africa Studies* 19, no. 2 (June): 183.

Naff, Alixa. 1985. *Becoming American: The Early Arab Immigrant Experience.* Carbondale: Southern Illinois University Press.

Najmabadi, Afsaneh. 2005. *Women with Mustaches and Men without Beards: Gender and Sexual Anxieties of Iranian Modernity.* Berkeley: University of California Press.

Naples, Nancy A. 1998. *Community Activism and Feminist Politics: Organizing across Race, Class, and Gender.* New York: Routledge.

Narayan, Kirin. 2003. "How Native Is a 'Native' Anthropologist?" In *Feminist Postcolonial Theory: A Reader,* edited by Reina Lewis and Sara Mills, 285-305. New York: Routledge.

Narayan, Uma. 1997. "Introduction." In *Dislocating Cultures/Identities, Traditions, and Third-World Feminism,* 3-38. London: Routledge.

Ngai, Mae M. 2005. *Impossible Subjects: Illegal Aliens and the Making of Modern America.* Princeton, NJ: Princeton University Press.

Odem, Mary E. 1995. *Delinquent Daughters: Protecting and Policing Adolescent Female Sexuality in the United States,*

1885-1920. Chapel Hill: University of North Carolina Press.

Omi, Michael, and Howard Winant. 1994. *Racial Formations in the United States.* New York: Routledge.

Ong, Aihwa. 2006. *Neoliberalism as Exception.* Durham, NC: Duke University Press.

Ono, Kent. 2005. "Asian American Studies after 9/11." In *Race, Identity, and Representation in Education,* edited by Cameron McCarthy, Warren C. Richlow, Greg Dimitriadis, and Nadine Dolby. Vol. 2, 439-52. New York: Routledge.

———. -Ono, Kent A., and John M. Sloop. 2002. *Shifting Borders: Rhetoric, Immigration, and California's Proposition 187.* Philadelphia: Temple University Press.

Pappe, Llan. 2006. *A History of Modern Palestine: One Land, Two Peoples.* Cambridge: Cambridge University Press.

Park, Kyeyoung. 1997. *The Korean American Dream: Immigrants and Small Business in New York City.* Ithaca, NY: Cornell University Press, 1997.

Parker, Andrew, Mary Russo, Doris Sommer, and Patricia Yaeger. 1992. "Introduction." In *Nationalisms and Sexualities,* edited by Andrew Parker, Mary Russo, Doris Sommer, and Patricia Yaeger, 1-20. New York: Routledge.

Pateman, Carole. 1983. "Feminist Critiques of the Public/Private Dichotomy." In *Public and Private in Social Life,* edited by Stanley I. Benn and G. F. Gaus, 118-40. London: St. Martin's Press.

Peace, Propaganda, & the Promised Land. 2004. Directed by Sut Jhally and Bathsheba Ratzkoff. Media Education Foundation.

Pedraza, Silvia. 2006. "Assimilation or Transnationalism? Conceptual Models of the Immigrant Experience in America." In *Cultural Psychology of Immigrants,* edited by Ramaswami Mahalingam, 33-54. Mahwah, NJ: Erlbaum.

Peters, Joan. 2001. *From Time Immemo-rial: The Origins of the Arab-Jewish Conflict over Palestine*. Chicago: JKAP Publications.

Povinelli, Elizabeth A. 2002. *The Cunning of Recognition: Indigenous Alterities and the Making of Australian Multicultural-ism*. Durham, NC: Duke University Press.

Power, Samantha. 2002. *"A Problem from Hell": America and the Age of Genocide*. New York: Basic Books.

Prashad, Vijay. 2000. *The Karma of Brown Folk*. Minneapolis: University of Min-nesota Press.

Puar, Jasbir K. 2007. *Terrorist Assemblages: Homonationalism in Queer Times*. Dur-ham, NC: Duke University Press.

Puar, Jasbir, and Amit S. Rai. 2004. "The Remaking of a Model Minority: Perverse Projectiles under the Specter of (Counter)Terrorism." *Social Text* 80, no. 3: 75-104

Rabinovich, Itamar. 2004. *Waging Peace: Israel and the Arabs, 1948-2003*. Princ-eton, NJ: Princeton University Press.

Radcliffe, Sarah A., and Sallie Westwood. 1993. *"Viva": Women and Popular Protest in Latin America*. International Studies of Women and Place. London: Routledge.

Radhakrishnan, R. 1992. "Nationalism, Gender, and the Narrative of Identity." In *Nationalisms and Sexualities*, edited by Andrew Parker, Mary Russo, Doris Sommer, and Patricia Yaeger, 77-95. New York: Routledge.

Rafidi, Abeer N., May Howell, and Manal Elkarra. 1999. *The Arab American Com-munity in San Francisco: A Community Needs Assessment*. San Francisco: Arab Cultural Center.

Rana, Junaid. 2007. "The Story of Islamo-phobia." *Souls* 9, no. 2: 148-61.

———. 2011. *Terrifying Muslims: Race and Labor in the South Asian Diaspora*. Durham, NC: Duke University Press.

Rana, Junaid, and Gilberto Rosas. 2006. "Managing Crisis." *Cultural Dynamics* 18, no. 3: 219-34.

Rawi, Mariam. 2004. "Rule of the Rapists." *The Guardian*, February 12.

Razack, Sherene H. 2008. *Casting Out: The Eviction of Muslims from Western Law and Politics*. Toronto: University of Toronto Press.

———. 2005. "Geopolitics, Culture Clash, and Gender after September 11." *Social Justice* 32, no. 4.

Reed, Betsy, and Katha Pollitt. 2002. *Noth-ing Sacred: Women Respond to Religious Fundamentalism and Terror*. New York: Thunder's Mouth Press/Nation Books.

Robnett, Belinda. 1997. *How Long? How Long? African-American Women in the Struggle for Civil Rights*, New York: Oxford University Press.

Rodriguez, Lilia. 1994. "Barrio Women: Between the Urban and the Feminist Movement." *Latin American Perspec-tives* 21, no. 3: 32.

Rose, Tricia. 1994. *Black Noise: Rap Music and Black Culture in Contemporary America*. Middletown, CT: Wesleyan University Press.

Rowson, Everett K. 2008. "Homoerotic Liaisons among the Mamluk Elite in Late Medieval Egypt and Syria." In *Isl-amicate Sexualities: Translations across Temporal Geographies of Desire*, edited by Kathryn Babayan and Afsaneh Najmabadi, 204-38. Cambridge, MA: Harvard University Press.

Roy, Sara. 2007. "Humanism, Scholarship, and Politics: Writing on the Palestin-ian-Israeli Conflict." *Journal of Palestine Studies* 36, no. 2: 54-65.

Rubin, Gayle. 1997. "The Traffic in Women: Notes on the 'Political Economy' of Sex." In *The Second Wave: A Reader in Feminist Theory*, edited by Linda Nich-olson, 27-62. New York: Routledge.

Saalakhan, El-Hajj Mauri. 1999. "Islam and Terrorism: Myth vs. Reality."

Washington Report on Middle East Affairs, April/May, 87-88.

Sabbagh, Suha. 1990. "Sex, Lies, and Stereotypes: The Image of Arabs in American Popular Fiction." ADC issue paper no. 23. Washington, DC: Anti-Discrimination Committee.

Said, Edward. 2003. "The Clash of Definitions." In *Identities: Race, Class, Gender, and Nationality*, edited by Linda Alcoff, 333-59. Malden, MA: Wiley-Blackwell.

———. 1981. *Covering Islam: How the Media and the Experts Determine How We See the Rest of the World*. New York: Pantheon.

———. 1993. *Culture and Imperialism*. New York: Knopf.

———. 1978. *Orientalism*. New York: Pantheon.

———. 1984. "Permission to Narrate." In *The Edward Said Reader*, edited by Moustafa Bayoumi and Andrew Rubin, 243-66. New York: Vintage Books.

———. 1979. *The Question of Palestine*. New York: Times Books.

Edward W. Said, Moustafa Bayoumi, and Andrew Rubin. 2000. *The Edward Said Reader*. New York: Vintage Books.

Saliba, Therese. 2003. "A Country beyond Reach: Liana Badr's Writings of the Palestinian Diaspora." In *Intersections: Gender, Nation, and Community in Arab Women's Novels*, edited by Therese Saliba, Lisa Suhair Majaj, and Paula W. Sunderman, 132-61. Syracuse, NY: Syracuse University Press.

———. 2011. "On Rachel Corrie, Palestine, and Feminist Solidarity." In *Arab and Arab American Feminisms: Gender, Violence, and Belonging*, edited by Rabab Abdulhadi, Evelyn Alsultany, and Nadine Naber, 184-202. Syracuse, NY: Syracuse University Press.

———. 1994. "Sittee (Or Phantom Appearances of a Lebanese Grandmother)." In *Food for Our Grandmothers: Writings by Arab American and Arab Canadian Feminists*, edited by Joanna Kadi, 7-17. Boston: South End Press.

Samhan, Helen Hatab.1999. "Not Quite White: Race Classification and the Arab-American Experience." In *Arabs in America: Building a New Future*, edited by Michael Suleiman, 209-26. Philadelphia: Temple University Press.

Samman, Khaldoun, 2005. "Towards a Non-Essentialist Pedagogy of 'Islam.'" *Teaching Theology and Religion* 8, no. 3: 164-71.

Sandoval-Sánchez, Alberto, and Nancy Saporta Sternbach. 2001. *Stages of Life: Transcultural Performance & Identity in U.S. Latina Theater*. Tucson: University of Arizona Press.

Scott, Joan W., and Debra Keates. 2005. *Going Public: Feminism and the Shifting Boundaries of the Private Sphere*. Champaign: University of Illinois Press.

See, Sarita Echavez. 2009. *The Decolonized Eye: Filipino American Art and Performance*. Minneapolis: University of Minnesota Press.

Shaheen, Jack G. 2001. *Reel Bad Arabs: How Hollywood Vilifies a People*. New York: Olive Branch Press.

———. 1984. *The TV Arab*. Bowling Green, OH: Bowling Green University Press.

Shakir, Evelyn. 1997. *Bint Arab: Arab American Women in the United States*. Westport, CT: Praeger.

Sharlet, Jocelyn. 2009. "Public Displays of Affection: Male Homoerotic Desire and Sociability in Medieval Arabic Literature." In *Islam and Homosexuality*, edited by Samar Habib, 37-56. Santa Barbara, CA: Praeger.

Sharma, Parvez. 2010. "Foreword." In *Islam and Homosexuality*, edited by Samar Habib, ix-xiv. Santa Barbara, CA: Praeger.

Shohat, Ella. 2001. "Area Studies, Transnationalism, and the Feminist Production of Knowledge." *Signs* 26, no. 4 (Summer): 1269.

———. 1998. "Introduction." In *Talking Visions: Multicultural Feminism in a Transnational Age*, edited by Ella Shohat, 1-64. Cambridge, MA: MIT Press.

———. 2006. *Taboo Memories, Diasporic Voices*. Durham, NC: Duke University Press.

Shohat, Ella, and Robert Stam. 1994. *Unthinking Eurocentrism: Multiculturalism and the Media*. New York: Routledge.

The Siege. 1999. Directed by Edward Zwick. Twentieth Century Fox Home Entertainment.

Silberstein, Laurence J. 1999. *The Postzionism Debates: Knowledge and Power in Israeli Culture*. New York: Routledge.

Simons, Geoff. 2002. *Targeting Iraq: Sanctions and Bombings in U.S. Policy*. London: Saqi Books.

Simpson, Audra. 2007. "On Ethnographic Refusal: Indigeneity, 'Voice,' and Colonial Citizenship." *Junctures: The Journal for Thematic Dialogue* 9 (Dec. 1): 67-80.

Sleeter, Christine E., and Peter McLaren. 1995. *Multicultural Education, Critical Pedagogy, and the Politics of Difference*. Albany: State University of New York Press.

Smith, Andrea. 2005. *Conquest: Sexual Violence and American Indian Genocide*. Cambridge, MA: South End Press.

———. "Heteropatriarchy and the Three Pillars of White Supremacy: Rethinking Women of Color Activism." In *The Color of Violence: The Incite! Anthology*, edited by Incite! Women of Color Against Violence. Boston: South End Press.

———. 2008. *Native Americans and the Christian Right: The Gendered Politics of Unlikely Alliances*. Durham, NC: Duke University Press.

Smith, Andrea, and J. Kehaulani Kauanui. 2008. "Native Feminisms Engage American Studies." *American Quarterly* 60, no. 2: 241-49.

Smith, Linda Tuhiwai. 1999. *Decolonizing Methodologies: Research and Indigenous Peoples*. London: Zed Books.

Smothers, Ronald. 1998. "Prosecutor Refuses to Enforce Subpoena in I.N.S. Case: A Palestinian Facing Deportation Wants to Uncloak Secret Evidence." *New York Times*, November 13.

Song Hyoung, Min. 2005. *Strange Future: Pessimism and the 1992 Los Angeles Riots*. Durham, NC: Duke University Press.

SOSC (Secretary of the State of California). 2000. *Juvenile Crime. Initiative Statute. 2000 California Primary Election Voter Information Guide/Ballot Pamphlet*. Secretary of the State of California.

Speed, Shannon. 2008. "Forged in Dialogue: Toward a Critically Engaged Activist Research." In *Engaging Contradictions: Theory, Politics, and Methods of Activist Scholarship*, edited by Charles R. Hale, 213-36. Berkeley: University of California Press.

Spivak, Gayatri Chakravorty. 1994. "Can the Subaltern Speak?" In *Colonial Discourse and Post Colonial Theory: A Reader*, edited by Patrick Williams and Laura Chrisman, 66-111. New York: Columbia University Press.

Stacey, Judith. 1998. *Brave New Families: Stories of Domestic Upheaval in Late-Twentieth-Century America*. Berkeley: University of California Press.

Stack, Carol. 1997. *All Our Kin: Strategies for Survival in a Black Community*. New York: Basic Books.

Stall, Susan, and Randy Stoecker. 1998. "Community Organizing or Organizing Community? Gender and the Crafts of Empowerment." *Gender and Society* 12, no. 6 (December): 729-56.

Stein, Rebecca. 2002. "Israeli Leisure, 'Palestinian Terror,' and the Question of Palestine (Again)." *Theory and Event* 6, no. 3.

Steinmetz, George. 2005. "Return to Empire: The New U.S. Imperialism in Theorical and Historical Perspective." *Sociology Theory* 23.4: 339-67.

Stiffler, Matthew. 2010. "Selling Arab at Church: Antiochian Orthodox Christians and Their Political, Cultural, and Religious Engagements with Arabness." Dissertation/Thesis, unpublished, University of Michigan.

Stockton, Ronald. 1994. "Ethnic Archetype and the Arab Image." *The Development of Arab American Identity*, edited by Ernest McCarus. Ann Arbor: University of Michigan Press.

Stoler, Ann. 2006. *Haunted by Empire: Geographies of Intimacy in North American History*. Durham, NC: Duke University Press.

———. 1989. "Making Empire Respectable: The Politics of Race and Sexual Morality in Twentieth-Century Colonial Cultures." *American Ethnologist* 16.4 (November).

Street, Linda. 2000. *Veils and Daggers: A Century of National Geographic's Representation of the Arab World*. Philadelphia: Temple University Press.

Suárez-Orozco, Carola, and Marcelo M. Suárez-Orozco. 1995. *Transformations: Immigration, Family Life, and Achievement Motivation among Latino Adolescents*. Stanford, CA: Stanford University Press.

Sudbury, Julia. 2000. "Building Women's Movements beyond 'Imperial Feminism.'" *San Francisco Chronicle*, March 27.

Suleiman, Michael. 1999. "Introduction: The Arab Immigrant Experience." In *Arabs in America: Building a New Future*, 1-24. Philadelphia: Temple University Press.

———. 1988. *The Arabs in the Mind of America*. Brattleboro, VT: Amana Books.

Tal, David. 2003. *War in Palestine, 1948: Strategy and Diplomacy*. London: Routledge.

Teaiwa, Teresia. 2001. "L(o)Osing the Edge in 'Native Pacific Cultural Studies on the Edge.'" *Contemporary Pacific* 13, no. 2: 343-57.

Terry, Janice. 1999. "Community and Political Activism among Arab Americans in Detroit." In *Arabs in America: Building a New Future*, edited by Michael Suleiman, 241-55. Philadelphia: Temple University Press.

———. 1985. *Mistaken Identity: Arab Stereotypes in Popular Writing*. Washington, DC: Arab-American Affairs Council.

The Thief of Bagdad: An Arabian Fantasy. 1940/2008. Directed by Michael Powell, Ludwig Berger, and Tim Whelan. Criterion Collection edition.

Traub, Valerie. 2008. "The Past Is a Foreign Country? The Times and Spaces of Islamicate Sexuality Studies." In *Islamicate Sexualities*, directed by Kathryn Babayan and Afsaneh Najmabadi, 1-40. Cambridge, MA: Harvard University Press.

Tripp, Charles. 2002. *A History of Iraq*. 2d ed. Cambridge: Cambridge University Press.

True Lies. 1994. Directed by James Cameron. Twentieth Century Fox Home Entertainment.

Tsoffar, Ruth. 2006. *The Stains of Culture: An Ethno-Reading of Karaite Jewish Women*. Detroit, MI: Wayne State University Press.

Tucker, Judith. 1993. *Arab Women: Old Boundaries, New Frontiers*. Bloomington: Indiana University Press.

United Nations Children's Fund. 1990. *The State of the World's Children 1990*. Oxford: United Nations Children's Fund.

Vertovec, Steven. 1997. "Three Meanings of 'Diaspora,' Exemplified among South Asian Religions." *Diaspora* 6, no. 3: 276-99.

Visweswaran, Kamala. 1994. *Fictions of Feminist Ethnography*. Minneapolis: University of Minnesota Press.

Volpp, Leti. 2003a. "The Citizen and the Terrorist." In *September 11th in History: A Watershed Moment?* edited by Mary L. Dudziak,147-62. Durham, NC: Duke University Press.

————. 2003b. "Feminism versus Multiculturalism." In *Critical Race Feminism: A Reader*, ed. Adrien Katherine Wing. Vol. 2, 395-405. New York: New York University Press.

Wadud, Amina. 2006. *Inside the Gender Jihad: Women's Reform in Islam.* Oxford: Oneworld.

Wall, Brenda. 1992. *The Rodney King Rebellion: A Psychopolitical Analysis of Racial Despair and Hope.* Chicago: African American Images.

Webb, Gisela. 2000. "May Muslim Women Speak for Themselves, Please?" In *Windows of Faith: Muslim Women Scholar-Activists in North America*, edited by Gisela Webb. Syracuse, NY: Syracuse University Press.

Werbner, Pnina. 2002a. *Imagined Diasporas among Manchester Muslims.* Santa Fe, NM: SAR Press.

————. 2002b. "The Place Which Is Diaspora: Citizenship, Religion, and Gender in the Making of Chaordic Transnationalism." *Journal of Ethnic and Migration Studies* 28, no. 1: 119-33.

Werbner, Pnina, and Tariq Modood, eds. 1997. *Debating Cultural Hybridity: Multi-Cultural Identities and the Politics of Anti-Racism.* London: Zed Books.

Wexler, Jon. 2002. "Free Jamil Al-Amin! Political Frame-Up of a Black Radical in Georgia." *The New Abolitionist* no. 24.

White, E. Frances. 1990. "Africa on My Mind: Gender, Counter-Discourse, and African-American Nationalism." *Journal of Women's History* 2, no. 1 (Spring): 73-97.

Williams, Brackette. 1996. "Introduction: Mannish Women and Gender after the Act." In *Women out of Place: The Gender of Agency and the Race of Nationality.* New York: Routledge.

Williams, Brackette F., and Paulette Pierce. 1996. "'And Your Prayers Shall Be Answered through the Womb of a Woman': Insurgent Masculine Redemption and the Nation of Islam." In *Women out of Place: A Gender of Agency and the Race of Nationality*, edited by Brackette F. Williams, 186-215. New York: Routledge.

Wingfield, Marvin, and Bushra Karaman. 1995. "Arab Stereotypes and American Educators." *Social Studies and the Young Learner*, March/April.

Wistrich, Robert. 2004. "Anti-Zionism and Anti-Semitism." *Jewish Political Studies Review* 16, nos. 3-4.

Young, Robert. 2001. *Postcolonialism: An Historical Introduction.* Oxford: Blackwell.

Zaborowska, Magdalena J. 1995. *How We Found America: Reading Gender through East European Immigrant Narratives.* Chapel Hill: University of North Carolina Press.

Zimmerman, Bonnie. 2000. "Arab Americans." In *Encyclopedia of Lesbian and Gay Histories and Cultures*, edited by Bonnie Zimmerman. Vol. 1. New York: Garland.

Zogby, James. 2000. *Arab American Population Highlights.* Washington, DC: Arab American Institute Foundation.

Area Arab Americans, 13, 66, 68–69, 75–78, 108–109; sexuality, 65, 78, 82, 83–87; socioeconomic class, 94–95, 109; unmarried women, 97–98; village-based organizations, 46–47; wealth through hard work, 26; weekends, 75; white middle-class norms, 93–94
cultural nationalism, 272n5
cultural racism, 135–136
cultural work, 239–242
culture: diasporic Arab feminist critique, 249; disaggregating religion from, 112, 121; hip-hop culture, 240; religion, conflation with, 121. *See also* Arab culture
Cyber AWSA, 59

Davis, Angela, 239
de-Orientalizing methodology, 14–15
Dearborn, Michigan, 39
Deb, Trishala, 261n5
debka dance, 223–224, 226, 267n5
"decolonizing methodologies," 14–15
Deeb, Lara, 113, 262n6
Democratic Party, 93
"Desert Storm" operation, 209–210
Diallo, Amadou, 152, 153
diaspora of empire, sense of belonging to, 60, 198
diasporas, 71–75; as coherent spaces, 245; family as marker of cultural distinction, 74; "fictions of purity," 74; *al-nas,* concept of, 101; privileging territorial homelands over, 198; sense of belonging to, 173; as states of consciousness, 172
diasporic anti-imperialism, 19, 48–51, 229–230
diasporic Arab feminist critique, 249–250
disidentification, 88–91
al-Durrah, Mohammad, 196–197
Dwyer, Kevin, 145

Egypt: British colonialism, 71, 72, 196; Christians in, 260n22; family, concepts of, 71, 72; gender, concepts of, 71; Islamic education, 118; marriage, concepts of, 72; national unity, 72; return to/travels in, 170; veiling, 136
Egyptian Americans, 47
endogamy, 67
Enlightenment, 85
equal rights, Islam and, 124
Executive Decision (film), 111

family, 64–75; Arab compared to American, 65, 68–69, 70; Arab culture, 64; Arab culture, conflation with, 70; Arab world, 67, 68, 71; Arabness as, 66–71, 73–75, 102; cultural authenticity, politics of, 65; Egyptian concepts, 71, 72; extended families, 67, 68; heteropatriarchal families, 67; heteropatriarchy, 84; LAM (leftist Arab movement) as, 158–159, 164, 169, 171–172; as marker of cultural distinction in the diaspora, 74; middle-class norms about, 92; Muslim First, Arab Second, 113; racialized concepts of, 71; second generation Bay Area Arab Americans, 68; unmarried individuals, 87
Fanon, Franz, 71–72
FBI, 38, 152
Federation of Islamic Associations of U.S. and Canada (FIA), 263n5
feminism, Islamic, 119–120, 126–127
feminist anti-imperialism, transnational, 228–234
feminist discourse, art as a mechanism for, 226–228
feminist ethnography, 253
feminist intersectionality, 229
feminist research on nationalism, 72
feminist scholars: "activist mothering," 216; Arab American, 252–253; "bridge work," 216; liberalism, 208; national liberation movements, 208; women's ties to grassroots constituencies, 215–216
feminist women of color theories, 17
feminists, Pacific Islander, 230
"fictions of purity," 74
FMLN (Farabundo Marti National Liberation Front), 171, 267n8

Foucault, Michel, 40
Fourth Geneva Convention, 269n13
France: Arab world, 268n11; colonial
  Algeria, 71–72, 194, 196; veiling,
  136–137
Freedom Archives, 243
Fusco, Coco, 272n5

Gaines, Kevin, 92
"gay" (the term), 87
gay rights, 237
gender: Arab culture, 64, 124; cultural
  authenticity, politics of, 78, 82;
  Egyptian concepts, 71; imagined
  differences between Arabs and
  Americans, 7; Islam, 119, 124–128;
  Islamophobia, 136; LAM (leftist Arab
  movement), 186, 188, 200, 207–208;
  middle-class norms about, 92; Muslim
  First, Arab Second, 113, 154; racialized
  concepts of, 71; racism, 92; second
  generation Bay Area Arab Americans,
  78; socioeconomic class, 190; U.S. and
  Israeli state violence, 182
gender egalitarianism, 120
gendered racism, 139
General Union of Palestinian Women's
  Associations (GUPWA), 179
Giacaman, Rita, 102
Gilmore, Ruthie, 143
Gilroy, Paul, 177, 181–182, 240, 272n6
Global Exchange, 157, 243
Global Fund for Women, 254
global Muslim consciousness: Bay Area,
  117; Bosnian Civil War (1992-1995),
  141–142; emergence of, 112; Muslim
  First, Arab Second, 18, 112; Muslim
  student activism, 10; Palestinians,
  support for, 146–147; second
  generation Bay Area Arab Americans,
  10–11
Gökariksel, Banu, 136
Goldberg, David Theo, 55, 135
Gopinath, Gayatri, 74, 197
Gulf War (1990-1991): anti-Arab
  sentiment/racism, 53; Iraqi refugees in
  Bay Area, 57; LGBT Arab Americans,

55–56; pan-Arabism, 116; political
  organizing around, 154

Hall, Stuart, 256n6
Hasso, Frances, 73
heteronormativity, 84–85, 85–86, 93
heteropatriarchy: Arab Americans, 93; Arab
  culture, 201; cultural authenticity, politics
  of, 82; family, 84; heteronormativity,
  84; intra-communal tensions, 159; in
  LAM (leftist Arab movement), 12, 160,
  184–193, 198, 199–200
heterosexuality, 83, 87, 93. See also
  compulsory heterosexuality
hip-hop, 240
Hodgson, Marshall, 264n13
homophobia: Arab culture, 85, 193–196,
  261n5; Arab families and communities,
  109; California, 225; in LAM (leftist
  Arab movement), 12, 161; Orientalism,
  4; Saadawi, Nawal El, 239
"homosexual" (the term), 85
homosexuality: America, the West
  conflated with, 85–87; Arab culture,
  84–85, 262n8; Arab world, 67–68;
  cultural authenticity, politics of, 84–87,
  98–99; as haram (forbidden), 99; Iran,
  85; Iraq, 68; Islam, 67–68
Hyndman, Jennifer, 214

Ibtisam, 128
"imagined community," 101–102, 108
immigrant generation Bay Area Arab
  Americans, 30–35, 40–46; anti-Arab
  sentiment/racism, 74; Arab Grocers
  Association, 44–46; assimilation, desire
  for middle-class, 40, 42–43, 44–45,
  108; church in community building,
  42; cultural authenticity, politics of, 13,
  66; entrepreneurship, 31–32; ethnic
  accommodation, 42–43; grocery
  store owners, 41; nostalgia for 1950s
  and 1960s, 34, 35; old-timers, 30–31,
  32–34, 38, 40–41, 42–44, 46, 51; old-
  timers, Palestinian, 42–44; stores in
  disadvantaged neighborhoods, 260n24;
  suburbs, movement to, 44; wealth, 44

Nadine Naber is Associate Professor in the Program in American Culture and the Department of Women's Studies at the University of Michigan–Ann Arbor. She is co-editor of *Race and Arab Americans* (2007) and *Arab and Arab American Feminisms* (2011).